CRIMINAL JUSTICE

Situations
and
Decisions

CRIMINAL JUSTICE

Situations
and
Decisions

Howard C. Daudistel
University of Texas at El Paso

William B. Sanders
San Diego State University

David F. Luckenbill
University of Illinois, Chicago Circle

Holt, Rinehart and Winston
New York Chicago San Franscisco Dallas
Montreal Toronto London Sydney

ACKNOWLEDGMENTS

Pages 197-200 reprinted from Abraham Blumberg, *Criminal Justice,* pp. 132-35. Copyright © 1967 by Abraham Blumberg and used by permission of the Publisher, Franklin Watts, Inc.

Excerpts on pages 220, 223, 241, 264, and 265 reprinted from Lynn T. Mather, "Some Determinants of the Method of Case Disposition: Decision-Making by Public Defenders in Los Angeles," *Law and Society Review* 8 (Winter 1973): 199-200, 204, 206-7. Used by permission of the copyright holder, The Law and Society Association.

Table 5-2, page 170, and Table 5-3, page 171, reprinted from Charles E. Ares, Anne Rankin, and Herbert Sturz, "The Manhattan Bail Project: An Interim Report on the Use of Pre-Trial Parole," *New York University Law Review* 38 (January 1963): 84,85. Used by permission.

Table, page 208, from Note, "Guilty Plea Bargaining: Compromises by Prosecutors to Secure Guilty Pleas," *University of Pennsylvania Law Review* 112 (April 1964): 901. Reprinted by permission of the *University of Pennsylvania Law Review* and Fred B. Rothman & Co.

Table 5-1, page 162, reprinted from Frederic Suffet, "Bail Setting: A Study of Courtroom Interaction," *Crime and Delinquency* 12 (October 1966): 321. By permission of the National Council on Crime and Delinquency.

Library of Congress Cataloging in Publication Data

Daudistel, Howard C
  Criminal justice: situations and decisions.

  Bibliographies.
  Includes index.
  1. Criminal justice, Administration of—United States. I. Sanders, William B., joint author. II. Luckenbill, David, F. joint author. III. Title. KF922.3.S22
345'.73'05   76-41970
ISBN 0-3-033051-3
Printed in the United States of America

890 039 987654321

To Our Fathers

PREFACE

This text was written to provide a fresh approach to the study of criminal justice. We did not want to write an introduction to criminal justice that describes what is *supposed* to happen in police stations, courtrooms, and prisons. There are already several books that adequately describe the "due process ideal." These traditional texts tell us about the law as it is written, but while concentrating on the ideal they gloss over the actual ways in which our legal system achieves "justice."

We prefer to analyze the interpersonal transactions that constitute the criminal justice process. Because legal agents "do justice," this text will focus on them. For example, we shall discuss how policemen decide to investigate crimes and arrest suspects; how procecutors decide what charges to file against defendants; how prosecutors and defense attorneys routinely settle cases; and how judges decide what sentences to give convicted offenders. While describing the nature of criminal justice decision-making we shall also discuss the impact these decisions have on the citizens caught in the criminal justice process. This latter concern is perhaps the most difficult to satisfy. Although most people demand uniformity in the application of the law, justice is highly individualized. Whatever our opinions may be, we cannot predict with any significant level of certainty what will happen to individuals caught in the arms of the law. We can, however, describe the kinds of things that are likely to happen to different types of persons who encounter the situations in which decisions about justice are made.

It is unfortunate that most students of criminal justice have little knowledge of how the criminal justice system actually operates. For example, even in law school very little is said about plea bargaining. Although policemen spend weeks learning the statutes codified in penal codes until they "hit the streets," few know much about real police work. Even though we are not specifically interested in teaching persons how to become policemen and lawyers, we hope those who are interested in criminal justice careers will gain a more intimate familiarity with the roles they will eventually play. Furthermore, persons who simply wish to know more about the legal system will find our approach refreshing and informative. Likewise, social scientists will see how sociological studies can and have contributed to our overall understanding of criminal justice.

All textbooks are selective of the topics they address, and, of course, this book is no exception. But we feel that we have provided the kind of detailed sociological analysis that is often missing from other criminal justice texts. Rather than just talking about trial, for instance, we have elected to talk about first appearances, bail, arraignments, charging, plea negotiations, and sentencing. Additionally, throughout all of the chapters we have used material from a variety of scholarly books, articles, studies, and commentaries. Although the large number of references may be tedious for some, they will help others who are especially interested in pursuing the issues we address.

The "tradition," if there can be said to be a tradition, behind our approach lies in the work of "interpretive" sociologists. Nevertheless, we were less concerned with demonstrating loyalty to any particular theoretical approach than describing accurately what goes on in the criminal justice system. Much of what we have to say is a result of our own research and study in this field. Nevertheless, we have borrowed ideas from several sources and have attempted to identify all of the contributions made by others.

Many persons, too numerous to name, were instrumental in our instruction and background, and still others let us into the inner sanctum of criminal justice agencies to study the process of their organizations. Several anonymous reviewers are due credit for correcting the many flaws in early drafts, and any oversights in this book cannot be attributed to their lack of scrutiny.

Svein Arber, Jim Bergin, and Herman Makler showed a good deal of patience and offered much needed help to complete the book. Our wives, Sandy, Eli, and Diane, were always understanding and willing to cope with our bizarre work schedules. We are grateful to them for their support.

It is customary to relieve those who we have acknowledged from any faults the book may have, and we do so, for we were the final judges of what would be included and omitted. However, instead of accepting joint responsibility for any of the book's shortcomings, each of us will blame the other two.

H.C.D.
W.B.S.
D.F.L.

CONTENTS

ix

part one

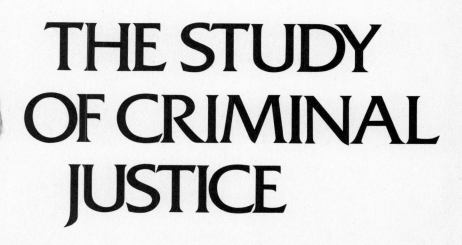

THE STUDY OF CRIMINAL JUSTICE

1
a SITUATIONAL APPROACH to CRIMINAL JUSTICE

The institution of criminal justice is a special kind of formalized social control. Intended to be a force to control crime and guard civil rights, the criminal justice system is actually a receptacle of all kinds of social problems that people encounter in their daily lives requiring intervention by an outside control mechanism. In addition to maintaining order and enforcing the law, police are expected to help locate lost children, escort pregnant women to hospital, and assist stranded motorists. Prosecutors are called upon to charge religious groups with brainwashing young adults even though the United States Constitution guarantees religious freedom. Correctional agencies are asked to "straighten out" children who have broken no laws, as well as to rehabilitate convicted felons.

Typically, people can control situations through informal means. Even in situations where a crime has been committed or order has broken down, they often prefer to handle problems themselves. However, when a situation comes to be defined as one in which the participants cannot resolve the problems without outside help, control is sought through the criminal justice system. As such, we can treat the criminal justice process as a device for "repair work" in social control when the normal social control processes break down.

WHAT IS CRIMINAL JUSTICE?

The study of criminal justice must begin with some understanding of what we shall be talking about in this book. Commonsense understandings of criminal justice include everything from a highly idealized image of Perry Mason rushing to the defense of innocent defendants to a critically cynical view of prisoners shackled in dungeons. The news media thrill us with a vivid newspaper account or live television coverage of a shoot-out between bank robbers and the police, or we are shocked to learn that the Attorney General of the United States has been indicted on criminal charges. We hear that the criminal justice system is hopelessly ineffective in the United States at the same time as we hear that it is the most just and democratic. Such dramatic events or arguments are the stuff that popular television shows and what some might consider good journalism are made of, but they really tell us little of the actual day-to-day operation and structure of criminal justice. Moreover, such perceptions tend to cloud the important issues and create contradictory realities of criminal justice.

In order to provide a clearer view of what we will be dealing with, it will be necessary to define our topic, explain how we are going to examine it, and, then, throughout the rest of the book, carry out our examination.

To begin our definition we must clearly identify the two basic components of criminal justice, namely, *criminal* and *justice.* The term criminal has its roots in the term crime, and so it is necessary to spell out exactly what a crime is, and then show how we are using "criminal" in the context of this book. Basically, *a crime is any act that violates the criminal law* (Sutherland and Cressey, 1974). While all crimes must be defined in criminal laws, not all laws refer to crimes; that is, some laws are "civil" and involve "torts" instead of crimes. Other laws involve everything from administrative procedures to the writing of contracts.

Legally defined, a "crime" is an offense against the state punishable by fine, imprisonment, or some other penalty (Kerper, 1972:30). The important aspect of this definition is that the act is considered to be *against the state* and *punishable by the state.* This distinguishes a crime from a tort in that a tort is *against an individual,* and any legal action taken against the defendant is in the name of the individual and not the state. Some may wonder why the complainant is the state when most crimes are, in effect, against individuals. For instance if Jones robs Smith's store, why isn't the case cited as *Smith v. Jones* instead of say, *Texas v. Jones*? After all, it wasn't the state of Texas that was robbed. The state is the plaintiff because the robbery is considered harmful to the entire society, not just to Smith. A crime is defined as a *public wrong* whereas a tort is a *private wrong;* therefore, when Jones robbed Smith, he committed a public wrong. But still, does the fact that the robbery was against Smith not make the robbery a private wrong as well as a public one? Of course it does. Not only could Jones be charged with a crime, but Smith could also take him to court on civil charges and sue him for the problems created by the robbery. Thus, Jones is responsible for both a crime and a tort. Typically, criminal defendants are only brought to court on criminal charges for a criminal offense, even though a victim of a crime could, in most cases, bring civil charges against a criminal.

If "crime" can be defined as any violation of the criminal law, then what is the criminal law? Sutherland and Cressey (1974:4) argue that the criminal law can be defined "as a body of specific rules regarding human conduct that have been promulgated by political authority, which apply uniformly to all members of the classes to which the rules refer, and which are enforced by punishment administered by the state." Four ideal features or elements of the criminal law set it off from other forms of rules regarding human conduct. These characteristics constitute ideals, and as we shall see throughout the book, what appears to be a neat, firm, unequivocal law is much more complex when it is applied in an actual situation. This does not mean that these ideals are irrelevant and unimportant. On the contrary, we find that criminal justice agents take them seriously. For example, even though it is often a struggle to decide what acts are crimes, policemen and prosecutors argue consistently that their decisions are prescribed by law. An act is a crime because the law specifically describes it as such. On close examination we will find however, that the ideal of specificity is accomplished by criminal justice agents. Thus, specificity is a quality attributed to laws rather than inherent in them.

Since the criminal law, as opposed to other forms of law (as well as other social norms), is technically the phenomenon we shall examine, we should understand something of the differences between them in a formal sense. In this way, even though we may show that the formal features do not exist in practice, at least we can differentiate criminal law from other law-like social phenomena. *Thus, we can define a criminal law as a specific rule whose infraction is against the society as a collective and is uniformly sanctioned in the name of the state by the state.*

First, is the feature of *politicality,* the fact that the rules are constructed by the "state" as a corporate body. Any rule or law that is not made by the state or enforced in the name of the state is not a law. For example, the Comanche Indians did not take action as a collective against members of their group who committed homicide (Hoebel, 1954:140). If a Comanche was murdered, the member's family was obliged to take action against the killer, not the tribe as a collec-

A criminal act is taken to be against society as a whole rather than a single individual even though most crimes involve specific individual victims. (© *1976 by Fred W. McDarrah*)

tive. Therefore, among the Comanche, killing was not a crime. This is not to say that vengeance was not taken against the killer or even that the Comanches thought that killing fellow Comanches was not wrong. Rather, because the action was taken to be against an individual and the response to the act was not in the name of the collectivity, it was not a crime. In fact, among the Comanche, the only thing that could be considered a crime in terms of politicality was excessive sorcery, since that action was considered a threat to the collectivity and sanctions against it were taken in the name of the collectivity.

A second ideal feature of criminal laws that distinguish them from other norms is that of *specificity*. Many norms and mores are vague, and we have only a general understanding of their exact meaning. In contrast, criminal laws are characteristically more precise in stating what must be done or not done if an act is to be a crime. Such specificity characterizes only certain types of acts as crimes. For example, during the development of modern mercantilism the laws defining larceny specifically stated that a person had to be in the possession of money legally before someone could steal it from him (Cressey and Ward, 1969:65). When more and more businesses began hiring clerks (trusted servants) to handle money in financial transactions, the money did not legally come into the owner's possession until it was turned over to him by a clerk. Thus, when clerks began taking money entrusted to them, the law did not define it as a crime since it was not in the owner's possession (Hall, 1952:35).

Third, criminal laws are ideally *uniform* in the sense that they are applied equally to everyone regardless of social status. We might not believe this when we consider the different treatment accorded certain former presidents and others in high places, but the ideal of law is that it is applied uniformly to all. There are no laws that state different penalties for the rich and the poor, black and white, urbanites and ruralites, but they state that *anyone* who breaks the law is subject to penal sanction.

A final feature of criminal laws is *penal sanction,* an aspect of the criminal law that entails both politicality and specificity in that the punishment for violating a law is performed in the name of the society as a collectivity and specifically tied to a given violation. If no penal sanction is tied to a rule, the act cannot be considered a criminal law. In an unusual example of what can happen when no penal sanction is tied to a law, consider what happened when Short Creek, Arizona, was raided by law enforcement officials in 1951. A fundamentalist Mormon community in Short Creek was still practicing polygamy in 1951, and state officials decided to raid the community and arrest those responsible for practicing and advocating polygamy. There was a problem, however. When Arizona enacted specific laws prohibiting polygamy someone forgot to include penalties for breaking the law. As a result, polygamy was not a crime (Maloney, 1953:30–31).[1]

We could discuss further legal definitions of crime, but we have decided not to do so here because it would deviate from our purpose. We want to examine how the criminal law is routinely applied in society, and avoid traditional legalistic conceptions of law. Therefore, instead of delving into the elements of a criminal act, we shall take as our topic the question of how a particular act comes to be seen as a crime in everyday interaction within and outside of the criminal justice process. But first we will examine the concept of justice.

> Defining justice has been one of the primary tasks of jurisprudence, philosophy, ethics and the social sciences since civilization began. Thoughtful men always have found it difficult to make clear and comprehensive statements of what justice is. Contemporary ideas can be traced back to the philosophy of ancient Greece, and to the Near Eastern wisdom expressed in biblical and rabbinic traditions and such early law codes as that of Hammurabi (Rosett and Cressey; 1976:71).

What is justice? In *The Republic,* Plato describes the dialogue

---

[1] Short Creek was raided that year, but not on the basis of the polygamy laws. Instead, the attorney general decided that the community constituted a conspiracy, and on the basis of the conspiracy laws and the penal sanctions attached to them a lawful raid was carried out.

between Socrates and Thrasymachus in which this is the central question. Analyzing this dialogue, Pitkin (1972:170) shows us that "Socrates answers the question as if it were about the meaning of the word 'justice'," while Thrasymachus makes a "kind of sociological observation about the things people call 'just' or 'unjust'." Further, according to Thrasymachus, justice is a label the powerful give to their legal actions. Thus, like an early legal realist, Thrasymachus points out that justice is what the ruling class defines it to be.

Speaking from a different perspective, Socrates does not give a single definition of justice. Nevertheless, his argument rests on the idea that a just state is one in which persons possess what properly belongs to them.

Even though Socrates and Thrasymachus engaged in a philosophical dialogue, Thrasymachus' ideas have a strong sociological sense:

> The most obvious modern successor to Thrasymachus is the
> Marxist doctrine of ideology as false consciousness. According to
> this doctrine, human culture is only a reflection, a super-
> structure on the economic base of a society; the accepted
> standards and values and meanings embodied in the culture are
> in fact a reflection of class interest. So what things people call
> "just" or "beautiful" or "good" is really determined by what is
> in the interest of the ruling class in any society (Pitkin,
> 1972:170–71).

Regardless of what passes for justice in concrete situations, is there some ideal form of justice? Ginsberg (1965:56) says there is. "Justice in the broadest sense consists in the ordering of human relations in accordance with general principles impartially applied." But what is to be done by, to, or for equals? On what grounds are persons equal?

Rosett and Cressey (1976) say justice is accomplished by criminal justice agents who are flexible. Therefore, not everyone is treated alike, and what is just depends on the circumstances of an act. A just punishment for a crime depends on variables associated with the act, not only the crime itself.

We will see, throughout our study of the criminal justice system, that discretion is the dominant theme of legal processing. So, although we cannot resolve the philosophical debate about justice, we can see how agents of the legal system try to achieve what is commonly called criminal justice. Even though criminal justice agents use discretion in their application of the law, the law (as it is written) is not unimportant. The law represents an ideal limitation of the power of the state. At least in principle the coercive power given to the agents of the state is exercised within certain legal limits. How these legal limitations are interpreted and applied will vary of course. Indeed, a variety of practices may violate a person's sense of justice yet be legitimated by criminal justice agents who argue they comply with "due process" requirements.

BASIC RIGHTS

While we shall continue to show that the rights of due process are constantly subject to situational interpretation, it is important to know what some of these basic rights are. In the United States, the basic rights are grounded in the United States Constitution and spelled out in the Bill of Rights. All of the rights in the criminal justice process can be shown to have some foundation, given the relevant interpretation, in the Constitution, and all case law (for example, *Miranda v. Arizona*) is ultimately justified in an interpretation of that fundamental document. These rights can be viewed as the "rules of the game" and as safeguards against injustice and obstacles to summary adjudication. The following "rules" are only the most essential and basic ones and constitute the basic guidelines in "doing criminal justice" (Kerper, 1972:193–94).

1. *The right against unreasonable searches and seizures.* This right prevents people from being searched without probable cause. In a criminal investigation, the police cannot search anyone they want to or go into a home unless they can give a good reason, usually to a magistrate, that the search is linked to a reasonable likelihood that the person in question has something hidden in the dwelling. Ideally, a search warrant signed by a judge must state what the police are looking for, where it is located in the dwelling being searched, and why they have a good cause to believe it is there. Of course, the idea of "probable cause" is grounded in commonsense notions about what any reasonable man would do in a given situation and certain legal decisions (case laws) documenting what certain judges have decided, but on the whole the notion of probable or reasonable cause is vague. Thus, since the right is forbidding *unreasonable* searches and seizures, there is the ever-present problem of either showing that any search is *reasonable* or *unreasonable* depending on the interpretation of the situation. This is true not only with searches and seizures but also with every application of the law and judgment on the acknowledgment of due process.

2. *The right of a person to be informed of his constitutional rights whenever suspicion is focused upon him.* This aspect of due process is essentially the protection against ignorance of one's rights. Known as the "Miranda warning," this right holds that before a person can be geared into the criminal justice system, he should be advised that he does not have to say anything and that anything he does say can be used against him in court. Further, if a criminal suspect so desires, an attorney can be present during all questioning, and if the suspect can-

not afford an attorney, one will be appointed without cost. The application of this right has been subject to many interpretations and uses. For example, if a criminal suspect blurts out a confession to the police but the police have not questioned him, some jurisdictions will allow the confession to be admitted as evidence in court. The argument is that since the police did not question the person, they did nothing illegal in obtaining the confession. In other cases, other jurisdictions, and other situations, there would be a different interpretation and application of the Miranda warning.

3. *The right against self-incrimination.* A person cannot be forced to be a witness against himself; that is, he does not have to talk to the police, the prosecutor, or even a jury in a manner that will divulge information that will implicate him in a crime. This right is spelled out clearly in the Fifth Amendment of the Constitution, and when criminal defendants "take the Fifth," they are exercising their right against self-incrimination.

4. *The right to an attorney during criminal justice proceedings where critical decisions are made.* In the landmark case *Gideon v. Wainwright*[2] the Supreme Court held that counsel was to be made available to felony defendants who could not afford one. Later, in the 1972 case of *Argersinger v. Hamlin,* this right was afforded to misdemeanor defendants who could possibly be imprisoned. There are still a large number of defendants accused of misdemeanors who do not have the right to free legal counsel, but given the interpretation of the Sixth Amendment in *Gideon v. Wainwright,* the trend in decisions has been to affirm the right of legal counsel to all who come before the criminal justice system. Whether this right will be extended to all defendants, though, is not yet decided.

5. *The right to reasonable notice of the nature of the charge against the defendant.* This right may seem to be superfluous since we might take it for granted that if a person was arrested the police and courts would "naturally" tell him why he was arrested. However, this right is extremely important, for where it does not exist, a person can be arrested for almost any reason. Additionally, if a defendant is not informed of the charges against him, it is difficult for him to defend himself since he does not know what he must defend himself against.

6. *The right to be heard.* A defendant has the right to tell his side of the story and present witnesses that will aid in his defense. This prevents the development of a one-sided case and promotes the adversary system of equal representation.

7. *The right of the defendant to confront the witness against him.* When one person accuses another of a crime, the accused can face the witness and learn exactly the nature of the accusation. Not only does

---

[2] This case is explained in detail in Anthony Lewis, *Gideon's Trumpet* (New York: Random House, 1964).

this provide the defendant with an opportunity to cross-examine the accuser but it also prevents him from being accused by anonymous witnesses.

8. *The right to a fair trial.* When a defendant is charged with a crime, he has the right to be tried on the basis of evidence developed and presented in court and to be tried in a location that will ensure a minimum of prejudice against him. For example, if a defendant is charged with child-molesting in a small town where everyone knows the child or its parents, but little if anything about the defendant, the chances of a fair trial in that town are undoubtedly not good. Therefore, the trial can be moved to another town or jurisdiction where emotions about the case may not be as intense, thus enabling the defendant to get a fair trial.

9. *The right to a jury trial.* In many countries the idea of a jury trial by a group of laymen is considered strange. They consider the American jury system based on judgment by the defendant's peers to be unusual in that the jurors are not legal experts. In Holland, for example, trials are held by a panel of three judges who weigh the legal evidence of a case based on what the prosecutor and defense present in court. For most offenses, criminal defendants have the right to a jury trial, but there is a good deal of variation in different states as to the right to a jury trial for several offenses, especially minor ones.

10. *The right to a speedy and public trial.* This right is especially important for those who are in jail awaiting trial. If this rule of speed did not exist, a person could be accused of a crime and incarcerated indefinitely before his trial. The time limit for a "speedy trial" is not specified, but in some states it is 180 days—about a half-year. This may not seem speedy enough to the jailed defendant, and there have been cases in which innocent persons were held in custody for this length of time before their trials began. In some cases where the defendant "waives time" (agrees to a longer amount of time for better preparation of his defense) he can spend even longer periods of time in jail before his trial.

Trials must also be public to avoid "backroom" trials in which the defendant's rights may well be violated by the officers of the court. Publicity is provided by the press in most instances, but any citizen has the right to attend a trial.

11. *The right against double jeopardy.* Once acquitted of a crime, a person cannot be retried for that crime. In cases of a "hung" jury, that is, a jury that cannot reach agreement as to the defendant's innocence or guilt, the person can be tried again until a jury decides his fate one way or another.

These eleven rules, though constituting only a partial list of due process rights, point to processes and procedures in criminal justice that are of possible interest and partial explanations of why things are done the way they are. However, as we shall see, the legal rules form only a background for the criminal justice process; if we decided to study merely the legal requirements of criminal justice, we would find it difficult to explain what happens within the system on a day-to-day basis.

THE CRIMINAL JUSTICE SYSTEM

The purpose of the criminal justice system is to process those who have been accused of criminal activities. At the outset, the police are responsible for gathering evidence and arresting suspected law violators. Next, the prosecutor is responsible for evaluating the evidence the police have gathered and deciding whether it is sufficient to warrant filing charges against alleged violators. Meanwhile, defense attorneys, whether privately retained or provided by the state, are responsible for defending the accused. At trial, the judge is an arbitrator in court who ensures that the defense and prosecution adhere to the legal requirements of introducing evidence and examining and cross-examining witnesses. Additionally, the judge supervises jury operations and pronounces sentences against those found guilty. Probation officers construct presentence investigations the judge will make use of in the determination of sentences, and also supervise convicted defendants placed on probation. If the defendants are convicted and sentenced to prison the prison system receives and keeps them until the parole board grants them parole or they have completed their sentences. Finally, the parole department assists released prisoners in their reintegration into the community.

This brief ideal description of the criminal justice system's work makes it appear to be a system-like process. The problem with treating the criminal justice agencies as a system, however, is that there are very few system-like features among these agencies. Ideally, a system is expected to have interrelated goals, but when we look at the goals of the various agencies (which are called part of the "criminal justice system") oftentimes we find that not only are the goals not interrelated but they are also often contradictory. For example, it is a police goal to clear as many reported crimes as possible, and to the extent the police are successful, the court's goal of clearing the calendar (processing defendants through the courts) is thwarted (Skolnick, 1966; Blumberg, 1967). Cooperation between the various agencies is haphazard and understanding of each other's problems is almost nonexistent. Defense and prosecuting attorneys blame the police for violating a defendant's rights, and the police accuse the attorneys of letting too many of the people they arrest go free. Agencies blame each other for not doing their jobs properly. Even though they are all supposed to be working together to achieve a single overall goal, a system-like process and organization remains an ideal instead of a reality. However, even

The Supreme Court of the United States interprets laws and cases in terms of the Constitution and Bill of Rights. The direction of the interpretations depends on who fills the positions on the Supreme Court. (*Fred Ward from Black Star*)

though we realize the agencies that make up the "criminal justice system" (structure) do not in fact constitute a system, we shall use the term since it denotes all of the agencies and processes as a whole.

THE SITUATIONAL APPROACH TO CRIMINAL JUSTICE

In examining the criminal justice process, we can identify three distinct and predominant approaches. The first, which we shall call the "administrative-legal approach," focuses on the ideal administration of justice. How the criminal justice system operates is explained in terms of how the law and administrative policies and procedures for carrying out various criminal justice duties say it operates. A major weakness with this approach is that it assumes that the criminal justice system operates basically according to the laws and policies set down in the ideal. It tends to reify the ideal in the description of actual workings. Those who are tutored under this system of legal-administrative idealism are disappointed when they see what actually takes place in criminal justice. Police often complain that they learned nothing useful in the academy, and only after "street experience" do they really know how to operate and understand criminal justice. Similarly, attorneys who are instructed in the case approach to law soon learn that the courthouse does not operate in terms of the fine points of law they studied in law school.

A second major approach to the study of criminal justice, the "critical approach" (Quinney, 1974:16–25; Chambliss and Seidman, 1971), is designed to expose the "official" explanations of criminal justice and show what the criminal justice system actually does to people. This approach is not content with merely exposing conventional or official ideology; it also advocates *radical* change of society. As Quinney (1974:17) explains:

> It is in a critical theory that we are able to break with the ideology of the age. For built into the process of critical thinking is the ability to think negatively. This dialectical form of thought allows us to question current experience. By being able to entertain an alternative, we can better understand what exists. Rather than merely looking for an objective reality, we are concerned with the negation of the established order. Through this negation we are better able to understand what we experience. Possibly only by means of this dialectic can the present be comprehended. Certainly the present cannot be surpassed until the dialectic is applied to our thought.

The critical approach to criminal justice focuses on the development of legal rules and their administration by state officials. The substantive and procedural law is conceptualized as the product of those social groups holding economic power working to have their particular interests formalized in law and supported by the state. The law as well as the formal and informal crime control policies shaped by those groups holding power are fundamental inputs to the organizations charged with the administration of law. That is, the legal rules provide reference points for the management of those types of disorder which the powerful deem threatening and wrongful. To be sure, officials may not literally adhere to the written word of the legal rules and policies but instead interpret them vis-à-vis concrete situations of action. Nevertheless, such rules do function as reference points to be employed.

A central problem with the critical approach is that it glosses the dynamics whereby critical decisions regarding the existence of crime, the guilt of suspects, and the proper disposition of offenders are made.

Our position, which we call the "situational approach" (Sanders and Daudistel, 1976:1–10), is grounded in a theoretical framework that points to "critical situations" in which actual decisions about processing persons are made. We do not rely on policy pronouncements or legal statements for conclusions. Instead, we look to empirical evidence concerning those occasions where criminal justice officials are engaged in the practical tasks of processing people and doing justice.

Our position is grounded in the phenomenological point of view. We focus on how events come to be *seen* as crimes (Schutz, 1967; Gurwitsch, 1965; Garfinkel, 1967). We do not treat the social world as a set of objective facts. We investigate society in terms of facts that are made by people in interaction. Criminal justice agents do not function like a computer that responds to electrical impulses running through its wires. Instead, they operate as people who are trying to make sense of others' acts in relation to the criminal law. From the first policeman to respond to a call for police intervention in a possible criminal matter to the parole officer who is trying to decide whether or not he should revoke a client's parole, criminal justice agents ask, "What's going on here?" and "What should I do about it?" They have to make decisions about complex, confusing, and contradictory accounts of events and people, and *these decisions* come to be treated as objective facts; therefore, instead of treating organizationally and socially constructed facts as though they are objective (cf. Wilson, 1970), we shall focus on how they are created.

We take the position that in order to understand how criminal justice gets done on a day-to-day basis, we must focus on those situations in which some kind of sense is made out of the array of materials, accounts, and people that are encountered by criminal justice agents. Thus, we view the work done by the criminal justice system as accomplished in situated and occasioned encounters between people (Zimmerman and Pollner, 1970; Goffman, 1961, 1963, 1974).

By pointing out that laws are defined when the conduct of persons is evaluated by criminal justice agents, we are forced to pay attention to the interpretive work done in applying the law. When policemen, prosecutors, judges, and others evaluate an act, they elaborate the meaning of the law in terms of the act, and the criminal or noncriminal nature of the act is affected by the definition given to the law. That is, the act and the law mutually elaborate one another in the talk about both. For example, consider two men in a bar hitting one another. We could talk about the hitting as "playing," "goofing off," or some other nonlegal activity. Or we could elaborate the actions in terms of law violation, such as "battery," "disturbing the peace," or "assault." There is no objective reality independent of the talk, since the talk points to some unseen interpretive scheme that informs observers of what is "really happening."

To further elaborate this point, what would happen if someone called the police when two men were hitting one another? When the police officer arrives he is likely to ask, "What the hell's going on here?" Now, he may see clearly the two men hitting one another, but this is not his only concern. Someone might tell him, "They're fighting" or "They're drunk" or "Joe's beating up Sam" or any number of other things that could be violations of the law. On the other hand, he may be told, "They're only playing" or "They're seeing who can hit the hardest" or "They're just showing off." Whether the act is a crime depends on what account is provided and accepted. The exact law that is violated depends on how the event is elaborated and accounted for. Therefore, we cannot understand why the law is applied unless we know how the act and the law were interpreted.

Alternative interpretations of acts are made by criminal justice agents according to information they gather about the circumstances surrounding acts. For example, in a reported burglary an investigating detective learned that the person believed to be responsible for the burglary was the estranged husband of the victim. By treating the alleged crime as a "divorce problem," the detective was able to provide an alternative sense for the event, and instead of proceeding to investigate the matter as a burglary, he suggested that the case be settled by the woman and her ex-husband in civil court (Sanders, 1977:94). Thus, by viewing the event in terms of a different scheme, the detective provided both the account for not applying the burglary law and a way of making sense of the concrete act itself. That is, even though a home had been illegally entered and furniture stolen, the illegal entry was not really a crime because the alleged criminal was once the husband of the victim. Rather than taking things like other burglars, the ex-husband was trying to take what he once owned.

The detective in the aforementioned case could have treated the

The initial critical situation in the criminal justice process occurs when someone "calls the cops." (*Wide World Photos*)

THE STUDY OF CRIMINAL JUSTICE

incident as a burglary rather than a civil problem. The elements of the burglary law were satisfied literally. For example, there was physical evidence that indicated someone broke into the dwelling and took furniture. But even though the man did not legally own the furniture he was not a typical burglar; he was an acquaintance who took things he felt were his. The biography of the culprit turned out to be a crucial variable in the decision-making process about this case. The man's marital status is technically irrelevant to the law, but as we can see, it was in fact very important in this case.

Since all accounts depend on some context for their specific sense, they are context-bound instead of context-free or objective (Wilson, 1970). Therefore, any and all applications of the law are tied to the context of their situated usage and cannot be treated as independent of this context. All attempts to make laws more objective or specific and literal eventually fail, for at least some contextual matters are necessary to make sense out of even the most specific statements. Furthermore, all laws are reflexively created in the situations where they are applied, for the meaning of the law is discovered in the situation in which they are applied (Wieder, 1974:167–170). Thus, instead of the talk about law violation being separate and independent of the situation, it constructs the sense of the situation so that it is understandable as a law violation. In this way we can understand the reality of law application, and instead of attempting to determine whether or not the application of the law is literal or according to the book, which is impossible anyway, we can concentrate on the ways in which the law works on a day-to-day basis in criminal justice.

The central theme to our approach is that interpretive work is necessary if one is to competently use the law. Even though the law is said to be specific, as we pointed out in our discussion of the characteristics of a criminal law, and although those acts which are asserted to be criminal are assumed to be outlined by the law, it cannot be claimed that the law is absolutely objective. Statutes are written in a manner that is claimed to be more objective than other social norms, but this "objectivity" is not available in the law itself. "Elements" of crimes cannot act as specific criteria which instruct one how to accurately label acts as criminal. The meaning of the elements of a crime are determined on the occasions in which they are used. No matter how many elements (or criteria) are outlined by the law, it is not automatically apparent to anyone who uses the law when the elements are represented in concrete acts and when they are not. The policeman, judge, attorney, or others who use the law to categorize persons as offenders must show that each element of a crime is present in the specific act committed by the accused. This work is not consciously viewed by the agents of the criminal justice system as work, but it is, and it is necessary for them to do it. The question is how this work, which we shall call "competent categorization of offenders," is accomplished. No matter how many criteria are written in the law, they cannot act as literal elements. In fact, the ideal of absolute specificity in the written law cannot be obtained. It is impossible to construct a rule which can be used literally as a guide for proper categorization, for it is not possible to specify beforehand all the occasions in which a rule may seem to apply. For instance, although the law says it is a crime to take the life of another with malice aforethought, it is not possible for the law to specify all the unique occasions in which that law may apply. Indeed, if a man were to kill his wife on October 15 at 9:00 A.M. at the corner of Elm and Main streets, he would probably be charged with the crime of murder even though the law says nothing about a man's wife, the date, or the corner of Elm and Main. Of course, one may point out that the law refers to killing anyone and there are a number of general conditions where it is not illegal to do so—for example, self-defense. Nevertheless, categorization of a behavior as a murder is not done without any effort. The person categorizing the behavior must construct the meaning or the law's elements and then determine whether they are found in the behavior in question. Importantly, the law does not specifically indicate what is concretely required of a unique act to be a crime. It merely provides a category (or type of act) which itself must be interpreted.

Other writers in the field of criminal justice point out that legal decisions are made by members of the criminal justice system who rely on a unique system of formal and informal rules. These rules, especially the informal ones, are used to explain why there is differential enforcement of laws. Explanations of decision-making center around these rules, for by arguing that legal agents adhere to an informal or formal set of rules, criminal justice researchers can "show" decision patterns in terms of these "rules." For example, observers of the courts have shown that "standard deals" exist in terms of an informal policy for adjudicating people in misdemeanor cases where the sentences were less than the punishment called for by the law. (Mendes and Wold, 1976:192–96). Of course, informal rules may exist, but we do not believe that the decision-making process can be explained entirely by reference to these rules.

We have found that when deciding what to do with a criminal case, criminal justice agents are always forced to provide accounts to characterize their decisions as rule-governed. They may make a variety of different decisions about similar cases, yet still argue that they were constrained by a specific rule. Agents legitimate decisions as rule-governed so they do not appear to be capricious in their treatment of offenders. In fact, however, they are very flexible and treat cases differently depending on the circumstances associated with them. Normative conceptions of rule use, especially those which rely on a cursory review of informal rules to account for patterns of decisions, frequently miss seeing this work as a fundamental process called criminal justice.

In a study of police-prosecutor discretion, Daudistel (1976) found evidence of the interpretive work we call "doing justice." This work was particularly apparent in police reports officers wrote about the cases they were assigned to investigate.

Any policeman writing an official report for the law enforcement agency studied had an opportunity to account for his categorization of a particular behavior as an instance of a crime. Heading the report form was a request that the officer classify the reported event in accordance with the penal code. He had to specify what type of crime or crimes he was documenting. When the officer documented the offense, arrest, or incident he was classifying, he filled in spaces in the report form which asked him to specify the elements of the crime. Following from this, the report form requested, among other things, the victim's name and address, the day and time the crime occurred, person who discovered the crime, location of the victim's property at the time of the offense, the point of entry, the method used to gain entrance, weapons used, and possible suspects. Finally, in a blank section taking most of the space on the form, referred to as the "narrative section," the officer was requested to "summarize the details related to the crime."

Since the narrative section provided a context through which officers and others interpret categorizations of crimes, it was the most important part of the form. Departmental attempts to construct a report form that omitted this space failed. An administrative officer who at one time was in charge of the records bureau contended that attempts to eliminate the task of writing out a narrative account (by supplying the officer with a structured form which gave him a finite set of preestablished categories to be checked if the alleged criminal event exhibited those features) failed because a definitive list of features of any given crime cannot be preestablished. "They have never been able to figure out what to put on those forms," the administrative officer reported. "Also the ones I've seen used by other departments seem to over-complicate things. I have always argued that a good report could be written on a blank piece of toilet paper."

An example of an instance where the particulars of one's action were interpreted differently when contexts were altered was offered by the police investigation of a crime report which alleged that the crimes of "assault with a deadly weapon" and "theft" had been committed. The initial patrol report labeled the incident as an assault, which in California is "An unlawful attempt, coupled with the present ability, to commit a violent injury on the person of another" (California Penal Code: 1971:43). This report said that a young female who had witnessed three other women (suspects) taking fruit from an orchard was assaulted by the thieves. When suspects saw the observer, it was alleged that they attempted to "run her down with their vehicle." Although the vehicle did not hit her, the girl had told her father about the incident. Believing an assault had occurred, he called patrol officers. Apparently the policemen agreed with the father and documented all of the elements necessary to charge someone with assault by including evidence in the report that was supposed to support the claim that a crime had taken place. Like other reports, this one was to act as an explanation for its writer's categorizing the specific act as an assault.

Because the patrol officer who wrote the report formulated a background in accordance with the assertion that an actual crime was committed, he searched the victim's story for documentary evidence that supported his "assault" label. The officer's notion of a typical assault provided a context through which particular features became relevant to the case. Consequently, the action "car headed in girl's direction" was used as a piece of evidence supporting the claim that an actual assault had been committed. But later, detectives, acting on the same report, formulated an alternative background which indicated that the particulars of the event did not point to a criminal act. Based on a story provided by the three suspects, they examined the same particulars of the case and determined that the evidence did not document any crime. Even though the victim claimed she had told the patrol officer that the automobile "had jumped the curb" and headed in her direction, this was not noted by the patrol officer. In the detectives' report, this feature (evidence) documented their interpretation that an attempt to run the girl down had not been made.

This case illustrates the mutually elaborative character of the elements of "act" and "intent." In the detectives' account, one of the suspects said that in the process of making a U-turn in order to leave the area, the automobile had "accidentally jumped the curb." The detectives' reformulation of circumstances altered the meaning of the particulars in the case and showed that other particulars not reported by the patrolman were important. These new relevant features altered the circumstances of the incident so that the patrolman's allegation that criminal intent was manifested in the acts of the suspects could not be supported by the evidence. Given a new noncriminal background within which the specific actions took place, these acts themselves became noncriminal.

What actions one sees in a crime scene depend on the context in which they are formulated, and the context as formulated depends on the social acts deemed relevant. The patrolman drew the inference of a criminal state of mind based upon his identification of relevant acts committed by the suspects. However, the detective made an inference of a noncriminal state of mind based on his assessment of the suspect's account of the events. This inference then made other acts relevant which in turn supported the noncriminal interpretation of the report.

The law itself seems to explicitly call for the use of the documentary method whenever one is attempting to establish the presence of criminal intent. For example, Section 21 of the California Penal Code reads:

> Intent How Manifested and Who is Considered of Sound Mind: The intent or intention is manifested by the circumstances connected with the offense and the sound mind and discretion of the accused.

Even though the law prescribes that a criminal charge can be sustained only when it is established that there is an "act," "intent," and congruence between them, the penal code section about intent suggests that the two cannot be separated. A crime cannot be identified if one examines its constitutent elements by extracting them from the context in which they occur. The existence of criminal intent cannot be established independently of specific acts that are said to reflect a criminal state of mind, and the existence of relevant acts cannot be established without some inference to the state of mind of the individual. Even in those cases in which it is claimed that criminal intent is established by the commission of a act, that is, general intent, criminal justice practitioners cannot establish general intent by only looking for a forbidden act. In order to discover the forbidden act there must be a perception of intent. Crimes, then, are not built out of elements that exist independently of one another. Any specific "act," if considered in isolation of its context, "may be affected so radically and by such deep-reaching modifications as to destroy its phenomenal or experiential identity" (Gurwitsch, 1964:114). The discovery of a criminal act is not possible through an examination of properties which belong to it per se.

THE DOCUMENTARY METHOD OF INTERPRETATION

The importance of the narrative section of police reports points to the role played by the officers' characterization of the circumstances of an incident. The previous examples showed that violations of the law (or the correct application of penal-code sections) are not found by simply matching the elements listed in the criminal law with a concrete situation. Because laws are used as titles descriptive of criminal acts, the argument is similar to Wieder's discussion of the use of names and titles: "If one examines the activity of employing criteria for using names or titles, he finds that the particular sense of the criteria are specific to the cases in which the criteria are employed" (1970:128). Rather than having a stable meaning across a set of cases that are classified by their use, criteria are matched against cases by elaborat-

The arrest situation brings people into the criminal justice process. Arrests are based on interpretations of people and events in terms of the law. (*Charles Moore from Black Star*)

ing the sense of the criteria or the case to encompass the particular occurrences that the name or title user faces.

The documentary method of interpretation is one conceptualization of the way in which police officers elaborate the sense of the elements of the law and the situation to which it is applied. Garfinkel identifies and defines the procedure as follows:

> The method consists of treating an actual appearance as "the document of," as "pointing to," as "standing on behalf of" a presupposed underlying pattern. Not only is the underlying pattern derived from its individual documentary evidences, but the individual documentary evidences, in their turn, are

interpreted on the basis of what is known about the underlying pattern. Each is used to elaborate the other (1967:78).

This mutually elaborative character of particulars and backgrounds has long been a concern of gestalt psychologists and others. For example, Gurwitsch (1964:114) comments that a "configuration cannot be accounted for in terms of the properties and attributes which its constituents display when they are extracted from the actual configuration and are taken isolatedly."

None of the police and prosecutors interviewed by Daudistel (1976) used the term "documentary method." Furthermore, none recognized that the specificity of the criminal law was accomplished through their own interpretive work. Nevertheless, they frequently indicated that they recognized the important relationship between particulars of action and the context in which the particulars occurred. Detectives who took pride in themselves as expert investigators were quick to point out that one should not ignore particular features of a crime scene even though, at the moment, they might not appear relevant to the investigation. What is relevant, it was said, depends on the "total picture" one has constructed about a crime. If that picture is incorrect, and one has formed an erroneous assumption about a crime, particular pieces of evidence will probably be ignored. In other words, if one has assumed a particular background and it is incorrect, the evidence available to the detective will be interpreted in accordance with a scheme that will lead him to an inappropriate conclusion. Detectives seem to recognize that a particular piece of evidence does not have a specific meaning; it can mean many different things.

Evidence of the officers' recognition of the interaction between backgrounds and particulars can be obtained readily by watching police photographers at the scene of an alleged murder as they work to photograph every aspect of the crime scene. Pictures and notes about them are said to provide the officers with a chance to "totally reconstruct" the crime scene long after the crime has occurred. Creating alternative contexts may "expose" new evidence that was initially overlooked. For example, if a man is found slain in the bathroom of his home, the particular features of the scene will probably be interpreted in terms of the background "murder." Then, what features are considered relevant—that is, what pieces of evidence are seen—will depend on the murder context. Likewise, the context of murder will be documented by the particulars. But suppose it is learned that the victim was despondent over a recent business failure? An alternative context of suicide may be used as an interpretive scheme through which the particulars are examined. By altering the context, one who reexamines the crime scene (through photographs) may actually see pieces of evidence that were originally overlooked (not seen) in the first investigation.

Further evidence of the detectives' recognition of the interaction between backgrounds and particulars was illustrated by an officer's written remarks about criminal investigations:

> Of prime importance is to approach the case with an open mind. On receiving a complaint or information, the investigator should think only "it is said such and such a crime has been committed at such and such a place." If an opinion is formed too early, the investigator may come up with a preconceived opinion which may be erroneous; and if it is erroneous and he holds to it, priceless time and valuable clues will slip by. And if a definite opinion is formed too late, the whole investigation is bound to be a flop.

In his statement the detective seems to recognize that if a background is prematurely formulated, many clues or particulars will not be noticed. Additionally, if no background is assumed, the particulars will be a swirl of meaningless perceptions, lacking any coherence or sense.

These cases illustrate that acts labeled as criminal depend on how evidence is formulated. Pieces of evidence by themselves do not necessarily document a crime. The problem is further complicated, however, because the law itself does not tell agents of the criminal justice system what features of a crime scene or citizen's report are relevant, nor does it specifically define what constitutes a violation of the law. Even though this is the case, it does not mean that what is written in the law is irrelevant. Police officers and prosecutors must account for their decisions by reference to the written law. Indeed, if the written law were completely meaningless, it would be hard to explain why officers insist that they are enforcing it.

KNOWING THE LAW

Knowledge of the penal code is one prerequisite to being a good police officer or prosecutor. It is assumed that anyone who knows the code can determine when a particular crime has been committed. Notice that knowledge of the law does not mean one *will determine* when an act is a crime; rather, this depends on the person's ability to "competently use the law." When an officer or prosecutor is characterized as a good cop or a good district attorney, that person is characterized not only as one "who really knows the law" but also as one who can be relied upon to know what to look for in order to correctly document that someone has violated a particular law.

Police crime reports are evaluated by persons in positions at various levels in the criminal justice system. For example, patrol reports are reviewed by patrol supervisors, detectives, and prosecutors, while detectives' reports are reviewed by supervisors in the investigative bureau and prosecutor's office. At all levels the major concern of the evaluator is to determine whether the report adequately documents a crime. If a report is not adequate it can be rejected, returned to the officer, or be reinvestigated by the evaluator or someone supervised by the evaluator. Whatever action is taken, if the report is negatively evaluated the evaluator must also account for his decision. This can be done by merely showing that the documentation in the report failed to support the particular charge the report asserted. Supervisors, detectives, and prosecutors do not need to establish the applicability of an *alternative* law or rule in order to convince others that the report is inadequate. Put simply, if a patrolman fails to convince detectives that the report he has written documents an actual crime, his failure is felt to have resulted from detectives' inability to accept his data as relevant facts supportive of a criminal categorization. The following case illustrates this review process.

Patrolmen filed a report coded as an "attempted armed robbery." A man had entered a local liquor store and asked the clerk for a bottle of Seagrams. When the clerk asked whether the man wanted "Seagrams-Seven or Seagrams VO," he replied, again, "Seagrams." The clerk turned his back to the customer and took a bottle off the shelf. At this point, the clerk thought he heard a gunshot and because of it dropped to the floor behind the counter. He left the bottle on the floor and ran to the back of the store as the customer ran out the front door. A detective who worked on the major crimes detail that handled this type of case said the report was a bad one because "[the case] did not appear to be a real 211 [robbery]."

The patrolmen's report of the "attempted robbery" included the following evidence in support of the allegation that the crime took place:

1. Victim: Clerk of the liquor store.
2. Criminal: Man who asked for bottle of liquor.
3. Act: Ineffectual overt attempt to complete robbery—gunshot and run out of the store.

In addition to the major crimes detective who evaluated the report as a bad one, two other detectives (one from the major crimes unit and another assigned to the burglary detail) agreed that "they could

A facsimile of an offense report, which is prepared by patrolmen and sent on by them to the detective division.

not see a 211 in the report" because the report did not supply the pieces of evidence they felt were needed to appropriately document a 211. In other words, the report was considered inadequate because it only *asserted* that a robbery took place. During their review of the patrolmen's account, detectives could not connect the evidence about the victim, the criminal, and the act to the elements of the law.

The major point of disagreement was the customer's status as a criminal. Detectives claimed, reasonably enough, that a person's presence in a store in which some crime may have occurred is not necessarily incriminating. In order to successfully label someone as a criminal the patrol officers needed to establish (1) that the actual behavior of the customer was an instance of an attempt to obtain the possessions of another by force or threat of force; (2) that the customer specifically intended to take the personal property in the possession of another; and (3) that "what may have been a gun shot" was an instance of the element of force.[3]

While establishing the factual existence of evidence that documents the elements of the crime, the patrol officers must also typify the event as a robbery. "The process of typification consists of ignoring what makes a particular object (or event) unique and placing that object in the same class with others that share some trait or quality" (Heeren, 1970:51). The strange aspects of the case had to be identified as either solid evidence of a crime or irrelevant to the case. Because the report did not characterize the crime in its normal form, detectives did not consider it as another instance of a typical robbery.

NORMAL FORMS OF CRIME

Reporting an event as a normal form of crime does not require completely unambiguous communications. Police officers, like others, expect that some parts of reports will be vague and that some remarks will be understandable only by considering the context in which they are written. But a police report, regardless of the context in which it is written, must also be constructed out of pieces of "factual evidence" that are generally available to all who investigate a case. Thus, the above case did not cease to be a "good case" simply because it had some unusual qualities. Indeed, it became a "good case" when a new investi-

---

[3] One explanation for the detectives' failure to accept this report could be that it did not establish the fact of a commission of a crime, that is, *corpus delicti*. However, the detectives' treatment of other cases does not support this argument, since they accepted many reports that included only partial evidence of the *corpus delicti*. For example, a victim's statement that a crime occurred is not proof of the *corpus delicti*, but on most occasions detectives accepted reports as documents of real crimes when the only evidence was such a statement.

gation typified the incident and made a connection between an unknown suspect and the act of robbery, thus saving the patrolmen's classification.

A detective was assigned to reinvestigate the case, to look for features that would further substantiate that a robbery attempt had occurred. If additional evidence could not be found, the officer was to close the case. After a brief investigation the detective concurred with the patrolman. Although the case seemed strange, the detective was able to typify it as being one of a series of attempted liquor store robberies that had been committed in a nearby city. When the detective discussed the case with another detective who was investigating these robberies, he was given a description of the suspect, which generally matched the one given by the liquor-store clerk.

The attempted robbery was more specifically typified when it was linked to a suspect perceived as a good (typical) robbery suspect. He was characterized as a young male who probably used drugs and therefore needed cash to purchase narcotics. In this case the gunshot was also accounted for by the biography of the suspect. Since anyone under the influence of narcotics could be expected to behave in a bizarre fashion, the unprovoked firing of the gun was no longer considered an unusual occurrence.

Typifications of events are not only done by detectives. The commonsense knowledge of patrolmen also consists of ideas about typical crimes. Consequently, they will search victims' stories for evidence that coincides with their typifications of crimes. Basically, even though officers feel their experience in law enforcement constitutes special knowledge not possessed by the average citizen, they assume that citizens will document their complaints with information that does not contradict commonly shared "repertories of what constitutes normal appearances in the culture" (Cicourel, 1974:86). Despite the fact that a wide variety of acts may be turned into, say, a typical burglary, patrol officers still expect to find some evidence to substantiate citizens' claims that they have been victimized. When evaluating citizens' reports, patrol officers, as well as detectives, are prepared to deal with some discrepancies between a victim's or suspect's idealizations of past events and their own, but they are not willing (or able) to let pass discrepancies that breach the "natural attitude" (Schutz, 1967:7). This means that officers assume there are some natural boundaries that distinguish between what is and what is not objectively possible.

When boundaries are breached by a citizen's report about a crime, policemen actively try to normalize the citizen's account. If they cannot typify the incident as an acceptable crime, they can treat the report as false and unfounded. For example, if a citizen violated the natural attitude by telling patrolmen that he saw an automobile going in two directions simultaneously, the officers would probably normalize the incident by labeling the citizen as a drug addict or "crazy person" who is hallucinating. A less extreme instance of the normalization process was observed when an event reported to officers as an armed robbery did not fit their notion of a normal armed robbery. The interpretive work officers did to specifically account for the odd story, rather than letting it pass, illustrates the officers' efforts to maintain their sense of typical crimes and sustain the natural attitude.

A woman who worked at a clothing store told patrol officers she was robbed while transporting the day's receipts from the store to the bank for deposit. She said that a man of medium height and build hid behind the seat of her pickup truck and forced her at gun point to give him the money from the bank deposit bags and drive to another location in the area where he got out of the vehicle. But, according to officers, the type of truck the woman was driving made it impossible for anyone to do what the victim claimed the robber did. She argued that the robber was behind the driver's seat and managed to conceal himself until she got in and began to drive.

Because the woman's story breached the officers' expectations about what was possible, the evidence she gave them was not treated as factual. Furthermore, the woman's story contradicted the officers' typification of a normal robbery. In order to restore the normal form of robbery, the officers searched for some account that would explain the differences between her story and their conception of how events in the world must naturally occur. This account was provided by a negative character evaluation of the woman. Because she had been previously arrested for drug possession, she was characterized as a drug user. This label, "drug user," turned an unbelievable story into a "typical attempt to cover up a crime." Now, with this biographical characterization the woman's original report was coded as "false and unfounded," but the case was not closed; it was reformulated as embezzlement. Also, the woman was no longer treated as a robbery victim; rather, she was reformulated as a suspect in the embezzlement (Sanders, 1977:101).

By treating the woman's story as one that was produced by a drug user who tried to embezzle money to support her expensive habit, officers no longer were faced with the discrepancies between the woman's idealization of the events and their own idealization of a normal robbery. Her story was no longer strange because she took the money, and there were no physical traces of the robber's presence behind the seat because a robber never existed.

When a district attorney[4] reviews reports, he too may reject cases because they fail to adequately document the charges. Cases judged to be inadequately documented are illustrated by the following example.

---

[4] In referring to the district attorney or "D.A.," we shall generally be talking about assistant district attorneys who screen or prosecute cases brought to the district attorney's office by the police.

A district attorney was handed a patrol report that was supposed to document the burglary of a motor vehicle. This report indicated that a young girl had been arrested and charged with "burglary," a violation of Section 459 of the California Penal Code.

The alleged burglary was said to have been committed on the freezer compartment of an ice-cream truck. The freezer was locked with a heavy padlock which was reported to have been broken off by the suspect. After the D.A. read the report, he said forced entry would be difficult to establish on the basis of what was written in the patrol report. Because the suspect was a female, he felt that the presence of tools used to commit the crime would have to be established. Apparently it was not enough, according to him, to say that the lock was broken by the suspect; there had to be some evidence that she was capable of doing so.

The D.A. said, "I thought everything was all right when I read the report. But I didn't find any mention of tools." Because the suspect was a female, because she was arrested at the scene of the crime, and because there was no mention of tools in the report, he concluded, "She could not have done it." However, the prosecutor did not deny that a crime took place. He accepted as factual that portion of the report which established that property was missing. In order to account for the missing property the D.A. asserted that the crime had to have been committed by someone else; in this case, he argued that a boyfriend of the suspect was probably involved.

This case shows that failure to document all of the elements of a crime can be a basis for others to argue that a report is inadequate. In this instance, there was no articulation between one of the elements—forceful entry—and the suspect's action. In order to establish that the woman committed an act of forceful entry, the patrolman had to describe the methods she used to break the lock on the ice-cream truck. In a manner similar to the cases previously discussed, the district attorney used the context of the crime to legitimate his decision. Again, the context partially consisted of a characterization of the suspect; that is, a typical female cannot possibly break a lock without help from someone else.

When a police report is reviewed by a district attorney, he can use the complaint man[5] to help solve ambiguities in police reports. For example, a D.A. who was reviewing a report that charged two college students with illegal entry and felony possession of marijuana considered the report inadequate because it did not accurately specify the amount of marijuana the suspects possessed. The report stated that they had entered a vacant apartment and were sleeping in it when the

---

[5] The "complaint man" is a representative from the police who takes cases to the D.A.'s office. He provides the D.A. with interpretive schemes for understanding problematic cases.

manager of the building apprehended them. As the officers were taking the two suspects into custody they discovered a small quantity of marijuana and a "½ square inch of hashish in their possession." The district attorney turned to the complaint man for help, asking him to find out what the weight of the confiscated drugs was.

After telephoning the police property room where the drugs were being stored, the complaint man ascertained that they weighed less than a half ounce. The amount of drugs possessed by the suspects was relevant to the attorney because the informal policy[6] regarding marijuana offenses instructed him to consider the amount of drugs when deciding whether or not to charge possessors with a crime. The policy stated that cases involving over an ounce of marijuana should be treated as felony possessions; persons apprehended with over a half ounce but less than one ounce were to be treated as misdemeanants, and persons arrested for possessing less than a half ounce were to be charged with misdemeanor possession of drug paraphernalia. The inadequacy of the patrol report, which charged felony possession, was a result of ambiguous information relevant to an informal policy and not the written law. Consequently, the charge "felony possession of marijuana" was dropped. The suspects were charged with 602n ("illegal entry") and misdemeanor 11555, Health and Safety Code ("possession of narcotic paraphernalia").

In order to legitimate his decision, the district attorney did not argue that the elements of the crimes were not satisfied by the information in the police report. Instead, he legitimated his decision by making a connection between this case and a rule, not a law but an informal departmental policy. Furthermore, by acknowledging the informal rule, the complaint man accepted the attorney's decision as one that naturally "stems from adherence to the informal rules of the organization" (Wieder, 1974:170).

District attorneys can account for their decisions by reference to both informal rules and the legal rules relevant to a case, as is illustrated by the following case. A complaint man and two district attorneys were evaluating a case coded by a patrol officer as a violation of Section 261.5 of the California Penal Code, which states in part: "Unlawful sexual intercourse is an act of sexual intercourse accomplished with a female not the wife of the perpetrator, where the female is under the age of eighteen years."

The circumstances of the alleged crime were very complicated. The narrative section of the report, which was over two pages long, indicated that an out-of-town family was visiting a local state park. While the parents were preparing their camp for the evening, the daughter had "gone down the beach with a boy she had met that same

---

[6] Today this policy has changed because now the law in California treats the amount of marijuana as relevant to the charge.

afternoon." When she did not return, her parents became concerned and called the police. Both parents and a police officer began a search of the beach, and found the daughter and boy friend "making love" on the beach. The complaint man handed the report to one of the two district attorneys on duty, and the following conversation among the three took place:

Complaint Man: (*After long pause.*) Well, the thing of it is in that case there the fact that the guy's twenty and she's sixteen you might say "contributing" instead of 261.5.
(*Pause while D.A. 1 continued reading in silence. Hands D.A. 2 a copy of the report.*) I guess she was all riled up. A case of bad judgment.

D.A. 2: (*Reads from the report.*) "She was a *willing* partner." (*Loud laughter; Long pause.*)

D.A. 1: You're not going to ask me for a complaint on this goddamn thing are ya?

Complaint Man: Well, no I'm not. Do we even have a 272 [contributing to the delinquency of a minor]?

D.A. 1: Not as far as I can see. (*Pause.*)

D.A. 1: There's not that much age discrepancy.

D.A. 2: Do you have a sperm count?

Complaint Man. No.

D. A. 1: Yea, you haven't got to that yet. That she has never had it [sexual intercourse]. That's unusual, because I've had gynecologists tell me that there's no way of telling.

Complaint Man: Well, we can always, if it turns out that way . . . we can always. . . .

D.A. 1: Well, there's no, well, they already took a sperm test and there was a complete absence in this case.

Complaint Man: O.K. give me an n/c on it.

D.A. 2: What's that?

D.A. 1: Insufficient evidence, no charge.

It seems obvious that the complaint man felt that the probability of getting a 261.5 P.C. complaint was very slim. His initial statement suggests that he did not feel the case constituted any form of crime. Whether or not there was in fact sufficient evidence to sustain the charge of illegal intercourse is not known. But the complaint man did not bring up the question of sufficient evidence when he presented the case to the attorneys.

The two district attorneys, however, specifically referred to the fact that no sperm were found in the vagina of the victim. Significantly, the law does not require that a male charged with illegal sexual intercourse or rape actually ejaculate; it says only that "penetration," however slight, is a necessary element of the crime. But prosecutors hold that the presence of sperm is the best way to substantiate penetration. However, if a victim of rape (not unlawful sexual intercourse where force is not an essential element) claimed that penetration occurred and that force was used, the case would be pursued. Nevertheless, if no evidence of force was discovered and if no semen was found on the female or on her clothing, detectives and prosecutors alike believe it would be difficult if not impossible to prove that rape or unlawful intercourse was committed. Clearly, the presence of semen is an extralegal requirement in cases of alleged unlawful intercourse. As such, it has characteristics different from the requirements of ordinary informal policies. Its status as a rule for providing sufficient evidence ties it to the law in such a way that its use is seen as legally required, rather than as a matter which necessarily provides "informal justice" or more efficient bureaucratic operations.

In this case, lack of evidence of intercourse was documented in the patrol report by quoting a physician who examined the "victim." According to him, the girl had "never had sexual intercourse." This statement, in addition to the absence of sperm, was taken as legal grounds for rejecting the charge of 261.5. But lack of sperm was more important to the prosecutors than the physician's claim that intercourse had never occurred. In fact, the physician's statement ("she had never had sexual intercourse") was viewed as unusual and a contradiction to other experts. The factual nature of the physician's claim was debated, but the reality of the sperm test was not.

In addition to the problem of trying to legally establish the *corpus delicti* of unlawful sexual intercourse, both the charge of 261.5 and the proposed charge of contributing to the delinquency of a minor were rejected on informal grounds. All the participants in the discussion agreed that "the girl may have been guilty of bad judgment" and that she was a "willing partner," both very important aspects of the case. But from a legal perspective they are irrelevant. The law specifically states that a female under the age of eighteen is not capable of willing her consent. It is a basic legal assumption that a young female is unable to make good judgments. Consequently, consent is not an element of unlawful sexual intercourse. It is, however, an element of the crime of 261 P.C. rape.

The age difference of the two parties was also cited as a relevant feature of this case, but again, the law makes no distinction between what is and what is not an acceptable age differential. The relevance of age is an extralegal policy, a rationale for evaluating cases which Skolnick and Woodworth state as follows:

> Another factor taken into consideration when deciding whether to report an offense is the perceived seriousness of the offense. A rough measure of seriousness may be made by calculating the difference between the ages of the girl and the boy. Let us assume that where the difference in ages is large, the relationship is less likely to be an ordinary teenage sexual relationship and more likely to involve some exploitation of youth by experience (1967:109).

The fact that the attorneys and complaint man found the case to be an amusing episode is an indication that they did not consider the alleged crime very serious. As one of the attorneys said, "It looked like nothing more than two kids 'getting it on' at the beach." They interpreted the alleged intercourse as insignificant, and the insignificance, in turn, elaborated the lack of sufficient evidence and reinforced their interpretation that no real crime had occurred. The suspect was treated as an ordinary boy and not negatively evaluated. This same type of documentary elaboration—where the extralegal particulars of the incident and the elements of the crime alter each other's character —was apparent in other cases. This case differs from most others because the officers accounted for their rejection of the report on the dual grounds of informal policy and legal requirements.

The cases discussed thus far illustrate that the circumstances of suspect events are important to police and prosecutors. In fact, part of the complaint man's job is to tell the prosecutor what cases are really about, and in order to do this, Daudistel found, he spent approximately two hours each morning organizing arrest reports. He carefully read them, searched for additional information that might "help" the D.A. decide what to do, and talked to detectives and patrolmen who might have been involved in the cases.

While the district attorney skimmed through the reports, the complaint man filled in the details of the crimes so that the D.A. would not have to scrutinize all of the narrative section. But even if the district attorney thoroughly studied the narrative section of a report and found it adequately accounted for the elements of the crime he could still ask for more information before making a decision. A report that alleged a burglary had been committed illustrates the importance of the complaint man. A complaint man handed a report to a D.A. and said: "This is the case of Angela Gonzales, a girl who was arrested yesterday in a high crime rate area for burglary of her parents' home."

To prove the charge of burglary, its commission has to include the illegal entry of a dwelling, the dwelling must not be owned by the person who entered it, and the entry must be made with the intention of committing a larceny, petit larceny, or felony.

The particulars in the written report included, among other things, a list of items taken from the home; the approximate time entry was made; how entry was gained; a statement from the mother, who said that her daughter was not given permission to enter the home; and a statement of a brother, who said he saw Angela in the area with a bundle of stolen garments.

The district attorney was not satisfied with the information given in the report. He did not argue that it was poor information, but he did ask the complaint man to tell him what the case was really all about, in effect inviting the complaint man to provide an interpretive scheme for the event. The complaint man described the circumstances of the crime by saying that the mother requested that the complaint be filed because Angela was not given permission to enter the home. Furthermore, Angela was living a "transient existence," had no permanent home, and was making money and finding places to stay at night by "going around and sleeping with numerous individuals in different apartments from night to night." Also, the complaint man added, the girl had a serious drug habit and use of narcotics had caused her "some serious mental problems."

The complaint man's remarks were used to index the typical character of the burglary. But in order to perceive the act as an actual burglary, the district attorney had to see that the features cited by the complaint man were similar to those features discovered in normal or typical burglaries. In this instance, the residential burglary was typified (given a normal form) by the following features: (a) a home was entered, (b) it was entered by a person who had no money and was using drugs, and (c) the person who entered the home lived in an area of the community that was "known as a neighborhood which was full of burglars." The latter feature was particularly important to this case. On more than one occasion police officers and district attorneys had commented, "Where there are burglars there are dopers." Therefore, because Angela was a drug user she could be typified as one who would commit burglaries.

From a legalistic perspective it would seem that the information given in the report adequately documented the elements of the law, that is, the events complied with the elements. The written report included a list of items that were taken, indicated how entry was made illegally, showed that the dwelling was not owned by the suspect, and indicated that the suspect committed a felony by revealing that she was seen in possession of the stolen items. However, more information about the circumstances of the crime was needed before the evidence was accepted as documenting the elements of the penal-code section.

The complaint man's and prosecutor's behavior may be the result of enforcing two principles at the same time. The practical application

We tend to think of criminals and crimes in terms of stereotypes that are "obviously" bad. However, even the most heinous crime and criminal is a social construct. (*Martin Adler Lenick from Black Star*)

of the law includes consideration of an act's circumstances and is therefore based upon neoclassical principles of justice, while the ideal of equal enforcement of objective rules is based on a classical model of law enforcement.

The first principle's application is indicated by the fact that higher courts frequently reexamine cases in an effort to determine whether the intent of the law has been upheld. This may not be decided by simply determining if all the elements of the law were *literally* satisfied. On the contrary, the circumstances of a crime may be used as grounds for arguing that an actual violation of the law has not occurred, a problem that daily concerns district attorneys. Occasionally, for instance, they drop charges against defendants on the grounds that the interests of the people (state) would not be served or the intent of law satisfied by prosecuting someone who could "technically" be charged with a crime (Miller, 1969:191–202).

This type of decision may appear to be divorced from what the law means, but it is not because the classical ideal of equal enforcement of objective and specific laws has been abandoned. Agents of the criminal justice system continue to uphold the ideal that their decisions are strictly governed by law by constructing the meaning of the law so that it includes consideration of the circumstances in which an act was committed.

SUMMARY

Earlier we claimed that specificity was an ideal feature of the criminal law. The specificity of the law (relative to other rules or norms) is said to be provided by elements or criteria which definitively "list" the qualities an act must have in order for it to be called a crime. We have found that the written law alone does not differentiate legal from illegal acts; people do.

Our basic purpose in applying the situational perspective is to critically evaluate decision-making. Only by looking at what policemen, prosecutors, judges, jurors, probation and parole officers, and correctional personnel do when they apply the law (or rules) can we begin to understand the criminal justice process. It is people who do justice, not rules.

Already we have seen how some criminal justice agents use rules. We found that what is written, in and of itself, is meaningless; consequently, it is the meaning given to what is written that is important and our topic of study.

We do not wish to imply that what is written in the law is irrelevant. What is especially interesting about our legal system is that in it the written law is revered and often perceived as a panacea. For example, if policemen are not behaving in ways deemed desirable, we usually write a rule or law to control their actions. Unfortunately the law cannot do what we want it to do. More rules simply call for more discretionary judgments.

People still hold fast to our legalistic ideal and expect agents of the criminal justice system to follow the rules. But because the rules don't solve problems, yet are still held in high esteem by the public and members of the criminal justice system, the system's agents always have to "prove" that their actions are legal ones. Even when decisions are obviously based on extralegal principles, we demand that legal decisons flow from the law. Therefore, we cannot understand the criminal justice process unless we understand how the legalistic ideal is sustained. We hope to shed new light and insights on this area rather than reify stereotypes.

REFERENCES

BLUMBERG, ABRAHAM
1967   *Criminal Justice.* Chicago: Quadrangle Books.

CALIFORNIA, STATE OF
1971   *Penal Code, State of California.* Sacramento: Printing Office.

CHAMBLISS, WILLIAM, AND ROBERT SEIDMAN
1971   *Law, Order and Power.* Reading, Mass.: Addison-Wesley.

CICOUREL, AARON
1974   *Cognitive Sociology: Language and Meaning in Social Interaction.* New York: The Fress Press.

CRESSEY, DONALD R., AND DAVID WARD
1969   *Delinquency, Crime and Social Process.* New York: Harper & Row.

DAUDISTEL, HOWARD C.
1976   *"Deciding What the Law Means: A Study of Police-Prosecutor Discretion."* Ph.D. diss. University of California, Santa Barbara.

GARFINKEL, HAROLD
1967   *Studies in Ethnomethodology.* Englewood Cliffs, N.J.: Prentice-Hall.

GINSBERG, MORRIS
1965   *On Justice in Society.* Baltimore, Md.: Penguin Books.

GOFFMAN, ERVING
1961   *Encounters.* Indianapolis, Ind.: Bobbs-Merrill.
1963   *Behavior in Public Places.* New York: The Free Press.
1974   *Frame Analysis.* New York: Harper & Row.

GURWITSCH, ARON
1964   *The Field of Consciousness.* Pittsburgh: Duquesne University Press.

HEEREN, JOHN
1970   "Alfred Schutz and the Sociology of Commonsense Knowledge," in Jack Douglas, ed., *Understanding Everyday Life: Toward a Reconstruction of Sociological Knowledge,* pp. 45–56. Chicago: Aldine.

HOEBEL, E. ADAMSON
1954   *The Law of Primitive Man: A Study in Comparative Legal Dynamics.* Cambridge: Harvard University Press.

KERPER, HAZEL
1972   *Introduction to the Criminal Justice System.* St. Paul, Minn.: West Publishing Co.

MALONEY, WILEY S.
1953   "Arizona Raided Short Creek—Why?" *Collier's* (November 13), pp. 30–31.

MENDES, RICHARD, AND JOHN WOLD
1976   "Plea Bargains Without Bargaining: Routinization of Misdemeanor Procedures," in William B. Sanders and Howard C Daudistel (eds.), *The Criminal Justice Process,* pp. 187–202. New York: Praeger.

MILLER, FRANK W.
1969   *Prosecution: The Decision to Charge a Suspect with a Crime.* Boston: Little, Brown.

PITKIN, HANNA F.
1972   *Wittgenstein and Justice.* Berkeley: University of California Press.

QUINNEY, RICHARD
1974   *Criminal Justice in America: A Critical Understanding.* Boston: Little, Brown.

ROSSETT, ARTHUR, AND DONALD R. CRESSEY
1976   *Justice by Consent: Plea Bargains in the American Courthouse.* Philadelphia: Lippincott.

SANDERS, WILLIAM B.
1977   *Detective Work: A Study of Criminal Investigations.* New York: The Free Press.

SANDERS, WILLIAM B, AND HOWARD C. DAUDISTEL, EDS.,
1976   *The Criminal Justice Process.* New York: Praeger.

SCHUTZ, ALFRED
1967   *Collected Papers I: The Problem of Social Reality.* The Hague: Martinus Nijhoff.

SKOLNICK, JEROME H.
1966   *Justice without Trial: Law Enforcement in Democratic Society.* New York: Wiley.

SKOLNICK, JEROME H., AND J. RICHARD WOODWORTH
1967   "Bureaucracy, Information, and Social Control: A Study of Morals," in David Bordua, ed., *The Police: Six Essays,* pp. 99–136. New York: Wiley.

SUTHERLAND, EDWIN, AND DONALD R. CRESSEY
1974   *Criminology,* 9th ed. Philadelphia: Lippincott.

WIEDER, D. LAWRENCE
1970   "On Meaning by Rule," in Jack Douglas, ed., *Understanding Everyday Life: Toward the Reconstruction of Sociological Knowledge,* pp. 107–35. Chicago: Aldine.

WIEDER, D. LAWRENCE
1974   "Telling the Code," in Roy Turner, ed., *Ethnomethodology,* pp. 144–72. Baltimore Md.: Penguin.

WILSON, THOMAS
1970   "Normative and Interpretive Paradigms in Sociology," in Jack Douglas, ed., *Understanding Everyday Life: Toward the Reconstruction of Sociological Knowledge,* pp. 57–79. Chicago: Aldine.

ZIMMERMAN, DON H., AND MELVIN POLLNER
1970   "The Everyday World as a Phenomenon," in Jack Douglas, ed., *Understanding Everyday Life: Toward a Reconstruction of Sociological Knowledge,* pp. 80–103. Chicago: Aldine.

SELECTED READINGS

KERPER, HAZEL. *Introduction to the Criminal Justice System.* St. Paul, Minn.: West Publishing Co., 1972.

A combination of a formal legal approach with a little sociological material. The author draws from Pound's theory of interests for sociological input.

NEWMAN, DONALD J. *Introduction to Criminal Justice.* Philadelphia: Lippincott, 1975.
A good example of a "functional approach" to criminal justice, stresses the functions of law enforcement, the courts, and corrections rather than the inter-organizational problems of these agencies. Like the situational approach though, it focuses on key decision-making situations.

PACKER, HERBERT L. *The Limits of Criminal Sanction.* Stanford, Calif.: Stanford University Press, 1968.
Provides two contrasting models of the criminal justice system, the adversary model stressing the rights of due process and the crime control model stressing bureaucratic goals of efficiency. Also included is an excellent discussion of "criminal tariffs," which are imposed unintentionally by the existence of criminal laws forbidding the "tariffed" goods and services.

QUINNEY, RICHARD. *Class, State and Crime: On the Theory and Practice of Criminal Justice.* New York: McKay, 1977.
Quinney provides asuccinct statement of the Marxist approach to criminal justice in a capitalist society. Alternatives to the current criminal justice system are seen in terms of restructuring society along socialist lines.

RAWLS, JOHN. *A Theory of Justice.* Cambridge, Mass.: Harvard University Press, 1971.
This work provides a compelling and complete theory of justice and the problems of coming to terms with justice in a complex, heterogeneous society.

2
the SOCIAL ORGANIZATION of CRIMINAL JUSTICE

In this chapter we will examine the criminal justice system as a unit of a larger organization—the legal system. Further, we will examine the relationship between the legal system and society.

It is important to understand the character of the legal system because it shapes the types of transactions in which members of the criminal justice system participate. We cannot look at the dynamics of any situational transactions or the micro-operations of criminal justice encounters in isolation, for they are located in a larger sociocultural context.

We shall review the models of society and formal organization that are used by social scientists. One should be aware of those ideas, developed by scholars who were not especially interested in criminal justice, that are useful to our study of the legal system.

We want to show that the legal system is influenced by other social institutions. Nevertheless, we will argue that local criminal justice agencies do not always operate as rational extensions of economic elites. We will see that members of local community-based criminal justice systems (police, prosecutors, and judges) typically do not operate as bureaucrats who are efficiently and rationally guided by the written law or rules of criminal procedure. In fact, it seems as if the formal law provides only loose and flexible boundaries for decision-makers. Therefore, even though one may "know the law," it is impossible to predict what specific decisions will be made by members of different "courthouse communities." The nature of the criminal justice system compels us, in later chapters, to analyze the decision-making processes of legal agents.

THE LEGAL SYSTEM

The relationship of the criminal justice system to its effective environment is very complex. The criminal justice system is a unit of a much larger, intricate organization, that is, the legal system, membership in which has some important implications for general criminal justice operations.

The legal system is a collective enterprise authorized and supported by the legitimacy and coercive power of the state to create and administer law.[1] It is first and foremost a formal system oriented to the control of human affairs (Davis, 1962:40–42, cf. Goulding, 1975:-9–12). The legal system consists of law-making organizations that function to create, revise, and abolish legal rules. Principal among such organizations are the state and federal legislatures. Also part of the legal system are the law-sanctioning or law enforcement organizations whose function it is to enforce the legal rules by detecting and sanctioning infractions. Typical among the law-sanctioning organizations are the local, state, and federal criminal justice systems, corporate regulatory agencies, correctional systems, and the like.

Formally, the legal system is organized hierarchically with units ranked in terms of the dimensions of authority and responsibility (Remington et al., 1969:12–13). In the United States, we typically think of the law-making organizations as occupying the preeminent position of authority and responsibility since they are supposed to direct and sanction the role performances of all other organizations in the system. The law-sanctioning organizations are considered as holding the lowest position of authority, whereas the appellate courts are conceived as occupying an intermediate position, for they function to resolve questionable applications of legal rules in concrete situations.

Although the appellate courts occupy a high-ranking position in the formal structure of the legal system, they are in fact ministerial units charged with the application of preexisting legal rules to "trou-

---

[1] The meaning of the legal system has been debated. A number of writers have held that it is a body of law and a set of supportive organizations (Friedman, 1969:1000; Schur, 1968). To hold that the legal system is coterminous with a body of law is to reify law, making it somehow independent of human action. We will argue that this may not be a valid means of conceptualizing law.

The prostitute being arrested symbolizes the impact of laws that are generated in the legal system and filtered into a situation where action is taken by the criminal justice system. (© *Michael Hanulak*)

ble" cases, that is, those cases in which the litigants disagree over the application of the law to their cases.[2]

Disagreement leading to appeal, of course, may stem from several sources, but perhaps ambiguity of legal rules and their conceptual properties is the foremost source of conflict (cf. Cohen, 1935). For example, in most states "murder" is defined as the unlawful killing of a human being with malice aforethought. But the conceptual properties of this definition are by no means clear. Is a fetus a "human being"? Precisely when is a person "killed"? When the heart stops beating voluntarily, or when the brain ceases to function? The concept of "malice" is also vague. Malice is typically considered to be "criminal intent," but how intent is established is equally equivocal. In California, for example, malice may be either expressed or implied. "It is expressed

---

[2] Chambliss and Seidman (1971:85–89) argue that the appellate courts deal with trouble cases, indicating those in which there is disagreement over the "primary" rules used in the case. A primary rule refers to one directed at the conduct of the citizen and the conduct of the criminal justice official. Hence, a law which states that one must not steal another's property also states that the judge shall punish the violator with a prison sentence. This a primary rule. We believe that in addition to debate over the primary rules there is debate over the "secondary" rules, rules of procedure. A scan of appellate cases yields evidence of attention to the adjudicative process by which defendants were tried. An error in police or court processing may result in either a mistrial or a reversal.

when there is manifested a deliberate intention unlawfully to take away the life of a fellow creature. It is implied when no considerable provocation appears, or when the circumstances attending the killing show an abandoned and malignant heart" (California Penal Code, 1974: § 188). We might ask what reference points indicate "deliberate intention." It can be manifested from vocal gesture to savage mutilation. What reference points indicate "provocation," and just what is a "considerable" amount of provocation? In this seemingly simple definition of murder lie a host of controversial issues, and the legal rules provide no ready recipes for rendering them concrete.

The procedural law (not unlike the substantive law) is also ambiguous. The police, for example, cannot arrest someone for a felony without "probable cause" to believe that a crime was committed and that the suspect is guilty of that crime. But just what are the boundaries of "probable cause"? Arrests have been invoked on the basis of hearsay statements of children and drunks, knowledge that the suspect has done similar things at other times, general suspiciousness, and on-view observations.

Thus, the appellate courts are met with cases in which ambiguities in the law are to be resolved, and the resolution of such troublesome cases requires considerable discretion on the court's part. The court must decide what properties of the law are at issue vis-à-vis the case at hand, and what constitutional rule or legal precedent should be used in accounting for the decision. In effect, in resolving troublesome cases, the appellate courts create legal rules or refashion from some existing rule a legal rule explicitly relevant to the case at hand.

In some cases, the court may find no specific rule covering the issue of debate, while in others the properties of the rule are not clearly shared with the case. In the former instance, the court "must determine what the appropriate form and content of the rule is to be. Instead of discovering a pre-existing norm, the court must actually create a norm" (Chambliss and Seidman, 1971:88). In *Stanley v. Georgia* (394 U.S. 557:1969), for example, the United States Supreme Court essentially had to create a rule stating that the private possession of obscene literature—films, books, pictures, and the like—was not unlawful. Justice Marshall for the Court cited the "philosophy" of the First Amendment as justification for its position:

If the First Amendment means anything, it means that a State has no business telling a man, sitting alone in his own house, what books he may read or what films he may watch. Our whole constitutional heritage rebels at the thought of giving government the power to control men's minds.
And yet, in the face of these traditional notions of individual liberty, Georgia asserts the right to protect the individual's mind from the effects of obscenity . . . . To some, this may be a

noble purpose, but it is wholly inconsistent with the philosophy of the First Amendment.

In other cases, the properties of the legal rule are not clearly shared with the case, and the court must refashion the rule, enlarging its scope and properties to include the case or constricting the scope and properties such that the case is clearly excluded. The latter was done in *Davis v. Commonwealth* (Court of Appeals of Virginia, 1922, 132 Va. 521, 110 S.E. 356), in which the defendant had been convicted of burglary and sentenced to prison. The defendant, it was charged, "broke and entered" the home of the victim and "feloniously and burglariously" stole $412.50. The point of debate centered on whether the defendant "broke and entered." She had been a long-time and intimate friend of the victim, and with the victim's consent and encouragement carried a key to the house with the understanding that the victim's home was also "her home." "Breaking," the court held, may be actual or constructive, "constructive" meaning that entrance was made by threat of violence, by fraud, or by conspiracy. The present case involved neither means. Moreover, "breaking" must result in an "entrance contrary to the will of the occupier of the house," a circumstance also not present in this case. As a consequence of the interpretations given the concept of breaking, the court held that the defendant could not have burglarized the victim's home. In this case, then, the court constricted the meaning of burglary by setting certain standards for the event, that is, actual or constructive breaking and entering.

In resolving trouble cases, then, the appellate courts operate as lawmakers in two ways. Resolving controversies over the "meaning" of a legal rule—whether an event is criminal, subsumed under this and not that statute, or whether the defendant's rights were legally upheld. Also, the appellate courts create or refashion from the bones of some constitutional rule, legal precedent, or philosophical position, from which the cases at hand can be decided.

THE OPERATION OF THE LEGAL SYSTEM

The legal system is not a static structure of roles, but a set of ongoing activities. It is an open system, which imports from its effective environment various inputs, transforms them, and exports them back to the environment, receiving feedback on its production (Friedman and Macaulay, 1969:698; cf. Katz and Kahn, 1966:17; Buckley, 1967).

Sketching this process, we begin by noting that people make certain demands on the law-making institutions. They write congressmen, sign petitions, and organize or contribute to special interest groups, demanding that new laws be created, that existing ones be revised, and that outdated or unjust ones be abolished. The law-making organizations transform some of these demands into changes in the system of laws: Legislators create, revise, and abolish statutes.

Whatever the impetus for legislation, the output of law-making organizations is directed at the activities of particular role-occupants engaged in the conduct under question, as well as law enforcement officers and law-sanctioning officials. A landlord, for example, is told that in the course of his role-related activities he cannot discriminate by denying blacks the right to housing. The police (or other law officers) are directed to detect and apprehend role-occupants engaged in the violation of the substantive legal rules, and the courts are to sanction them.[3]

Like other open systems, the legal system attends to feedback from agencies within and outside the system concerning its activities and decisions through a number of channels by which the system can then adjust its operations. An interesting example regarding the criminalization of drugs illustrates one channel that links particular role-occupants to the law-making organizations. The first formulations of the Marihuana Tax Act brought strong opposition by the manufacturers of hempseed oil and the birdseed industry, which used approximately four million pounds of hempseed a year (Becker, 1963:144). While the manufacturers of hempseed oil were quickly accommodated by winning an exception to the basic law, the birdseed industry was not. Government witnesses argued that the seed contained the active substance of the drug that could be used for smoking. Nevertheless, as Becker points out:

> Faced with serious opposition, the Government modified its stern insistence on the seed provision, noting that sterilization of the seeds might render them harmless: "It seems to us that the burden of proof is on the Government there, when we might injure a legitimate industry" (1963:145).

Once the legislature had accomodated both sets of potential role-occupants, the bill passed easily:

> Marihuana smokers, powerless, unorganized, and lacking publicly legitimate grounds for attack, sent no representatives to the hearings and their point of view found no place in the record. Unopposed, the bill passed both the House and Senate. . . . (Becker, 1963:145).

---

[3] The affected role-occupant, as well as the larger public of which he is a part, may react to the law-making institutions by voicing either further demands or support.

A second channel of feedback links role-occupants to law enforcement agencies. This mode of feedback, for example, may take the form of a concerted effort by some community group to dissuade officials from treating individuals engaged in certain types of activities as criminals. Groups may protest that some activities are not really criminal; hence, treating them as such would be a gross injustice. The efforts of large business enterprises and corporations to persuade criminal justice officials that their violations of certain regulations are not really criminal are illustrative of this form of feedback (cf. Aubert, 1952), as are the efforts of local religious groups to persuade the police and courts not to treat bingo games and raffles as "gambling" on the basis of their essential noncriminality.

A third feedback channel links law enforcement agencies to lawmaking organizations. Just as citizens react to laws and operational activities of the legal system, law-enforcement agencies respond to laws they are to enforce and by which they are to act. This feedback may take the form of direct demands made upon lawmakers for immediate legal changes. Donald Dickson's (1968) study of the Federal Bureau of Narcotics demonstrates that this agency pressured the federal legislature to exact additional drug laws favorable to the agency's interests. Initally, the functions of the bureau were limited: "to enforce registration and record-keeping of narcotic drugs, the violation of which could result in imprisonment for up to ten years, and to supervise revenue collection" (Dickson 1968:149). Being a government agency, the bureau relied on Congress for its budget. But due to its reasonable success in controlling drug violations in the early 1930s, the bureau began to feel the pinch of a diminishing budget. Because of steadily decreasing funds, "the bureau responded as any organization so threatened might react: it tried to appear more necessary, and it tried to increase its scope of operations" so as to receive an increased budget (Dickson, 1968:155). Consequently, the bureau promoted the passage of legislation that would increase its powers, an effort successfully capped by Congress's passage in 1937 of the Marihuana Tax Act. Subsequently, the "violations and seizures under the Marihuana Tax Act contributed substantially to the bureau's totals, which had been declining for some time" (Dickson, 1968:155).

Similarly, many local police forces have organized lobbies to promote their interests in community and sometimes state legislative arenas (Stark, 1972:208–12). Police associations, for example, have been quite effective in shaping policy on law enforcement matters. Stark's investigation provides the following examples:

In New York City, Mayor John Lindsay has lost to the police lobby in the state legislature in his proposals to have police cadets take over traffic patrol duties, the use of one-man squad cars, and the consolidation of precincts.

Different organized groups come into conflict over the promotion of their interests.
(© *1976 by Fred W. McDarrah*)

[In Boston] . . . the PBA [Policeman's Benevolent Association]
lobbied vigorously against Mayor Kevin White's decision to
place civilians in most jobs occupied by traffic patrolmen, a
move which would have freed men for crime work. The city
council, which had to approve the change, sided with the police.
The mayor then went to the state legislature but the police
lobby again prevailed and White lost. In November 1968, the
PBA again prevailed over the mayor when the city council
substantially altered the police component of White's Model
Cities Program. Changes included removal of a plan to allow
citizens to receive (not judge) complaints against the police and
removal of references to the need to recruit blacks to the police
force (1972:210).

Feedback from law-enforcement agencies to the law-making bodies may also take an indirect form. Concerted efforts by the police to
shape the makeup of law-making organizations are really efforts at
influencing the kinds of laws such bodies make (Stark, 1972:209).
Efforts include their wearing of campaign buttons on their uniforms,
the placing of bumper stickers on patrol cars (both prominent in the

1964 presidential campaign), as well as their participation in political fund-raising events.

The feedback link between bar associations and the legal system is similar to the links between police departments, legislatures, and the courts. Uniquely, bar associations have secured some power in judicial selection. In areas where judges are selected through elections, the bar usually holds "bar primaries," polls where lawyers vote on the fitness of candidates for office. The results are publicly announced in the hope that the electorate will be influenced. When judges are selected through appointment, the bar usually seeks to influence the officials charged with the appointment. In these cases the bar screens each possible candidate and makes a recommendation to the official.

As our discussion suggests, the legal system does not operate in a void. The rules created, revised, or abolished by law-making organizations and directed at both citizens and law enforcement agencies are shaped by the demands of others. It is important, consequently, to understand whose demands are taken into consideration in the construction and interpretation of law.

TWO MODELS OF SOCIETY

Sociological discussions about the role of the legal system in society are grounded generally in one of two ideal conceptions of society.[4] The *integration-consensus* perspective characterizes society as a functionally integrated, relatively stable system held together by a basic consensus on values (cf. Parsons, 1951). Social order is seen as more or less permanent, and people can best achieve their interests as well as optimize their life chances through cooperation. Thus, society appears as a very large voluntary association. Social conflict is considered the unnecessary struggle between people who have not yet attained sufficient collective understanding of their common interests and basic interdependence. The *conflict-coercion* perspective, in contrast, characterizes society as consisting of tenuous, dynamic sets of groups marked by conflict and dissensus on values, and held together by some members who coerce others (Dahrendorf, 1958; 1959). Social order, in this view, is seen as temporary and unstable. At most, there is a precarious balance of power in which one group effectively subjugates all others. Because each group strives to maximize its own interests and life chances in a world of limited resources and goods, social conflict is viewed as intrinsic to the interaction and relations between groups.

When these two perspectives are applied to the legal system, not

---

[4] The following discussion uses an argument in a paper by Austin Turk (n.d.), but a somewhat similar discussion may be found in Chambliss (1976).

unexpectedly, quite disparate conceptions of its basic role result. On the one hand, the integration-consensus perspective conceives the legal system as a neutral framework for maintaining societal integration. As Parsons (1962:57–58) argues: "It serves to mitigate potential elements of conflict and to oil the machinery of social intercourse." With the growing complexity of social relations occasioned by natural environmental changes, technological innovation, and human variability, those who accept an integration-consensus perspective believe it is necessary for society to supplement informal with formal mechanisms for generating and sustaining interpersonal cooperation (Turk, n.d.: 11–12). This need is met by the creation of the legal system. Thus, the legal system operates to formalize collectively shared norms derived from commonly held values, and ensure that moments of conflict and dispute are settled in the interests of the public at large (cf. Zeigenhagen, 1970: 27).

On the other hand, the conflict-coercion perspective sees the legal system as a "weapon in the hands of the dominant class" (Chambliss and Seidman, 1971:53; cf. Quinney, 1974 and a). From this perspective, the movement from a single, relatively homogeneous social group to a network of specialized groups brought about the evolution of both distinct sets of interests—values, conduct norms, and ideological orientations considered important for the existence and welfare of the group —and differences in effective power between groups. When particular groups come into conflict, they compete to have their interests protected and perpetuated, which is best achieved through the formalization of such interests in law and social policy. Thus, the legal system is a tool used by those groups to protect and perpetuate their interests, even at the expense of the interests of groups with less power (Quinney, 1970:40; cf. 1969:30–40).

These dialectical models—integration-consensus and conflict-coercion—of society are ideal types. Taken toward the operation of the law-making organizations, there may be an element of truth in both. In this regard perhaps an eclectic approach is best. Nevertheless, we favor the conflict-coercion approach because it emphasizes the role of special interest groups. We feel it is important to focus attention on how the wishes of relatively few persons affect everyone.

In response to a multitude of particularly heinous tales in the mass media about the attack and molestation of women and youngsters by men characterized as perverse and crazed, community-action groups sprang up around the United States during the 1930s and 1940s to resolve the problem. These action groups, generally led by psychiatrists, sought to curb the seeming epidemic surge of sexual psychopathy by promoting special legislation that provided for the incarceration of sexual psychopaths in mental hospitals instead of prisons. Sutherland's (1950) investigation of the sexual psychopath laws demonstrates that the psychiatrists had a special interest in such laws and their implementation. The laws stipulated that the diagnosis for the court be made by psychiatrists, and that sexual psychopaths be treated as "patients" or "mental cases," not simply as "criminals" to be confined in prison. Thus, passage of these laws in the name of community safety brought psychiatrists added business as well as a strengthened position in the political sphere.

The history of the "great experiment" known as Prohibition, established by the Volstead Act and ratified by the Eighteenth Amendment, similarly involved special interest groups that arose in the latter 1800s to crusade against the evil and immoral ways of urban folk that were epitomized in their consumption of alcohol. These groups, which included the Prohibition Party, a third political party organized against drinking, the Anti-Saloon League, and the Women's Christian Temperance Union, lobbied effectively and brought pressure through the power of votes on national legislators which led to bringing passage of state and local bans on drinking (Sinclair, 1964).

The creation of anticontraceptive laws in the United States in the last century was the outcome of pressure exerted by various interest groups seeking to maintain what they considered to be high moral standards (cf. Best, 1972:36–38). The 1870s witnessed passage of a series of antiobscenity laws intended to restrict dissemination of obscene materials. Included in these laws were bans on the dissemination of contraceptives. "The decision to treat contraceptives as a type of obscene material was based on the theory that they could be employed to allow illicit sexual activity without risking pregnancy," hence giving way to an epidemic of immorality (Best, 1972:37). Led by Anthony Comstock, these moral crusaders included such prominent individuals as P.T. Barnum and such organizations as the YMCA and the Committee for the Suppression of Vice. While the movement sought to give legal recognition to a widespread attitude on obscenity, it nevertheless formalized its particular interest in opposition to a minority interested in maintaining complete freedom of the press (Brooks, 1966:3).

The power of economic and commercial interests to influence legislation is shown in the history of vagrancy statutes. A vagrant is an idle person, one who begs or wanders about without the ability to give a "good" account of himself. Chambliss' (1964) investigation of the law of vagrancy found that the crime originated in early English laws, the first of these statutes coming into existence in 1349, and aimed at punishing the able-bodied who were unemployed. The stimulant for this legislation, Chambliss argues, was the Black Death, a plague that struck England about 1348.

> Among the many disastrous consequences the Black Death had upon the social structure was the fact that it decimated the labor force. It is estimated that by the time the pestilence had run its course at least fifty percent of the population of England

had died from the plague. This decimation of the labor force would necessitate rather drastic innovations in any society, but its impact was heightened in England where, at this time, the economy was highly dependent upon a ready supply of cheap labor (1964:69).

The unavailability of an adequate labor force was further aggravated by the wholesale movement of workers from rural areas to the towns where they found work in the new weaving industry. By threatening criminal punishment for being able-bodied and unemployed, a condition that existed when peasants were in the process of moving from the land to the towns, the vagrancy law served "to force laborers (whether personally free or unfree) to accept employment at a low wage in order to insure the landowner an adequate supply of labor at a price he could afford to pay" (Chambliss, 1964:69).

The breakdown of the feudal order and the diminishing power of the landowners brought a period of dormancy in the enforcement of

Vagrancy laws came about because of the power of commercial interests to have them enacted. (*Peter Martens/Nancy Palmer Photo Agency*)

THE STUDY OF CRIMINAL JUSTICE

and concern with the vagrancy statutes. This dormancy, however, did not last, as a major economic shift toward commerce and industry brought about their revision and revival. When political power shifted to industrialists, the laws were redefined in such a manner that their focus was not on the regulation of labor but on the management of "criminal" activities. "With commercialism came considerable traffic bearing valuable items" (Chambliss, 1964:72), and with the dramatic increase of commercial transportation came a dramatic increase of highway robbery. The vagrancy statutes were revised to control the activities of those preying upon powerful merchants by making liable to criminal punishment " 'rogues,' 'vagabonds,' and others who were suspected of being engaged in criminal activities" (Chambliss, 1964:76). The growth of commercial and industrial interests, then, is tied to the redirection of vagrancy statutes, from the protection of landowners to the protection of commercial transportation.

The appellate courts are also influenced by special interest groups. Even when pressure is not explicitly applied by others, the courts' decisions are essentially value-choices. As Peltason argues:

> When a judge makes a decision he gives his support to one pattern of activity as against another. He becomes, however, temporarily and for whatever reason, an important member of an interest group. Litigation, like legislation, is a stage in the accommodation of interests. Judicial decision-making is one stage, not the only nor necessarily the final one, in the process of determining which of several conflicting activities shall be favored (1953:51).

Not only are the courts involved in political questions, but decisions seem to be shaped toward the interests of the more powerful. This contention is indirectly supported by several lines of research. First, the selection of appellate court justices seems to follow more from their politics than from their legal competence. Justices have been appointed, or nominated for confirmation, on the basis of party affiliation. It has been observed that when one party repeatedly wins the presidency, the judiciary tends to reflect this predominance. "From 1865 to 1933 the judiciary was predominantly Republican; since Franklin Roosevelt's administration it has been predominantly Democratic. Eisenhower's administration brought the partisan affiliation of judges to an almost even balance by his appointment of Republicans. President Kennedy once more made the judiciary predominantly Democratic: 93 percent of 108 appointments went to fellow Democrats" (Jacob, 1972:106–8).[5]

---

[5] Sometimes justices have been appointed as a favor to either the candidate or the candidate's sponsor. Politicians charged with appointing judges have

The election of appellate justices may be either partisan, in which the candidate runs on a party ticket, or nonpartisan, in which he or she runs without party affiliation. In the former case, party connections are very important. To win a judgeship, the candidate must first win the party nomination, which itself is a considerable task. Winning the nomination often requires considerable financial contribution to the party, campaigning for various politicians, and the like. Party influence is somewhat weaker in cases of nonpartisan election; yet even then, as Jacob indicates, party affiliation is not completely absent.

> In Michigan a place on the nonpartisan ballot can only be won by nomination at a party convention. In other states party organizations make a fairly vigorous although secret effort to select their man under the guise of nonpartisanship. . . . It is fair to estimate, however, that in about half of the eighteen states that use nonpartisan judicial ballots, parties play some role in the selection of judges (1972:108–9).

Second, once judges have secured their positions, the elements of party loyalty and political partisanship do not necessarily diminish, since most see their position as a career to be maintained through reelection or as a stepping stone to higher judicial or political station. Consequently, justices maintain their political ties when in office (Levin, 1972). In addition, it has been documented over the last decade that judicial decisions reflect in part a judge's political perspective. Ulmer's (1962) investigation of the Michigan supreme court, for example, showed that the different political ideologies of its justices, and their different party affiliations, correlated with different decisions in the same case. He found that the Democratic justices were more sensitive to the claims and position of the unemployed and the injured than were the Republican justices.

In a series of studies of state supreme court judges, Nagel (1964) concludes that justices with a perspective leading to or derived from their affiliation with the Democratic Party brought decisions significantly different from justices with a perspective leading to or derived from their Republican affiliation. Nagel reports:

> Democratic judges sitting on the same courts with Republican judges were more prone to favor (1) the defense in criminal cases, (2) the administrative agency in business regulation cases, (3) the private party in regulation of non-business entities, (4) the claimant in unemployment compensation cases, (5) the broadening position in free speech

---

also sought out those candidates who favor their views. Franklin Roosevelt's attempt to "pack" or expand the Supreme Court was essentially an attempt to appoint justices favorable to his position.

cases, (6) the findings of a constitutional violation in criminal-constitution cases, (7) the government in tax cases, (8) the divorce seeker in divorce cases, (9) the wife in divorce settlement cases, (10) the tenant in landlord-tenant cases, (11) the labor union in labor-management cases, (12) the debtor in credit-debtor cases, (13) the consumer in sales-of-goods cases, (14) the injured party in motor vehicle accident cases, and (15) the employee in employee injury cases, than were the Republican judges (1964:242–43).

Judicial selection, then, is based in partisan politics, which in turn influences decision-making along lines not necessarily consistent with conceptions of the public good.

Third, while everyone has the right to appeal an adverse decision, not everyone can. The appellate process is a long and tortuous one. Consequently, only wealthy litigants or those supported by reasonably powerful groups can profitably undertake such a venture. Additionally, through "test cases," pursuit of which are also excessively expensive, powerful social groups may protect and further their interests. In such cases, either a group marshals support for the cause of some litigant or purposely has someone break a particular rule so they may appeal the case and secure some formal change of policy. They may additionally provide *amicus curiae* ("friend of the court") briefs to the court. As Jacob observes:

> *Amicus curiae* briefs involve groups more casually than do test cases. They parallel to a striking degree the principal technique of lobbyists before executive agencies and legislatures, for they rely on the utility of information. It is hoped that giving the courts information will incline them to rule in favor of the group's interest. Furthermore, an *amicus curiae* brief is an effective means of showing a group's support for a particular cause that has reached the court through someone else's initiative (1972:35).

In summary, the law-making organizations of the legal system formalize as law the particular interests of those with the power to have their claims realized.

PERSPECTIVES ON ORGANIZATIONS

Law enforcement agencies are traditionally characterized as the units that operate to detect law violations and sanction violators. If the law-making organizations serve only the interests of some groups at the expense of the less powerful, are we then justified in contending that the law enforcement organizations necessarily serve the interests of the more powerful? To help us answer this question, we should consider two conceptions of formal organizations which are employed by students of the criminal justice system.

Generally speaking, the *rational-goal model* treats formal organizations such as law enforcement agencies as a rational tool for the achievement of formally articulated goals. More specifically there are two generic features in this scheme. First, the formal organization is charged with the effectuation of a set of formal goals constructed and announced by those in the organization's leadership. Second, the formal organization is itself a strategy for organizing and binding people in the rational and efficient pursuit of formal goals. This particular strategy of organization corresponds closely with Max Weber's "ideal" conception of the rational-legal mode of bureaucratic administration. An organization based on this mode of administration is characterized by the following:

1. There is a clear-cut division of labor in which activities required for the achievement of organizational goals are distributed on the basis of a fixed scheme of official duties (Weber, 1946:196).
2. Offices are hierarchially organized. That is, each lower office is under the control and supervision of higher offices (Weber, 1947:331).
3. The performance of organizational duties is governed by a system of formal, abstract rules. These rules define the duties of each member, the relationships between members, and the system of rewards and punishments (Weber, 1947: 330).
4. The assignment of roles is based on candidates' technical qualifications for the position as these are ascertained through formalized and impersonal precedures such as educational certificates and competitive testing (Weber, 1946: 198).
5. Organizational officials perform their specialized duties impersonally. They act without hatred or passion, with affection or enthusiasm (Weber, 1947:340).

Thus, a bureaucracy organized in this "ideal" way would be highly differentiated and rationally organized. The rational and efficient achievement of formal goals is made possible by a neat package of formal rules that delineate members' duties and relationships, and the sanctions for rewarding or punishing members' performances. Additionally, rational operation is made possible by bureaus of trained experts whose specialized roles are coordinated by a hierarchial chain of command. As Weber (1946:214) suggests, "the fully developed bureaucratic mechanism compares with other organizations exactly as does the machine with the nonmechanical modes of production." It is, from a purely technical standpoint, "capable of attaining the highest degree of efficiency" (Weber, 1947:337).

The *organic model,* fashioned on the arguments of Chester Barnard (1938) and extended by Philip Selznick (1943, 1948, 1949), does not treat the formal organization as a perfectly ordered structure for the rational achievement of professed ends. Rather, to proponents of the organic model, formal organizations are like organisms, developing, changing, and declining over time. While the rational-goal model implies that organizations efficiently pursue goals by formally articulated and sanctioned means, the organic model argues that organizational operation entails the practical pursuit of secondary and informal goals by informally articulated and sanctioned means. Furthermore, while the rational-goal model implies that organizations are relatively stable closed systems, the organic model holds that organizations are dynamic and open systems.

The organic model argues that the character of organizational operation is shaped by the varied contingencies of its effective environs, both internal and external. For example, the model emphasizes that members do not always perform specialized tasks in strict accordance with formal prescriptions. Members of an organization may place various demands on the operation of the larger organization. In contrast to the implications of the rational-goal model, "individuals have a propensity to resist depersonalization, to spill over the boundaries of their segmentary roles, to participate as wholes" (Selznick, 1948:26). Consequently, organizational role performances are flavored with the particular interests and commitments of its members.

Furthermore, the operation of a formal organization is shaped by the acts of informal work groups. These groups, which are collections of members sharing common interests and intimate contact, serve to control the behavior of persons in the group. According to Selznick (1943:47), within the larger context of the organization, the informal group acts as "a mechanism for the expression of personal relationships for which the formal organization did not provide." Frequently, informal groups modify formally stated goals and procedures for purposes of solving their own special problems. For example, rather than produce the prescribed number of units, a work group may pressure members to limit their output, a move that both asserts their "power" over the organization and makes their work a bit easier. Informal groups and relationships may additionally assist the enterprise in making necessary corrections in operation not provided by formal rules (Caplow, 1964:21; cf. Blau, 1963). This is the central point of Selznick (1943): The actual procedures and goals of every formal organization are modified, abandoned, deflected, or elaborated through the process of informal structure and its attempt to find operationally relevant solutions to the daily problems of organizational existence.

Organizational operations are also shaped by contingencies posed by the external world. The very maintenance and survival of the organization requires continuous adjustment to changes in its immediate environment. All organizations require resources or energy input, even if this consists only of the time people could have used doing something else (Stinchcombe, 1967:160–64). "Resources" are anything the organization requires for its operation, including raw materials to be processed into finished goods, facilities and tools necessary for processing, human labor, transportation and communication networks, and capital investment. Not only must resources be administered within the organization, but, just as important, they must also be imported and continuously replenished. Importation and replenishment, in turn, require the establishment and maintenance of organizational links to environmental sources. A breakdown in such a relationship brings either the cultivation of new sources of resources, or degeneration of the organization. Thus, changes in sources of resources bring changes in organizational action.

A second condition to which organizations must adapt is changing markets. As stated, all organizations must export their finished products to some segments of the environment, whether to the consumers of their goods or services or other organizations making use of their output. For example, the interests of auto consumers changed significantly with the energy crunch in 1973. While the market for large, luxury cars had been reasonably good before this time, their interest now shifted toward smaller, more economical cars. Consequently, the American auto industry had to make a quick turnaround toward the production and marketing of smaller cars. A few years later, however, the consumer turned around and demanded the big car again even though gasoline prices were double the early-1973 price.

A third condition to which organizations must adjust is the particular interests of their powerful audiences. Barnard recognized long ago that all organizations need an air of legitimacy, that they must be judged as right and proper by those groups powerful enough to control significant resources and markets. To win support from powerful interest groups, organizations must adjust to their interests. This may be accomplished through formal cooptation of such segments—absorbing these elements into the leadership or policy-making structure—or informal cooptation—adjusting operations to their specific demands with absorption (Selznick, 1949:217, 226, 259–61). For example, even as the federal government took legal action to force the Crown-Zellerback Corporation to integrate its work force, the firm's leadership continued to adapt to the demands of the white community of Bogalusa, Louisiana, by segregating its white and black workers (Perrow, 1972:193–94).

In sum, the organic model holds that organizations take on a life of their own, growing, adjusting, and declining as do other forms of life. While the formal organizational blueprints may show the operation as the rational pursuit of professed goals by formal means, in fact the operation is the outcome of continuous adjustments to multivaried conditions. As Perrow observes:

> The explanation for organizational behavior is not primarily in the formal structure of the organization, the announcements of goals and purposes, the output of goods and services. It lies also in the myriad of subterranean processes of informal groups, conflicts between groups, recruitment policies, dependencies upon outside groups and contingencies, the striving for prestige, community values, the local community power structure, and legal institutions (1972:180).

On inspection, the *formal* structure of the criminal justice enterprise stands close to the ideal of the rational-goal model. First, the system is provided with an explicit set of formal goals that it is charged with achieving, namely, enforcement of the substantive law and "doing justice" by adhering to the procedural law. Second, the system is supposed to operate as an organization bonded by a complex set of procedural laws for the processing of people. At each processing stage, organizational officials are to act in conformity with a variety of rules and procedures. When a suspect is interrogated by police, for example, he is entitled by constitutional right to have an attorney present and may be silent during questioning. The police, furthermore, must abide by rules of search and seizure, and arrest only when they have probable cause or a warrant. An individual arrested for a crime should be taken before a judicial magistrate "without delay" for purposes of attaining counsel, hearing the state's charges, and allowed release on bail. A defendant cannot be denied trial. These and a multitude of other procedural laws, created in both the legislatures and the appellate courts, constitute the formal rules that are supposed to govern the officials of the organization.

Third, agencies in the criminal justice system are also organized on the principle of hierarchy, a characteristic feature of the rational-goal model best exemplified by police departments. In most police agencies in the United States there is a formal chain of command, and a set of demarcated ranks in which the lower ranks are always under the control and supervision of the upper ranks.[6]

Students of the criminal justice system disagree about which model of complex organization—the rational-goal or the organic—best characterizes the actual operations of the criminal justice system. On

---

[6] On another level, the criminal justice system is itself organized on the principle of hierarchy. That is, the agencies are differentially ranked, with the lower ones subject to the control and supervision of the upper ranks. For example, the police are ultimately under the control of the courts. The lower courts are subject to the directions of the trial courts, and the trial courts are subject to the directions of the appellate courts.

the one hand, some have implied that the system functions as a rational machine in support of the ruling class. On the other hand, some have argued that the system adjusts to a variety of contingencies in addition to those embodied in legal rules. We shall examine each argument in turn.

LAW ENFORCEMENT FOR WHOM?

Several sociologists have argued that law enforcement agencies are not organizations oriented to protecting all by the just administration of the criminal law. Rather, it has been proposed that criminal justice agencies operate as a repressive arm of the ruling class, oriented toward the maintenance and perpetuation of the elite's economic interests as well as the capitalist mode of production characteristic of the United States.

According to Marxist scholars, a variety of "reproductive mechanisms" have been created and employed by the state for purposes of preserving and perpetuating capitalism, hence preserving and perpetuating the economic positions of the bourgeoisie. Reproductive mechanisms are "those aspects of capitalism which tend to perpetuate traditional forms of institutions and behavior, as well as stabilizing new ones" (Wolfe, 1971:19). One of the most important functions of the state is to create and employ such mechanisms. Perhaps one of the most powerful of reproductive mechanisms is repression, "the physical use of force or the threat of force by those in power to meet challenges to their legitimacy" (Wolfe, 1971:19). Quinney comments:

> The legal system provides the mechanism for the forceful and violent control of the rest of the population. . . . The agents of the law (police, prosecutor, judges, and so on) serve as the military force for the protection of domestic order. Legal order benefits the ruling class in the course of dominating the classes that are ruled (1974:52).

Law enforcement agencies, these writers argue, are best seen as rational bureaucracies constructed to serve the ruling class at the expense of the remainder of the populace. "The state creates a complex of bureaucratic agencies in the course of establishing control over the population . . . . The administrative, coercive, and judicial agencies of the state, and the people who function within them, reinforce the state's political and economic objectives" (Quinney, 1974:105).

As with all formal organizations, the effectiveness of the criminal justice system's operations—the achievement of professed goals—is never perfect. The crime control policies established by law are never

Bureaucratic organization in criminal justice is typified by computer assisted dispatch in this police headquarters. (*Wide World Photos*)

fully followed in fulfillment of the system's repressive goal. As a consequence, there have been marked attempts over the last decade to increase the effectiveness of law enforcement and judicial administration.

Hence, the Omnibus Crime Control and Safe Streets Act of 1968, the District of Columbia crime bill of 1970, and the Organized Crime Control Act of 1970 were attempts to further add to the repressive operation of the criminal justice enterprise. The various programs and recommendations made by advisory commissions further complemented the movement toward increased effectiveness in the repression of revolutionary challenges to the social order. Such agencies as the Law Enforcement Assistance Administration (LEAA) as well as the various presidential crime commissions have consisted of members who are also members or servants of the ruling elite (cf. Quinney, 1974: 75–93).

Detailed empirical studies of law enforcement agencies from this critical perspective are as yet few. Silver's (1967) provocative essay on the creation of the police in England, however, provides support to the general thesis that the enterprise was constructed to preserve the capitalist order and protect the propertied. The early 1800s witnessed a growing concern among the propertied with the "dangerous classes," that is, the unattached and unemployed, the "agglomerations of the criminal, vicious, and violent—the rapidly multiplying poor" (Silver, 1967:3). To thwart the challenge posed by the seemingly widespread existence of the dangerous classes, the propertied classes created the London police in 1829, an organization that was bureaucratic from the beginning.

> One of their tasks was to prevent crime by regularly patrolling beats, operating under strict rules which permitted individual discretion. The police also had a mission against the "dangerous classes" and political agitation in the form of mobs or riots (Silver, 1967:7).

More importantly, "the peaceful and propertied classes appreciated two other advantages of the modern police: they relieved ordinary respectable citizens of the obligation or necessity to discharge police functions, especially during emergencies; and they also made less likely a resort to the military for purposes of internal peacekeeping" (Silver, 1967:8–9). Thus, the propertied classes insulated themselves from violent uprising and attack by turning toward a bureaucratic police organization that drew attack and animosity upon itself. The police, then, were created and subsequently operated to fulfill a mission: to repress those who would challenge the authority and position of the economically powerful. The most effective means of achieving that mission, moreover, was through the institution of a rational bureaucracy in which members were bound to strict rules.

The use of the police for strike breaking in the 1920s and 1930s illustrates how law enforcement agencies can be used to impose the will of the powerful. Similarly, during the antiwar movement in the 1960s and early 1970s, the police were used to put down student strikes and political protests.

While we maintain that the law-making organizations generally operate to formalize the interests of the powerful at the expense of the nonpowerful, *the implication that law enforcement agencies operate as a set of rational bureaucracies which administer the law, thus supporting the ruling classes that shape the law, is questionable.* Officials enforce the law selectively and therefore sanction only some cases of law violation. Indeed, powerful persons who have committed crimes are frequently set free by police officers, prosecutors, and judges, but it is incorrect to assume that all persons who are given "breaks" are politically powerful. Ennis (1967) shows that cases are usually sifted out of the criminal justice system rather than tried in court. Although it is efficient to minimize time and resources spent on criminal cases, it is clear that reducing and dropping charges is also a way to do justice which is not always accomplished by strict application of the law.

Three additional lines of argument, two of which are consistent with an organic model of organization, suggest that the criminal justice agencies are not fully constrained by the legal rules imposed by the law-makers. First, research has shown that members of law enforcement agencies adjust their performances to various organizational and personal needs not accommodated by the formal organizational design. Second, the agencies themselves adjust their operations to the power structures of their effective environment, and these typically include the *community's* political culture, which may be very different from national or state politics. Third, organizational members order and give meaning to the concrete rules which they are to enforce and by which they are to operate. We will examine each argument in turn.

A number of writers have demonstrated in whole or in part that law enforcement officials adjust their task performances to the needs of the organization and to the demands of their own careers. Their various efforts share certain common features. First, each emphasizes the development of informal rules and goals that have been substituted for the formal, professed rules and goals. Second, each emphasizes that this process of substitution occurred as a function of adjustment to organizational needs and the needs of the organizational agents in light of legal and organizational obstacles. Third, the informal structure takes on a life of its own.

Specifically, officials shape their activities to enhance or sustain their personal careers, and they shape their activities to further the survival of the organization. But because legal and organizational obstacles often make the satisfaction of these ends difficult, members develop informal ways to circumvent them. Two empirical studies have investigated this problem.

Skolnick (1966) examined police work and found officers are supposed to be constrained by two formal goals. First, they are expected to use skill and initiative to efficiently enforce the substantive law, that is, make "good busts." Second, they are expected to conform to the procedural law when they enforce the substantive law. However, Skolnick found that officers routinely violate the procedural law in order to enforce the substantive law.

Why do police officers arrest people when doing so often necessitates violating the procedural law? According to Skolnick, they use legally deviant means to arrest persons because their superiors use arrest rates to evaluate individual officers' competence. In order to maintain their tenure as well as secure promotion within the department, policemen must build up "good stats" that is, they must make many arrests.

Blumberg (1967) examined criminal-court operation in a major American city and found that the court's formal goals had been replaced by informal ones, a result, Blumberg explains, of several contingencies that operate on the court and its members. For one, like any other complex organization, members of the courthouse community strive for security and personal gratification. Members of the court strive to maintain and enhance their careers by managing efficient and productive appearances. Specifically, prosecutors try to maintain a good "batting average" (a high rate of convictions), trial judges try to minimize appellate reversals, and public defenders try to reduce case backlogs. But because they face an additional problem—intolerably large numbers of defendants who must be handled by a limited number of court personnel—it is difficult for the court and its members to manage competent and efficient appearances.

Blumberg (1967) outlines a number of techniques used to expedite the processing of criminal cases. One practice is the routine screening of cases deemed troublesome and time-consuming regardless of whether the evidence in the case supporting guilt is legally strong or weak. Another common practice is the negotiated guilty plea, whereby the defendant agrees to plead guilty to the state's charges in exchange for some concession in punishment. Through plea negotiation, court members are spared the task of taking cases to trial.

In summary, both Skolnick and Blumberg demonstrate that the criminal justice operation does not correspond to the formal blueprints designed by law-makers. Officials replace the goal of enforcing substantive law by adherence to procedural law with the goal of maintaining organizational and personal security.

Legal inconsistency and organizational overload are not the only contingencies shaping operation of criminal justice operations. To achieve organizational and personal security and survival requires that agencies and officials accommodate the demands of groups that hold power in areas where the agencies operate. Just as the law-making organizations respond to demands of the very powerful in creating legal rules, so too do criminal justice agencies accommodate to the demands of the very powerful in their operation. But research has shown that the powerful groups that directly shape the operation of criminal justice agencies are *not* always the same groups that shape the law-making process.

The principal law-making organizations are state and nationally based and respond to demands from groups holding power at these levels. The criminal justice system, however, is principally community based and draws its basic resources, budget and manpower, from the community. Therefore, criminal justice agencies must accommodate the demands of local groups.

In his investigation of the police in eight communities, Wilson (1968) found that the "political culture" of a particular community shapes the general policies and goals of the police department in that community. For example, the police departments in cities with professional, "good-government" regimes under the control of professional city administrators took on a "legalistic" style of enforcement. This mode of operation produced a large number of arrests for crimes that in similar circumstances would have been ignored by officers in other cities.

Chambliss (1975), in a study of law enforcement, found that gambling, prostitution, drug distribution, pornography, and usury flourished with the compliance, cooperation, and encouragement of both local political officials and law enforcement officers. Local criminal organizations, as Chambliss showed, often controlled vice and pressured local officials to cooperate in the management of illicit businesses.

Examining the administration of vagrancy laws in Philadelphia, Foote (1956) found that the desires of the central business community shaped the enforcement and court processing of vagrants. When local businessmen defined the number of vagrants who loitered and panhandled in the central business district as a nuisance, they brought pressure on the police and courts to increase enforcement and confine the vagrants. This pressure led to the arrest of more vagrants and severe sanctioning of their law violations.

In his examination of one San Francisco county, Swett (1969)

Criminal justice operations are intertwined with the communities they serve, but there are different views as to the nature of the relationship. (*John Launois from Black Star*)

found community attitudes (particularly those of the more influential residents) regarding the seriousness of using marijuana became more tolerant. Many persons regarded marijuana use as a trivial matter. With this change in community attitudes prosecutors rarely brought marijuana cases to court and judges were more likely to dismiss those cases that did enter the court.

We discussed aspects of a third line of argument, which suggests that law enforcement and sanctioning organizations are not *fully* constrained by what is written in law when we portrayed the appellate courts as law-makers rather than mere law-finders and appliers. The core of this argument rests on the nature of rules themselves. Bittner comments:

> The main reason why the abstract formulations of the police mandate cannot be brought closer to the conditions of actual practice by more detailed rule-making, even when such more detailed rules are devised under aegis of in-principle-practicality, is that all formal rules of conduct are basically defeasible. To say that rules are defeasible does not merely admit the existence of exceptions; it means asserting the far stronger claim that the domain of presumed jurisdiction of a legal rule is essentially open ended. While there may be a core of clarity about its application, this core is always and necessarily surrounded by uncertainty . . . . No matter how far we descend on the hierarchy of more and more detailed formal instruction, there will always remain a step further down to go, and no measure of effort will ever succeed in eliminating, or even in meaningfully curtailing, the area of discretionary freedom of the agent whose duty it is to fit rules to cases (1970:3–4).

Although law-making has been of interest to sociologists and political scientists for a long time, their tendency to adopt a macro perspective, by and large, has limited their studies to the social forces, groups, and interests influencing what is *written* in the statutes and court decisions. There is nothing wrong with obtaining a more thorough understanding of this legislative and judicial process. However, because what is written in statutes and court decisions is always being defined, expanded, specified, and interpreted by those who are far removed from the law-making process, those events that influence legislators and courts are indirectly related to the everyday decisions made by policemen, prosecutors, defense attorneys, clerks, and others. Agents of local criminal justice agencies determine what is criminal by their interpretation of what is written in statutes; often there is a big difference between these two.

The claim that agents of the criminal justice system *make* law rather than find it is not a new discovery. Legal scholars such as Holmes, Pound, Llewellyn, and Frank noted long ago that there is a vast difference between the "law on the books" and the "law in action." The early legal realists argued that agents of the legal system make decisions on the basis of extralegal ideas and beliefs. Furthermore, they have said that decision-makers make their decisions reasonable and rational to others by spelling out a connection between their decisions (no matter what they may be) and the law. Essentially the legal realists argued that decisions are "rationalized" by ad hoc and ex post facto reference to the written law. The legal realists recognized that even though the circumstances of a crime, the character of a suspect, or notions of justice may contribute to a judge's decision, he must somehow show that it is in accordance with the law.

In his study of police-prosecutor decision-making Daudistel (1976) shows that the legal realists were right in arguing that laws were made to fit decisions rather than specifically guide them. But unlike the legal realists, Daudistel's study emphasizes that the meaning of law itself is created when it is applied. That is, when policemen and prosecutors legitimate their decisions, they formulate what the law means. Essentially, they go beyond what is written to formulate the "true meaning" of the law. Importantly, the legal realists at least imply that legal agents are deviating from the law. Underlying this argument is the assumption that somehow the law could be applied appropriately if it were followed literally. Put another way, legal agents would not be deviating from the law if they followed what was written in statutes. Referring back to Bittner's comment, we have to admit, however, that it is unclear what the written law means. And Daudistel's research shows that no law has only one "correct" meaning.

Rosett and Cressey (1976) show that applying the law to all offenders (sanctioning all defendants in the same manner) is equal in a purely objective sense but is often unfair. Agents do not apply the law in a mechanical fashion. If they did they would always punish persons who should not be negatively sanctioned. A written rule cannot specify exactly (in writing) all of the actions to which it applies. Therefore, the nature of rules themselves means that persons applying them may do so according to varying conceptions of what they mean.

SUMMARY

Thus far we have portrayed the legal system as a set of units authorized to maintain social order under the aegis of the law. Rather than being arranged in a hierarchical order of authority, with the legislature on top, the appellate courts in the middle, and the criminal justice agencies on the bottom, the units of the system are mutual and simultaneous partners in crime definition and the implementation of crime control procedures (Newman, 1975:62). Particular groups of the environment place demands on the law-making institutions and the law-enforcement agencies, and the law-makers transform such demands into legal rules that are then placed on particular role-occupants and the criminal justice agencies.

REFERENCES

AUBERT, VILHELM
  1952 "White-Collar Crime and Social Structure," *American Journal of Sociology* 58 (November): 263–71.

BARNARD, CHESTER
  1938 *The Functions of the Executive.* Cambridge, Mass: Harvard University Press.

BECKER, HOWARD S.
  1963 *Outsiders: Studies in the Sociology of Deviance.* New York: The Free Press.

BEST, JOEL G.
  1972 "Moral Change: A Study of the Invention and Vindication of Deviance." Ph.D. diss., University of California, Berkeley.

BITTNER, EGON
  1970 *The Functions of the Police in Modern Society.* Rockville, Md.: National Institute of Mental Health.

BLAU, PETER M.
  1963 *The Dynamics of Bureaucracy,* 2d ed. Chicago: University of Chicago Press.

BLUMBERG, ABRAHAM S.
  1967 *Criminal Justice.* Chicago: Quadrangle.

BROOKS, CAROL F.
  1966 "The Early History of the Anti-Contraceptive Laws in Massachusetts and Connecticut," *American Quarterly* 18 (Spring): 3–23.

BUCKLEY, WALTER
  1967 *Sociology and Modern Systems Theory.* Englewood Cliffs, N.J.: Prentice-Hall.

CAPLOW, THEODORE
  1964 *Principles of Organization.* New York: Harcourt, Brace and World.

CHAMBLISS, WILLIAM J.
  1964 "A Sociological Analysis of the Law of Vagrancy," *Social Problems* 12 (Summer): 67–77.
  1975 "The Political Economy of Crime: A Comparative Study of Nigeria and the USA," in Ian Taylor, Paul Walton, and Jock Young, eds., *Critical Criminology,* pp. 167–80. London: Routledge and Kegan Paul.
  1976 "Functional and Conflict Theories of Crime: The Heritage of Emile Durkheim and Karl Marx," in William J. Chambliss and Milton Mankoff, eds., *Whose Law, What Order: A Conflict Approach to Criminology,* pp. 1–28. New York: Wiley.

CHAMBLISS, WILLIAM J., AND ROBERT B. SEIDMAN
   1971   *Law, Order, and Power.* Reading, Mass.: Addison-Wesley.

COHEN, FELIX S.
   1935   "Transcendental Nonsense and the Functional Approach," *Columbia Law Review* 35: 809–49.

DAHRENDORF, RALF
   1958   "Toward a Theory of Social Conflict," *Journal of Conflict Resolution* 2 (June): 170–83.
   1959   *Class and Class Conflict in Industrial Society.* Stanford, Calif.: Stanford University Press.

DAUDISTEL, HOWARD C.
   1976   "Deciding What the Law Means: An Examination of Police-Prosecutor Discretion." Ph.D. diss. University of California, Santa Barbara.

DAVIS, F. JAMES
   1962   "Law as a Type of Social Control," in F. James Davis, Henry H. Foster, C. Ray Jeffery, and E. Eugene Davis, *Society and the Law: New Meanings for an Old Profession,* pp. 39–61. New York: The Free Press.

DICKSON, DONALD T.
   1968   "Bureaucracy and Morality: An Organizational Perspective on a Moral Crusade," *Social Problems* 16 (Fall): 143–56.

ENNIS, PHILIP H.
   1967   "Criminal Victimization in the United States: A Report of a National Survey," in *Report of a Research Study to the President's Commission on Law Enforcement and Administration of Justice, Field Surveys II.* Washington, D.C.: Government Printing Office.

FOOTE, CALEB
   1956   "Vagrancy-Type Law and Its Administration," *University of Pennsylvania Law Review* 104 (March): 603–50.

FRIEDMAN, LAWRENCE M.
   1969   "Legal Culture and Social Development," in Lawrence M. Friedman and Stewart Macaulay, eds., *Law and the Behavioral Sciences,* pp. 1000–16. Indianapolis Ind.: Bobbs-Merrill.

FRIEDMAN, LAWRENCE M., AND STEWART MACAULAY, EDS.
   1969   *Law and the Behavioral Sciences.* Indianapolis, Ind.: Bobbs-Merrill.

GOULDING, MARTIN P.
   1975   *Philosophy of Law.* Englewood Cliffs, N.J.: Prentice-Hall.

JACOB, HERBERT
   1972   *Justice in America: Courts, Lawyers, and the Judicial Process,* 2d ed. Boston: Little, Brown.

KATZ, DANIEL, AND ROBERT L. KAHN
   1966   *The Social Psychology of Organizations.* New York: Wiley.

LEVIN, MARTIN A.
   1972   "Urban Politics and Policy Outcomes: The Criminal Courts," in George F. Cole, ed., *Criminal Justice: Law and Politics,* pp. 330–63. North Scituate, Mass. Duxbury Press.

NAGEL, STUART S.

1964 "The Relationship between the Political and Ethnic Affiliation of Judges and Their Decision-Making," in Glendon Schubert, ed., *Judicial Behavior: A Reader in Theory and Research,* pp. 234–59. Chicago: Rand McNally.

NEWMAN, DONALD J.

1975 *Introduction to Criminal Justice.* Philadelphia: Lippincott.

PARSONS, TALCOTT

1951 *The Social System.* New York: The Free Press.

1962 "The Law and Social Control," in *William M. Evan,* ed., *Law and Sociology: Exploratory Essays.* New York: The Free Press.

PELTASON, JACK W.

1953 "A Political Science of Public Law," *Southwestern Social Science Quarterly* 34, no. 2: 51–56.

PERROW, CHARLES

1972 *Complex Organizations: A Critical Essay.* Glenview, Ill.: Scott, Foresman.

QUINNEY, RICHARD

1969 *Crime and Justice in Society.* Boston: Little, Brown.

1970 *The Social Reality of Crime.* Boston: Little, Brown.

1974 *Critique of the Legal Order: Crime Control in Capitalist Society.* Boston: Little, Brown.

1974a *Criminal Justice in America: A Critical Understanding.* Boston: Little, Brown.

REMINGTON, FRANK J., DONALD J. NEWMAN, EDWARD L. KIMBALL, MARYGOLD MELLI, AND HERMAN GOLDSTEIN, EDS.

1969 *Criminal Justice Administration: Materials and Cases.* Indianapolis Ind.: Bobbs-Merrill.

ROSETT, ARTHUR, AND DONALD R. CRESSEY

1976 *Justice by Consent: Plea Bargains in the American Courthouse.* Philadelphia: Lippincott.

SCHUR, EDWIN M.

1968 *Law and Society: A Sociological View.* New York: Random House.

SELZNICK, PHILIP

1943 "An Approach to a Theory of Bureaucracy," *American Sociological Review* 8 (February): 47–54.

1948 "Foundations of a Theory of Organizations," *American Sociological Review* 13 (February): 25–35.

1949 *TVA and the Grass Roots.* Berkeley: University of California Press.

SILVER, ALLAN

1967 "The Demand for Order in Civil Society: A Review of Some Themes in the History of Urban Crime, Police, and Riot," in David J. Bordua, ed., *The Police: Six Sociological Essays,* pp. 1–24. New York: Wiley.

SINCLAIR, ANDREW

1962 *Prohibition: The Era of Excess.* Boston: Little, Brown.

SKOLNICK, JEROME H.

1966 *Justice without Trial: Law Enforcement in Democratic Society.* New York: Wiley.

STARK, RODNEY
1972   *Police Riots: Collective Violence and Law Enforcement.* Belmont, Calif.: Wadsworth.

STINCHCOMBE, ARTHUR L.
1967   "Formal Organizations," in Neil J. Smelser, ed. *Sociology: An Introduction,* pp. 154–202. New York: Wiley.

SUTHERLAND, EDWIN H.
1950   "The Diffusion of Sexual Psychopath Laws," *American Journal of Sociology* 56 (September): 142–48.

SWETT, DANIEL H.
1969   "Cultural Bias in the American Legal System," *Law and Society Review* 3 (August): 79–110.

TURK, AUSTIN T.
n.d.   "Law, Conflict, and Order: From Theorizing toward Theories," unpublished paper, mimeographed.

ULMER, S. SIDNEY
1962   "The Political Party Variable in the Michigan Supreme Court," *Journal of Public Law* 11, no. 2: 352–62.

WEBER, MAX
1946   *From Max Weber: Essays in Sociology,* trans. and ed. Hans H. Gerth and C. Wright Mills. New York: Oxford University Press.
1947   *The Theory of Social and Economic Organization,* trans. A. M. Henderson and Talcott Parsons. New York: Oxford University Press.

WILSON, JAMES Q.
1968   *Varieties of Police Behavior: The Management of Law and Order in Eight Communities.* Cambridge: Harvard University Press.

WOLFE, ALAN
1971   "Political Repression and the Liberal Democratic State," *Monthly Review,* 23 (December): 18–38.

ZIEGENHAGEN, EDUARD A.
1970   "The Reconceptualization of Legal Systems and Processes," in James R. Klonoski and Robert D. Mendelsohn, eds., *The Politics of Local Justice,* pp. 26–35. Boston: Little, Brown.

SELECTED READINGS

BLUMBERG, ABRAHAM S., *Criminal Justice.* Chicago: Quadrangle, 1967.
    An empirical investigation of a metropolitan criminal court. As a complex organization, the criminal court generates a multitude of needs that are not formally accommodated, such as organizational production and efficiency. These needs lead to the replacement of formally prescribed practices with informal practices sanctioned by informal rules.

CHAMBLISS, WILLIAM J., AND ROBERT B. SEIDMAN, *Law, Order and Power*. Reading, Mass.: Addison-Wesley, 1971.
Employs an open systems approach in sketching the operations of the legal system and relationships between organizational units of the legal system.

DAHRENDORF, RALF, "Toward a Theory of Social Conflict," *Journal of Conflict Resolution* 2 (June 1958): 170–83.
A critical examination of the consensus and conflict models of society.

FEELEY, MALCOLM M., "Two Models of the Criminal Justice System: An Organizational Perspective," *Law and Society Review* 7 (Spring 1973): 407–25.
Outlines and evaluates the rational-goal and functional-systems approaches toward the social organization of the American criminal justice system.

part two

INITIAL ENCOUNTERS WITH CRIMINAL JUSTICE

3
THE POLICE: OCCASIONS of CONTACT with the CRIMINAL JUSTICE SYSTEM

Social scientists have addressed several issues in their study of the police. Generally speaking, sociologists and legal scholars have studied many police departments and police officers in an attempt to describe and explain police behavior. For example, researchers have tried to describe accurately the role police play in our society, and they have asked if the police can provide efficient social services and enforce the law. Among many other things, social scientists have evaluated police training schools, the effectiveness of mobile patrol, enforcement of vice and narcotic laws, and they have studied police encounters with juveniles, gang members, and prostitutes.

Of course, all of the above issues are important. But it is our contention that the key to understanding police work is knowledge about police decision-making. The police are decision-makers who have the power to enforce resolutions to a variety of problems, some of them legal but most not. Nevertheless, the police are called to intervene in many situations in which they can exercise their power to make consequential decisions about other persons' lives.

POLICE DECISIONS

A plethora of studies have analyzed police decision-making. Studying decision-making on Skid-Row, Bittner (1967) found that policemen must constantly decide what to do with persons who are disturbing the peace. According to Bittner a competent police officer is one who is able to maintain the peace without necessarily using his power of arrest. In fact, Bittner points out, arresting someone is only one of many tools available to the officer who must solve problems on the street.

Skolnick (1966) describes how detectives make decisions regarding narcotic and vice violations. His findings indicate that whether or not someone is arrested depends significantly on the type of crime they are accused of committing, whether or not they can provide detectives with information about more serious crimes, or whether they are defined by officers as "good pinches," that is, good arrests.

Piliavin and Briar (1964) discuss why juvenile officers arrest some youngsters for delinquent acts while they define others' similar behavior as nondelinquent. They describe the informal cues that police officers attend to when deciding what to do about a juvenile who is a "problem." Styles of dress and racial characteristics, for example, may be variables that bias an officer's decision.

Wilson (1968) studied police organizations and found that they can be categorized into three different styles of department. These types of organization—"watchmen," "legalistic," and "service"—have a profound effect on routine police decisions. For instance, departments characterized as "legalistic" are more likely to arrest persons for minor offenses than are "watchmen" departments, which are more concerned with keeping the peace.

Goldstein (1960) claims that police decisions have "low visibility," that is, policemen make routine decisions that are not often scrutinized by the courts or other social control agencies. Unless someone accused of a crime is prosecuted in the criminal courts, police arrest techniques, searches, and seizures are not critically examined. This is important because a defendant may waive his or her right to trial and plead guilty to a lesser offense when they may have been found innocent of all charges in a court trial. Police abuse of power may become systematic because policemen are not rewarded for obtaining convictions in a court of law. Rather, they are rewarded for "clearing crimes." This means that they only have to apprehend someone they feel is guilty. Illegal searches may give a policeman enough evidence to satisfy his own standard of proof yet fail to legally establish guilt in a court of law.

Like several other sociologists we want to contribute to the social scientific knowledge and understanding of decision-making. In doing so we will divide police work into two general categories: proactive and reactive.

It cannot be overemphasized that this distinction is an artificial one and is used here because of its common usage in the literature about police. Generally, on the one hand, proactive refers to police activity initiated by the police themselves. On examination one will find, however, that almost all police work is reactive, that is, work initiated by citizens' calls to the police. So, even though detectives may initiate undercover narcotic investigations, commonly regarded as proactive police work, they are probably doing so because special interest groups have demanded that drug laws be enforced and that users of narcotics be arrested. Additionally, when a patrol officer stops persons on the street and questions them, he is taking the initiative and searching for crime. Although field interrogations are usually thought of as proactive, they may be in response to influential citizens' demands that "undesirables" be kept off the streets.

CITIZEN DISCRETION IN APPLICATION OF THE LAW

Because policemen decide whom to arrest and whom to set free, many scholars treat police decisions as the first stage in the criminal justice process. A review of the academic literature written about the police shows most authors have assumed that a citizen's fate is determined by the police, an assumption that is incorrect. Although one should not minimize the significance of police power and discretion, the

Most citizen requests for the police are for services other than law enforcement activities. (*United Press International Photo*)

citizen's role in the decision-making process must be examined. Whether persons are apprehended by the police and arrested for committing crimes depends on the willingness of citizens to *give information* to law enforcement officers. The citizens' role in the criminal justice system is indexed by the fact that approximately 80 percent of all police activity is initiated by them. This means that most of the information gathered about criminal and noncriminal matters comes from citizens. "In this sense, citizens may be regarded as enforcers or nonenforcers of the law and its moral order" (Reiss, 1971: 65).

We can look at the findings of victimization surveys to get an idea of how much crime is not reported to the police. These surveys attempt to obtain accurate estimates of the amount of crime committed in the United States. Because researchers have found that many persons do

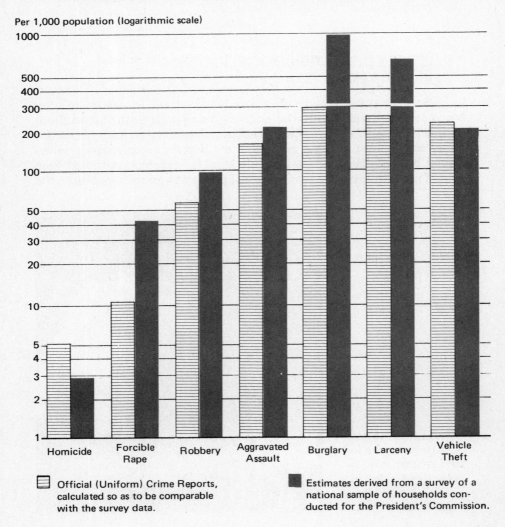

Per 1,000 population (logarithmic scale)

☐ Official (Uniform) Crime Reports, calculated so as to be comparable with the survey data.

■ Estimates derived from a survey of a national sample of households conducted for the President's Commission.

INITIAL ENCOUNTERS WITH CRIMINAL JUSTICE

not report crimes to the police (Biderman, 1967), it is estimated that criminal statistics compiled by the Federal Bureau of Investigation in the *Uniform Crime Reports* underestimate the amount of crime in the United States. Rather than asking the police how many crimes they know about, survey researchers have asked citizens how many times they have been victimized by criminals, and whether they reported their encounters to the police. Using this technique, researchers have determined that a great number of crimes are not reported to the police. Therefore, a large number of crimes are never investigated and many criminals never apprehended.[1] The graph on page 80 indicates the difference between crime rates reported in the *Uniform Crime Reports* and the rates estimated by surveys of households.

There are a number of examples which demonstrate that citizens can significantly affect the criminal justice process. In 1973 victimization surveys of households and businesses were undertaken by the Bureau of the Census for the Law Enforcement Assistance Administration. The findings from these surveys dramatically substantiate our point.

In 1973 it was estimated that 159,670 rapes and attempted rapes were committed in the United States. But according to victims only 44 percent or 69,920 of these crimes were reported to the police. Therefore, approximately 89,740 rapes and/or attempted rapes were not known to the police. In other words, approximately 56 percent of these crimes did not result in any police action.[2]

In 1973 it is estimated that there were 6,433,030 burglaries in the United States, but victims reported only 46 percent of these crimes to the police. As a result, 3,429,190 burglaries were not reported to the police by victims.

The National Crime Panel found (for the twelve months prior to the first quarter of 1974) in Oakland, California, as many as 86 percent of some crimes were not reported to the police.

The reasons why people do not report crimes to the police are varied. With only a few exceptions, victimized persons most frequently

---

[1] We must exercise caution when using data gathered by victimization surveys. In many cases citizens report incidents to researchers that are not actually criminal matters. Therefore, it is possible to overemphasize slightly citizens' failure to call the police. Reiss has pointed out: "Many incidents citizens regard as criminal must, by law, be handled otherwise, since they do fall into the category of civil or private matters. The police superficially may appear to exercise discretion in civil or private matters, in which citizens and police actually have very little control" (1971:77).

[2] It is possible that some victimizations did come to the knowledge of the police even though they were not reported to them by citizens who were victimized. Witnesses not directly involved may report criminal incidents to the police. Interestingly, however, in the past several years the number of crimes known to the police actually were less than the number of crimes citizens said they reported to the police. Apparently policemen do not record all criminal matters as crimes (cf. Ennis, 1967).

Table 3–1 OAKLAND: PERCENT OF VICTIMIZATIONS REPORTED TO THE POLICE, BY SECTOR AND TYPE OF CRIME

SECTOR AND TYPE OF CRIME	PERCENT
PERSONAL SECTOR, ALL CRIMES	36
Crimes of violence	45
Rape	54
Robbery	53
Robbery and attempted robbery with injury	65
From serious assault	71
From minor assault	59
Robbery without injury	60
Attempted robbery without injury	31
Assault	40
Aggravated assault	49
With injury	64
Attempted assault with weapon	43
Simple assault	31
With injury	41
Attempted assault without weapon	27
Crimes of theft	31
Personal larceny with contact	47
Purse snatching	67
Attempted purse snatching	17[1]
Pocket picking	42
Personal larceny without contact	29
HOUSEHOLD SECTOR, ALL CRIMES	49
Burglary	57
Forcible entry	77
Unlawful entry without force	51
Attempted forcible entry	32
Household larceny	27
Less than $50	14
$50 or more	48
Amount not available	24[1]
Attempted larceny	24
Motor vehicle theft	77
Completed theft	92
Attempted theft	33
COMMERCIAL SECTOR, ALL CRIMES	78
Burglary	77
Robbery	83

[1] Estimate, based on about 10 or fewer sample cases, is statistically unreliable.
SOURCE: Law Enforcement Assistance Administration, *Criminal Victimization Surveys in Thirteen American Cities,* June 1975, p. 174.

fail to report crimes because they think nothing can be done about their victimization. For example, according to researchers, in 1973, 22 percent of the time victims of rapes and attempted rapes did not report these crimes to the police because they felt nothing could be done.

Additionally, some rapes were not reported because the victims feared reprisal, while others were not reported because the victims did not feel the police "wanted to be bothered" or felt the police did not "want to take the time." Whatever their reasons for not reporting crimes to the police, it must be concluded that citizens play an integral part in the criminal justice process.

The citizens' role in the criminal justice process is not limited to calling the police. After the police learn about crimes, citizens can still influence the outcome of legal decisions. For example, Black's (1971) research has shown that citizen complainants have a strong affect on the outcome of police-suspect encounters (see Table 3–2). Black states: "Arrest practices sharply reflect the preferences of citizen complainants, particularly when the desire is for leniency and also, though less frequently, when the complainant demands arrest."

Several studies, the most notable being Piliavin and Briar's (1964), have indicated that police officers attend to persons' dress and physical appearance as cues to their character. For example, a black juvenile dressed in shabby blue jeans and a black leather jacket is more likely to be viewed as a delinquent than a well-dressed white youth. As we shall see later in this chapter, police assessments of character are consequential for all citizens. Negative evaluation of character not only influences whether or not one is arrested but also effects the policeman's judgment about what acts are crimes. There is some evidence that character evaluations based on physical appearance of suspects also influence citizens' judgments about whether or not to take action and report crimes.

Following the work of Darley and Latane (1968) and Latane and Darley (1970, 1970a), Bryjak (1970) completed a field experiment in which he studied the effect of physical appearance on witnesses to crime. In the experiment, Bryjak varied the appearance of a thief (a confederate of the researcher) whose crimes were witnessed by subjects.

All of the thefts were carried out in the same manner. The thief would be standing at the checkout counter of the liquor store leafing a magazine. On the counter next to the magazines would be a bottle of bourbon that had been set there by the thief. As soon as a customer approached the counter the clerk [also a confederate of the experimenter] would ask the robber if he could help him. The thief would then request some imported beer: "Do you carry Lowenbrau by the case?" "Yes, we do, would you like light or dark?" would be the clerk's reply. Upon hearing the robber's choice the clerk would say that he was going to the back room and get a case. Leaving the robber and the subject alone in the store the clerk would go to the back room and presumably look for the Lowenbrau. Waiting approximately ten seconds after the cashier was out of sight the robber would pick up the quart, look at the label and remark to

TABLE 3-2 ARREST RATES IN CITIZEN-INITIATED ENCOUNTERS ACCORDING TO TYPE OF CRIME, RELATIONAL TIE BETWEEN COMPLAINANT AND SUSPECT, AND COMPLAINANT'S PREFERENCE

		FELONY				MISDEMEANOR	
Relational Tie	Complainant's Preference	Total Number of Incidents	Arrest Rate in Percent	Relational Tie	Complainant's Preference	Total Number of Incidents	Arrest Rate in Percent
Family Members	Prefers Arrest	20	55	Family Members	Prefers Arrest	15	80
	Preference Unclear	8	(6)		Preference Unclear	13	38
	Prefers No Arrest	10	0		Prefers No Arrest	8	(0)
Friends, Neighbors, Acquaintances	Prefers Arrest	5	(4)	Friends, Neighbors, Acquaintances	Prefers Arrest	11	64
	Preference Unclear	8	(6)		Preference Unclear	15	40
	Prefers No Arrest	0	(0)		Prefers No Arrest	20	5
Strangers	Prefers Arrest	3	(3)	Strangers	Prefers Arrest	15	87
	Preference Unclear	2	(2)		Preference Unclear	15	47
	Prefers No Arrest	3	(2)		Prefers No Arrest	5	(0)
All Family Members		38	45	All Family Members		36	47
All Friends, Neighbors, Acquaintances		13	77	All Friends, Neighbors, Acquaintances		46	30
All Strangers		8	(7)	All Strangers		35	57

SOURCE: Donald Black, "The Social Organization of Arrest," *Stanford Law Review* 23 (1971): 1066. Copyright © 1971 by the Board of Trustees of Leland Stanford Junior University.

INITIAL ENCOUNTERS WITH CRIMINAL JUSTICE

nobody in particular, "He'll never miss one bottle" and head for the door (1970:4–5).

Comparing customers' responses to an "extremely sloppy male" and a "uniformed marine carrying a cane and walking with a noticeable limp," Bryjak found that 46.6 percent (n=30) of the subjects responded immediately to the shabbily dressed thief and reported his behavior to the clerk while only 13.3 percent (n=30) responded immediately to the limping marine.

Interestingly, 56.7 percent of the subjects who witnessed a "neat male" committing a crime never reported the incident (even after the clerk asked what happened) while even more (80 percent) who witnessed the marine take a bottle of liquor never said anything to the clerk about the crime.

PROACTIVE PATROL

It is important to note that *appearances* are the basis for many police activities and that the decision about whom to stop and interrogate is usually made on the basis of how that person "looks" to the officer. That is, all the policeman generally has available to him are the visible cues of scenes, and he organizes and assesses such cues in order to determine whether all is in order or if trouble is imminent (Sacks, 1972; cf. Goffman, 1971). Wambaugh, reporting on events that led up to the death of a Los Angeles police officer, describes how the police decided to stop a particular automobile:

> It was now 10 P.M. and the unmarked Plymouth police car known as Six-Z-Four was emerging from the alley onto Carlos when the coupe crossed their headlight beam and they saw the two gaunt young men with their jackets and snap-brim leather caps in their little car with Nevada plates.
> They would have aroused the suspicions of almost any policemen in Hollywood that night. It was patently obvious that they were *not ordinary* out-of-town tourists cruising the boulevard. The caps were rare enough, but with the matching leather jackets, they were almost absurdly suspicious, even contrived . . . .
> This little Ford looked "too good," which in police jargon means it looked too bad, too suspicious, a "good shake." It had to be stopped and a reason found to search (emphasis added) (1973:139–40).

Goffman has devoted much study to the topic of appearances, and any analysis of police work would benefit from a familiarity with his works.[3] By appearances, Goffman means more than the clothing one wears or the physical features that distinguish someone. It is useful to think of appearances as contextual matters that include a number of variables; for example, a person's appearance is affected by the time and place in which he is seen, the clothing he is wearing, the behavior he is engaged in, and so forth. These are just a few basic elements all of which contribute to how one is perceived by others. To put it simply, "normal" appearances are those features of a person or situation that convey to others the feeling that all is "okay," typical, proper, and that "nothing is out of the ordinary" (Goffman, 1971).

Importantly, the unique characteristics of a scene or encounter may be noted by persons and not reacted to as being abnormal. Everyone has encountered others with whom he is not familiar but with whom he can interact easily. Sometimes, however, the other's behavior may provide the observer with a feeling that "something is wrong." On these occasions (when others' actions are viewed as threatening or unusual), alarm and possibly defensive action seem necessary. For example, should one individual begin to run down a busy sidewalk or engage in a shoving match with another, pedestrians will probably notice this behavior. In such circumstances, persons are likely to feel "something is up" that could be a threat to personal security. Although we are all somewhat attentive to appearances, Sacks (1972) has pointed out that the policeman has been trained to be particularly watchful and is more intent than others in his observations. Sacks has called the method that officers use to discover others who are a danger the "incongruity procedure."

The incongruity procedure basically consists of an interpretation of witnessed events in terms of their familiarity. For example, an officer assigned to patrol a sector of a city will become familiar with the routine activities of those who live and work in his beat. If the officer on patrol notices that something is different from the routine (that is, incongruous), he will attempt to specify how it is different and if it is serious enough to be investigated. Should things seem extremely odd, further information will be sought to account for the strangeness of the situation. For instance, should an officer recall that a particular light that is usually burning is out, he will probably inspect the scene to determine if things are all right. It must be noted that it is not simply the fact a light is out that calls for investigation. Rather, it is the fact that a particular light in a particular context is not burning that indicates the need for further explanation.

Similarly, when a police officer encounters persons, he is measuring them against their surroundings:

> A policeman is chronically suspicious and he is forced, by the
> nature of the duty with which he is entrusted, to make snap

---

[3] We do not intend to provide a summary of Goffman's work. Rather we wish to acknowledge his contribution to our ideas on this subject.

decisions about the appropriateness of what people are doing. Since he is looking for the unusual, his decisions are environment-specific; what action he takes depends upon what is perceived to be common for that area (Bayley and Mendelsohn, 1968: 93).

Whether a policeman stops persons because he feels their presence on the street is not normal, or because he has been provided with a description of a criminal suspect that may "match" a pedestrian, his decision to stop and interrogate is still made on the basis of appearance. Although this is a crude method of investigation, the pressure to maintain a high clearance rate and the limited access to private settings have led the police to rely on this technique.

Numerous studies have found that many citizens resent the use of this technique and consider it police harassment. While the police do not define their efforts as harassment, the fact remains that such law enforcement actions generate considerable public hostility toward the police. For instance, the United States Commission on Civil Rights reported (in *Mexican Americans and the Administration of Justice in the Southwest*) that "many complaints were heard—some from law enforcement officials—concerning the frequency of arrests on suspicion or for investigation and dragnet stop and frisk practices in Mexican American neighborhoods" (United States Commission on Civil Rights, 1970: 10). The upset and anger of those who are stopped is easy to understand. Although there are no laws against walking the street at night, to do so in certain neighborhoods at certain times is to stand a very good chance of being questioned by patrolling officers. Such an interrogation, although it may be legal, is an inconvenience and constitutes a momentary loss of freedom.

A stop may be made even though there is no evidence that the person being questioned has committed a crime. Indeed, a person may be interrogated even though the officer has no information to indicate that any recent crime has been committed. Because they are told to be on the lookout for anything that may be out of the ordinary, officers consider these stops to be reasonable. They view a stranger's presence on the street late at night as suspicious enough to be investigated. The officer's concern with those who appear out of the ordinary is indicated by a patrol sergeant's comments to a researcher:

> The guys are getting a little tired of this shift [work time assigned to a patrol squad]. During the day it's hard to figure out what's going on. Everybody is out on the street. At least late at night if you see a guy at 3:00 A.M. you can be fairly confident that a stop is needed (Daudistel, 1976).

Were the policeman's task to see only what is out of the ordinary, it would be less difficult than it actually is. One can imagine that individuals who are "up to no good" can use normal appearances to their advantage. And indeed, consequently, the policeman's task is complicated by the fact that those whose intentions might ordinarily cause alarm (were they to appear out of the ordinary) frequently are aware of the importance of their appearance and attempt to normalize it. A culprit may carefully assume a normal everyday appearance to gain illegal entrance into homes. During the 1960s, the Boston Strangler, for instance, was able to gain access to his victims' homes by posing as a repairman sent by the phone company. Persons who saw him at a door would have had reason to believe that he was, in fact, a repairman because he was wearing working clothes. Similarly, burglars may be successful by posing as moving men. If no one is at home and if little communication exists between neighbors, most persons in the area of a house will assume that men carrying furniture out of it to a truck during the daylight hours are simply doing their job.

Most police officers are keenly aware of the ability some persons have to cover up their "true" intentions, and police training emphasizes the problem. Most officers have been told many stories that document the importance and, at the same time, the unreliability of appearances. All are familiar with cases in which a bank robber has stolen money from a teller without others in the bank knowing that a robbery was taking place.

Because training and field experiences emphasize the tenuousness of appearances, policemen have come to adopt standards of suspiciousness that are quite different from those of the average citizen. The extent to which police standards are more accurate than those of citizens is not known, but it is clear that if a citizen is stopped and interrogated on the basis of cues that he either does not consider suspicious or is unaware of, some antagonism between the police and the citizen will result.

Police officers recognize the difference between their perceptions and those of citizens (Skolnick, 1966: 42). A study of decision-making in law enforcement by Daudistel (1976) has found that officers acknowledge that there is a qualitative difference between the grounds they use to decide whether someone is acting suspiciously and those commonly accepted by the public. In this regard, it is not rare to hear police officers exclaim they have a "sixth sense" that allows them to "see" what others ignore. Interestingly, it seems, the notion of a sixth sense is merely an indication of the fact that a unique subcultural perspective has developed in most police departments. Because sociologists and anthropologists have found similar phenomena when they have done analyses of sense perception, it is apparent that the ability to notice things that others ("outsiders") do not see is not a supernatural power. For example, Cantril, in extensively exploring the influence of social expectations on an individual's perception, found that cultural values and previous experience determine what an observer actually sees:

> Numerous investigations in the fields of sociology and social
> psychology have shown over and over again how the particular

A police officer, lying in a doorway, dons the appearance of a skid row bum. Such decoy tactics are used mainly in proactive police work. (*United Press International Photo*)

characteristics we have learned to attach to a particular individual or particular group of individuals determine both our awareness of and our reactions to them. It has been found, for example, that persons who are highly prejudiced against the Negro, who have learned to attach unfavorable significance to a person with black skin, will more quickly spot a Negro if he is mixed in with a group of white people, but that these same prejudiced individuals are less able than others to distinguish between one Negro and another (1950: 76).

Considering the influence of occupational values and working conditions on the policeman's "working personality," Skolnick observed that the police "tend to develop ways of looking at the world distinctive to themselves, cognitive lenses through which to see situations and events" (1966: 42). According to Shibutani:

A perspective is an ordered view of one's world, what is taken for granted about various physical objects, events, and human nature. The environment in which men live is a unity of order, not merely an aggregate of things. The substitute world consists of a set of meanings, and behavior is predicted upon all kinds of understandings about the attributes of various categories of objects. Perceptual cues arouse hypotheses about the characteristics of an object, many of which cannot actually be seen (1961: 119).

Even though many police officers persist in calling their abilities a sixth sense, these studies have indicated that unique perceptions are explicable on "sociological grounds." The physician, for example, has been trained to see specific things that others may not be able to see. That is, persons share in many different perspectives, all of which act as "filters" that channel observations.

Because officers share a unique perspective and because they are trained to pay attention to appearances that many citizens find unalarming, they are faced with the problem of convincing others that their actions follow from a reasonable assessment of a situation. If an officer has developed an ability to see and attend to features of scenes that most other persons do not notice, how can he show that it is "reasonable" to stop and question a citizen?

The legal issue here is an extremely complicated one. The police have a legal right to stop and question persons even though they may not, at the time, have probable cause to make an arrest. According to Bassiouni, "the right of the police and investigatory agencies to inquire under reasonable circumstances as to the identity of a person, or to ask certain limited or relevant questions of a suspect, has long been recognized as a necessary adjunct to law enforcement" (1969: 357). An examination of criminal cases will confirm this finding and show that courts are willing to accept evidence that is less than "probable cause for arrest" as justification for the stopping and interrogation of a suspect. The difficulty remains, however, because the court in its acceptance has failed to specify a "verbal formula to describe the probability of guilt requisite for stopping and questioning" (Remington, 1962: 18).

Within this complicated legal context, police officers have been asked to control crime. In the effort to achieve such control, police departments have been encouraged by public and governmental agencies to become more professional. This has meant that governmental agencies have come to reward officers for developing new skills and abilities that others do not have. Policemen trying to be professional, which means having skills that laymen do not share, have continued to develop unique ways of recognizing suspicious persons by appearances and have trained one another to pay attention to extremely obscure cues that they deem identify those who are up to "no good." Consequently, they have found that the difference between their observations and those made by the average citizen has continued to increase. The special perspective that has grown around police work makes it impossible for officers to explain adequately to others many of their actions. Indeed, through training and experience, they have developed observational skills, but they have not achieved a concomitant ability to communicate the basis for their suspicions to outsiders.

The fact that officers often cannot explain the reasons for their actions does not mean that they are always covering up for one another or that they always capriciously stop citizens on the street. It appears that most of the time, those who stop and question persons do so only if they feel that an interrogation might lead to discovery of a crime. The concern with clearing crimes and making many arrests, however, has led to stopping some persons more frequently than others. "According to Jess Cuellar, a probation officer in Phoenix, Arizona, and a former policeman in that city, Mexican Americans living in South Phoenix, a predominantly Mexican American area, will be picked up for questioning by the police, sooner or later, even though they may have no police record" (United States Commission on Civil Rights, 1970: 10). So, although the frequent stopping of blacks and chicanos, for example, may be viewed by the police as legitimate and necessary, this practice has also generated conflict in our society (President's Commission on Law Enforcement and Administration of Justice, 1967a: 183; Stark, 1972; United States Commission on Civil Rights, 1970).

Simply stated, the police and the public may not see "eye to eye"; therefore, the significance of events or behavior may be interpreted quite differently by each group.

We have already suggested that reasons for these differences are not too difficult to understand. Policemen, because they are members of a specific occupational group with unique goals, have come to develop and share particular conceptions and views of the world. But this perspective is difficult to describe because it is neither definite nor static. It is possible, however, to demonstrate that policemen and citizens are likely to view many actions differently. Thus, interaction between them can produce conflict. If, for example, the members of a black community and the white policeman assigned to patrol their neighborhood view things differently, it is likely that police-citizen interaction in the neighborhood will result in some complaints and accusations of police abuse. Most often the police do not see these complaints as legitimate, frequently responding to them by commenting, "If you were in our shoes you'd understand why we, the police, did what we did." Similarly, citizens frequently reject the officers' justification of police behavior and often simply state, "If you were in our shoes you'd be upset about the treatment you received at the hands of the police."

Allegations of police misconduct are not always made by citizens who are asserting that the police acted illegally when performing their duties. In fact, quite frequently police actions that are legally sanctioned generate many complaints from concerned citizens. For example, on May 17, 1974 the Los Angeles Police Department and the F.B.I. were involved in a fiery gun battle with members of a revolutionary group called the Symbionese Liberation Army (S.L.A.). After the smoke had settled, six occupants of the house that stood near the intersection of 54th Street and Compton Avenue were dead. Only hours after this well-publicized incident occurred, many Los Angeles area citizens and community groups complained about the way the police had dealt with the situation, questioning whether it was necessary for the police to engage in a shootout with the suspects. Most complainants, interestingly, did not argue about the legality of the law enforcement effort. Some community leaders acknowledged that the S.L.A. did shoot at the officers, and the policemen's legal right to return fire was not questioned. However, people did wonder if the agencies involved had exhausted the many alternative tactics available to them. Although tear gas was used first, community groups contended that the police were too quick to respond to the situation with automatic weapons fire. The debate was not a legal one, but one in which many citizens inquired about the necessity of using gunfire to apprehend the S.L.A.

The charges voiced against the Los Angeles police and the responses to them by law enforcement officials are evidence of the discord between citizen and police perspectives. These differing outlooks lead both groups to define the same situation differently. For instance, prior to the S.L.A. shootout, the police publicly announced that the S.L.A. was an extremely violent and irrational organization. Whether this characterization was correct is not important. The fact remains that many police officials seemed to have believed that a shootout was inevitable. Based upon this belief, when the S.L.A. was surrounded, the decision of the police to fire at the house was seen by them as the only way to deal with the fugitives. Those who complained about the police action, on the other hand, believed that more important than immediate apprehension was concern for the safety of neighborhood residents. They thought the police should have tried to capture the revolutionaries without any bloodshed. Because of the basic difference between the police and citizen definitions of the situation, the debate that followed the shoot-out reached a major impasse in which the debating groups were unable to undertake a reasonable consideration of the event.

The decision to use force and the assessment of how much is needed depends on how each specific instance of police-citizen interaction is defined by the policeman. This does not mean that others who are interacting with a police officer do not influence his judgment about the use of force. According to Reiss:

> In general, persons officers regarded as being in a deviant offender role or who defied what the officer defines as his authority were the most likely victims of undue force. Thirty-nine percent openly defied authority by challenging the legitimacy of the police to exercise that authority, 9 percent physically resisted arrest, and 32 percent were persons in deviant offender roles, such as drunks, homosexuals, or addicts (1971: 149).

There is no code book that can be used to specify definitively what behavior is to be handled with force. The unique character of each encounter must be evaluated by the officer. Based upon what he sees, he is given the legal right to use the amount of force (less than deadly) he interprets as necessary to accomplish his task. Even in cases where deadly force may be used, the law does not specify what behavior requires the use of such force to obtain control of the situation. That is, the instructions the courts use to evaluate the need for deadly force still require that the officer do a great deal of interpretive work. Confronted with a person who resists his commands, the police officer must decide: (1) Is the suspect (whether accused of a crime or not) likely to cause "great" bodily harm to others? (2) Is gunfire needed to prevent the escape of a suspect accused of a forceful felony? Such a decision is based upon the officer's past experience and the evidence of the moment. The information available to each officer is limited, and even one who is familiar with the many court decisions about the use of force will find that he must use discretion.

Evidence from a report by Black and Reiss (1967) clearly indicates that the vast majority of all police-citizen encounters are executed with few problems and little evidence of antagonism during the transaction. Even though most contacts go smoothly, other studies have shown that minorities are more likely than whites to report unfavorable experiences in their personal contact with the police (Campbell and Schuman, 1968; Stark, 1972: 109). For example, in their supplemental study for the National Advisory Commission on Civil Disorders, Campbell and Schuman (1968: 43) found that blacks viewed many police stops as unnecessary and unjustified. In response to questions that asked if persons felt "the police frisk or search without good reason," if it "happens to people in your neighborhood," and if it "happens to you," the investigators obtained the pattern of responses shown in Table 3–3.

Although during stops the police may act civilly and in a business-like manner, many minorities still regard their behavior as illegitimate (Wilkins, 1966). Importantly, differences in opinion are not always due to legal issues. More often than not, police officers have a legal right to stop and interrogate people, and the studies of Reiss (1971) and Black (1971) indicate that the majority of officers do not violate the law during these encounters. To the citizen, these encounters are consequential. When one is stopped and questioned, whether legally or not, he has experienced an undeniable momentary loss of freedom.

Because minorities are stopped more frequently than whites, there is a greater possibility that they will be arrested or cited by officers. Forslund (1970: 216), in his examination of criminal justice statistics, found that "regardless of the type of [crime] rate considered,

Table 3–3   "BELIEFS ABOUT USE OF SEARCH AND FRISK TACTICS"

	NEGRO			WHITE		
	Men	Women	Total	Men	Women	Total
Yes	22	3	13	6	6	4
No	36	55	45	16	24	20
Don't know	1	2	1	0	0	0
Don't think it happens in their neighborhood	41	40	41	78	75	76
	100	100	100	100	100	100

SOURCE: Angus Campbell and Howard Schuman, "Racial Attitudes in Fifteen American Cities," in *A Supplemental Study For The National Advisory Commission On Civil Disorders* (Washington D.C. Government Printing Office, 1948), p.43.

Negro rates are substantially higher than those for whites. . . . Negro male rates range from 5.8 times the white male rate for separate individuals arrested to 9.8 times the white male rate for persons sent to correctional institutions."[4] Although criminal statistics are not too reliable, they do indicate who gets arrested. In the case of blacks, the *Uniform Crime Reports* (*UCR*) supplied by the F.B.I. also indicate that they are arrested more frequently than whites. "While blacks, in 1967, comprised only one-tenth of the population, they constituted nearly one-third of persons arrested for all offenses (computed from UCR, 1967: 126, using total population arrest figures)" (Wolfgang and Cohen, 1970: 31). A similar pattern was discovered by Stewart, who found that "the amount of Indian criminality relative to population size seems to be exceptionally large. For the nation as a whole, the rate of Indian criminality is nearly seven times that of the national average" (1964: 61).

There is a considerable amount of literature that addresses the question of how race is associated with crime (Geis, 1965; Wolfgang and Cohen, 1970). In these studies criminologists seem to agree that the disproportionately high crime rate attributed to minority groups is predominantly a function of police procedures (cf. Morales, 1970). For certain groups, such as blacks, chicanos, and native Americans, the crime rate attributed to them develops in a "snowball" fashion. "It is commonly believed, and nowhere convincingly refuted, that police surveillance is much more extensive in the residential areas of the lower economic class. There may be sound reasons for this . . . but for what-

---

[4] Forslund is only reporting what available statistics indicate. He does not claim that, in fact, blacks are more criminal than whites.

ever the reason, frequency of patrols in these areas is bound to apprehend a greater proportion of those groups who live in these areas . . ." (Colorado Commission on Spanish Surnamed Citizens, 1967). The more crime that is perceived to take place in these areas, the more patrols are allocated to police these communities. With increased patrols the probability of apprehending a violator is greatly increased. As Geis comments:

> A belief, based on real or imagined information, that a particular minority group commits more crime than other groups will often lead to a greater saturation of this group's neighborhood by police patrol. Such saturation will likely turn up more crime and produce a larger number of arrests of persons belonging to the group, though it will also often inhibit some kinds of criminal activity because of the increased likelihood of apprehension (1965:146).

All of this does not mean that crime does not take place in minority neighborhoods; indeed, a large amount of criminal activity takes place in the ghetto. However, the fact is that crimes are also committed by whites. In truth, police statistics that indicate a higher crime rate for blacks than whites show only that blacks are apprehended more frequently than whites. "No one really knows whether blacks, as socially defined, commit more crime than whites; but we do know that, according to official police statistics, more persons with the designated status of Negro than with the status of white are arrested" (Wolfgang and Cohen, 1970: 37).

Systematic discrimination is the most critical problem that results from the dependence on appearances as grounds for investigating and interrogating a citizen. The "incongruity procedure" described by Sacks (see p. 86) contributes to a self-fulfilling prophecy that most minorities are criminal. Because blacks, for example, cannot blend into a crowd that is predominantly white, there is no doubt that their presence in many areas will be readily noticed by the police. This is illustrated by the police investigation of a notorious set of crimes called the "Zebra Case." In 1974 several white residents of San Francisco were randomly gunned down in the streets. At the time there were few clues to the identity of the murderers. It was known, however, that in several cases the assassins were blacks. During the early stages of the case, officers attempted to interrogate all blacks found on the streets of the city. Although it is evident that police administrators did not feel this dragnet was very efficient, they did feel that it was tactically possible to attempt such a sweep of the town. The Zebra program was possible only because noticeable physical characteristics distinguish most blacks from whites. While the stopping of blacks by the police was conceived to be a reasonable investigative technique, it is doubtful that such a widespread dragnet would have been attempted if a description of a suspect established that he was Caucasian. Even though the police have defended the tactic, contending that similar dragnets have been instigated in search of white suspects, the probability of a white person being stopped in such searches is not as great as it is for a black. Because there are more whites in the population, even extensive dragnets will not affect the white population as much as the black. For example, in San Francisco, many blacks complained that they were stopped three or four times by officers. Occasionally, it was even reported that the same white police officer would stop the same black person more than one time.

Furthermore, the differential effect of a dragnet can be accounted for by the significant difference between racial minorities' and whites' ability to escape noticeability. In an interview with a chicano (Lohman et al., 1966:86), it was mentioned that "just because your face is brown and you are wearing tennis shoes, you are subject to arrest whenever a 'Mexican' commits a crime."

A person's ability to escape from a crime scene is directly related to his ability to disappear into the population. If a white male, for example, has committed a crime in a white neighborhood and all that is known about him is that he is Caucasian, the chance of his making contact with the police on the street is less than if he were black. Even if a description is not available, a black is not able to appear as a member of a white neighborhood. In other words, in a white neighborhood, a black may be apprehended simply because he is black, while a white person (if there are others on the street) will be stopped only if *other* features of his appearance can be used to differentiate him from others. If a suspect is described as a white male with long hair and a beard, these features can be used by the police as identification devices. It is possible, however, that a bearded suspect can eliminate this feature, thus depriving the police of a useful clue in their attempts to apprehend him. On the other hand, there is no doubt that a white person seen in a black community will also arouse suspicion. Indeed, if a crime has been committed and the police know that a white person is a suspect, any white who happens to be in the area is likely to be stopped and questioned. Like the black in a white neighborhood, the white in a black community also has a limited ability to blend into the environment. For example, in mid-March of 1974, members of the Symbionese Liberation Army were discovered in Los Angeles. After the shoot-out between the S.L.A. and the police in May of that year, newspaper reporters asked the residents of the black neighborhood in which the event took place if they had noticed any strangers in the area. The most common reply was typified by a black woman's response: "Sure I noticed them, they were the only whites around, I knew they were strangers."

Although both blacks and whites may "blend in" in the right neighborhood, the black citizen is more likely than the white to find himself in areas where he does not "blend in," a result of the fact that there are a greater number of "solidly" white neighborhoods than there are areas completely populated by blacks. Additionally, blacks need to use white areas of a city more often than whites need to use black communities. There has been considerable concern expressed by black leaders that social services are not conveniently located in ghetto areas. This means that to carry out the everyday tasks common to all persons blacks have to enter white areas, although the reverse is not true. For example, in the predominantly black community of Watts in Los Angeles, there are few supermarkets. After the riots of the 1960s the large supermarkets destroyed in the area were not rebuilt. Thus, if Watts residents wish to pay the lower prices for food that are available in larger markets, they must travel to other sectors of the city and these incursions increase the possibility of their being stopped by patrol officers. Wolfgang and Cohen (1970:74) have shown some of the consequences of this state of affairs. They describe an ongoing study by Sellin and Wolfgang which, in tracing 10,000 males over eleven years, has shown that "more than half the Negroes, compared to only a third of the whites, had at one time or another been taken into police custody." A study by Werthman and Piliavin (1967:56) also indicates that blacks are more often viewed as "out of place" than are whites. They illustrate this condition through the remarks of a black juvenile who reported to them: "If the boys from Hunters Point or Fillmore [Negro neighborhoods in San Francisco] go in all white districts, the police will stop you and ask where you are from. If you say Fillmore or Hunters Point, they'll take you down to the station and run checks on you. Any burglaries, any purse snatchings, anything" (1967:79).

In addition to their limited ability to escape notice by police officers, minority-group members are stopped more often than whites because policemen feel that their interrogations of them are more likely to result in arrest. Because they are rewarded for writing citations and making arrests, officers believe that they must be practical in the allocation of their efforts, and the records available to the police, showing that blacks commit a large number of crimes, validate such efforts. Therefore, when deciding whom to stop, police officers will probably select a black or other minority-group citizen before they pick a white. And the more stops they make, the greater the possibility that they will discover violations. Because these violations are recorded and make up a significant part of the crime rate, members of minority groups will be viewed as persons who should be stopped and interrogated. Consequently, officers find such field interrogations profitable.

As one might imagine, when a large number of crimes are attributed to any population group, there is a greater probability that members of that group will be stopped more often than others. For the police these field tactics are justified by crime statistics. But the justification for this practice is weakened if one recognizes that the crime statistics do not reflect the actual amount of crime in a society and that these statistics contribute to policing techniques that promote public hostility toward law enforcement.

REACTIVE PATROL

Emphasizing that most police work is "reactive," Reiss (1971) has called attention to the important role the police dispatcher plays in the criminal justice system. Most police mobilizations develop in three stages. First, a citizen calls the police department, and the dispatcher decides whether the situation requires police help. Second, the dispatcher reacts by allocating law enforcement resources to handle the citizen's call, categorizing the call into the police radio code and assigning the matter to the nearest free patrol car. The actual arrival of police officers on the scene constitutes the third stage of this process. At this point it is their task to gather information and make a determination about what course of action they think should be taken.

Reiss did not investigate the nature of the dispatcher's influence on police officers' legal decisions, but important and critical decision-making is a routine part of dispatch work. The dispatcher must code calls into penal code categories, decide whether patrol cars should be sent to a scene, decide which cars should be sent, and decide how many and when additional cars, if any, should be sent as "back-ups" to others.

Most importantly, the dispatcher gives patrolmen assessments of character which act as interpretive schemes for evaluating citizens' complaints. Despite the small amount of information dispatchers receive from citizens who request police aid, they make character assessments, however tentative, and pass their evaluations on to officers in the field.[5] Yet, with the exception of Rubinstein's (1973) recent work, the role of dispatchers in the labeling of citizens' behavior has been virtually ignored.

Rubenstein emphasizes that "what the dispatcher tells a man when he gives him an assignment is all the patrolman knows about what he will find until he actually arrives. The dispatcher must tell him everything relevant to the job in the most economical way, to avoid wasting air time . . . . The patrolman must have faith in the skill and experience of the dispatcher because what this unseen person relates

---

[5] Here "character" refers to type of person. In this sense the categories of character are very general. For example, the dispatcher tries to differentiate between "good" and "bad" people. We use the term character to emphasize that policemen (as well as others in society) search for clues to what a person is "really like." They treat roles as inadequate indicators of character. To police officers and officials, character is not necessarily associated with particular roles.

to him establishes his initial expectations and the manner of his response to the assignment" (1973:88).

During their research, Daudistel and Sanders (1976), Sanders and Daudistel (1974), and Daudistel (1976) learned that when calls are received by dispatchers, a request that the caller identify himself or herself is routine. The reporting party's ("R.P.") name is used as a way of identifying the report and locating the source of information. If it is determined that a patrolman should investigate a crime or render public service, he is told where he is needed and whom to contact. The patrolman who is dispatched also records the R.P.'s name, address, and other information he deems relevant to the case. The information about the reporting party is said to be necessary because the victim of a crime or the person who needs help is not always the reporting party.

Unless the R.P. is a victim or a suspect, information other than name and address is not *officially* requested by most police departments. Nevertheless, information about all reporting persons is sought by personnel in a dispatcher's office and officers in the field. This does not mean, of course, that dispatch personnel (or "desk sergeants") directly ask callers to outline their own character. Rather, officers attempt to infer character from the speech of the caller, for example, accent, voice inflection, and the like. Further, after learning the names and addresses of those involved in a case, they consult others to determine if anyone knows anything about the involved parties. Even the

Uniformed police patrols are generally "reactive" in that they receive requests from citizens for action rather than proactively "drumming up" their own business. (© 1976 by Fred W. McDarrah)

area in which the caller resides significantly influences patrolmen's interpretations of calls and evaluations of crimes assigned to them.

The following radio communication recorded during research in a California police agency illustrates how a dispatcher's assessment of character is communicated to officers in the field:

Dispatcher: 21–52 Mountainbeach.
Patrol Car: 21–52.
Dispatcher: 21–52, contact Mrs. Davis, who sounds 5150, in regards to suspicious circumstances at 5794 Thomason Street.
Patrol Car: 21–52, 10–4.

The number "5150" is taken from the California Welfare and Institutions Code and refers to the section dealing with those who are mentally disturbed. Prior to arriving at Mrs. Davis' home, officers knew nothing specific about the "suspicious circumstances," but they were provided with a biographical context in which to view the scene and interpret everything said by the reporting party. During an interview the case was discussed by an officer:

Researcher: What happened on the call the other night on Thomason Street about the suspicious circumstances?
Officer: Aha, oh nothing, the lady who lives there is really old, she just wants some attention.
Researcher: What did she call about?
Officer: Oh, I'm not sure, something about a prowler.
Researcher: Did they check it out?
Officer: I'm sure they took a quick look.
Researcher: How did they write it up?
Officer: Field report, I think it would be a field report of an F&U [false and unfounded] prowler.

The official report filed by the responding officers listed Mrs. Davis' claim as false and unfounded, which means that no criminal event took place. This disposition would not be particularly interesting if all the reports involving prowlers were recorded as "F&U" when no one is seen or apprehended by officers, and when no physical evidence of prowling is seen either. However, Daudistel's (1976) examination of patrol reports written over a three-month period showed that many citizens reported to the police that they had been victimized by a prowler. During the research it was impossible to make an exact count, but very few cases in which no prowler was apprehended were recorded as false and unfounded. On the contrary, most were filed by patrol officers as incidents of 647 P.C. or 647 (H) P.C.. These California Penal Code sections say:

Every person who commits any of the following acts is guilty of disorderly conduct, a misdemeanor:

Who loiters, prowls or wanders upon the private property of another, in the nighttime, without visible or lawful business with the owner or occupant thereof.

(H) Who, while loitering, prowling or wandering upon the private property of another, in the nighttime, peeks in the door or window of any inhabited building . . . .

Although our data are not conclusive, we can suggest there is a strong possibility that the F&U judgment in the Davis case was made because of the victim's character. After the dispatcher alerted them with the number 5150, the investigating officers expected to encounter a woman who was not competent and therefore could not reliably report what happened. There was no way to know if a prowler actually had been in her yard. The officers who responded to the call may have been absolutely correct in their characterization of it as a false report, but having been provided by the dispatcher with the characterization of Mrs. Davis as a 5150, they were indirectly told to see no crime. Further, this label provided a context in which the victim's talk to police officers was to be interpreted. Given this background, the officers merely documented the delusional character of the victim rather than seeing or hearing evidence of crime. Importantly, without some evaluation of the victim's character, the absence of physical traces or clues pointing to the past actions of a prowler may not have been used to document the mentally unstable character of the victim.[6]

Naturally not everyone who calls a police department is negatively evaluated by radio dispatchers. The majority of callers do not give dispatchers any reason to believe they are not "ordinary" citizens. Other than character evaluations officers may construct after they have been given a person's address by a dispatcher (for example, he is probably a drug user if he lives in a certain area or he is probably an average citizen if he lives in another section of town), dispatchers usually do not tell patrolmen what they think of callers. But, in a sense, when a dispatcher does not give officers in the field a biographical characterization, they assume (at least temporarily) that the reporting party and victim are, like most other citizens, typical persons requesting police help.

Occasionally police dispatchers explicitly characterize a report-

---

[6] Wilson points out that patrolmen evaluate the legitimacy of citizens' complaints differently. "Middle-class victims who have suffered a street attack (a mugging, for example) are generally considered most legitimate; middle-class victims of burglary are seen as somewhat less legitimate (it *could* be an effort to make a fraudulent insurance claim); lower-class victims of theft are still less legitimate (they may have stolen the item in the first place); lower-class victims of assaults are the least legitimate (they probably brought in on themselves)" (1968:27).

ing party and victim in a positive way (Daudistel, 1976).[7] Unfortunately, it is difficult to evaluate the impact such characterizations may have on the officers' evaluation of events.

The following transcribed broadcast by a police dispatcher suggests the impact a positive characterization may have on officers' categorization of events:

Dispatcher: Control one-A-6 Mountainbeach.
Patrol Car: A-6.
Dispatcher: A-6 contact off-duty officer Smith in front of Thrifty Mart [shopping center] parking lot in regards to two blacks selling pumpkin pies.

After the initial call was assigned to unit A-6, two other patrol cars radioed that they would "swing by" the location to help out. Earlier in the week in which this call was recorded there were calls from ordinary citizens complaining about the same individuals. The initial complaints were rapidly handled by a single patrol officer who did not arrest any of the blacks after learning that they were members of an out-of-town religious group selling their pies to shoppers as a means of raising money for their religious activities. However, when the event was said to have been reported by an off-duty policeman, four officers in three separate cars went to the shopping center, investigated the incident, and determined that a crime had been committed. Because the suspects did not have a license to sell the pies, each was given a misdemeanor citation.

The routine assessment of character must be emphasized. Anyone with access to the settings in which legal decisions are made will be struck by the prominence of this activity. Not all the character evaluations are made by an assessment of "here and now" pieces of information. That is, the quality given to someone's character may be created by more than an examination of their presentation of self. Even if one appears to be quite normal, of sound mind, and reputable character, a negative evaluation may be made by law officers. For example, records of prior contacts between the police and citizens are often consulted by officers and used in character assessments. So, even if one's immediate behavior is interpreted as not necessarily indicative of a faulty character, past behavior that is recorded may be used to construct negative evaluations.

In several cases, studied by Daudistel (1976) the character of a victim changed a crime into no crime. One case involved a man who hailed a Highway Patrol car and told the driver that his car had just been stolen. Accepting the man's story as factual, the officer called his

---

[7] Because so few positive characterizations were provided by dispatchers, it was difficult to judge their significance as compared to routine instructions that implicitly depict reporting parties as ordinary citizens.

office, described the stolen automobile, and gave the victim's name so that the license number of the car could be confirmed by vehicle registration records. The Highway Patrol dispatcher assembled the information given to him by the patrolman and rebroadcast it to all other patrol cars in the area. This procedure assures that all Highway Patrol officers will be aware that a particular vehicle has been stolen. Further, other police agencies monitor the Highway Patrol's radio frequency, and when they hear the description of a recently stolen auto they relay it to their own officers in the field so all agencies can be on the lookout for the stolen car. All officers who have any relevant information about the theft are expected to contact their dispatcher so that others (particularly the officer who "took the report") can be given the new information.

In this case a dispatcher in a sheriff's substation heard the call, telephoned the Highway Patrol dispatcher, and gave him information about the victim of the auto theft. The Highway Patrol dispatcher then relayed the following to the officer who had originally assessed the case as a factual one.

Dispatcher: 341 Sierra Blanca.
Patrolman: 341.
Dispatcher: 341 Mountainbeach Sheriff just called and said he [referring to victim] has been arrested numerous times 23102 CVC. Also a little bit 5150. He probably misplaced the vehicle.

The designation "23102 CVC" refers to the California law concerning driving under the influence of alcoholic beverages and, again, "5150" refers to the California Welfare and Institutions Code regarding those who are not mentally competent. The communication of this discreditable information introduced the possibility to the investigating officer that his original assessment of the situation and categorization of the incident as a criminal one was incorrect. In fact, the attribution of poor character was so influential that he did not complete a stolen auto report.

Evaluations have a formal character when official police records indicate someone has been previously arrested. An informal character evaluation is made when the communications between two patrol cars involves sharing information constructed by an officer who has had past experiences with someone at a residence, business, or neighborhood. Sometimes these unofficial evaluations are shared by many officers and consist of "well-known information" in a department. Many individuals are known to be "troublemakers" to officers even though the information the officers share about them is stereotyped and not included in any law enforcement files.[8] This information about some-

---

[8] This point is illustrated by an officer's remark made during research conducted by Daudistel and Sanders (1976). After arresting an adult male; the

one increases the likelihood that he will be negatively characterized and also increases the chance that he will be arrested, cited by those officers who come into contact with him. For example, according to Chambliss (1973), a gang of young men in a community he studied were perceived by citizens and the police as problem youngsters. Consequently, they were often arrested for conduct that was overlooked when committed by other young men in the same community who were not portrayed as delinquents. Chambliss states:

> [The police knew,] with all the confidence necessary to be a
> policeman, that these boys were engaged in criminal activities.
> They knew this partly from occasionally catching them, mostly
> from circumstantial evidence ("the boys were around when
> those tires were slashed"), and partly because the police shared
> the view of the community in general that this was a bad bunch
> of boys. The best the police could hope to do was to be sensitive
> to the fact that these boys were engaged in illegal acts and
> arrest them whenever there was some evidence that they had
> been involved (1973:28).

Sharing of informal evaluations is facilitated by the fact that communication systems allow patrol officers to monitor some of the calls to other patrol officers. In their radio communications officers may specify character by commenting on the setting in which persons are located. This information is considered relevant to the evaluation of persons encountered in a particular location until behavior compels reinterpretation of their character. For example, if a patrol car is dispatched to a popular bar, the dispatcher may say, "Disturbing the peace: loud music" and give the address of the bar. But immediately after a patrol car receives the call, other officers may tell the responding patrolman about the types of persons who can be found at that location. With the knowledge that a particular bar is frequented by certain types of persons, the officer is able to typify the people he will encounter when he arrives at the scene of the disturbance.

This information is immediately functional in two ways: (1) it warns against potential danger and (2) it negatively characterizes the persons in the bar. We can be certain that it does the latter because policemen treat all persons as potential threats. However, dispatchers do not amend their calls with statements like, "Be advised that's been a hangout for the workers from the electronics factory" or "the teachers at the high school." When no one makes an explicit characterization of those about to be encountered in a setting, the officer assumes that he will contact "ordinary citizens" who could be dangerous but will not be so if things are normal. In the case of an explicit negative

---

officer said, "Jesus, everyone knows this kid is a real fuck-up. Anybody here would be happy to rip him off if they could."

INITIAL ENCOUNTERS WITH CRIMINAL JUSTICE

characterization that is grounded in some shared typifications (including a real or imagined image of violence), officers expect to encounter dangerous people who are always a threat, even if things are normal.

Information about persons and locations can be institutionalized if it is circulated long enough. Just as a citizen's reputation may be known by many officers even though most have never interacted with him, various locations come to be viewed by many if not all officers as places where those of disreputable character congregate. The character of citizens at such locations is assumed to be bad, therefore, those who are encountered by officers at such places must prove their integrity. In other words, they have to account for their presence on the scene by representing themselves as outsiders or as somehow different from those who regularly frequent such establishments or areas. Bittner (1967:678) makes a similar point when he states:

> What patrolmen view as normal on Skid Row—and what they also think is taken for granted as "life as usual" by the inhabitants—is not easily summarized. It seems to focus on the idea that the dominant consideration governing all enterprise

A Detroit police officer holds the gun of the man he has just shot and killed while his partner searches two other suspects. Character assessments in such situations are far more consequential than the typical occasions in which the police must make action decisions. (*John Colleir from Black Star*)

and association is directed to the occasion of the moment. Nothing is thought of as having a background that might have led up to the present in terms of some compelling moral or practical necessity. There are some exceptions to this rule, of course; the police themselves, and those who run certain establishments, are perceived as engaged in important and necessary activities.

Such assessment of character by area location plays a part in producing the differential arrest rates that are common in all communities. On the one hand, those encountered in environments that have not been negatively evaluated will be judged by their presentation of self. On the other, those who are encountered in places that are negatively characterized are judged and handled as if their location is prima facie evidence of their criminality (cf. Sacks, 1972). From one police officer's perspective, such persons "start with one point against them."

Certain parks, streets, and even large areas of a community may be designated by officers as places that are full of crime and, therefore, of bad people. They expect to be treated negatively and disrespectfully by persons there. For example, in a report completed for the President's Commission on Law Enforcement and Administration of Justice (Lohman, 1966:125), a police officer stated that his colleagues expected problems in certain areas of the community:

> Statistically it is lower-class people who have the higher crime rate and different types of crimes. But you take a middle-class section of the city where the middle-class people live, you generally have less police problems there than you do in the lower class. To work in a residential area of middle-class people, the majority of your job would be friendly, nice, courteous things that you could do for people. When you work in a lower-class section of the city, of any city for that matter, or predominantly in a racial-group area of the city where the crime rate is higher and less devotion to city government is by the individual down there, your job is 180 degrees away from the other. . . .

Our observations of police-citizen interactions in places that were characterized negatively by police officers suggest that an individual's status as a disreputable character is not absolutely guaranteed by residence in a neighborhood. Daudistel's (1976) observations of police officers found they sometimes made statements indicating positive evaluations of persons despite negative feelings about the community. For instance, a detective commented: "See, the citizen wasn't such a bad guy, not like the rest of the assholes out here."

It is true, of course, that, from time to time, officers reevaluate the evidence of character supplied by assessment of physical location. Negative characterizations, especially, are reviewed and revised in particular cases. Both evaluations of locations and the people encountered in them mutually elaborate one another in ways such that a reevaluation of one forces a change in the other.

REACTIVE DETECTIVE WORK

Even if everyone, including citizens and patrolmen, agrees that a citizen's complaint is about a crime, complete police investigation of the matter is not guaranteed. Assessing a citizen's crime report is a complicated process, and, basically, a judgment about the crime's "seriousness" is the crucial step that determines whether a thorough police investigation will be pursued (Sanders and Daudistel, 1974). Understanding the assessment process will contribute to an understanding of how police services are allocated, and in this section we shall describe how determinations of seriousness are made.

In many instances, law enforcement officers regard citizens' complaints as criminal in nature but evaluate their reports as of "little significance" and not worth investigating. Often, in their initial investigations the police may support a citizen's claim that a crime was committed (Sanders and Daudistel, 1974) but in later investigative work come to feel that time should not be wasted on such a petty matter. To the investigating officer such disposition of a case is a reasonable way of coping with the organizational demands placed upon him. If, for example, a patrol officer is dispatched to two or three calls at a time, it is not unusual for him to make an assessment of the seriousness of these calls in order to determine how much time should be spent investigating each one. Similarly, if a detective is given a large number of reports that document the occurrence of many crimes, it is not surprising to find that he also evaluates the "workability" of each case in an effort to determine how much time should be allocated to each one. For example, the *Policy Manual of the Los Angeles Police Department,* 1972 (Sec. 540.20), explicitly deals with the allocation of resources to follow-up investigations: "As it is not feasible to expend equal time and energy in the investigation of all reported crimes, priority of investigation and allocation of resources must be based upon the relative seriousness of each reported crime."

A study by Sanders and Daudistel (1974) investigated how detectives decide whether or not to "work" a case and outlined the methods they use to evaluate the merits of a citizen's complaint. This study examined cases in which the patrolman agreed with citizens in identifying events as criminal matters. In terms of investigative work, it was found that this mutual agreement about the situation was not that important. The investigation of a case was not ensured if patrolmen agreed with citizens and characterized their complaints as criminal. In most jurisdictions, particularly large metropolitan areas, investigative work is conducted by detectives. Consequently, their formulation of the event as criminal or noncriminal (real or "phony") is most crucial. Thus, the agreement of patrolman with citizen as to criminality does not guarantee that the case will be thoroughly investigated by detectives. For instance, when a citizen reports that his home has been burglarized, patrol officers usually conduct a preliminary investigation of the incident. Their report provides information that will aid others in a complete investigation of the crime. Among other things, therefore, the initial patrol report consists of the name and address of the victim, items that were taken, the possible time the crime occurred, and a specification of the physical evidence indicating that an illegal entry was made. Although this information is very important, neither apprehension of the perpetrator nor location of the stolen property are likely without further investigative work. Most calls for help in criminal matters are not ultimately resolved by patrol officers; in fact, most police departments instruct their uniformed officers that their job is to respond to citizens' calls for help, not to investigate crimes fully. Therefore, if a patrol report is not followed up by detectives, resolution of a case is unlikely.

In order for a detective to feel that investigative time should be allocated to a citizen's complaint, it is essential that he formulate the reported event as a "real" crime. Once this evaluation is made, he must also decide whether the particular crime is "significant" enough to be worked, a judgment usually based upon the official record provided in the patrol report. Occasionally, however, in addition to the official patrol report, the detective will be given information by others which he can use to determine the factuality of a complaint. For instance Daudistel and Sanders (1976) describe a report on a series of incidents classified by patrol officers as "burglary" and "assault with a deadly weapon" that was forwarded as a matter of routine to the detective investigators they studied. The report was given a case number that routed it to a file containing numerous reports of similar incidents that took place in one family over a brief period of time. Detectives assigned to handle this file said that the new report was only one of a series of family complaints asserting that a "madman was harassing them." One report indicated that while the daughter-in-law (who lived at her in-laws' address) was cleaning up the bathroom, a man suddenly came from behind and grasped her, placed his hand over her mouth, slipped a rope over her head, then around her neck, and began to choke her. She was reportedly found by her mother-in-law lying in the bathroom with "blue skin color and purple lips" (Daudistel and Sanders, 1976: 102).

All of this suggested that the report was a genuine account of a crime, but the officer who wrote it attached an "unofficial" narrative account that provided a context for assessing the crime as a "phony." He said that many other reports of harassment made by this family had led to numerous police "stake-outs" of the house, but no one had ever been seen around the home. Then the officer analyzed the particulars of the incident, establishing what he took to be "evidence" that a crime could *not* have taken place as reported:

1. Rope could not have been placed around the victim's neck while the suspect kept his hand over her mouth.
2. Location of the mirror in the bathroom would have allowed the victim to see the suspect.
3. (Even though there was some irritation on the neck), no irritation could have been seen on rear of victim's head or neck, because her hair would have been in the way.
4. Report that victim had purple lips and blue skin was inconsistent with slight irritation on neck.

The officer could have left these particular features unstated (since they were not in the official crime report) as minor details that were interesting but irrelevant because alone they did not deny the possibility that an actual crime had occurred. Certainly other reports of violent crimes were received by detectives and treated as valid even though certain details seemed "odd" or "unlikely." But in this case a determination was made that this family habitually reported crimes that "just don't happen this way." By unofficially providing detectives with his assessment to aid them in their formulation of the case as "workable" or not, the patrol officer was providing another context in which his report could be interpreted.

In many cases, although detectives may see reported events as criminal matters, they may not agree with a patrolman's specification of the law that was violated. Take, for example, a case in which detectives received a patrol report of an attempted murder (Daudistel and Sanders, 1976:105). The report stated that a man threatened to kill his wife and had performed acts against her that might have been lethal. When a detective sergeant read the report, he characterized it as a "glorified domestic." A "domestic" is a family argument that is categorized as a crime under the Penal Code section pertaining to "Disturbing the Peace." Typically, disturbing the peace is not considered a "significant crime," and unless the involved citizens demand that it be investigated, such a complaint would not be worked by detectives. Similarly, detectives viewed this case as a crime, but not, as the patrol officer had specified, as attempted murder. Because it was reformulated, the event, even though it was viewed as a crime, was thought to be too minor to warrant thorough study.

In the same study, it was found that the significance of a crime was judged in connection with several contingencies including (1) actual or potential physical or "social" harm; (2) victims' loss (property); and (3) the availability of investigative "leads." The decisions made by burglary detectives illustrate this process of evaluation. These detectives receive a large number of cases and must, out of necessity, decide which ones to investigate. Since time would not permit a complete investigation of each case, the decision to work a case is based primarily on the amount of loss to the victim, leads, and harm.

However, one cannot establish easily a formula based upon the three elements by which to predict which crimes will be investigated. Decisions are based on a variety of features that change from one context to another. Crimes that involve small economic loss are frequently investigated, generally in cases where the patrol report provides a number of "substantial leads." In cases involving no leads but substantial loss, on the other hand, the fact that there is little information to work with may not stop officers from investigating the cases. In these instances, detective work usually concentrates on the items that were stolen. Officers in charge of such work will attempt to determine the exact extent of loss and to obtain an accurate description of the property in the hope that if the stolen items are recovered, they can be returned to the owner and used to locate the culprit.

Making decisions about which cases to investigate involves gathering information about alleged crimes. Sanders (1977) studied detectives' formulation and use of information in detail. Included in his work is an analysis of police officers' techniques for gathering and using evidence which documents the contextual (ad hoc) quality of evidence. Here we would like to stress the role character evaluations play in the detectives' interpretation of information. Like patrolmen, detectives evaluate character on the basis of information they gather during interviews with citizens, what other officers tell them they think of a particular suspect or victim, or appraisal of official records.

The importance of character evaluation is illustrated by the following case. A burglary detective received a patrol report indicating that a woman's home had been burglarized and that a very valuable ring had been stolen. The detective drove to the woman's home to interview her about the burglary. The fact that the detective interviewed the victim indicates that he initially believed that a crime had been committed. However, during the interview the woman did not show too much concern for her ring. Although she "wanted something done," as the detective talked to her she constantly changed the subject and discussed her impending move to another house. She said that she was moving because she had recently divorced her husband and no longer needed to live in a large house. After the interview the detective said that he was puzzled about the victim, and described her as "kinda crazy." Even though she showed him a broken window and claimed that the burglar entered through it, he did not think a crime had been committed. Furthermore, he said that because the woman was "sorta flaky" she probably misplaced her ring and used the broken window as a way of convincing others that a break-in occurred. Finally, after saying that he did not blame her husband for leaving her, the detective decided that the case was not workable because it was a "phony report," one that did not document a real crime.

A few days after the detective decided that the burglary of the woman's house had not occurred, she telephoned him to report that a person who had been looking at her house with a view to buying it probably saw the ring and came back to steal it when she was not at home. The officer decided to see if the suspect had been previously arrested for any crimes. After receiving the suspect's "rap sheet," he changed his mind about the case since the suspect has been arrested many times and was characterized as a criminal. He decided that the physical evidence (the broken window) may have actually been the point of entry for the burglar, because the suspect previously had been arrested for burglary. Biographical evidence about the suspect forced the detective to reevaluate the physical evidence as well as the victim's character, that is, perhaps she wasn't crazy after all. He commented to another officer:

> **Detective** (investigating officer): I thought this case was kinda hinky until I saw his rap sheet.
>
> **Detective** (member of burglary detail): Changed your attitude, did you?
>
> **Detective** (investigating officer): Yea, I might want to work it now.

This case illustrates the fact that a retrospective evaluation of physical evidence is not always based upon new physical evidence. A revision can also come from new biographical evidence. Oddly, this means the existence of physical evidence is tied to characterizations of suspects and victims. This is strange because the concrete objects that constitute physical evidence have no "objectively verifiable" connection to member's ideas about others in the society.

An object is seen as evidence, and perhaps seen at all, only when it is presented as such by an officer. An object is not evidence unless it is grounded in a socially constructed background which may or may not consist of other pieces of physical evidence. This background may be an interpretation of a biography that can be made independently of the particular criminal event in question, yet be intimately tied to it. Consequently, what is evidence of a crime may depend on the biography of the victim, and what constitutes relevant features of a biography may depend on the physical evidence observed in a crime scene. What is seen can be one thing at one time and something else at another time.

In addition to the informal evaluations that are communicated among patrol officers and detectives, official documents and records serve as information detectives use as a basis of characterizations. This phenomenon had already been illustrated. Here it will be emphasized that the use of such official information is routine among detectives whose work frequently requires them to compile lengthy reports about crime investigations.

While telling about a murder investigation, a detective noted some of the consequences an official police record may have for a victim.

> A check of their [Kentucky State Police] police records showed that Henderson had served time in prison for bank robbery in 1955. He had also been recently released from a Kentucky jail where he was in custody for the armed robbery of a supermarket. On that occasion, his arrest had been preceded by a running gun battle with the police. Learning the identity of the victim [Henderson] and his background caused officers to dig deeper into his more recent activities.

Once Henderson's biography had been constructed, officers determined that his murder was not a typical criminal homicide. In fact, he became much more than a victim; now he was a "suspect" in organized crime. Consequently, the investigation into his death was more of an investigation into his criminal activities than into his murder.

Commenting on the use of official juvenile records by the police, Lemert (1969:364) points out, interestingly, that the "police tend to pay more attention to prior offense records of juveniles and their demeanor than do probation officers." Although he emphasizes the importance of a juvenile's demeanor, Lemert also comments that the police make a distinction between the "normal" delinquent and "hard-core types" (1969:365). Arrest records are the primary source of information upon which this judgment is made. The hard-core types are more likely to be processed in juvenile court than are normal delinquents, who are likely to be handled informally.

The influence of official records on police investigations was also indicated by a detective who was "working a case of possible embezzlement." The act of embezzlement, like most illegal acts, cannot be considered a crime if the element of criminal intent is not present. The specific intention to feloniously appropriate funds or property in one's control, but not in one's ownership, must be established if one is to be considered guilty of this crime. In the case at hand, the officer reported that he had been investigating an incident involving an employee of a large foreign-car parts store. According to the detective, the employee had taken many car parts without paying for them. He did not sell the parts but, instead, used them for his own automobile, which he was restoring to running condition. After interviewing the suspect (who had been arrested at the request of the employer), the detective reported that he did not believe the suspect had committed a crime. Because the suspect kept a record of the parts he took from the store and filled out company receipts for them, the detective believed he intended to pay for them. He said he thought that the suspect was "only relying on the credit which he assumed he had with his employer." The "criminal intent" element was missing, so no crime had been committed.

But the employer had not explicitly extended credit to his employee and alleged that he had taken various products without permission. Because of the employer's claims, the detective felt that it was possible that the suspect had "technically committed the crime, but it [was] still a weak case." Further, the detective's skepticism about the suspect's guilt was increased by the suspect's contention that he had never been arrested or convicted of a crime. The detective said the suspect was very cooperative during the initial investigation, characterizing him as "a very nice guy."

The detective's initial feeling that the case was not "really a criminal matter" was changed by his discovery that the suspect did, in fact, have a criminal record indicating that he had a past conviction of theft. On the basis of this knowledge, the detective decided to "reopen the case," to put together a complete report on the incident (including a copy of the suspect's "rap-sheet") and forward it to an assistant district attorney for review. Although the officer still felt the case was not a very strong one, his knowledge that the suspect had previously been arrested persuaded him to pursue the case and let the district attorney decide if it should be prosecuted.

PROACTIVE DETECTIVE WORK

Proactive detective work typically involves the enforcement of laws usually associated with "private offenses" (Stinchcombe, 1963) or "crimes without victims" (Schur, 1965). Because crimes of this kind are not likely to be reported to the police, the police themselves must search for and uncover crimes hidden from their view. Persons who consent to use the services of a prostitute, drug dealer, loan shark, or gambler are not likely to complain to police about their criminal activity. When a person is victimized by a prostitute who takes all of his money, or a drug dealer sells a user inferior narcotics, such persons are usually reluctant to seek police assistance because reporting such events to the police indicates their own complicity. Skolnick says:

The vice squad is not concerned with those criminal activities where the malefactor is an assailant. Indeed, the crimes which it seeks to control or redress typically have no "victim" or, more precisely and neutrally, no citizen complainant. Thus, when a policeman investigates a strong-arm robbery, a rape, or a forgery, he ordinarily does so at the request of an aggrieved citizen. By contrast, when a vice control officer arrests a bookmaker, a prostitute, or a seller of narcotics, the gambler, the "trick," or the user are typically not interested in having an arrest made. Since the vice control squad deals with crimes for which there are usually no complaining witnesses, vice control men must, as it were, drum up their own business (1966:115–16).

There are several studies that describe various aspects of the detective's role (for example, Banton, 1964; Westly, 1970; Cain, 1973; Pepinsky, 1975; Skolnick, 1966) but few have thoroughly investigated the routine operations of "proactive detectives." There are many reasons why these detectives have been ignored by sociologists even though they have exemplified popular conceptions of police work. The fact that little police work is actually proactive and proactive detective bureaus are usually very secretive about their work are the two most important reasons.

Even though proactive detective work is an extraordinary type of law enforcement activity, certainly it is of consequence for many citizens, as Skolnick's (1966) work on narcotics and vice detectives clearly documents. For example, whether one is prosecuted for crimes related to drug use may depend on whether or not he or she can supply detectives with information about more "serious" criminal activity. In other words, criminal culpability may be tied to one's ability to help police officers apprehend others who are better "pinches" (Skolnick, 1966). Furthermore, if an arrestee is involved with criminal organizations and the police want to "bust" the organization, they may release the defendant in return for information about the criminal group or undercover access to the organization. According to Skolnick (1966:129), "In general, burglary detectives permit informants to commit narcotics offenses, while narcotics detectives allow informants to steal."

The informer system is a commonly disputed type of citizen-police bargain (Goldstein, 1960). But the growth of the practice of granting immunity from prosecution in return for information has probably resulted from community pressure to control crime, police officials' desire to maintain a good image of their departments, and the perceived difficulty of solving victimless crimes in accordance with the law. Because the police cannot control such crimes as narcotics and vice by depending on citizens' complaints and information, it is only by locating criminals themselves that the police can make a significant number of arrests and crime clearances. Also, because vice and narcotics crimes usually involve well-organized operations, arrest of those who are instrumental members in these organizations necessitates that the police gain access to settings that are normally guarded and private. For example, a narcotics officer writing on the importance of drug investigations summarizes his feelings about the necessity to deal with informants: "Clearly, relationships with informants occasionally border on moral and legal issues; however, considering the character of narcotics investigations, without them enforcement would be severely hampered" (Bishop 1972:57).

In many instances, the use of someone who has gained access to

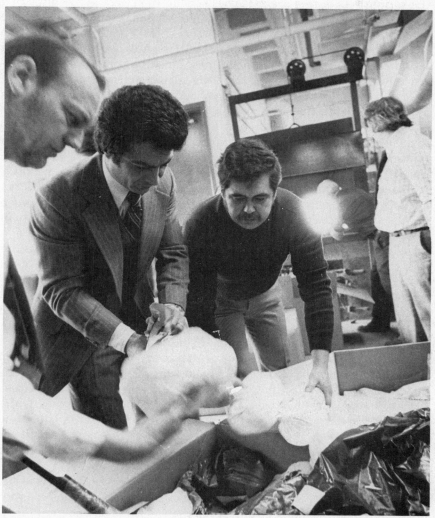

"Proactive" detective work. Here detectives incinerate more than $500,000 worth of confiscated drugs. (*Paul Kein from Black Star*)

these settings is the only possible way of obtaining arrests for these crimes. Although undercover police officers are frequently used, many criminal organizations will accept as members only persons who are well known to other criminals. Consequently, the police must use an inside man as a source of information. Since the inside man is usually an arrestee, it is not likely that he will be a "good citizen" who altruistically offers to help in an investigation. Rather, in return for information about the criminal activity of others, he is given the valuable opportunity to avoid punishment and, as previously indicated, the chance to continue his illegal behavior with full police knowledge. But the seriousness of this practice goes beyond the unequal handling of a few cases. In the case of narcotics crimes, it has been shown that the granting of immunity for informants violates the law. According to Goldstein (1960:568), "The narcotics statutes, unlike comparable legislation concerning other specific crimes, make no provision for obtaining information by awarding immunity from prosecution." But "the narcotics squad has ignored this, and adopted an informer policy which appears to constitute a usurpation of the legislative function."

Proactive detective work is more likely than reactive work to involve abuse of police power. The tools used to dig for violations of the law may breach constitutional limitations on police investigations. The use of illegal wire taps and "bugs," illegal searches and seizures, bribes, and unnecessary force are much more likely to occur when information about crimes is scarce. Furthermore, proactive detective bureaus, such as vice and narcotic details, are tied typically to intelligence units in police departments.

Not only the types of investigative techniques used but the matters that are investigated by proactive detectives often violate legal restrictions and community expectations about legitimate police activity. During the late 1960s and early 1970s, more and more local police agencies were involved in gathering information about political activities initiated by antiwar groups, protesters, and reformers. In many cases this information was not related to criminal activity, but was used to squelch legitimate political dissent. Although it is clear the police have always been used to help sustain political power, with the advent of computer technology and "scientific crime control devices" their role has continued to expand in the area of political crimes (Quinney, 1974). In many cases the police in our society have actually become counterinsurgency forces directed against not only "radical" political activities but also against persons who are committed to democratic principles.

How the police define their role and task is central to this issue. Certainly, law enforcement intervention in the lives of citizens does not occur unless policemen can interpret their actions as criminal (or at least potentially criminal) and their own roles as, say, guardians of the good life. For example, many police agencies have established organized crime task forces. But because these forces have adopted a very broad definition of organized crime, many of them are almost completely concerned with political dissent. There is no doubt that some groups have actually committed serious criminal offenses. Here our point is that proactive police agents often fail to distinguish between those groups that clearly pose a threat to personal safety and freedom and those who simply question the political status quo.

SUMMARY

As we saw in this chapter, police officers receiving calls from citizens or observing situations needing investigation try to gather information in order to answer two interrelated questions: determining what kinds of events they face and what should be done about them.

The process of answering these questions requires that the officer fit together his observations with abstract categories of the law or types of situations he has experienced in the past or been told about by other officers. For example, a policeman must determine whether the physical objects he sees point to a crime. Likewise, when giving aid to citizens, he must decide whether the situation is a dangerous one like others he knows about in which policemen or citizens were hurt. To make these decisions the policeman attends to particular features of situations and individuals he has learned are important. Certainly an officer's knowledge about what is important is learned during his socialization into the police occupational culture. Policemen learn to gather information about suspects and victims that may reflect on their character, and they learn how to evaluate evidence given them by "good" citizens as well as "bad" ones.

Indeed, plenty of evidence indicates that policemen (like others) develop subcultural perspectives. But we must be careful with this conclusion, since perspectives are always changing and developing. Understanding police work, therefore, requires more than knowledge about the police subculture; it also requires understanding the decision-making process.

Understanding the nature of police decision-making permits us to evaluate two features of the criminal law. First, that the enforcement of the criminal law is *uniform* is highly questionable. Seemingly identical events can be categorized differently depending on how persons are evaluated by the police. Acts that appear to be crimes may not be categorized as such by police officers. Second, that the law is *specific* is also questionable. In reality the law is a vague set of categories that cannot specify when a particular act is a crime. Policemen must always fit specific events into these categories. We must conclude, therefore, that police discretion is unavoidable and essential just as interpretation is essential for all human conduct. No matter how specific one tries to make the law, it always has to be applied by someone who must interpret what is written. Naturally, what constitutes an appropriate interpretation of what is written is always open for debate.

REFERENCES

BANTON, MICHAEL
1964 *The Policeman in the Community.* London: Tavistock.

BASSIOUNI, CHERIF
1969 *Criminal Law and Its Process.* Springfield, Ill.: Charles C. Thomas.

BAYLEY, DAVID, AND HAROLD MENDELSOHN
1968 *Minorities and the Police: Confrontation in America.* New York: The Free Press.

BIDERMAN, A.D., ET AL.
1967 *Field Surveys 1: Report on a Pilot Study in the District of Columbia on Victimization and Attitudes toward Law Enforcement.* Washington, D.C.: Government Printing Office.

BISHOP, CHARLES
1972 "Metro Narcs: A Collective Effort," *Police Chief,* 39:10.

BITTNER, EGON
1967 "The Police on Skid-Row: A Study of Peace Keeping," *American Sociological Review* 32 (October): 699–715.

BLACK, DONALD
1971 "The Social Organization of Arrest," *Stanford Law Review* 23 (June): 1087–1111.

BLACK, DONALD, AND ALBERT REISS
1967 "Patterns of Behavior in Police and Citizen Transactions." In *President's Commission on Law Enforcement and the Administration of Justice, Studies of Crime and Law Enforcement in Major Metropolitan Areas,* Vol. II, Section I. Washington D.C.: Government Printing Office.

BRYJAK, GEORGE
1970 "Bystander Intervention as an Effect of the Physical Appearance of a Thief," unpublished paper.

CAIN, M.E.
1973 *Society and the Policeman's Role.* London: Routledge and Kegan Paul.

CAMPBELL, ANGUS, AND HOWARD SCHUMAN
1968 "Racial Attitudes in Fifteen American Cities." In *Supplemental Studies for the National Advisory Commission on Civil Disorders.* Washington D.C.: Government Printing Office.

CANTRIL, HADLEY
1950 *The "Why" of Man's Experience.* New York: Macmillan.

INITIAL ENCOUNTERS WITH CRIMINAL JUSTICE

CHAMBLISS, WILLIAM J.

1973 "The Saints and the Roughnecks," *Society* 11 (November-December): 24–31.

COLORADO COMMISSION ON SPANISH SURNAMED CITIZENS

1967 *Report to the General Assembly: The Status of Spanish Surnamed Citizens in Colorado.* Boulder: Colorado Government Printing Office.

DARLEY, JOHN, AND BIBB LATANE

1968 "Bystander Intervention in Emergencies: Diffusion of Responsibility," *Journal of Personality and Social Psychology,* 62: 377–83.

DAUDISTEL, HOWARD C.

1976 *Deciding What the Law Means: An Examination of Police-Prosecutor Discretion.* Ph.D. diss. University of California, Santa Barbara.

DAUDISTEL, HOWARD C., AND WILLIAM B. SANDERS

1976 "Application of the Law: An Examination of Rules Use by Police Officers," in William B. Sanders and Howard C. Daudistel, eds., *The Criminal Justice Process,* pp. 96–107. New York: Praeger.

ENNIS, PHILIP

1967 "Criminal Victimization in the U.S.: A Report on a National Survey." In *Report of a Research Study to the President's Commission on Law Enforcement and Administration of Justice, Field Surveys II.* Washington D.C.: Government Printing Office.

FORSLUND, MORRIS

1970 "A Comparison of Negro and White Crime Rates," *Journal of Criminal Law, Criminology, and Police Science* 61 (June): 214–17.

GEIS, GILBERT

1965 "Statistics Concerning Race and Crime," *Crime and Delinquency* 11 (April): 142:50.

GOFFMAN, ERVING

1971 *Relations in Public.* New York: Basic Books.

GOLDSTEIN, JOSEPH

1960 "Police Discretion Not to Invoke the Criminal Process: Low Visibility Decisions in the Administration of Justice," *Yale Law Journal* 69 (March): 543–94.

HOOD, ROGER, AND RICHARD SPARKS

1970 *Key Issues in Criminology.* New York: McGraw-Hill.

LATANE, BIBB, AND JOHN DARLEY

1970 "Situational Determinants of Bystander Intervention in Emergencies," in J. Macauley, ed., *Altruism and Helping Behavior,* pp. 13–27. New York: Academic Press.

1970a *The Unresponsive Bystander: Why Doesn't He Help?* New York: Appleton-Century-Crofts.

LAW ENFORCEMENT ASSISTANCE ADMINISTRATION

1975 *Criminal Victimization Surveys in 13 American Cities.* Washington, D.C.: National Criminal Justice Information and Statistics Service.

LEMERT, EDWIN

1969 "Records in the Juvenile Court," in Stanton Wheeler, ed., *On Record: Files and Dossiers in American Life,* pp. 355–87. New York: Russell Sage Foundation.

LOHMAN, JOSEPH, ET AL.

   1966   *The Police and the Community, Field Survey IV,* Vol I. *The President's Commission on Law Enforcement and the Administration of Justice.* Washington D.C.: Government Printing Office.

LOS ANGELES POLICE DEPARTMENT

   1972   *Policy Manual of the Los Angeles Police Department,* Vol. I.

MORALES, ARMANDO

   1972   "Police Deployment Theories and the Mexican-American Community," in *Ando Sangrando (I Am Bleeding): A Study of Mexican American-Police Conflict,* pp. 47–57. La Puente, Calif.: Perspectiva Publications.

PEPINSKI, HAROLD

   1975   "Police Decision-Making," in Don Gottfredson, ed., *Decision-Making in the Criminal Justice System: Reviews and Essays,* pp. 21–52. Rockville, Md.: NIMH Publication.

PILIAVIN, IRVING, AND SCOTT BRIAR

   1964.   "Police Encounters with Juveniles." *American Journal of Sociology* 70 (September): 206–14.

PRESIDENT'S COMMISSION ON LAW ENFORCEMENT AND THE ADMINISTRATION OF JUSTICE

   1967   *Task Force Report: The Police.* Washington, D.C.: Government Printing Office.

   1967a   *The Challenge of Crime in a Free Society.* Washington D.C.: Government Printing Office.

QUINNEY, RICHARD

   1974   *Critique of Legal Order: Crime Control in Capitalist Society.* Boston: Little, Brown.

REISS, ALBERT

   1968   "Police Brutality, Answers to Key Questions." *Trans-action* 5 (July-August): 10–19.

   1971   *The Police and the Public.* New Haven: Yale University Press.

REMINGTON, FRANK

   1962   "The Law Relating to 'On the Street' Detention, Questioning and Frisking of Suspected Persons and Police Arrest Privileges in General," in Claude Sowle, ed., *Police Power and Individual Freedom: The Quest for Balance,* pp. 11–20. Chicago: Aldine.

RUBINSTEIN, JONATHAN

   1973   *City Police.* New York: Ballantine.

SACKS, HARVEY

   1972   "Notes on Police Assessment of Moral Character," in David Sudnow, ed., *Studies in Social Interaction,* pp. 280–333. New York: The Free Press.

SANDERS, WILLIAM B.

   1977   *Detective Work: A Study of Criminal Investigations.* New York: The Free Press.

SANDERS, WILLIAM B., AND HOWARD C. DAUDISTEL

   1974   "Detective Work: Patterns of Criminal Investigations," in William B.

Sanders, ed., *The Sociologist as Detective: An Introduction to Research Methods,* pp. 166–83. New York: Praeger.

SCHUR, EDWIN
1965 *Crimes Without Victims: Deviant Behavior and Public Policy.* Englewood Cliffs, N.J.: Prentice-Hall.

SHIBUTANI, TAMOTSU
1961 *Society and Personality: An Interactionist Approach to Social Psychology.* Englewood Cliffs, N.J.: Prentice-Hall.

SKOLNICK, JEROME
1966 *Justice without Trial: Law Enforcement in Democratic Society.* New York: Wiley.

STARK, RODNEY
1972 *Police Riots: Collective Violence and Law Enforcement.*

STEWERT, OMER
1964 "Questions Regarding American Indian Criminality," *Human Organization* 23 (Spring): 61–66.

STINCHCOMBE, ARTHUR
1963 "Institutions of Privacy in the Determination of Police Administrative Practice," *American Journal of Sociology* 69 (September): 150–60.

UNITED STATES COMMISSION ON CIVIL RIGHTS
1970 *Mexican Americans and the Administration of Justice in the Southwest.* Washington D.C.: Government Printing Office.

WAMBAUGH, JOSEPH
1973 *The Onion Field.* New York: Delacorte Press.

WERTHMAN, CARL, AND IRVING PILIAVIN
1967 "Gang Members and the Police," In David Bordua, ed., *The Police: Six Sociological Essays,* pp. 56–98. New York: Wiley.

WESTLEY, WILLIAM
1970 *The Police: A Study of Law, Custom and Morality.* Cambridge: MIT Press.

WILKINS, ROY
1966 "Stop and Frisk," *New York Post,* May 28.

WILSON, JAMES Q.
1966 "Crime in the Streets," *The Public Interest* 5 (Fall): 26–35.
1968 *Varieties of Police Behavior: The Management of Law and Order in Eight Communiies.* Cambridge: Harvard University Press.

WOLFGANG, MARVIN, AND BERNARD COHEN
1970 *Crime and Race: Conceptions and Misconceptions.* New York: Institute of Human Relations Press.

SELECTED READINGS

BITTNER, EGON. *The Functions of the Police in Modern Society.* Rockville, Md: National Institute of Mental Health, Center for Studies of Crime and Delinquency, 1970.

A short book that analyzes police work from an "interpretive" perspective. Bittner argues that the "open-ended" and vague character of rules makes control of police conduct by rules and policy problematic.

DAVIS, KENNETH CULP. *Police Discretion.* St. Paul, Minn.: West Publishing Co., 1975.
A law professor's study of police discretion. Davis' work is particularly interesting because he claims that discretion is essential and addresses how to control excessive selective enforcement.

REISS, ALBERT J. *The Police and the Public.* New Haven: Yale University Press, 1971.
Reiss reports findings from an extensive observational study of police encounters with citizens. Includes a section on the discretionary decisions of citizens to mobilize the police.

RUBINSTEIN, JONATHAN. *City Police.* New York: Ballantine, 1973.
A detailed description of police work which is notable for its description of police dispatchers' decision-making and how police officers learn to be competent policemen.

SANDERS, WILLIAM B. *Detective Work: A Study of Criminal Investigations.* New York: The Free Press, 1977.
A sociological analysis of reactive detectives, their organization, and the process of criminal investigations.

SKOLNICK, JEROME. *Justice without Trial: Law Enforcement in Democratic Society,* 2d ed. New York: Wiley, 1975.
One of the first complete sociological studies of police discretion. Skolnick argues that policemen work in an environment of conflicting demands, one to "rule by law," the other to "efficiently clear crimes." He shows that police officers (especially those on vice squads) are likely to violate the law when it helps them to "solve" crimes.

4
CHARGING

This and the three chapters that follow focus on the processing of criminal defendants through the criminal court system. This processing encompasses the movement of defendants through a multitude of "fateful" situations. In fateful situations, defendants are confronted with several alternate lines of action, each of which has important consequences for their future reputation and identity (Goffman, 1967:214–39). The prosecution, adjudication, and sentencing of defendants certainly constitute significant decision-making points that encompass several alternatives, each of which has important ramifications for both the reputation and identity of defendants.

Before we move directly into detailed examinations of each of the recurrent, fateful decision-making points in court processing, we should sketch briefly the formal process in its entirety. It is important to note at the outset that no singular presentation of the criminal court process can be applicable to all jurisdictions in the United States. Indeed, the rich diversity in the substantive and procedural law applicable to different jurisdictions precludes such a possibility. Nevertheless, as Newman (1975:105) notes, there are a core series of *decision-points that are roughly comparable in all jurisdictions, and it is with these that we shall concern ourselves.*

••

THE FORMAL PROCESS

Court processing begins with *initial charging,* a stage that revolves about two principal decisions, each made by the prosecutor. Should the suspect be charged with the commission of a crime? If so, what specific charge or charges should be levied against him? Initial charging may result from two different processes. First, a citizen may come directly to the prosecutor and ask him to institute a criminal proceeding against a suspect not yet in custody. If the prosecutor decides to charge, he then requests the magistrate to issue a warrant commanding the police to arrest the suspect. The second and more typical process finds the police arresting a suspect, either on "reasonable grounds" or on a citizen complaint, without a warrant.

Following arrest, the law requires that a suspect be brought before a judicial magistrate (a judge) without "unnecessary delay." At this stage—*the initial appearance*—the suspect is apprised of the state's charges. What is accomplished in the initial appearance depends on the severity of the criminal charges. When charges are minor and triable by a magistrate, the defendant is asked to plead to the charges. If he pleads guilty to the charges, the magistrate sentences him immediately. However, if he pleads not guilty, then he may be tried by the magistrate in a summary fashion. When charges are serious and not triable by a magistrate, the magistrate must decide whether the defendant should be released without posting bond, released on posting bond, or simply remanded to custody. In those jurisdictions that use preliminary hearings, the magistrate asks the defendant if he wishes a preliminary hearing. If he does, then the magistrate will set a date for the hearing. If the defendant waives the hearing, then the magistrate may transfer the case directly to the trial court.

The third stage in court processing involves review of the prosecutor's decision to charge and the specific charges brought against the defendant. Such a review may take one of two forms, depending on the particular statutes and customs of the jurisdiction. First, the case may be taken before a magistrate for a *preliminary hearing,* which serves three basic functions: (1) "to determine whether there is probable cause to hold the defendant for trial, (2) to afford the defense an opportunity to learn about the state's case, and (3) to enable the state to preserve the testimony of witnesses who may later balk at testifying" (Miller and Remington, 1962:122). If the magistrate decides that the evidence does not establish "probable cause" that the defendant committed a crime, the case will be dismissed. Conversely, if "probable cause" is

Following arrest and booking, a criminal suspect must be brought before a judicial magistrate without "unnecessary delay." A suspect may not be delayed for purposes of police interrogation. (© *1976 by Fred W. McDarrah*)

established, the defendant will be bound over to the trial courts. In some states, a second form of review is made. This review, done by a grand jury, differs from preliminary hearings. The grand jury's decision to hold the defendant for trial is made solely from the evidence submitted to them by the prosecutor. The defendant or his counsel are not admitted to grand jury proceedings. If a majority votes to return an indictment, the defendant is bound over for trial.

Following the preliminary hearing or grand jury proceeding, the defendant makes his first appearance before the trial court. This appearance is termed the *arraignment*. Here the trial judge reads the formal accusation to the defendant, outlines the punitive consequences of each charge if convicted, and notifies the defendant of his constitutional rights, especially his right to counsel. At this stage, the defendant is asked to plead to the formal accusation, and several alternatives are available to him. First, he may plead guilty to the formal accusation.[1] Second, on permission of the trial judge, he may enter a plea of *nolo contendere* (no contest), which is essentially a plea of guilty that cannot be used as an admission of guilt for subsequent civil litigation. A third alternative a defendant may select is to plead not guilty. In this situation, the trial judge responds by ascertaining whether the defendant wishes a trial by jury or by the bench, and sets a date for commencement of the trial.

A plea of not guilty sets in motion an additional step in court processing not experienced on pleas of guilty or no contest. This is the *criminal trial*. The trial is the occasion in which the judge or jury, depending on the type of trial selected, decides on the guilt or innocence of the defendant. Their decision is to be grounded on the assessment and evaluation of the arguments and evidence bearing on the case presented by the prosecution and defense.

A final stage in court processing is *sentencing*. In approximately ten states, the jury may determine the sentence of convicted defendants. Generally, however, the trial judge must decide within broad statutory limits the type of punishment to be administered. His decision-making efforts are aided by the operation of the probation department. On his order, a presentence report prepared by the probation department is often made of the convicted defendant, and a recommendation regarding the suitability of probation is given to the judge.

On conviction and sentencing, the defendant has the right to appeal his case to at least one appellate court. If the defendant was convicted in a magistrate's court, he has the right to appeal his conviction by requesting a new trial in the trial courts. One convicted in the trial courts has the right to appeal the adverse decision to the intermediate appellate courts. Lastly, if the defendant loses at the intermediate level, he may appeal his case to the highest appellate court of the jurisdiction, in many states called the supreme court. Unlike the previous levels of appeal, however, the supreme court has the right to

---

[1] In capital cases, however, the trial judge may refuse to accept pleas, and enter pleas of not guilty.

accept or reject cases for consideration. Generally, it will review cases only when constitutional issues are involved, or when there has been some dissent or points of debate in the intermediate levels of appeal with regard to the cases involved.

In some states, the prosecution may appeal an acquittal only as it involves the clarification of the law. An acquittal itself marks the end of court processing on that particular charge. A cornerstone of our system of justice is the rule against double jeopardy, that is, the prohibition against a defendant's being tried more than once for the same crime. There are some subtle qualifications to this cornerstone, though. A defendant may be tried on separate charges such that his acquittal on one charge in one trial does not preclude his being brought to trial for another of the charges. An illegal act may additionally violate the laws of two jurisdictions. Thus, acquittal in the state court system does not preclude a trial in the federal court system, for each is considered a distinct jurisdiction.

THE CHARACTER OF COURT DECISIONS

The decision-making points we have described vary along several dimensions. In some areas, for example, charging precedes the initial appearance while in other areas it follows the appearance. Decision-making points may vary in their ordering within the same jurisdiction. On weekends, defendants may be released on bail prior to charging while on weekdays they may be released on bail after charging. Some decisions are made during occasions that are strictly bounded in time and place, a case found with initial appearances and trials.

All decisions are the product of considerable interpretive work on the part of the relevant decision-makers. Members must first interpret the particular case as an instance of some larger category, and subsequently invoke a recipe strategy on the basis of that interpretation. How a case is interpreted, moreover, is subject to a product of varying amounts of negotiation between relevant members. Consequently, all cases are in fact "trouble" cases demanding some degree of interpretation and thought.

In all cases there are several alternatives to every decision. Which alternative is selected and initiated, however, is not a matter of chance or fiat. Rather, decisions during court processing share the quality of being ad hoc constructions forged toward the achievement of individualized justice with limited organizational resources. That is, those alternatives that prove through experience to be pragmatic means to the achievement of justice vis-à-vis the case at hand and to the conservation of limited resources will be selected for initiation.

Just as the police must assess situations and suspects for purposes of order maintenance or law enforcement, so too must court officials assess concrete cases for purposes of deciding whether defendants should or should not be subjected to criminal proceedings and state-administered punishment. The assessment of cases is not a mechanical process, simply a literal matching of the penal code and the case at hand. This is so because the penal code is no more than a conceptual scheme making reference to flexible, open-ended categories of action, the basic properties of which are not literally specified. For example, in the California Penal Code, robbery is defined as "the felonious taking of personal property in the possession of another, from his person or immediate presence, and against his will, accomplished by means of force or threat." This definition makes reference to a class of human activities that share the properties "taking of personal property in the possession of another," "against his will," and "by means of force or threat." These code properties are themselves categories, the particulars of which are not specified in the statutes. To what "taking of personal property in the possession of another," "against his will," and "by means of force or threat" refer is simply unstated. Robbery could conceivably refer to everything from "taking the candy from the hands of a child" to "taking at gunpoint the cash from the register of a liquor-store owner."

Two points follow from this recognition of the abstract character of the code. First, because the code categories are inherently abstract, members of the enterprise must develop typifications that represent these categories they recurrently use in order to effectively process their cases. Such typifications include a multitude of specific properties learned and developed through organizational experience. Officials gain "knowledge of the typical manner in which offenses of given classes are committed, the social characteristics of the persons who regularly commit them, the features of the settings in which they occur, the types of victims often involved, and the like" (Sudnow, 1965:-259). They learn the routine types of crimes and criminals, and attribute to most offenders typical kinds of personal biographies, criminal histories, psychological characteristics, and social backgrounds. Consequently, when members are confronted with concrete cases, they approach them from the perspective of their typifications, not from the literal meanings of statutes.

Second, because penal code categories are inherently abstract, and because concrete cases are always unique in time, space, and configuration, officials must, to achieve their authorized tasks, engage in an interpretive process through which cases and penal code categories fit together. That is, members must categorize the event as an instance of some routine typification to which there is a particular sanctioned recipe disposition.

To be sure, the specific properties officials attend to in their interpretation of cases cannot be specified in so many words. Nevertheless, a number of basic properties appear relevant in officials' assessment of cases. On the basis of various empirical investigations, three basic types of properties officials attend to in their assessment stand out— the character of the defendant, the character of the event, and the ramifications of processing for the organization.

CHARGING

Some have argued that charging is the most fateful of all decisions in court-processing. Indeed, the fatefulness of charging is captured in the opening pages of Miller's monograph on *Prosecution:*

> The charging decision has obviously serious implications for the individual involved. Not only does a decision to charge represent an affirmation of the need to condition the personal freedom of the accused on his ability to provide bail; it is also the decision that the accused should bear the economic and social costs of trial. . . . On the economic side, loss of earnings and the loss of preparing a defense may be considerable. On the social side, temporary loss of prestige and position are certain, and permanent damage to reputation not unlikely (1969:3).

The court officials responsible for charging decisions vary from one jurisdiction to another. In some areas, the police are responsible for both the arrest and the charging of suspects. In such systems, the public prosecutor learns of cases at the point of the preliminary examination (Oaks and Lehman, 1968:28–35; McIntyre, 1968). Most often in the United States, the charging decision is the province of the prosecutor. In this pattern of operation the police typically arrest presumed malefactors, screen those deemed unsuited for formal charges, and advance those judged suitable for processing to the office of the prosecutor.

Members of the prosecutor's office enjoy a reasonable degree of autonomy in their decisions of charge. But while the prosecutor enjoys a degree of autonomy in performing his tasks, we must notice that other officials have an impact on his decisions. Investigations of Oakland and Seattle, for example, demonstrate that the police and prosecution frequently discuss cases prior to charging; thus, whatever the decision on charge, it is the product of the prosecution-police negotiation (Skolnick, 1966:199–201; Cole, 1970). Neubauer's (1974) investigation of "Prairie City" shows that while the prosecutor reviews cases without the presence of the police, the police nevertheless "indirectly influence . . . the charging decision by virtue of their role as suppliers of information" (1974:117). Cole (1970:334) notes that the prosecutor's power to determine the disposition of cases "is limited by the fact that usually he is dependent upon the police for inputs to the system of cases and evidence." Consequently, because the police both shape the basic information prosecutors use when making charging decisions and serve as ready sources of reference for enlightening the prosecutor of details of the case, they significantly influence his decisions (cf. Reiss, 1971:114–20).

Charging includes two basic decisions. First, officials must decide whether the defendant should be charged with the commission of a crime or released without prosecution. Second, given a decision to charge, officials must then decide what specific charge or charges should be levied against him.[2]

A defendant will generally be charged with a crime when the official defines (1) the event as an instance of a "real" crime; (2) the defendant as an instance of a "real" criminal who engaged in that criminal event; and (3) the case as an instance of one that poses little difficulty to the organization. A defendant will probably be released from prosecution when the official defines (1) the event as an instance of some "noncriminal," albeit dubious, class of action; (2) the defendant as an instance of a "noncriminal" type of person, who may not have even performed the event in question; and (3) the case as an instance in which prosecution poses difficulty to the organization. When deciding whether an act is a crime, officials evaluate the behavior in question in terms of what they consider to be the "true" meaning and "intent" of the criminal law. Indeed, when officials decide to charge, they may legitimate that decision by saying it definitely follows from an extant rule or standard. Similarly, when they decide not to prosecute a particular case, they can proffer to superiors, colleagues, and others rules indicating the logic and rationality of their decision. But that which is codified and revered in the penal code is in fact a flexible tool for accomplishing the practical task of doing justice under the banner of authority.

Technically, an official files charges only when a case meets the standard of "probable cause," which refers to the reasonable basis to believe that a crime has been committed and that the defendant committed it. But in the law, the meaning of probable cause is not specified. As Miller notes:

> The probable cause requirement might be interpreted to
> mean either that enough evidence must be presented to
> convince the magistrate that the defendant is probably guilty of
> an offense, or that, even though sufficient facts could be

---

[2] Officials often approach the charging decision with the central orientation of "doing justice," or "fair" processing. Consequently, they do not ask themselves if they should charge a suspect with a crime, and, if so, what specific charges they should file. Rather, they ask what it is the particular defendant "deserves," what, in all fairness, the state should do to the defendant (Rosett and Cressey, 1976).

presented to show guilt, the defendant must be dismissed at the preliminary hearing when it is unlikely that he could be convicted at trial (1969:94).

While charging officials may talk about the probable cause standard when arriving at their charging decision, in fact they operate according to other standards. Neubauer (1974:117–19) found that Prairie City prosecutors ask themselves if the case at hand has a good chance of conviction at trial. Officials chart the likely reactions of a judge and/or jury toward the particular case and the evidence that can be marshaled in support of the state's case. Not only are the imputed reactions of judge and/or jury assessed, but the officials also consider the possible defense strategies that could be presented in opposition to the state's case. Kaplan (1965:183–84) indicates several features of a case that may make it, in the eyes of officials, weak, that is, nonconvictable at trial. These include cases in which the state's witnesses are reluctant or unwilling to testify, those in which the state's witnesses may be attacked by the defense because they were convicted felons or were themselves involved with the defendant in the present case (but turned state's evidence), and those in which critical pieces of evidence could not be introduced because they were illegally gathered. If the official assesses the case as one in which there is a bleak chance of conviction at trial, then charging is unlikely.

The prosecutor's office sorts through all of the incoming cases and decides which ones meet the office's criteria for filing charges. (*Freelance Photographers Guild Inc.*)

If the district attorney prosecutes too many weak cases, an inordinate strain is put on limited organizational resources. Put simply, it costs money to bring cases to trial.

Prosecuting weak cases not only costs money, it also costs the individual decision-maker. Because he is an organizational member, the charging official must maintain a favorable set of relations with those for whom he works. Furthermore, prosecutors do not wish to sport a losing record. Reporting the findings of his study of a federal prosecutor's office in California, Kaplan says:

> There were also some very personal reasons for the assistant to exercise caution in authorizing prosecution. Although he was under relatively little supervision in his daily activities, he had to be careful to stay in the good graces of the United States Attorney, who, holding an essentially political position, was very sensitive to the criticism of the press, the judges, and the defense bar, all of whom were quick to note a rising number of acquittals and ascribe this to either incompetence in the staff or to overzealousness in the choice of targets for prosecution (1965:181).

Officials may not prosecute when doing so creates inordinate strain in the office's working relations with other officials or offices. For instance, the decision not to prosecute may be made because of pressure placed on the office by judges or police. The prosecutor may not charge when a defendant is an informant who provides the police with information concerning the identities or criminal activities of colleagues or acquaintances. Or, the defendant may be asked to help the police by purchasing illicit goods or services from others who are under investigation.

What is costly to the prosecutor's office varies. With regard to the prosecution of weak cases, cost refers to the expenditure of resources (time and manpower) as outweighing the consequences of prosecution. With regard to the prosecution of cases that bring political pressure, either from the powerful segments of the community, from the office itself, or from other officials, cost is something quite different. Here, cost refers to the possible disruption of critical relationships, hence organizational persistence and members' tenure.

Failure to charge cannot be explained solely in terms of organizational cost. Indeed, there are situations in which officials file charges in weak cases and those that are quite costly. The orientation of "doing justice," of fitting charges to a case bringing what officials deem the defendant deserves, best accounts for these cases. (A multitude of cues, whether legally admissible or not, may critically influence a prosecutor —rumor, hearsay, illegally secured materials, as well as confessions and witness accounts). For instance, no matter what the legal strength of the case, if it is felt that the defendant is innocent, prosecution is generally dismissed, for the defendant is simply not a criminal deserving punishment (cf. Miller, 1969:42).

Officials will generally not charge a defendant when the punishment contingent on prosecution and conviction is considered unduly harmful and severe in relation to the suspect event. In confronting concrete cases that are not considered to be serious, officials may feel that further processing is unjust. For example, prosecution is unlikely when

> the alleged criminal act was the result of some quarrel between neighbors and all parties were equally at fault; the alleged criminal act was the result of some minor domestic dispute; where an overzealous creditor attempting to pervert the criminal process for the purpose of collecting a civil debt; [or when] a person may have committed a technical violation of the law, and a warning may be sufficient to prevent further infractions . . . (Wright, 1959:293).

Officials confronting events assessed to be criminal but not serious may respond by either dismissing charges or by invoking some alternate procedure aimed at resolving whatever conflict brought the case into the judicial process in the first place. These alternate procedures include restitution for bad checks, payment plans for nonsupport cases, attending marriage counseling sessions, voluntary commitment to psychiatric therapy, and the like. In such instances, it is felt that defendants deserve some type of aid, not the punishment contingent on criminal conviction. As suggested before, prosecutors develop conceptions of the "normal" criminal involved in crime, which is constituted by knowledge of the offender's character, including his social life and position in the community and psychological makeup. When officials encounter defendants who do not measure up to their conception of the normal criminal performing some event, then routine charging is unlikely. In situations where the defendant is assessed as an essentially "noncriminal" type, charging may be dismissed. More specifically, cues that are taken as indicators of a noncriminal character include the following:

> 1. *Standing in the community.* To charge an upstanding person with a crime, let alone convict him, brings punishment far beyond what is necessary.
> 2 *Prior offenses.* In many cases, first-time offenders are not seriously committed to crime as a way of life.
> 3 *Age and health.* The rigors of processing may impose a severe hardship on defendants who are old or in ill health. Furthermore, when the physical condition of the accused

substantially precludes the ability to maintain criminal conduct, the need for punishment is reduced (Kaplan, 1965:190).

The analytical distinction between an official's assessment of a defendant's character and the crime as they enter into his decision concerning charge and punishment blurs an important point, namely, that these contingencies cannot be viewed independently of others. A seemingly petty offense may not be judged as an instance of "real" crime when performed by a first-time offender who is an established citizen of the community. Yet, the same offense may be judged as such an instance when the defendant is known to be a persistent offender. Similarly, the taking of glass ornaments from a department-store display may be viewed as "theft" when performed by a young male resident of a lower-class ghetto, while it is seen as a "prank," or sign of mental illness, when performed by a respectable middle-class resident.

If a prosecutor decides that a defendant deserves some sort of state-administered punishment, then he must also decide what charge or charges should be filed to attempt to bring the desired outcome. Several alternatives are available. Of course, as will be discussed later, charges can be subsequently changed. First, the official may file as many charges as he can justify, given the evidence. For example, if a woman is forcibly raped, her offender may be charged with forcible rape, kidnapping, and assault. If an armed person breaks into a family-owned store, assaults one of the family members, and takes the money from the cash register, he may be charged with breaking and entering, assault, armed robbery, and carrying a dangerous, possibly concealed, weapon. Second, the official may file only one of the several possible charges contained in the event. Thus, our armed robber may be charged with armed robbery or breaking and entering. Third, the official may file a lesser charge. For example, a person who shot and critically wounded another person may be charged with simple assault instead of aggravated assault or attempted murder. We cannot say with certainty which of these alternatives is most frequently selected. Chambliss and Seidman (1971:398) argue that "prosecutors invariably initiate prosecutions for the highest degree of crime that the evidence can sustain." Once officials decide to prosecute, the strategy is to expediently process such defendants; to do otherwise is to make inefficient use of limited resources. Trials are to be avoided, and this is best accomplished by securing guilty pleas at arraignment. Thus, "aware that a bargaining session with a defense counsel is ahead, prosecutors invariably bring the highest charge that the facts will permit" (Chambliss and Seidman, 1971:405). Full charging, then, is considered a strategy for inducing guilty pleas: initiate full charges and at a future stage offer a reduction in exchange for a guilty plea. Newman discovered such a strategy in several jurisdictions, which is aptly demonstrated in the comments of one prosecuting attorney:

The other day the bargaining prosecutor came in and told us: "For God's sake, give me something to work with over there. Don't reduce these cases over here; let me do it over there or many of these guys will be tried on a misdemeanor." What he was referring to is, if we had graded a case at the lowest charge in the class of offenses in which it logically belonged, a defense attorney could conceivably get his man to plead to even a lower crime, a misdemeanor, for example (1966:81).

Some argue that officials rather routinely initiate charges for less than what could be filed, given the available evidence. In a study of the lower courts Mileski (1971:510–11) found that some 28 percent of the defendants were charged with crimes substantially less than the substance of their criminal performance. Of course, this pattern can also be explained in terms of organizational requirements for expedient processing. For certain types of cases, initiating lesser charges reduces the potential strain on organizational resources. Reducing felonies to misdemeanors, for example, permits more expedient processing because cases handled in misdemeanor courts can be adjudicated in minutes, whether the defendant wishes a trial or not (cf. Mileski, 1971). Initiating lesser charges also circumvents the possibility of added courtroom battles over particular legal points raised by additional charges. As Miller (1969:340) notes, this also eliminates the extra court appearances of those police and officials involved in the case. Of perhaps greatest significance is the use of undercharging as a tool for inducing guilty pleas. To initiate a lesser charge, one coupled with a lesser maximum penalty, is to wave a carrot before a hungry defendant. A reduced charge may induce the guilty defendant to grab the "bargain" by pleading guilty; to plead not guilty is to provoke the prosecutor to refile and bring full charges. This strategy seems implicit in Newman's (1956) early study of plea negotiation. Those defendants previously involved in the criminal justice process were familiar with court routines. They knew that to upset officials, by asking for an attorney, or pleading not guilty, was to earn their wrath, and likely to result in full charging or severe sentences. Consequently, they would enter a guilty plea to the prosecution's charges without causing any trouble.

Which of the practices is routine in the United States is an academic question. Whether officials normally initiate full or lesser charges varies both across and within jurisdictions. What is critical is not so much the organizational necessity of securing guilty pleas (since this contributes to the efficient use of limited resources) but the concern with ensuring that defendants receive the treatment they justly deserve. Newman (1975:195) argues that "the actual decisions of the prosecutor in charging . . . do not involve automatic application of the full force of statutes in all cases, but rather the fair use of his authority to make just and sensible distinctions among cases . . . ."[3] That is, officials may *not fully* charge defendants in a variety of situations. For one, reduced charges may be filed when full charging precludes negotiation over sentence. For example, officials often avoid charging defendants with crimes that carry mandatory sentences. In some states, burglary-at-night is a nonprobationable offense; those convicted must be sentenced to a minimum prison term. If the prosecutor does not feel the particular case warrants imprisonment, he may charge the suspect with a burglary-during-daytime, a crime that does not carry a mandatory sentence.

Second, charging officials routinely reduce charges when it is felt that full charging would cause the defendant undue harm (Miller, 1969:207–12). In such instances, a reduction of charges does not necessarily mean a reduction of penalty. Rather, the objective is to avoid those negative consequences that may accompany "rightful" punishment. For example, it is customary in some areas to reduce felony charges for youthful, first-time offenders engaged in reasonably minor offenses in order to avoid stigmatizing them with felony records. Newman (1966:109) provides a good illustration:

> *Illustration No. 5:* Two young men in Kansas entered a liquor store and stole some beer. In the process of removing the beer from the store they were spotted by a policeman who chased them. In attempting to hide, one of the boys jumped into a parked automobile and, noticing that the keys had been left in the ignition, drove off. He and his partner were later apprehended and charged with burglary with the additional count in one case of auto theft. The deputy county attorney, however, discovered that neither offender had a prior record and said: "I hate very much giving felony records to these young men. I think they have learned a lesson and there's no point in putting a blight on their whole future." He then reduced the charges to misdemeanors and both defendants pleaded guilty and received bench parole.

Third, charges are also reduced for purposes of avoiding collateral harm in cases that are sexually oriented. As Miller (1969:209) argues, "prosecution for offenses against morality may result in severe injury to the defendant's reputation, while a conviction creates a more harmful criminal record than is true of offenses of other types." Consequently, a defendant who has committed statutory rape may be charged with common assault; one who has committed adultery may

---

[3] Schrag (1971:164) makes a similar point: "The prosecutor's role is not simply to obtain convictions but to judge the merits of each case in terms of the public interest and to arrive at a just disposition.

be charged with disorderly conduct, as may one who has committed sodomy.

A final pattern of charging is to fully charge defendants. Here, officials file the severest charge or the most charges they can justify. This course of action reflects a variety of contingencies; nevertheless, it is found in situations in which officials judge the defendant as rightfully deserving that punishment contingent on conviction while, at the same time, serving particular organizational ends. Let us note three typical situations of full charging.

First, a defendant may be fully charged when there is a "strong desire by officials to separate the offender from the community" (Miller, 1969:287), a disposition that is the product of the official's assessment of both the event and the defendant. "If the circumstances of the offense are particularly heinous, such as a combination murder-rape, full enforcement is likely. . . . But even when the offense is not particularly heinous, a number of factors in the suspect's personal history may make officials especially anxious to 'put him away' for a long time" (Miller, 1969:287). There are cues to which officials attend in assessing the defendant as one who should be removed from the community. If the defendant is seen as a nuisance to enforcement agencies and the community, or if he is viewed as a persistent offender, such as a professional thief or a drug marketer, who has in the past

Only under certain circumstances will a defendant be charged on all of the crimes for which the police have listed in the arrest. (*Bureau of Public Information, Police Department, City of New York*)

flagrantly violated the law with impunity, prosecutors will probably want to "send him away." Those defendants who have been arrested many times, particularly for violent crimes, as well as those with fewer "priors" but who are uncooperative with the police and others in the criminal justice system, are also seen as "bad actors" who deserve to be sent to the "slammer."

Second, a defendant may be fully charged when there is considerable notoriety surrounding a case. Highly publicized crimes as well as those committed by well-known criminals may eventuate in full charging of the apprehended parties. In such situations, officials feel their hands are tied. Even if the case is weak, that is, when evidence is less than satisfactory or adequate, they feel pressed to fully charge. "As one deputy [prosecutor] noted, 'In that case [murder and molestation of a six-year-old girl] there was nothing that we could do. As you know the press was on our back and every parent was concerned. Politically, the prosecutor had to seek an information" (Cole, 1970:335). Miller provides another illustration:

> *Illustration No. 2:* The suspect had committed several armed
> robberies in Milwaukee. Newspapers gave the case more than
> the usual amount of publicity. An assistant prosecutor approved
> the police recommendation for three warrants, each charging
> one of the robberies (1969:281–82).

An important idea derives from this situation. When the facade of day-to-day organizational operation is penetrated by mass media and public observation, officials feel constrained to "follow the book," that is, to cover themselves by appearing to adhere to formal rules of law. Full charging, lengthy pretrial motions, jury trial, and the like become the order of the day. But, while charging may be full in such cases, this is not to suggest that, like the previous situation, sentencing will be more severe. Indeed, full charging may be used simply to satisfy the appetites of certain powerful groups. But once the case becomes old news, officials may bring the type and degree of punishment they feel the defendant deserves. For example, in one of the cases Miller reports, the Detroit press demanded that the police "clean up the bums" and charge them with misdemeanor repeater violations. Some 150 were arrested and so charged. "Of the 150 bums charged as repeaters in response to the newspaper criticism, only about twenty were sentenced as repeaters. All of the sentences, including the twenty, were no more than they would have been without the repeater charge . . . " (Miller, 1969:282).

Third, full charging may be used as a tool for promoting a defendant's cooperation with enforcement agencies. As a "tool," full charging serves several ends. It may, as Chambliss and Seidman (1971) argue, serve as a lever for prompting a defendant to plead guilty in

        INITIAL ENCOUNTERS WITH CRIMINAL JUSTICE

exchange for such concessions as reduced charges. Full charging is a threat to be initiated on a defendant's failure to cooperate; as such, it is a punishment:

> *Illustration No. 9:* During the several months since he had been released from prison, the suspect had committed six major burglaries. In exchange for being charged with only one of the six offenses, he had agreed to plead guilty and to testify against two of his accomplices and their fence. After being charged, the suspect refused to perform his part of the bargain. Two more burglary charges were brought against him (Miller, 1969:286).

Full charging serves officials by reinforcing their power in negotiation. Just as corporal punishment was considered a symbol telling others what would happen to them under certain circumstances, so too is full charging a cue telling defendants and defense counsel what would happen if negotiated agreements are violated. In this situation, then, full charging is a course of action that buttresses a particular relationship of trust between role players.

A final note about full charging. While the legal strength of a case is an important contingency to which officials attend, and serves as an agreed upon rationale for releasing or reducing charges when the case is weak, legal strength may be of secondary importance in cases finding full charging. In notorious cases, for example, where the public is acutely aware of the processing of a defendant, the prosecutor may take the case through the process even though he feels the case is legally shoddy. Furthermore, officials will fully charge, or at least take to court, serious cases, those deemed particularly heinous. As Kaplan (1965:181–82) found:

> In the case of the more serious crimes, it was often felt that the accused should be put on trial even though prosecution might routinely be declined for a lesser crime where conviction was equally uncertain. In fact, in a few cases where the defendant was believed to be guilty of previous offenses and likely to commit future ones unless prevented, the assistant concluded that he was justified in taking a considerably greater chance of losing the case in order to attempt conviction.

Again, when legal strength and officials' assessments of the defendant as someone deserving state-administered punishment are weighed, the latter seems to dominate.

We should be cautious in concluding that under certain conditions officials will decide on one particular line of charging action and not another. The concrete contingencies—those instances of the broader categories of defendant, event, and organizational ramification —are in fact everchanging. What is a legally "weak" case, for example, cannot be specified in so many words. One instance of murder may be weak because the body is never found. Another case may be weak because detectives mishandled critical evidence. Yet another may be weak because the only eyewitness dies. For an official to assess a case as weak means that he has constructed it as weak; it is a hypothesis constructed from various cues and subject to reality-testing. The "value" of these concrete contingencies for any given case also fluctuates. Sometimes, notoriety is marked and brought to the attention of the charging official; other times, it is irrelevant for it is not brought to his attention. For certain kinds of cases, the presiding judge is critical because he is well known for dismissal of such cases. For other kinds of cases, who the presiding judge is makes little difference. The character of the defendant or the event is also flexible, subject to reassessment with the addition of negation of particular cues. Furthermore, the substantive basis for charging decisions is subject to varying degrees of debate and negotiation.

Not only is the charging official's decision affected by his relations to other officials and offices; his decisions are also of consequence to the operations of other officials and offices. Taking the prosecutor as the charging official, his decisions are efficacious to both the police and courts, the two offices linked by his office. On the one hand, charging practices affect the preceding decision of arrest. It is certainly true that the police mold the quantity and quality of input to the prosecutor's office. But it is also true that the prosecutor molds the quantity and quality of the police operation eventuating in arrest and bindover to court processing.[4]   LaFave (1965:103) reports that the persistent refusal by prosecutors to charge for certain cases is taken by police as a cue that future arrests and bindovers for similar cases will prove futile. Consequently, fewer arrests and bindovers for such cases are made. To be sure, the substantive basis for the prosecutor's refusal vary. In some cases, refusal is based on the poor quality of police work, that is, arrest or the gathering of evidence may have been of a dubious or illegal nature. Or the evidence gathered in support of the case may be unduly weak and inconclusive. In both cases, prosecution of a case may be a fatuous venture ending in dismissal. In other cases, refusal is based on the desire to avoid a substantial backlog of cases. In still other cases, refusal is made on the grounds of the noncriminal character of certain offenses. Whether the source is political or organiza-

---

[4] Note that arrest does not necessarily mean bindover to the prosecution for court processing. As Bittner (1965) aptly points out, for vagrants, drunks, disturbers-of-the-peace, pandhandlers, and the like, police consider arrest the first and final action of the criminal justice enterprise. In situations where the police have no intention of binding defendants over for prosecution, the practical effects of the prosecutor's demands are quite minimal.

tional, the prosecutor informs the arresting officer or the complaint man that certain types of offenses are really noncriminal, and hence should not be prosecuted. Thus, the decisions of the prosecutor feed back to the arrest and bindover operations of the police.

On the other hand, the charging decision shapes the basic material with which the courts work. How cases are sorted and processed in succeeding stages is influenced, in part, by the quantity and quality of input (Oaks and Lehman, 1968:180). Take, for example, the quality of the input. A change in the kinds of cases the prosecution passes on affects the basic dispositions rendered. Taking legally weak cases to court may increase the number of dismissals rendered at the preliminary examination. Conversely, dismissing cases at the prosecutorial stage usually brings greater numbers of convictions. Furthermore, the prosecution can regulate the flow of cases to successive stages. As Cole (1975:234) argues, "he [the prosecutor] can regulate the length of time between accusation and trial, hence hold cases until he has the evidence that will convict." Such regulation may provide the prosecution with a means of ensuring that court processing eventuates in conviction. Conversely, "he may also seek repeated adjournment and continuances until the public's interest dies down, witnesses become unavailable, or other difficulties make his request for dismissal of prosecution more easily justifiable" (Cole, 1975:234).

One consequence of the prosecutor-court relationship should be noted. Because the prosecutor's office provides the fundamental input to the court, it structures the "stuff" from which fundamental typifications of crime and criminals are developed. Consequently, changes in what and who are passed on to court bring changes in the basic conceptions court officials hold for the relevant objects, as well as, but not necessarily, the "rates" and trends of local crime. For example, a small suburb deals regularly with such minor events as vagrancy, drunk driving, burglary, and assaults, yet deals infrequently with auto theft. This is so, perhaps, because the police routinely discipline the youthful joyriders who make up the bulk of auto thieves. One day, however, the prosecutor demands that future cases of auto theft be referred to his office for possible action. The police comply, and the prosecutor initiates action against a number of offenders. In consequence, the court may be deluged by a sudden "surge" of auto thieves; perhaps ideas of a professional ring of auto thieves fill the courthouse air. Conceptions of the infrequent joyrider shift to conceptions of young hoods, professional thieves, and the like. Penalties on conviction may sour, the community becomes worried, and the police may become more intent on arresting those now deemed real criminals.[5]

---

[5] The process we have illustrated here has been termed a "self-fulfilling prophecy" by Merton. The practical effect for such defendants is likewise fateful. As Becker and others of the "labeling" persuasion argue, treatment as

SUMMARY

In this chapter the model of the actor involved has been that of a pragmatic organizational member oriented toward doing justice within the framework of organizational demands. The basic contingencies to which the relevant decision-makers attend concern the character of the defendant, the event, and the ramifications for the organization. And as we have sketched those particular sets of contingencies, they bring different dispositions.

We can treat the prosecutor as the most important person in the charging process. Yet, as we have shown, he does not make critical decisions in a vacuum. The prosecutor is one who must balance competing demands from within the courthouse community and from politically powerful persons outside the criminal justice system. Furthermore, the prosecutor must behave in a way that can be justified as legal. As politically motivated as a prosecutor may be, it is very rare to find one who is not at all concerned with using the law to legitmate his decisions. Doing justice may of course mean the prosecutor legitimates his decisions using odd interpretations of the law. When this happens, others' interpretations of the law may be violated. In such cases, for example, judges may reject a prosecutor's information because they feel no law has been violated. Naturally, however, judges are also operating within the framework of organizational and political demands so their decisions also reflect an interpretation of the law. What the law means is always a matter for judgment.

What makes legal decision-making so interesting is the nature of law itself. No matter how much appears in statutes or case law, what is written will never in itself make decisions. All criminal charges are made by role-players who react to an infinite variety of variables. Put bluntly, charging decisions are produced by an evaluation of "the things" associated with actors and their acts.

REFERENCES

BITTNER, EGON
  1967 "The Police on Skid Row: A Study of Peace Keeping," *American Sociological Review* 32 (October): 699–715.

CHAMBLISS, WILLIAM J., AND ROBERT B. SEIDMAN
  1971 *Law, Order, and Power.* Reading, Mass.: Addison-Wesley.

"criminal" rather than "playful" may produce "criminality" rather than transient deviance. For a fine case study of deviance and crime amplification, see Young (1971).

COLE, GEORGE F.

1970 "The Decision to Prosecute," *Law and Society Review* 4 (February): 331–43.

1975 *The American System of Criminal Justice.* North Scituate, Mass.: Duxbury Press.

GOFFMAN, ERVING

1967 *Interaction Ritual: Essays on Face-to-Face Behavior.* Garden City, N.Y.: Doubleday-Anchor.

KAPLAN, JOHN

1965 "The Prosecutorial Discretion: A Comment," *Northwestern Law Review* 60 (May-June): 174–93.

LAFAVE, WAYNE R.

1965 *Arrest: The Decision to Take a Suspect into Custody.* Boston: Little, Brown.

MC INTYRE, DONALD M.

1968 "A Study of Judicial Dominance of the Charging Decision," *Journal of Criminal Law, Criminology, and Police Science* 59 (December): 463–90.

MATHER, LYNN M.

1973 "Some Determinants of the Method of Case Disposition: Decision-Making by Public Defenders in Los Angeles," *Law and Society Review* 8 (Winter): 187–215.

MILESKI, MAUREEN

1971 "Courtroom Encounters: An Observation Study of a Lower Criminal Court," *Law and Society Review* 5 (May): 473–538.

MILLER, FRANK W.

1969 *Prosecution: The Decision to Charge a Suspect with a Crime.* Boston: Little, Brown.

MILLER, FRANK W., AND FRANK J. REMINGTON

1962 "Procedures before Trial," *Annals of the American Academy of Political and Social Science* 339 (January): 111–24.

NEUBAUER, DAVID W.

1974 *Criminal Justice in Middle America.* Morristown, N.J.: General Learning Press.

NEWMAN, DONALD J.

1956 "Pleading Guilty for Considerations: A Study of Bargain Justice," *Journal of Criminal Law, Criminology and Police Science* 46 (March–April): 780–90.

1966 *Conviction: The Determination of Guilt or Innocence without Trial.* Boston: Little, Brown.

1975 *Introduction to Criminal Justice.* Philadelphia: Lippincott.

OAKS, DALLIN H., AND WARREN LEHMAN

1968 *A Criminal Justice System and the Indigent: A Study of Chicago and Cook County.* Chicago: University of Chicago Press.

REISS, ALBERT J.

1971 *The Police and the Public.* New Haven: Yale University Press.

ROSETT, ARTHUR, AND DONALD R. CRESSEY

1976 *Justice by Consent: Plea Bargains in the American Courthouse.* Philadelphia: Lippincott.

SCHRAG, CLARENCE
  1971 *Crime and Justice: American Style.* Rockville, Md.: National Institute of Mental Health.

SHIBUTANI, TAMOTSU
  1961 *Society and Personality: An Interactionist Approach to Social Psychology.* Englewood Cliffs, N.J.: Prentice-Hall.

SKOLNICK, JEROME H.
  1966 *Justice without Trial: Law Enforcement in Democratic Society.* New York: Wiley.

SUDNOW, DAVID
  1965 "Normal Crimes: Sociological Features of the Penal Code in a Public Defender Office," *Social Problems* 12 (Winter): 255–76.

WRIGHT, DOUGLAS B.
  1959 "Duties of the Prosecutor," *Connecticut Bar Journal.* Vol. 33.

YOUNG, JOCK
  1971 "The Role of the Police as Amplifiers of Deviancy, Negotiators of Reality and Translators of Fantasy: Some Consequences of Our Present System of Drug Control as Seen in Notting Hill," in Stanley Cohen, ed., *Images of Deviance,* pp. 27–61. Harmondsworth, Eng.: Penguin.

SELECTED READINGS

COLE, GEORGE F., "The Decision to Charge," *Law and Society Review* 4 (February 1970): 331–43.
An empirical investigation of the charging decision in the Seattle prosecutor's office. Cole focuses on the impact of the police and the public on charging.

GROSMAN, BRIAN A., *The Prosecutor: An Inquiry into the Exercise of Discretion.* Toronto: University of Toronto Press, 1969.
A sociological examination of prosecution in Canada. Charging, as well as other prosecutorial practices, is related to the organizational context of the prosecutor's office and the criminal court.

KAPLAN, JOHN, "The Prosecutorial Discretion: A Comment," *Northwestern Law Review* 60 (May-June): 174–93.
A study of charging among federal district attorneys. Kaplan analyzes the criteria on which various types of charging decisions are based.

MILLER, FRANK W., *Prosecution: The Decision to Charge a Suspect with a Crime.* Boston: Little, Brown, 1969.
An investigation of the charging practices in Kansas, Michigan, and Wisconsin, the focus is on the alternatives available to prosecutors and the conditions under which different alternatives are employed.

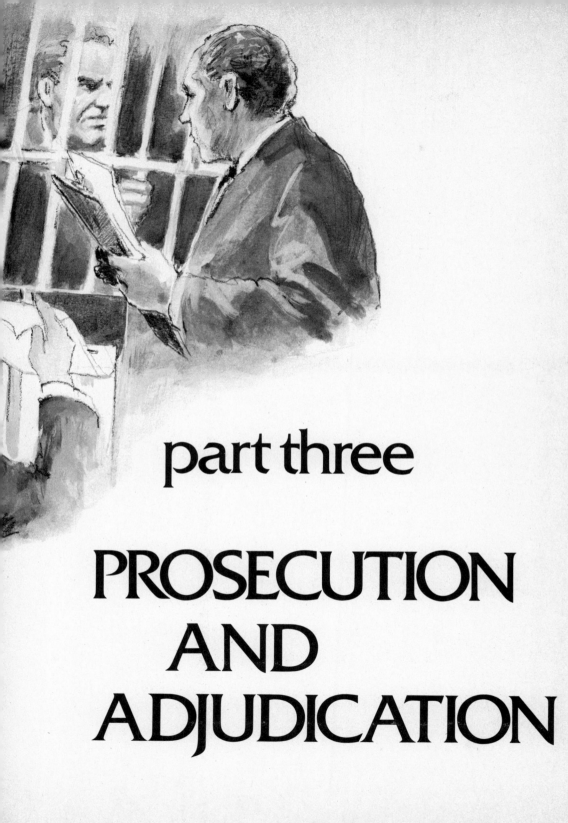

part three

PROSECUTION AND ADJUDICATION

5
FIRST COURT APPEARANCE and FORMAL CASE SCREENING

In this chapter we shall examine several stages of the criminal justice process that we group under the rubric "formal case screening." Here we shall study the judicial review of charges instigated by the police and prosecutor. We shall go on to look at grand jury proceedings to see how they are critical decision-making points in the criminal justice process. We shall also see what kinds of variables influence the setting of bail, and how they affect defendants.

Because the decision-making process associated with the case screening is by no means stable with respect to the critical contingencies that officials assess in arriving at their varied dispositions, we should emphasize that "it is difficult to determine the exact motivation of a decision-maker when he selects one alternative over another" (Cole, 1975:237). As Cole argues, an agent of the criminal justice system probably cannot specify what variables caused him to make a particular decision, and it may very well be impossible to ferret out the interactive effects an infinite variety of variables have on each other as well as on decisions.

FIRST APPEARANCE

After arrest defendants are to be taken before a judicial magistrate without unnecessary delay for their first court appearance. Although there is considerable variation between jurisdictions, the first court appearance is termed "initial appearance" when the case is a felony or serious misdemeanor, such as breaking and entering, many narcotics offenses, robbery, aggravated assault, murder, and rape. The first appearance is termed "arraignment on the warrant" when the case is a minor misdemeanor or summary offense,[1] such as a city-ordinance violation, a breach of the peace, intoxication, petty larceny, resisting arrest, and simple assault. The different labels are more than cosmetic; they denote fundamental differences in importance.

The initial appearance signifies that the offense is serious enough to be within the trial jurisdiction of the trial courts. Consequently, the initial appearance has a limited purpose. The defendant is informed of the charges lodged against him, advised of his constitutional rights, asked whether he wishes a preliminary hearing (at least in those jurisdictions employing this method of screening), and released on certain conditions pending trial or remanded to jail.

The arraignment on the warrant signifies that the offense is within the trial jurisdiction of the magistrate. Consequently, on a first appearance, the defendant is not only informed of the charges against him and advised of his constitutional rights but he is also asked to plead to those charges. In many cases, defendants plead guilty, and the magistrate responds by immediately passing sentence.[2]

In some cases, though, defendants plead not guilty; two alternatives are available to magistrates in such an event. For summary offense cases, if the arresting officer and complainant are present in court, and the defendant does not wish defense counsel, the magistrate may try the case and pass sentence immediately on conviction. If the arresting officer and complainant are absent from the proceeding, or the defendant wishes an attorney, the magistrate will set a date for trial and release the defendant on certain conditions pending trial. Nonsummary cases in the trial jurisdiction of the magistrate may be set for trial by jury or by the bench, whichever the defendant chooses,

---

[1] A "summary" trial is one a jury is not authorized to hear. Thus, in some cases, such as vagrancy and intoxication, trial is by the magistrate alone. The defendant cannot request and receive a jury trial.

[2] It has generally been found that defendants arraigned on a warrant plead guilty far more often than do defendants processed for serious misdemeanors and felonies at their arraignment. Mileski (1971:493) reports that in one lower court, 89 percent of minor misdemeanants plead guilty while 68 percent of serious misdemeanants and 44 percent of felons plead guilty. In Detroit, for 1965, 60 percent of minor misdemeanants plead guilty while "very few" felons plead guilty at their arraignments; much the same pattern was found for Baltimore (President's Commission on Law Enforcement and Administration of Justice, 1967: 133–35).

or may be sent to specialized court (Subin, 1966:69). Trial is by the magistrate in the context of the magistrate's court. We may find at this singular stage, then, the entire adjudicatory process: arraignment, trial, and sentencing.

It may be useful to portray the basic context in which the initial appearance is made. The following description is of the Recorder's Court in Detroit:

> *The Decorum in Early Sessions.* The Recorder's Court courtrooms are large and well lighted; the area between the bench and the bar is about 40 square feet, and there is seating capacity for about 120 spectators. But the proceedings in the early sessions branch make no attempt to retain the dignity that could be captured from the physical setting. The spectator's area is often overflowing, and many persons must stand along the side and back walls. The area before the bench is similarly crowded. Police witnesses, sometimes numbering as many as 35 or 40, crowd into the jury box and mingle about in a corner. Clerks, court reporters, and jail and probation personnel wander

Courtrooms are often crowded and confusing during first appearances. (© *1976 by Fred W. McDarrah*)

about, seemingly impervious to the proceedings, and the five or six court policemen do little to correct the disorganization.

At the beginning of each session there were a great many police officers present because the arresting officer must be present in all cases, even drunk offenses. All of the policemen were sworn in a group at the beginning of each session; some who were smoking in the room behind the bench poked their arms out into the courtroom at that time. Prisoners were brought up in groups of 25 from a detention room in the basement and placed in a dimly lighted cubicle outside the courtroom. When their cases were ready to be heard, they formed a line stretching from the side door of the courtroom to the front of the bench. Each prisoner was led forward as his name was called by a court policeman.

When a defendant decided to plead not guilty, all of the other prisoners had to stand during the trial. As each group was processed, another group was brought up to take its place. The cases were called in a regular order: first the drunks, vagrants, and beggars, then the prostitutes, then the gamblers and loiterers, and finally the petty larceny and simple assault cases. The principal value in the process appeared to be speed rather than deliberation; sentence followed conviction, and case followed case without pause. And the noise and confusion was so great that the judge often had to raise his voice to be heard by the prisoner (President's Commission on Law Enforcement and Administration of Justice, 1967:134).

The Apprising of Rights

By law, magistrates must inform defendants not only of the charges levied against them and their consequences[3] but also of their various constitutional rights: they have the right to remain silent, to have defense counsel, if indigent, to have defense counsel present, and to have bail. Investigations of urban lower courts suggest that instead of being apprised of their rights in a one-to-one encounter with the magistrate, defendants are generally not informed of their rights or are informed in groups (President's Commission on Law Enforcement and Administration of Justice, 1967:30). In observations of the Baltimore lower court, the President's Task Force found that although one magistrate took great care to advise petty misdemeanor defendants of their rights, "in the cases observed no defendant was told that he had a right to remain silent or that the court would appoint a lawyer to represent him if he were indigent" (1967:124). In observations of the Detroit lower court, the Task Force found that when petty misdemeanor defendants wished

---

[3] Some report a failure on the part of magistrates to inform petty misdemeanants, not suspected felons, of the charges and conviction consequences. (See Foote, 1956.)

PROSECUTION AND ADJUDICATION

trial, "the judge made no effort to explain the proceedings to the defendants or to tell them of their right to cross-examine the prosecution's witnesses or of their right to remain silent" (1967:134). In the misdemeanor courts of Los Angeles, Nutter (1962:216) states that "defendants are informed of their constitutional rights in crowds ranging from 100 to 300 defendants" (cf. Mileski, 1971:481–86).

The Presence of Defense Counsel

By law, criminal defendants have the right to have a defense attorney present, whether privately retained or provided by the state, at their first court appearance. As one may expect, there is considerable variation between jurisdictions regarding the presence of counsel at initial proceedings. In some courts there is widespread participation of defense attorneys at the first appearance. In Washington, D.C., for example, Subin (1966:68–69) found that while defendants are almost always without counsel, the court readily appoints one usually from a group of attorneys regularly present in court awaiting assignment. But, examining the Detroit Recorder's Court, Warren (1971) found that attorneys for the defense were present in only 22 percent of the cases. Research has indicated, however, that defendants charged with more serious crimes are represented more often than those charged with petty misdemeanors (cf. President's Commission on Law Enforcement and Administration of Justice, 1967:121–38). In the lower court studied by Mileski (1971:487), it was found that "only 12 percent of the misdemeanor suspects were professionally represented, whereas over five times as many (64 percent) of the felony suspects were represented." For those charged with petty misdemeanors the first court appearance typically signals the last court appearance. For defendants to ask for counsel is only to prolong, if not worsen in their estimation, sentencing by the magistrate; for the court to provide counsel would place undue strain on courtroom routine and processing. Conversely, for those defendants charged with more serious offenses which are to be tried in trial courts or by the magistrate at other times, the provision of counsel may be more desirable. But in both types of cases defense counsel can provide a host of services to defendants at their first appearance. For felony and serious misdemeanor cases, counsel can lobby for reasonable bail, explain confusing constitutional rights to clients, and guard them against self-incrimination. For minor misdemeanors and summary offenses, both of which are triable by the magistrate, counsel can guard clients from faulty application of the statutes, cross-examine whatever witnesses comprise the state's cases, and, of great importance, bring to the court's attention particular circumstances that mitigate charges (Kalodner, 1956:342; Mileski, 1971:491–92).

The Decision on Preliminary Hearing

As we shall see, a preliminary hearing serves to protect defendants from unfounded accusations by the state. Its basic function, as Karlen (1967:145) points out, is "to provide an early and independent check on the initial decision of the police or the district attorney to prosecute." At the hearing, the prosecution need only produce enough evidence to support a prima facie case that there is sufficient evidence to believe a crime was committed and that the defendant was responsible for it.

The hearing also provides the defense with an opportunity to examine the state's case, namely, its physical evidence and witnesses, and gives the state an opportunity to evaluate its evidence and witnesses under trial-like conditions.

Unlike the English system of criminal justice, in the American system a defendant can waive the preliminary hearing where he is entitled to have one. Although the preliminary hearing is considered, theoretically at least, a critical stage in processing, we generally find a high rate of waivers of such hearings at the first appearance. Subin (1966:83–84) reports that in Washington, D.C., about half of all defendants entitled to a preliminary hearing waive this step. Miller (1969:84) found even higher rates. In Kansas, 66 percent of the defendants waived the hearing; in Wisconsin, some 90 percent; and, in Michigan, 72 percent. Why defendants waive the preliminary depends on one or more conditions related to the particular case as well as the particular courthouse community.

First, courtroom personnel may persuade defendants to waive the hearing. Miller (1969:120–22) found several cases in which such officials as police, bailiffs, and court clerks suggested to confused defendants without counsel that they should waive the hearing. The following is a case in point:

Illustration No. 1: Two women were charged with embezzling $2,500 from a department store. They entered the court without counsel for their initial appearance. As they stood before the bench they were asked whether they waived a preliminary examination. The judge repeated the question and then said, "Now, again, ladies, I ask you, what do you want to do? Do you want me to adjourn this matter so you can think it over, or do you want to waive the preliminary examination. It's up to you." The women shrugged their shoulders and, looking about in a somewhat puzzled fashion, said, "Gee, we don't know what to do." The judge replied, "Well, I'll give you a few minutes to discuss this among yourselves and then you let me know if you want to waive the preliminary hearing." As the judge left the bench, a police detective said to the defendants, "Look, there is nothing to this procedure. Take my word for it, just waive. When the judge gets back, tell him you waive." A court attendant said, "Look, we're not trying to influence you in this matter whatsoever, but the best thing for you to do is to waive the preliminary examination. When the judge comes back, tell him you waive the preliminary examination." When the judge returned, the women waived the preliminary (Miller, 1969:120).

Second, ignorance of the option may lead the defendant to waive the preliminary. In some jurisdictions, if a defendant is asked to plead and he pleads guilty, this is taken as a waiver of the hearing.

Third, even when the defendant is represented, the hearing may be waived out of tactical consideration, as when the defense believes the prosecution will reward such cooperation by reducing the charge or sentence, or disclose critical pieces of the state's case without the necessity of formal motions for disclosure or discovery.

Fourth, preliminary hearings are waived when they are considered a waste of time and energy. If the defendant intends to plead guilty anyway, the hearing simply costs time that could be spent more profitably in working off a sentence. Furthermore, discovery of the state's case may be best accomplished through informal discussions with the prosecutor. Indeed, to establish a prima facie case the prosecutor need only present part of all the state's evidence. Consequently, the defense may discover more through informal than formal procedures.

Lastly, "there are certain situations in which a preliminary examination is a genuine detriment to the defendant" (Miller, 1969:129), especially if he is privately represented or must take time off work to attend the hearing. But it can also be quite harmful to him when particularly grisly details of the offense are publicly released.

In some cases, though, even when the defense waives the preliminary hearing, the prosecution may move for a hearing. This is done in cases in which the state wishes to get on the official record the testimony of witnesses who are uncooperative, in poor health, or may change their accounts as a result of monetary enticement or physical coercion.

Pretrial Release

If there is no final disposition of a case at the first appearance (a situation found in felony and some misdemeanor cases), what is done with the defendant is of signal importance. Specifically, the magistrate has one of three alternatives: (1) He can remand the defendant to jail without the possibility of release. (2) He can release the defendant on his own recognizance. Sometimes called a "personal bond," the defendant is released on the explicit promise that he will appear at later proceedings. (3) He can release the defendant on bail or a bail bond, wherein the defendant promises to pay the state a specified sum of money ("cash bond") or piece of real estate ("property bond") if he fails to appear at later proceedings. Not only is this the principal method of securing release pending further proceedings; it is also the typical course of action taken by magistrates. As we shall see, each alternative has significant ramifications for both the defendant and his case.

Bail

The modern institution of pretrial release on the condition of bail evolved from a practice that originated in pre-Norman England, and was refined through English common law (*Yale Law Journal,* 1961; Goldfarb, 1965:23, 93).[4] Although the original justification for releasing defendants on bail pending trial is not altogether certain, it probably developed "from the medieval sheriff's desire to avoid the costly and troublesome burden of personal responsibility for those in his charge" (*Yale Law Journal,* 1961:966). In time, though, additional purposes took supremacy.

Our system of criminal justice is based on the presumption of innocence, conviction before punishment, and the right of the accused to remain at liberty for purposes of preparing a defense. To imprison defendants pending trial and conviction is troublesome for the state in terms of cost, but, more importantly, it runs counter to the ideological framework upon which our adversarial system of justice is constructed. If this set of basic presumptions were given full effect, we expect all defendants (save those involved in capital offenses) would be unconditionally released pending trial. Yet, unconditional release of defendants has been and continues to be rare. This is so because the state must ensure that defendants will reappear at later proceedings. Supposedly, posting a financial security serves as a deterrent to flight. It is assumed that defendants will hesitate to flee even the most dismal of cases because they have a financial stake in reappearing. However, this assumption may be incorrect. It may be inapplicable to a large number of defendants who pay a commercial bail bondsman to provide the court with the necessary security. The bondsman's fee, which is generally between 5 and 15 percent of total security posted, is not returned to defendants when they appear at later proceedings, since it is payment for a service rendered. Consequently, the state does not have a financial hold over such defendants. In addition, those persons who are capable of posting large amounts of bail money may not be deterred from flight because the amount may be petty in comparison to the day-to-day earnings they realize from crime. For such defendants, flight and consequent forfeiture of bail brings little if any financial discomfort.

Landes (1974) found that the relationship between bail and reappearance is very weak. Take, for example, two groups of defendants matched on the severity of charge, prior felony record, and probation or parole status. One group secures release on high bail, and the other

---

[4] This discussion is based in part on *Yale Law Journal* (1961:966–69) and Goldfarb (1965:23–31, 93–95).

secures release on low bail. We cannot accurately predict on the basis of the financial stake alone which will have the greatest number of disappearances and which will have the greatest number of reappearances. Other conditions must be considered.

In his investigation of bail administration in New York City, Foote (1958:706) found that a defendant is generally a good bail risk if he "has lived and worked in the same community for a number of years and is currently employed, if he has a family with whom he lives, and if he belongs to a church, or to a union or to other social organizations." Thus, it appears that one's job, family, and friends tie him to the community and to reappearance more than the financial stake of bail.

The possibility of successful flight has probably diminished over the years, thereby precluding a number of attempts. In the past, one could find anonymity among drifters, and persecuted minorities, and establish an identity that was difficult to verify. Today, new methods of identification, and information networks such as the National Crime Information Center and the System for Electronic Analysis and Retrieval of Criminal Histories, make it very difficult for criminals to disguise their identity. Therefore, the claim that bail serves as an effective deterrent to flight is questionable.

Beyond the failure of bail to ensure a defendant's reappearance lies a further problem. The bail system does not enable all people to gain pretrial freedom. In a national survey of bail administration, Silverstein (1966:621, 626–27, 630–31) found that while the proportion of defendants unable to make bail varied from place to place, it is often quite substantial:

Large counties	
Cook (Chicago)	75
Hennepin (Minneapolis)	71
Jefferson (Louisville)	30
Philadelphia (Philadelphia)	14
Small counties	
Brown (Kansas)	93
Rutland (Vermont)	83
Putnam (Missouri)	36
Anchorage (Alaska)	28
Catoosa (Georgia)	6

Two conditions, operative in most jurisdictions, account for these figures. First, most of the defendants are indigent and cannot afford the services of a commercial bail bondsman, let alone the money for posting the entire bail amount. In New York, for example, Foote (1958:707) found that 51 percent of all defendants could not furnish bail, either personally, through relatives, or through bondsmen. He found that 28 percent of those defendants required to make $500 bail failed to do so; 38 percent could not make $1000 bail; 45 percent could not afford $1500 bail; 63 percent could not afford $2500 bail; and, 75 percent failed to make $5000 bail. Because the bondsman's fee was 5 percent of the total bail amount, these figures indicate that 25 percent of those required to make $500 bail could not even muster up $25 for the bondsman.

Second, magistrates can effectively deny release to defendants by one of several means. They may simply deny bail and remand the defendant to jail until the case is successfully appealed, or they may set bail at such an exorbitant amount that the defendant is, in effect, denied release. What amount is "necessary" for ensuring reappearance, of course, cannot be specified in so many words. Nor can it be proven beyond a shadow of a doubt that some specific amount is more than is necessary to ensure reappearance. Consequently, the authorized discretion to set bail at whatever amount the magistrate deems necessary for reappearance can be used as a tool for denying bail to all but the very rich.

If bail generally fails to achieve its lawful goals, why does it persist as an institutionalized practice? Why aren't "good risks" simply set free? Many researchers have pointed out that bail setting has come to serve a number of other, albeit dubious, ends. Although these ends vary over time and space, we can identify several recurrent ones.

First, magistrates may set bail at an inordinate level in order to give defendants a taste of jail. Here the idea is to exact a measure of pain and suffering prior to conviction. A magistrate may feel that several nights in jail are worth the proverbial pound of cure. A night in jail may drive home the bitter consequences of crime. Goldfarb (1965:47) provides a good illustration from a report of the New York City Bar Association:

> *The Court:* . . . Now, these boys, as I see it, have gone
> beyond children's acts. This is something that shows they don't
> know when to stop. Maybe a couple of days in jail may solve the
> problem. I don't know. I'm going to set $5,000 bail on each.
> Now, I'm leaving word that if a bond is presented, the matter is
> to be sent back to me, and I'll tell you right now, if they put up
> $5,000 bail, I'll make it $10,000, and if they put up ten, I'll
> make it $25,000. I want these boys to spend one or two nights in
> jail. Maybe that is the answer.

One of the most prominent ends served by either denying bail altogether or setting it beyond what the defendant can afford is that of preventive detention. This practice has been used against a rather broad class of defendants, including political demonstrators, subversives, professional criminals, and hard-core recidivists. Decisions to deny or set bail at high amounts may be perceived as "self-defense." Defendants may commit additional crimes in order to pay their attorney's fee, or they may seek out witnesses or complainants to persuade them to drop or alter their testimony.

Defendants may be characterized as threats to the political order. In the civil rights demonstrations of the early 1960s, for example, it was not uncommon for magistrates to set bail at $15,000 or more in cases of trespassing, inciting an insurrection, and curfew violations. In a study of the legal processing of rioters in the Detroit civil disturbance of 1967, the *Michigan Law Review* found that the most recurrent bail amounts were $10,000 and $25,000. The reasoning behind such figures was clear:

> The initial decision on the bond policy seems to have been made by Wayne County Prosecutor William Cahalan some time during the first Sunday of the disorder. He publicly stated that his office would ask for bonds of $10,000 and up on all persons arrested "so that even though they had not been adjudged guilty, we would eliminate the danger of returning some of those who had caused the riot to the street during the time of stress" (1968:1549).

We should note another function of bail which explains why it is set despite its apparent inability to ensure the appearance of the accused at trial. Suffet (1966) found in New York City that bail is a way to "diffuse the responsibility for the release of the defendant" (1966:-305). The criminal court is not, as we saw in Chapter 2, a "closed system." That is, the operation of the court takes into account the community in which it is embedded. Consequently, "judges are sensitive to public pressure, and some will admit they fear an adverse reaction from the press should they make a mistake" (Suffet, 1965:329). As Judge Francis Morrissey states:

> If you let [the defendant] out on personal recognizance, with the understanding that he would reappear again for trial, and then the victim was badly injured, or killed, you have the problem of the newspapers coming in a very critical vein. You have to have some security for the particular judge (Suffet, 1965:330).

Setting bail instead of release on recognizance serves to diffuse the responsibility of release with the bondsman, defendant's family, and the defendant himself. Bail, then, functions as a buffer between courthouse officials and a potentially troublesome public.

The Bail-Setting Process

The amount of bail is not supposed to exceed that necessary to ensure the reappearance of the accused. What amount will magistrates think ensures reappearance of a defendant? In most states the procedural law declares that the amount of bail should be set with regard to

Most of the people in jail have not been convicted of a crime and are there because they cannot afford bail. (© *1976 by Fred W. McDarrah*)

the seriousness of the offense and the defendant's prior record. Yet there are no precise written standards and formulas for setting bail. It is not unusual, then, to find that magistrates develop their own criteria for determining bail amounts and, more generally, the pretrial status of defendants. Consequently, in his investigation of Detroit's Recorder's Court, McIntyre (1967:121) found considerable variation in judges' policies:

> Judge A. sets very high bond in all cases where a revolver or dangerous weapon is involved in the alleged crime. He also sets unusually high bond in purse-snatching cases, because several years ago his wife was the victim of this type of crime. Judges B. and C. set very low bonds on gambling and frequently will put a defendant on his own recognizance. Neither of these judges will go over $500 in a gambling case. Judge D. never fixes a personal bond (own recognizance) against a defendant. Judge E. is generally low in the bonds he fixes in most felony cases, but fixes very high bonds in gambling cases, sometimes as high as $5,000. Judge E. is also noted for his very thorough inquiry into the facts and circumstances of the case before he fixes bond. He follows this procedure to a greater degree than any of the other judges.

Similarly, Neubauer (1974:146–54) found substantial variation among magistrates in their bail setting for similar types of cases. Is variation in policies an indication that bail setting is haphazard, or a function of the magistrate's whim? Not at all. Several studies have shown that magistrates consciously attend to particular kinds of information in setting bail. Of the information that could be used in setting bail, magistrates generally pay special attention to the seriousness of the offense charged, the defendant's prior record, and, in some cases, the defendant's ties to the community (Suffet, 1966; McIntyre, 1967: 120–22; Neubauer, 1974:148–54; Landes, 1974). Several generalizations seem warranted on the basis of available evidence. First, the greater the seriousness of the offense charged, the more likely bail will be high, or the defendant detained. Suffet (1966) found that when defendants were charged with serious offenses, such as murder, forcible rape, and robbery, their average bail was $3,220. Those charged with minor offenses, such as assault, burglary, carrying a deadly weapon, larceny, and statutory rape, were released on an average bail of $1,010. While 22 percent of those charged with minor offenses received release on their own recognizance (R.O.R.), only 2 percent of those charged with major offenses received a comparable disposition (see Table 5–1).

Second, if a defendant has a history of arrests, his bail is likely to be high, or preventive detention is imposed, especially so if his previous arrests were for felonies or violence. Suffet (1966) found that when

TABLE 5-1 BAIL DISPOSITION ACCORDING TO CHARGE, PRIOR RECORD, AND PRESENCE OF R.O.R. RECOMMENDATION

MAJOR CHARGE[a]

Disposition	PRIOR RECORD[b]				NO PRIOR RECORD			
	No R.O.R. recommended		R.O.R. recommended		No R.O.R. recommended		R.O.R. recommended	
	%	No.	%	No.	%	No.	%	No.
Remand	10.0	18	c	1	14.0	8	0.0	
Bail	89.4	161	c	2	82.5	47	87.5	7
(Average amount)	($3,863)				($3,085)		($2,714)	
R.O.R.	0.6	1			3.5	2	12.5	1
	100.0	180		3	100.0	57	100.0	8

MINOR CHARGE

Disposition	PRIOR RECORD				NO PRIOR RECORD			
	No R.O.R. recommended		R.O.R. recommended		No R.O.R. recommended		R.O.R. recommended	
	%	No.	%	No.	%	No.	%	No.
Remand	4.1	29	1.3	1	2.2	6	0.6	1
Bail	92.1	654	49.4	39	68.3	185	21.2	35
(Average amount)	($1,587)		($732)		($961)		($760)	
R.O.R.	3.8	27	49.4	39	29.5	80	78.2	129
	100.0	710	100.1	79	100.0	271	100.0	165

[a] Major charges include homicide, forcible rape, and robbery. Minor charges include assault, burglary, carrying a deadly weapon, forgery, larceny, receiving stolen property, and statutory rape.
[b] Prior record includes any record of arrest, conviction, or prison. No prior record means never previously arrested.
[c] Number of cases is too small for percentage to be meaningful.

suspects had a prior record of arrests they were released on an average bail of $2061. Yet, those with no prior record were released on an average bail of $1880. While there is no real difference in Suffet's sample between the two categories in the proportion remanded to jail, there is a difference in their release on recognizance. While 7 percent of those with a prior record receive R.O.R., 42 percent of those without a prior record receive R.O.R. (see Table 5–1).

Third, some magistrates attend to the defendant's ties to the community—permanent residence, stable occupation, family and friends, and the like—in determining his pretrial status and conditions of release. While definitive data on the issue are few, we can hypothesize that if the defendant has stable ties to the community, the more likely the setting of low bail or imposition of R.O.R. Conversely, if the defendant is a transient member of the community with few stable ties, the more likely the setting of high bail or imposition of detention. For Detroit, McIntyre found that "in estimating the probability of reappearance following release on bail, many judges emphasize the work record of the defendant, including his length of employment in his present job. Other judges place more stress on his marital and family status and whether the defendant owns property" (1967:121). Whatever the particular emphasis, strong roots in the community is reason for minimal bail or personal bonds. Certain kinds of defendants are released on minimal bail because magistrates assume their criminality itself ties them to the community:

> A numbers writer was brought before the magistrate for the setting of bail. Without inquiry into any of the specific facts of this case, the magistrate immediately set an extremely low bail. "These people would not leave town if an atomic bomb were dropped on it," he remarked (Remington et al., 1969:493).

Of course, a variety of other pieces of information may be attended to in the setting of bail. Magistrates may, for example, consider the defendant's chances of conviction, given the available evidence. If it appears that the defendant will surely be convicted given the state's case, then bail may be set inordinately high. Or, if it appears that the chances of conviction are quite low, bail may be minimal or the defendant may receive R.O.R. The following is a case in point:

> A Negro defendant was brought before the magistrate, charged with felonious assault. The magistrate examined the case report and noted that the assault was on another Negro and that there was no other witnesses. He released the defendant on his own recognizance. "There'll probably be no

conviction here," he noted. "In these cases the victim usually 'forgets' what happened. I don't think the defendant will run" (Remington et al., 1969:493).

To be sure, the significance of this kind of information varies from area to area, for the evidence of the case is not always available to the magistrate at the initial appearance.

It may appear as though we have worked ourselves into a paradox. On the one hand, we have noted that there is considerable variation in magistrates' pretrial dispositions and bail-setting practices. This included variation in the amount of money set for bail as well as in the conditions of release for similar kinds of cases. On the other hand, we have noted that particular values of certain kinds of variables account for certain patterns of pretrial disposition. Hence, there seems to be inconsistency in our argument. For several reasons this observation is not as problematic as it may seem. First, magistrates do not interpret concrete cues similarly. What one may define as serious may not be defined as serious by another. A magistrate in a rural court, for example, may define the use of marijuana as a serious offense demanding considerable concern. A magistrate in a metropolitan court, in contrast, may view the use of marijuana as a normal, petty offense demanding only a reprimand. What one may define as a serious prior arrest record may be defined as a petty arrest record by another.

What constitutes a defendant's ties to the community is also subject to differential interpretation. McIntyre (1967:121), for example, observed that while some magistrates look at the defendant's work record in assessing his ties to the community, others look at the defendant's family life and property holdings. As we saw earlier, how an act, a defendant's prior record, and his ties to the community are interpreted makes a difference in what a magistrate will deem appropriate conditions of pretrial release. If this is so, then magistrates holding different cognitive perspectives will interpret similar kinds of cues differently and arrive at different decisions on the conditions of release.

While we certainly find variation in policies and practices *among* magistrates, we also find that they change their own policies from time to time. No one's cognitive perspective is fixed or stable; rather, it continually changes to meet the needs of a changing world. Consequently, what a magistrate sees as a petty offense today he may see as a serious one tomorrow. Magistrate X, for example, routinely set bail for those charged with gambling at a minimal amount, for he viewed gambling as a petty vice in which even his friends occasionally engaged. But, after his brother was beaten severely by a loanshark for failure to pay a gambling debt, and he himself was cheated by an astute gambler, his conception of gambling charged from its being a petty vice to a serious offense. Subsequently he set very high bail for those charged with gambling, a practice consistent with his reinterpretation of the event.

Second, while a magistrate determines the pretrial status of a defendant and the specific conditions of release, his decision is influenced by the police, the prosecutor, the defense counsel, and the commercial bondsman. These courtroom actors influence his decisions in at least two interrelated ways. For one, they may control the flow of information needed for decision-making. The court's workload and other practical obstacles typically preclude a magistrate from cultivating extensive and detailed information regarding defendants' community ties, the character and seriousness of prior records, and the circumstances and seriousness of the present offenses. Instead, information is typically confined to that supplied by various courthouse actors—police reports about offenses, defendants' "rap" sheets, and information the police, prosecutor, defendant, and defense attorney proffer. Often, such information is incomplete. At the time of his initial appearance, for example, a defendant charged with burglary may not have a prior record of arrests. Categorizing the accused as a "first offender," the magistrate may release the defendant on $1000 bail. However, during the interim between the initial appearance and the preliminary hearing, if the police discover that the defendant has a substantial record of burglary in other cities, the magistrate may reclassify the accused as a "professional" needing substantially higher bail. Obviously, if the prior record were introduced at the initial appearance, a different disposition would have been made. McIntyre's investigation of the Detroit Recorder's Court substantiated the fact that information about prior arrests supplied by policemen can make a difference in the judge's decision:

> Two defendants were arraigned for unarmed robbery and pleaded not guilty. The arresting officer advised the court of the defendants' previous records and that a "hold" was now on for them. The officer also stated that these individuals were known criminal characters. The judge set bond at $3000 each (1967:120).

Various bail projects, such as the Manhattan Bail Project, have had the effect of providing the magistrate with detailed information regarding the defendant's ties to the community. In the Manhattan Bail Project, Suffet (1966) found that magistrates will generally follow suit when R.O.R. is recommended by the project's staff. Even in those cases where magistrates decide against R.O.R. when it is recommended, bail amounts are generally kept quite low regardless of prior record.

Various courthouse actors can influence the magistrate by making known and justifying their positions toward pretrial release. More than simply providing information (as when the police inform the magistrate of the defendant's arrest record), persons may attempt to influence the magistrate's disposition so that it favors their own position. The police, for example, may ask the magistrate to jail a defendant because they believe he will try to destroy evidence in the case or intimidate key witnesses.

The prosecutor and the defense attorney are the most influential courthouse actors. As one might expect, the prosecutor typically asks that bail be set at a high level, and the defense typically asks that bond be reasonable or based on personal recognizance. Both also make somewhat different interpretations of the available information. While the prosecutor may emphasize the defendant's prior record of serious offenses, his potential dangerousness to the community, or the seriousness of the charge, the defense attorney may focus on the defendant's community ties, on his upstanding character, or on the hardships of excessive bail on his client. Of the two attorneys, the prosecutor is certainly the most influential in the bail-setting process. As Silverstein (1966:623) pointed out, in many areas the prosecutor, in effect, sets the bail. He makes recommendations to the magistrate, and the magistrate almost always follows the suggestions.[5]

In a detailed study of the issue, Suffet (1966) found several interesting things. First, in those situations in which a prosecutor or defense counsel made a bail suggestion and did not encounter opposition from the other, the magistrate disagreed with the prosecutor's recommendation in 9 percent of the cases while disagreeing with the defense counsel in 24 percent of the cases. Second, in those situations in which a prosecutor or the defense counsel made a bail suggestion and encountered opposition from the other, the magistrate sided with the prosecutor in 80 percent of the cases while siding with the defense in less than 50 percent of the cases. These patterns are accentuated when we find that the prosecutor makes far more suggestions than the defense attorney. Thus, when the defense attorney does make a bail suggestion, he has less chance of making it stick than does the prosecutor. This is so, Suffet (1966:328) argues, because the prosecutor and magistrate share a similar perspective toward the pretrial management of defendants. They subscribe to similar bail-setting standards, disagree far less often than either disagrees with the defense attorney, and show the same concern for the interests of the dominant public. While the magistrate is theoretically a neutral "referee" between the state and the accused, he is, like the prosecutor, an officer of the state who, among other

---

[5] In an investigation of the lower court in Washington, D.C., Subin (1966:79) also noted that magistrates usually defer to the prosecutor's bail recommendations.

things, strives to maintain control of defendants pending trial (Dill, 1975). Like the prosecutor, he has a stake in the pretrial movements and activities of defendants. If a defendant flees, commits a serious crime, or destroys valuable evidence while his case is pending trial, this may be taken by those in power, as well as the community at large, as a sign of the magistrate's incompetence. Consequently, to avoid potential outrage and the loss of tenure, he diffuses responsibility for the defendant by opting for bail instead of personal bond, and high instead of low bail.

It should be noted that in many cases the decision regarding pretrial release is actually a two-step process. First, as we have discussed, the judicial magistrate decides between remanding the defendant to jail, releasing him on his own recognizance, or releasing him on bail. In most cases, he selects the last alternative. Furthermore, in most of these cases, defendants must rely on the services of a commercial bail bondsman; that is, most cannot afford the financial security required by the court and must hire a bondsman to post the security. Thus, a second phase involves the bondsman's decision to either post bail for a defendant or simply let him remain in jail pending trial. In his investigation of such decisions by bondsmen, Dill (1975:660–62) found that bondsmen make their decisions on the basis of information other than that routinely employed by magistrates. He found that the character and seriousness of the offense and the possibility that the defendant will commit additional crimes if released were not significant variables. Rather, the critical variable is the assessment of whether the defendant can afford to pay the premium required for the service. For example, those who have substantial financial holdings that can be placed as collateral or have strong ties to the local community will be more readily defined as good risks and bailed out. Those who already owe a considerable amount of money to the bondsman for past services or have few if any ties to the community will be more readily defined as poor risks and refused bail. The point, then, is that the bondsman can oftentimes veto or ratify the official decisions of magistrates. This situation has been subject to recent scrutiny among students of the criminal justice process, and to a certain extent has been circumvented by recent reform measures to be discussed shortly.

The Fatefulness of Pretrial Release

We have alluded to the fatefulness of the magistrate's decision on the defendant's pretrial release at several points, a decision that is consequential for both the government and the accused. That is, it makes a difference, on a number of dimensions, to the government and the accused whether the accused is detained pending trial—either through preventive detention or the inability to make high bail—or secures release—either through R.O.R. or bail.

It is consequential to the government whether the defendant secures release or is detained. Detention itself is quite costly. Freed and Wald (1964:39–45) found that in New York City in 1962, "58,458 persons spent an average of 30 days apiece in pretrial detention, or a total of 1,775,778 jail days, at a cost to the city of $6.25 per day, or over $10,000,000 per year." The construction of new jail facilities to accommodate the potential or real overcrowding of current facilities by those awaiting trial is also costly.

Releasing a sizable proportion of defendants who now while away the hours in jail would mean a significant savings to the government. The San Francisco Commission on Crime (1970:145), for example, estimated that the O.R. [Own Recognizance] Bail Project wherein defendants with strong community ties were released on their own recognizance saved the city over a million dollars per year. Specifically, 425 defendants who ordinarily would have remained in jail because they could not make bail were released each day.

It is consequential to the defendant whether he secures release or is detained. For one, detention is itself punishing since the jail setting is far from pleasant. As LaFave (1965:497) observes:

> The conditions in most American detention facilities are deplorable. Many are overcrowded, lack proper sanitation equipment, lack recreational facilities, and indiscriminately mix together offenders of all kinds. Persons awaiting trial ordinarily are not confined separately from or treated differently than those who have been convicted. Conditions in these jails are far inferior to those in state penitentiaries.

Indeed, unlike most prisons, jails are designed for little more than detention. The *1972 Survey of Inmates of Local Jails,* published in May 1975, reported that most jails in the United States are small. Approximately 2901 of the nations 3921 jails have fewer than 21 inmates. In these small facilities approximately 2750 have no medical facility, and about three-fifths have no recreational equipment at all. In some, the recreational facilities consist of only a record player or a radio. Recreational opportunities were totally lacking in 1308 small and 187 medium-sized jails (medium-sized jails contain 21 to 249 inmates). In three large jails in Georgia, Indiana, and Ohio, over 250 inmates have no recreational facilities or equipment at all. Few jails have social and rehabilitative programs, and even when such programs, funded by the federal government, do exist, only a fraction of the jail population have access to them.

The unpleasantness of the jail setting is compounded by the typical length of detention. Freed and Wald (1964:39–45) found that there is variation between areas in the average length of detention, but it was often over a month. Those awaiting trial in the District of Columbia jail in 1962, for example, averaged 51 days. In Philadelphia, in 1964, the average was 26 days, in Los Angeles, 78 days. Smaller communities witness even longer periods of detention. In 1961 in Passaic, New Jersey, for example, grand jury defendants spent an average of four months in jail. It is no wonder, then, that defendants, such as the following, interpret detention as unjust chastisement:

> [Detention is] punishment before trial. I did six months—about 5½ months that I never get back in my life. How can they give me that back? They can't give it back! (Casper, 1972:68)

Second, pretrial detention takes its toll on the economic well-being of the defendant and his family. He either loses his job or whatever income he would ordinarily receive during the period of detention if he were free (Wald, 1964:632). If the defendant's income is cut off, it may prevent him from hiring a private attorney, since most criminal attorneys require a fee in advance. And, because a sizable number of defendants are close to indigence, it is likely that the sudden loss of income will cause their families to seek outside financial support from friends or the government.

Third, a detained defendant cannot prepare as effectively for his defense as can a released defendant. As suggested above, those who are detained and not working are generally unable to afford a private attorney or finance an adequate pretrial investigation of their cases. Moreover, as Foote aptly points out:

> The defendant's opportunity to obtain witnesses in his behalf is also greatly restricted. His attorney is confronted with the task of seeking out and conferring with witnesses without the benefit of the defendant's presence. Situations arise where acquaintances of the defendant are reluctant to divulge information which might be helpful in the preparation of the case when questioned by the attorney, a total stranger (1958:725).

Detention may also impede the attorney's contacts with his client. Conversely, defendants who are free on bail or their own recognizance can make good use of their liberty. As Wald (1964:633) observes, defendants are available on a twenty-four-hour basis to consult with counsel. Defendants may be able to locate and persuade witnesses to testify, and they can assist in tracking down crucial evidential leads.

Fourth, the probabilities of conviction and prison sentence are greater for those detained pending trial than for those who secure their release (Foote, 1954; Ares et al., 1963; Rankin, 1964; Single, 1972;

Landes, 1974). Ares et al. (1963) found significant differences in New York City between detained defendants and those at liberty in the proportions convicted and not convicted. As reported in Table 5–2, those who secure their release pending trial are either acquitted or dismissed significantly more often than those held in jail. In a follow-up investigation, Rankin (1964) found much the same pattern. While 47 percent of those at liberty were acquitted or dismissed, only 27 percent of those detained were not convicted. Similarly, in his investigation of pretrial detention in New York City, Single (1972) found that 50 percent of those who secured their release were not convicted while only 20 percent of the detained defendants received the same disposition.

Detained defendants are also more likely to receive a prison sentence than those defendants who are at liberty. Again, Ares et al. (1963) found significant differences in the severity of sentence between those in detention and those at liberty (see Table 5–3). Single (1972) discovered a similar relationship in his investigation. Although the difference was not as great as other jurisdictions for those convicted of felonies, 21 percent of the detained defendants received no jail sentence while 27 percent of those released received no sentence. More significantly 29 percent of the detainees received a short sentence while only 10 percent of those released received a short sentence; and 26 percent of the detainees received a long sentence while 4 percent of those released received a long sentence. For those convicted of misdemeanors, 12 percent of the detainees received no jail and 35 percent of those

TABLE 5–2   CASE DISPOSITIONS BY JAIL STATUS AND CHARGE

	AT LIBERTY			DETAINED		
Charge	Percent Convicted[a]	Percent Not Convicted[b]	Total Cases	Percent Convicted[a]	Percent Not Convicted[b]	Total Cases
Assault[c]	23	77	126	59	41	128
Grand Larceny[c]	43	57	96	72	28	156
Robbery	51	49	35	58	42	100
Dangerous[d] Weapons[d]	43	57	23	57	43	21
Narcotics[d]	52	48	33	38	62	42
Sex Crimes[e]	10	90	49	14	86	28
Others[e]	30	70	47	78	22	23
			409			490

[a] By trial or plea.
[b] By dismissal or acquittal.
[c] Difference significant at .001 level.
[d] Difference significant at .05 level.
[e] Too few cases to compute Chi Square.

released received no jail; 65 percent of the detainees were given a short sentence while only 19 percent of those released were given a short sentence; and 7 percent of the detainees were given a long sentence while none of the released received a long sentence.

While the relationship between pretrial status and the case disposition and sentence is clearcut, its explanation is debatable. On the one hand, Landes (1974) argues that even though the size of the bail bond, hence the probability of detention, is directly related to severity of sentence, the relationship is not a causal relationship. Rather, the size of the bond, hence detention, and severity of sentence are outcomes of the magistrate's prior assessment of the defendant's chances of conviction and the degree of punishment the defendant warrants:

. . . at the time bond is set judges are forecasting the likelihood of the defendant's conviction and the appropriate

TABLE 5–3   SENTENCE BY JAIL STATUS AND CHARGE

Charge on Which Guilt Determined	AT LIBERTY			DETAINED		
	Suspended Sentence Percent[a]	Prison Percent	Total Cases	Suspended Sentence Percent	Prison Percent	Total Cases
Felonies						
Assault	42	58	26	6	94	73
Dangerous Weapons[d]	30	70	10	9	91	11
Larceny[c]	42	48	40	7	93	107
Narcotics	41	59	17	–	100	16
Robbery	22	78	18	3	97	59
Others	43	56	14	12	88	17
			125			283
Misdemeanors[b]						
Assault[c]	63	32	134	13	87	159
Dangerous Weapons	49	51	65	25	75	43
Larceny[c]	72	28	193	14	86	357
			392			559

[a] With/without probation.
[b] Although all charges enter the court as felonies, the charges are often reduced and defendants plead guilty to misdemeanors.
[c] Significant at .001 level.
[d] Significant at .05 level.

punishment. The forecast is then incorporated into the bail-setting process by setting bond at relatively higher values for persons expected to receive more severe sentences, and setting bond at relatively lower values for persons likely to receive negligible sentences (Landes, 1974:336).

While detention itself may have an adverse effect on sentence, it is the magistrate's forecast that is crucial.

On the other hand, a number of researchers preceding Landes have found that detention has an adverse effect on case disposition and sentencing independent of other conditions. In an extensive investigation of the issue, Rankin (1964) examined the causal relationship between previous record, bail amount, type of counsel, family integration, and employment status of defendants to the case disposition and sentencing for different kinds of offenses. The first three variables showed a pronounced relationship with both detention and case disposition, but the latter two did not. Yet, when the values of these variables were held constant, the difference between probabilities of conviction-acquittal and prison–no prison remained. That is, irrespective of the severity of charge, prior record, type of counsel, and bail amount, those released fared considerably better than those detained. This is especially interesting given Landes' argument that a magistrate's decision that a defendant will probably be convicted and punished severely brings, independently of one another, the setting of high bail, the finding of guilt, and a prison sentence. Rankin, however, found that even when the bail amount is held constant, controlling in part the magistrate's assessment of chances of conviction and severe sentence, the difference between detained and released defendants in case disposition is considerable.

Examining the issue from a somewhat different angle, Ares et al. (1963) found that detention itself has an adverse effect on the defendant's case. Defendants who shared a number of characteristics relevant to bail-setting were divided into two groups. Those in the "parole" group were recommended for R.O.R. and magistrates usually followed the recommendation. Those in the "control" group, although qualifying for R.O.R., were not recommended, and many were consequently detained pending trial. The researchers found a significant difference between the released and detained defendants in case disposition and sentencing.

Why detention itself brings such an adverse effect on the defendant's case is easy to understand. As Goffman (1969) argues, in a "strategic" interchange actors seek to control the information others receive of them in order to maximize their particular ends. They attempt to manage impressions of themselves that further their particular ends. In a court of law, those detained are hampered in their efforts to present impressions of themselves as "noncriminal" and "respectable" members of the community who are not deserving of conviction and punishment. As Skolnick (1967:65) observes:

> . . . there is usually a difference in manner and appearance of defendants who make bail and those who do not. The man in jail enters the courtroom under guard, from the jail entrance. His hair has been cut by a jail barber, and he often wears the clothes he was arrested in. By contrast, the "civilian" defendant usually makes a neat appearance, and enters the court from the spectator's seats, emerging from the ranks of the public.

Because people act in terms of their definitions of situations, it is not surprising that judges and juries act toward those appearing respectable as if they are respectable and those appearing criminal as if they are criminal.

Bail Reform

In recent years there have been various reforms in the administration of pretrial release. Perhaps the most notable of these measures, and certainly the most inspirational, was the Manhattan Bail Project in New York City. Conducted by the Vera Institute, New York University School of Law, and the Institute of Judicial Administration, the project operated from 1961 to 1964 until it was taken over by New York City. This was a release on recognizance project. If defendants appeared to be good risks, R.O.R. recommendations would be made. In 60 percent of the cases recommended for R.O.R., magistrates released the defendants without bail; magistrates released defendants on their own recognizance in only 14 percent of the cases where R.O.R. was not recommended by the project staff made up of law students from New York University. The success of the project was extraordinary. There were four times as many defendants released pending trial than before, and significantly fewer defendants failed to reappear than those who actually secured their release by posting bail. This program demonstrated that many defendants can be released without a financial stake.

Similar programs have been established in other cities across the nation. In San Francisco's project, established in 1964, the staff met with all arrested defendants, secured information relating to their community ties, and asked for three references. If a defendant met certain established criteria, a recommendation for R.O.R. was made to the magistrate. Magistrates followed such recommendations in 85 percent of the cases. Once defendants were released, the staff maintained contact with them. Defendants were notified before they were to appear in court of the time and place for appearance, and they were offered assistance in securing defense counsel. Between 1964 and 1968, this project obtained the release of 6377 persons, only one percent of whom failed to reappear. Compared to the 6 percent of those released on bail who failed to reappear, this project brought freedom to many defendants as well as a higher rate of reappearance.

Another type of bail reform has provided some indigent defendants with release without assistance of commercial bail bondsmen. To gain freedom for large numbers of defendants, as well as eliminate the commercial bondsman and the sometimes dubious practices he brings to the process, several states and the federal courts have developed a system of court-administered bail. In this system, if a defendant is not released on his own recognizance, then he is released after posting with the *court* 10 percent of the total bail amount. If he appears in court at the designated time, 90 percent of the money posted is returned and the remainder is kept for administrative purposes. Thus, if bail is set at $1000, the defendant need only deposit $100 with the court to secure release. When his case is finished, the court will return $90 and keep the remaining $10 (Neubauer, 1974:147).

Another type of bail reform has developed from an alternate system of bringing defendants to trial. The underlying idea for this type is that for many offenses the arrest and confinement of suspected perpetrators pending the setting of bail is simply not warranted. Not only is such a procedure costly and time consuming to the government but it also imposes severe hardships on defendants. Consequently, several states, such as California and Washington, and the federal courts have replaced the widespread use of arrest and confinement of those charged with misdemeanors and ordinance violations with the "summons" and "citation" (President's Commission on Law Enforcement and Administration of Justice, 1967:40–41). The summons is an order issued by a judicial officer upon complaint of the prosecutor to appear in court at a designated time. The citation, in contrast, is an on-the-spot order issued by a police officer to appear in court at a designated time. In both procedures, defendants are saved the bitter experiences of arrest, booking, initial appearance, and the posting of bail or detention in jail, and the government is saved the time and cost of proceeding and housing defendants.

A related, albeit less inclusive reform measure has been to cut down the period of confinement pending the setting of bail. It is common today to find the operation of "stationhouse" bail:

> Some formal arrangement between police and courts is required so that the police can act on behalf of a judge in releasing persons pending their initial appearance in court. Usually, judges have chosen to deal with this by providing the

police with a "bail schedule" which, in effect, authorizes them to release designated categories of offenders who are capable of posting a specified amount of bail (Goldstein, 1968:16).

There are, of course, problems with this procedure. It does little to circumvent the real shortcomings of the traditional mode of pretrial release. As with the traditional practice, those unable to post the bond set by the bail schedule must either seek out a bondsman or spend their days in jail.

Thus far, we have noted reform measures revolving about inequities in the bail system. There is, however, another side to the issue. Arguments that certain categories of defendants commit additional crimes while awaiting trial, routinely flee when released, or pose extreme danger to the community have led to proposals for "preventive detention." To be sure, for decades magistrates have detained those considered dangerous or unreliable by setting bail beyond their financial reach. But, as Kaplan (1973:320) aptly points out, "Once we develop a substitute for the bail system which guarantees the defendant's appearance at trial without imprisoning the indigent, we will no longer be able to imprison the dangerous ones along with the much larger number who are not dangerous." As a consequence, we find over the recent years proposals (such as the now-abandoned New York Criminal Procedure Law) and a statute (the District of Columbia Court Reform

Skid-row drunks are sentenced at their first appearance and their entire court appearance averages only a few seconds. (*Michael Lloyd Carlebach*)

Act of 1970) that authorize the detention without bail of defendants who are considered likely to commit additional crimes or flee if released. While detainees are to be expediently tried, so as to minimize the punishing effects of confinement, a number of serious questions remain. How does one know that a particular defendant will commit additional crimes or flee if released? Can the behavioral sciences equip judicial practitioners with such predictive techniques? Does the chance of predictive error outweigh the punishing effects of preventive detention? And is preventive detention constitutionally valid?

THE PRELIMINARY HEARING AND THE GRAND JURY PROCEEDING

As we have seen, most defendants charged with petty offenses are arraigned, adjudicated, and sentenced at their first court appearance. For those charged with more serious offenses, the first court appearance signals the occasion in which rights are read, counsel is appointed to indigents, and, most importantly, decisions on pretrial release are made. The next stage in the court process that these defendants encounter, either directly or indirectly, is the occasion in which the prosecution seeks a formal charge or accusation.

While a complaint or warrant is typically used to institute the prosecution of those charged with petty offenses, before any defendant can stand trial on a felony charge he must be formally accused. (To be sure, the nature of the formal charging process varies from one jurisdiction to another.) Generally, a formal accusation is produced in one of two principal ways. First, based on statements made by the police, the prosecutor can prepare a formal charging document termed an *information*, and test it before a magistrate in a preliminary hearing. This method is common in most states west of the Mississippi River. Second, the prosecutor can appear before a grand jury and ask them to return a formal accusation against a defendant. The formal charging document produced in this proceeding is the *indictment*. This method is very common in most states east of the Mississippi River.[6]

In this section our goal is to examine the official role of the magistrate and grand jury in deciding on the formal charge. In other words, our primary concern is with the preliminary hearing and the grand jury proceeding.

Although the preliminary hearing and grand jury proceeding

---

[6] Some areas use a mixture of both methods. In Chicago, for example, defendants charged with serious offenses first encounter a preliminary hearing, which is part of their initial court appearance, and are then bound over to the grand jury who makes the formal accusation (cf. McIntyre, 1968). Neubauer (1974: 131–34) found a similar routine in Prairie City.

vary in many respects, both events similarly serve at least one function. They are the occasions for an independent check on the police or on a prosecutor's decision to hold a defendant for trial on a particular charge or set of charges. Whether charges are tested before a magistrate in a preliminary hearing or before a grand jury, both evaluate the state's evidence and the probability of conviction and decide whether further court processing is warranted. Ideally these official proceedings filter out weak and unfounded cases from the court process. How this screening is accomplished and its effectiveness (as well as what kinds of cases are routinely screened from further processing) are questions that will draw our attention.

The Preliminary Hearing

The preliminary hearing typically requires the participation of at least four actors—the assistant prosecuting attorney, the defendant, or if secured or appointed, his counsel, their respective witnesses, and the magistrate.

The preliminary hearing is usually swift and routine.[7] Generally, the transaction begins when the assistant prosecutor asks the first state's witness, usually an arresting officer, to summarize "the circumstances leading up to the arrest, what a search of the defendant produced, and the results of any laboratory analysis of physical evidence" (McIntyre, 1968:473). Civilian witnesses, victims or complainants, may then be asked to recount the details of the event. "The victim states what transpired and identifies the defendant as the offender" (McIntyre, 1968:473). For the most part, testimony is given in an informal fashion without much interruption except when witnesses omit critical elements of the case. At the conclusion of the prosecutor's questioning the defense may cross-examine witnesses.

Cross-examination is aimed typically at challenging witnesses' identification of the defendant as the offender and assertions that a crime had in fact been committed. After the prosecutor rests the state's case, the defense (the defendant or his counsel) may present a modest case generally restricted to the defendant's (and witnesses', if any) account of the event. Witnesses for the defense are subject to cross-examination by the prosecutor, as are the state's witnesses by the defense.

At the conclusion of the hearing, the magistrate, before whom the prosecutor and defense performed, will announce immediately one of four dispositions. (1) The defendant can be bound over to a felony trial court on felony charges (either the original or some other felony charge). (2) He can be bound over to the grand jury for consideration

---

[7] The following characterization of the proceeding is drawn from McIntyre (1968:473–74).

and formal charging. (3) He can be released by dismissal or by a qualified discharge. (4) Or he can be brought to trial on misdemeanor instead of felony charges and disposed of either by an immediate plea of guilty or transfer to another lower court for trial.

We must emphasize that the preliminary hearing is not an inquiry aimed at determining the defendant's guilt or innocence. This decision is reserved for trial. Rather, the inquiry is aimed at establishing "probable cause," that is, whether there is *sufficient evidence* for any reasonable and prudent person to believe a crime has been committed, and whether the defendant committed it.

Of course, what is sufficient evidence to establish probable cause is problematic. McIntyre (1967:124) underlines the inherent ambiguity of sufficient evidence and probable cause in his investigation of the Detroit criminal justice process. "The amount of proof required to establish that a crime has been committed, and that probable cause exists to believe the defendant committed it, varies with the demands of each judge of Recorder's Court." For instance,

> Judge A insists that there be some direct evidence (and not by inference) that a defendant charged with breaking and entering *intended* to commit a specific crime at the time. A case was recalled where a man and wife returned from a movie one night and found a strange man in their living room. The stranger simply pushed his way past the man and his wife, explaining that he was in the wrong house. An investigation of the house revealed nothing stolen or disturbed. The judge refused to bind this man over for trial on the charge of breaking and entering because there was no proof that he intended to commit a crime after he had entered the house. The assistant prosecutor felt sure that the other judges of Recorder's Court would have inferred from the presence of the defendant in the complainant's house that he had intent to commit breaking and entering (McIntyre, 1967:124, emphasis added).

A second, yet generally unstated function of the preliminary hearing is to screen those cases for which further felony processing is considered unjust and inappropriate even though the evidence is more than sufficient. In some cases, the magistrate may reduce the charge to a misdemeanor, a charge that brings a punishment more in line with what the defendant deserves. In other cases, the magistrate may dismiss the case, feeling punishment is simply not warranted. McIntyre provides an interesting example:

> An elderly man was charged with indecent liberties with a child. The public defender was assigned. Before the parties could

be sworn the mother of the girl—the chief complaining witness —volunteered that she did not wish to prosecute. The state's attorney interceded, saying that he would object to a withdrawal of the case since the complaint had been made, the defendant arrested, and several witnesses, all present, had been put to the bother of appearing in court. The judge asked for a summary of the case. The state's attorney said that five witnesses saw the defendant put his hand under the eight-year-old girl's dress. In answers to questions put to her by the court, the mother said the defendant was a neighbor and no damage was done to the child. At this point the court suggested that a plea to a lesser offense appeared to be called for. This was objected to by the public defender who emphasized the harmlessness of the old man and the desire of the state's witness to let the matter drop. The judge said: "All right then, I'll give it an SOL [Stricken Off with Leave to Reinstate]. Take the defendant home." Two of the state's witnesses took the old man by the arm and led him out of the courtroom (1968:480).

Thus, just as the prosecutor strives to do justice by fitting the punishment routinely administered on conviction for certain charges with the particular case, so too does the magistrate in the preliminary hearing strive to fit the case with what he deems it deserves (Remington et al., 1969:523–24).

Third, for those defendants who want to contest the charges at trial, the preliminary hearing provides an occasion to discover the state's case against them. In the course of establishing probable cause, the prosecutor must reveal, in part at least, the evidence he holds against the defendant. Furthermore, the defense is given the opportunity to cross-examine the state's witnesses. Out of this interchange the defense may secure a reasonably good idea of what they are up against, and prepare their case accordingly.

Finally, the preliminary hearing serves the prosecutor by providing an occasion in which he can firm up and strengthen his case. The preliminary is an arena within which the prosecutor can "test" his witnesses. That is, by observing their performance under questioning and cross-examination, he can evaluate how credible they may appear to a trial judge or jury, and adjust their future performance to suit his needs.

While the preliminary hearing could be a useful device for screening out the weak and unfounded cases and those cases for which further processing is unjust, is it an "effective" tool? Is it in fact more than a ritual in which the magistrate simply "rubber stamps" the prosecutor's decision to prosecute on particular charges? Do magistrates carefully weed out those cases that should not be tried as felonies or tried at all? Are a lot of cases screened out (as demonstrated by high rates of dismissals and reductions to misdemeanors)?

In some areas, magistrates make only a cursory examination of the cases, and almost all defendants are bound over for further felony processing. In others, magistrates seriously scrutinize cases, and a large proportion of defendants are dismissed or brought to trial on misdemeanor charges. The variation in general effectiveness of the hearing can be accounted for in terms of two generalizations.

First, in those jurisdictions where the prosecution actively screens cases before the hearing, the hearing itself will be little more than a rubber stamp of the prosecution's decision to prosecute on particular charges and there will be a high rate of bindovers. In other words, where the prosecution has decided that the defendant did not commit the crime in question, the event performed was not a real crime, the defendant does not "deserve" punishment which conviction on the charge normally entails, and he actively screens such cases prior to the hearing, then the hearing does little more than affirm those cases he does bring. This course of action was found in a number of recent studies. In his examination of the Washington D.C. criminal justice process, Subin (1966:83–84) found a high rate of waivers of the hearing and a low rate of dismissals at the hearing. This is so, Subin argues, because "most cases have been rather thoroughly screened before presentation in court as felonies . . . ." McIntyre (1968:124) found that of all the preliminary examinations he observed in Detroit Recorder's

Waiting outside of the courtroom before a preliminary hearing are witnesses and police officers who will provide the state's evidence. (© *1976 by Fred W. McDarrah*)

Court, "not one resulted in a dismissal of the case." The assistant prosecuting attorney permanently assigned to the court of the examining magistrate "estimated that approximately 95 percent of all preliminary examinations result in the defendant's being bound over for trial. The reason for this is the rather extensive screening process through which the case has passed before" (McIntyre, 1968:124).

Examining the preliminary hearing in Kansas, Wisconsin, and Michigan, Miller (1970:64–136) found a high rate of waivers of the hearing and a high rate of bindovers at the preliminary, ranging from 83 to 90 percent of all cases. His explanation of this pattern is clear: "Because of excellent police and prosecutor screening, there is little need for further evidence-sufficiency screening by the time most cases reach the preliminary examination stage" (Miller, 1969:78). Similarly, Neubauer (1974:131) found in Prairie City that when cases are reviewed prior to the filing of charges, the intended functions of the hearing are eclipsed.

Second, in those jurisdictions where the prosecution does *not* actively screen cases before the hearing, the hearing itself serves as a critical occasion in which cases are seriously scrutinized by the magistrate and prosecutor, and there will be a higher rate of dismissals and charge reductions. In other words, the hearing will serve much the same function as prosecutorial screening at the earlier charging stage. Chicago's criminal justice process best exemplifies this generalization. In that city, there is very little screening of felony cases by the prosecution prior to the preliminary hearing, having the major responsibility for initiating the criminal charge. This is normally the prosecution's job elsewhere. And "in deciding to invoke the criminal process the police are guided by the strong belief that analysis of the evidence, both in regard to its admissibility and its weight, are matters that should be decided by higher authority" (McIntyre, 1968:469). Consequently, the hearing is the forum in which substantial screening occurs. As McIntyre has indicated (1968:475), over 40 percent of all felony cases brought to the preliminary hearing are discharged, either by outright release or by a qualified release (including the SOL—Strike Off with Leave to Reinstate). In addition, between 16 and 40 percent of all cases were reduced to misdemeanors (the number of cases reduced to misdemeanors by a *nolle prosequi* is not clear).[8]

In examining these comparatively high rates of charge reductions and discharges, McIntyre (1968) argues that the examining magistrates assess each case on several dimensions. First, assuming a "crime" has been committed, is it serious enough to warrant felony

---

[8] A *nolle prosequi* is a formal entry on the court record in which the prosecutor states he will not proceed any further with a case, some of its counts, or some of its defendants.

processing? In other words, does the defendant pose a genuine threat to the community? Often the answer is no. Under certain circumstances some crimes are defined as less serious than the charge suggests and punishment contingent upon conviction warrants. Domestic quarrels among ghetto dwellers, barroom brawls between drinking partners, and burglaries and robberies among skid-row drunks are more often defined as "private matters" to which leniency is more apt than serious crimes deserving substantial punishment.

Second, can the state be reasonably assured of a conviction should the case go to trial? Is the case factually and legally "strong"? If the answer is no, discharge is likely. For example, if eyewitnesses fail to make an adequate identification of the defendant, if the complainant or witness has poor credibility, if the police made an illegal search or failed to inform the defendant of his rights, and the like, then discharge is likely.

Thus, the preliminary hearing in Chicago, unlike that in Washington, D.C., Detroit, and Prairie City, is an effective screening stage in the criminal justice process. In effect, it functions very much like the prosecutor's charging decision in other jurisdictions, except that it is principally performed by the magistrate. In Chicago we find substantial screening of cases. Screening decisions, furthermore, are based on assessments of factual and legal guilt of "real" crime, whether defendants deserve conviction and punishment for their crimes, and, if so, what degree of punishment is appropriate. Consequently, those that are bound over to the grand jury as felonies are cases in which "(1) the evidence is strong enough to sustain a conviction, and (2) the defendant's conduct and background indicate that he is a genuine threat to society" (McIntyre, 1968:481).

The Grand Jury Proceeding

A second formal procedure for screening certain defendants from further processing and bringing others to trial is the grand jury proceeding, which England abolished in 1933. While all of the states retain the grand jury in theory, about half use it as a major procedure for screening certain felony defendants and bringing others to trial. In the remainder of the states, the information–preliminary hearing is the major procedure for screening and formal accusation, and the grand jury is used only on special occasions.

There are many ways grand jurors are selected. In most jurisdictions they are picked from voter lists by judges. Whatever particular selection technique is used, several studies indicate that blacks, Mexican Americans, the young, and the poor are generally excluded from serving. Carp comments on jury selection in Texas:

Texas grants jury commissioners almost unlimited discretion to compile a small list of names from which the grand jury is impaneled. Very little is known about these jury commissioners and about the criteria by which these officers of the court select prospective grand jurors. However, preliminary evidence suggests, first, that a significant disproportion of the commissioners are upper-middle class Anglo-Saxon white males; and, second, that the commissioners tend to select as grand jurors their friends and neighbors who have similar socioeconomic characteristics (1975:826).

In our contemporary criminal justice process, the functions of the grand jury proceeding are much broader than those of the preliminary hearing. To be sure, the grand jury, like the preliminary hearing, is supposed to serve as a forum in which criminal cases are examined, evaluated, and disposed of. But, unlike the preliminary hearing, the grand jury proceeding is not confined only to considering criminal cases brought to its attention by the prosecution. Although its scope of investigation varies, it is empowered to inquire into the operations of local government, such as that of the county treasury, city planning, public parks, and the criminal court system. Like the police, the grand jury is empowered to *investigate* crime and identify those suspected of committing crime within its jurisdiction. Certainly one of its most celebrated functions is that of investigating corruption and misconduct by local officials. As Richard Younger (1963:208) observes:

Under extraordinary circumstances grand juries proved that they could, if necessary, unseat an entire municipal administration and, using their power of indictment, take over and run a city in the name of the people. In both Minneapolis and San Francisco, grand juries governed the city for long periods while they rooted out crime and corruption. City bosses, corrupt officials, and racketeering criminals learned to fear the grand jury inquest, but to citizens seeking to rid their city of corruption, it was often the only hope.

Similarly, grand juries in recent years have gained some notoriety through their investigations of illegal campaign contributions, the burglarization and bugging of political-party campaign headquarters, and the bribery of public officials by multinational corporations.

While the grand jury has the right to investigate crime, whether this be in government, politics, big business, or on the street, it is seldom invoked.

In our vast, urban society [grand] jurors have no intimate knowledge of the goings-on within the community. They must depend, therefore, upon the facts and knowledge brought before them from extrinsic sources. They have no investigative skills or resources of their own and thus the task of gathering facts must be performed for them by the professional investigative agencies at their disposal—law enforcement agencies (Campbell, 1973:178).

Thus, the grand jury proceeding primarily serves as an occasion in which a body of facts is developed, ordered, and presented by a prosecuting attorney; a decision is made; and a formal document either charging the suspect or calling for no prosecution is prepared.

There is also dissimilarity between the grand jury proceeding and the preliminary hearing with respect to their dynamics. The grand jury proceeding usually requires the active participation of the prosecuting attorney, his witnesses, and the grand jurors. Unlike the preliminary hearing, a judicial magistrate is not needed, all screening and bindover decisions being performed by the lay jury.

The grand jury is most often convened at the request of the court or prosecutor. Once the jury is assembled, the prosecutor's task, as in the preliminary hearing, is to demonstrate to it that there exists "probable cause" to believe that a crime has been committed and that the suspect is guilty of committing it. To this end, he presents briefly the state's case. As in the preliminary hearing, he may call upon the arresting police officer, the victim, and other key witnesses to answer questions regarding the event and identity of the suspected offender. The facts presented to the jury as evidence, however, need not conform to the rules of trial admissibility. That is, the jury can hear and make decisions on facts that may not be admissible at trial, such as hearsay and illegally seized evidence. Furthermore, the proceeding is nonadversarial: the defendant and his counsel are not allowed access to the proceeding, and, consequently, they can neither cross-examine and challenge the state's witnesses nor can they present their side of the case.[9]

Once the prosecutor concludes his presentation, he will generally ask the jury to return an indictment on a particular charge or set of charges. After a short period of deliberation, in which the grand jury is to consider the strength of the state's case and whether further processing of the case is just, it may return a "true bill" or indictment on some or all of the charges, or a "no bill" or refusal to indict.

---

[9] Under certain circumstances, such as when the defense can demonstrate a particularized need, the defense may be shown all or part of the minutes of the proceeding.

Theoretically, the grand jury proceeding functions as a check on the decisions of criminal justice officials to prosecute. It has been argued, however, that the grand jury proceeding is an ineffective screen, that the jury often "rubber stamps" the prosecutor's requests. Over forty years ago, Wayne Morse (1931) found, in his survey of grand jury operations in twenty-one states, that the grand jury honored the prosecutor's request for an indictment in all but 5 percent of the cases. Similarly, a survey conducted by the *Columbia Law Review* (1966) reports that grand jury rejections of prosecutors' requests for an indictment ranged from 1 to 10 percent. In their investigation of the Cook County Grand Jury, Oaks and Lehman (1968:44) found that "of the 4239 indictments sought in 1964, the grand jury returned true bills in 3862 instances and no-bills in 377 (9 percent)." In Prairie City, Neubauer (1974:134) reports that grand juries rarely return no-bills. During 1968, for example, the grand jury returned only four no-bills, and only one of these was in direct opposition to the prosecutor's request.

Winnowing from further processing approximately 5 to 10 percent of the cases may give the impression that the jury opposes prosecuting a substantial number of cases. This is not so. In those cases where the grand jury refuses to indict, their decision is often in accordance with the prosecutor's wishes.[10] For example, a prosecutor may not want to prosecute a case because he has weak evidence or because he feels further processing is unjust. However, he may confront substantial pressure from the news media and powerful community groups to prosecute the case and exact the proverbial pound of flesh (Campbell, 1973:178).

Many no-bills made by the grand jury may not reflect any real screening of cases. For example:

> At preliminary hearing, a defendant may be bound over on several charges. If these charges arose from "the same act or on two or more acts which are part of the same comprehensive transaction" (such as assault, kidnapping, and murder combination), the Code of Criminal Procedure allows them to be embodied in a single indictment with multiple counts. The defendant, meanwhile, has been held by the jailor on three separate mittimi [warrants of commitment to prison], one for

---

[10] In some cases, the prosecutor may make his position against further processing known explicitly. Other times, he may make his position known implicitly: "If the prosecutor does not believe a case is strong, he can and sometimes does convey this subtly to the jury. To quote one assistant, the grand jurors "get the feeling when we're not pressing a case real hard." One does not have to be overt to communicate to the grand jurors what you think of a case" (Neubauer, 1974:134).

each charge. To extinguish the two surplus mittimi, the grand jury enters a no-bill on two of the charges (Oaks and Lehman, 1967:45).

In this situation, then, a no-bill reflects a change in the record-keeping devices rather than careful screening.

Explanations of the rubber-stamp nature of the grand jury proceeding have taken several forms, but all essentially make the same point: the prosecutor *controls* the information on which the grand jury is to base its decision, and, hence, exerts enormous control over the decision itself (Lemert, 1945; Antell, 1965; Campbell, 1973; Neubauer, 1974:133–34; Johnston, 1974). As we have seen, the proceeding is nonadversarial. The defense can neither challenge the state's case nor present to the jury an alternate case. The jurors hear only the prosecutor's case. Furthermore, although the jury, through its foreman, is supposed to conduct the proceeding, the transaction is under the effective control and direction of the prosecutor:

> The prosecutor selects which witnesses the grand jury will subpoena, what evidence it will hear, which documents it will examine, and which suspected criminal violations it will consider. It is the prosecutor who will explain and construe the myriad of laws that the grand jury is charged to enforce. Moreover, this representative of the executive branch of government will also instruct the jury as to the quantum of proof necessary to justify an indictment (Campbell, 1973:177).

In his investigation of Los Angeles County grand juries, for example, Lemert (1945:755) found that the majority of the seventeen juries he studied were closely controlled by the district attorney. They were dependent on the prosecutor for the substantive and legal information pertinent to the cases under investigation as well as for secretarial, investigational, and interrogating personnel and services. He also found that prosecutors could not only persuade the juries to pursue certain public "whipping boys" but also they could block or squash other, sometimes independent investigations by concealing incriminating information. In a more recent investigation, Neubauer (1974:134) found that in Prairie City "the grand jury is the creature of the state's attorney." The prosecutor decides which cases the jury will hear, which witnesses will testify, and the general tone of the transaction. In effect, the jury will indict those persons the prosecutor wants indicted, and will not indict those he does not wish to proceed against. The point, then, is that the prosecutor controls what the jurors see and hear so as to receive findings consistent with his dispositions toward cases.

Some argue, however, that the ineffectiveness of the grand jury proceeding is not as obvious as it may seem. First, we would expect a high rate of true bills from the grand jury. Before a case reaches the grand jury proceeding, it has already been scrutinized and passed on for further processing by the arresting police officer, perhaps his superior, and the prosecutor and judicial magistrate or both. Each of these officials has decided, in preceding stages of the criminal justice process, that the defendant deserves prosecution, conviction, and some type of punishment. Consequently, if a case has survived the screening operations of these officials, the probability is high that some offense has been committed and that the defendant committed it (Johnson, 1974:168). A high indictment rate, then, should be taken as an indication that the police, prosecution, and perhaps lower courts are effectively screening the weak, the unfounded, and those cases for which further processing is unwarranted. Conversely, we would expect a comparatively higher rate of no-bills when the police, prosecution, and lower courts are failing in their screening tasks. Thus, when the grand jury returns a no-bill in opposition to the requests of the prosecutor, in some 1 to 5 percent of the cases, this may reflect some very real screening by the jury.

Second, the grand jury proceeding may be an effective means by which certain kinds of cases can be prosecuted. In California, for example, it was found that the proceeding is an effective means for bringing to trial those who have evaded apprehension and whose statute of limitations would bar any information requiring their presence (*California Law Review,* 1964:116). The proceeding may also be an effective means for prosecuting cases involving political corruption, election fraud, perjury, and the like. If, for political reasons, a prosecutor may be reluctant to tackle such cases on his own, he can avoid ignoring such sensitive cases by using the grand jury as a means of investigating and bringing formal accusations against suspected wrongdoers without taking full responsibility himself. Or, the proceeding may be an effective means for quashing the prosecution of notorious, albeit weak or unfounded cases. The prosecutor may not wish to prosecute a particularly weak or unfounded case, yet does not want to take full responsibility for refusing prosecution because of its notoriety. Consequently, he may shift the burden of responsibility to the jury by having them bring a no-bill. Thus, just as the grand jury proceeding may provide some prosecutors with a tool for oppressing some groups and protecting others, so too may it provide other prosecutors with a smoke screen behind which they can check the government without fear or harrassment.

Third, the proceeding provides an arena in which cases can be scrutinized without exposing the defendant to harsh publicity. Because the proceeding is secret, particularly heinous details of the suspected offense, the character of the accused, and other newsworthy tidbits are not made public. Thus, defendants are not made to suffer the consequences of unfavorable pretrial publicity, such as the loss of employment, divorce, loss of friendships, and difficulty in selecting a favorable jury.

SUMMARY

The criminal justice process does not begin with arrest and immediately advance to trial and, if one is convicted, to prison. We found several decision-making points where critical judgments are made about the fate of defendants that are not included in such simplistic outlines of the criminal justice process. Although the process is more complex than most persons realize, we also found that many critical decisions are made rapidly and on the basis of extralegal considerations or biases of the courthouse community. Persons granted pretrial release, for example, are defendants who appear to be good risks. This, of course, is a discretionary judgment. In most jurisdictions decisions about bail are based on unverified assumptions about a defendant's character.

As in other stages of the criminal justice process, some cases are screened out of the system because the evidence substantiating them is weak. It seems, however, that judgments about legal strength are influenced by informal evaluations of character. Evidence in cases involving citizens who are characterized as "bad guys" may be viewed differently than evidence in cases involving persons who are not negatively evaluated. We suggest, therefore, that the first appearance, grand-jury, and preliminary hearings are best viewed as character assessment proceedings. Those cases screened out are not only weak ones but are also those that involve defendants who do not deserve to be punished.

REFERENCES

ANTELL, MELVIN P.

1965 "The Modern Grand Jury: Benighted Supergovernment," *American Bar Association Journal* 51 (February): 153–56.

ARES, CHARLES E., ANNE RANKIN, AND HERBERT STURZ

1963 "The Manhattan Bail Project: An Interim Report on the Use of Pre-Trial Parole," *New York University Law Review* 38 (January): 67–95.

CAMPBELL, WILLIAM J.
   1973 "Eliminate the Grand Jury," *Journal of Criminal Law and Criminology* 64 (June): 174–82.

CARP, ROBERT A.
   1975 "The Behavior of Grand Juries: Acquiescence or Justice?" *Social Science Quarterly* 55, no. 4 (March): 853–70.

CASPER, JONATHAN D.
   1972 *American Criminal Justice: The Defendant's Perspective.* Englewood Cliffs, N.J.: Prentice-Hall.

COLE, GEORGE F.
   1975 *The American System of Criminal Justice.* North Scituate, Mass.: Duxbury Press.

COMMENT
   1964 "The California Grand Jury: Two Current Problems," *California Law Review* 52 (March): 116–28.

DILL, FORREST
   1975 "Discretion, Exchange, and Social Control: Bail Bondsmen in Criminal Courts," *Law and Society Review* 9 (Summer): 639–74.

FOOTE, CALEB
   1954 "Compelling Appearance in Court: Administration of Bail in Philadelphia," *University of Pennsylvania Law Review* 102 (May): 1035–38.
   1956 "Vagrancy-Type Law and Its Administration," *University of Pennsylvania Law Review* 104 (March): 603–50.
   1958 "A Study of the Administration of Bail in New York City," *University of Pennsylvania Law Review* 106 (March): 685–730.

FREED, DANIEL J., AND PATRICIA WALD
   1964 *Bail in the United States.* Washington, D.C.: National Conference on Bail and Criminal Justice.

GOFFMAN, ERVING
   1969 *Strategic Interaction.* New York: Ballantine.

GOLDFARB, RONALD
   1965 *Ransom: A Critique of the American Bail System.* New York: Harper & Row.

JOHNSON, ROBERT G.
   1974 "The Grand Jury: Prosecutorial Abuse of the Indictment Process," *Journal of Criminal Law and Criminology* 65 (June): 157–69.

KALODNER, HOWARD I.
   1956 "Metropolitan Criminal Courts of First Instance," *Harvard Law Review* 70 (December): 320–49.

KAPLAN, JOHN
   1973 *Criminal Justice: Introductory Cases and Materials.* Mineola, N.Y.: Foundation Press.

KARLEN, DELMAR
  1967 *Anglo-American Criminal Justice.* New York: Oxford University Press.

LAFAVE, WAYNE R.
  1965 *Arrest: The Decision to Take a Suspect into Custody.* Boston: Little, Brown.

LANDES, WILLIAM M.
  1974 "Legality and Reality: Some Evidence on Criminal Procedure," *Journal of Legal Studies* 3 (June): 287–338.

LEMERT, EDWIN M.
  1945 "The Grand Jury as an Agency of Social Control," *American Sociological Review* 10 (December): 751–58.

MC INTYRE, DONALD M.
  1967 *Law Enforcement in the Metropolis.* Chicago: American Bar Association.
  1968 "A Study of Judicial Dominance of the Charging Decision," *Journal of Criminal Law, Criminology and Police Science* 59 (December): 463–90.

MILLER, FRANK W.
  1969 *Prosecution: The Decision to Charge a Suspect with a Crime.* Boston: Little, Brown.

MILESKI, MAUREEN
  1971 "Courtroom Encounters: An Observation Study of a Lower Criminal Court," *Law and Society Review* 5 (May): 473–538.

MORSE, WAYNE L.
  1931 "A Survey of the Grand Jury System," *Oregon Law Review* 10 (February, April, June): 101–60, 217–57, 295–365.

NEUBAUER, DAVID W.
  1974 *Criminal Justice in Middle America.* Morristown, N.J.: General Learning Press.

NOTE
  1961 "Bail: An Ancient Practice Re-examined," *Yale Law Journal* 70 (April): 966–77.

NOTE
  1968 "The Administration of Justice in the Wake of the Detroit Civil Disorder of July 1967," *Michigan Law Review* 66 (May): 1544–1630.

NUTTER, RALPH H.
  1962 "The Quality of Justice in Misdemeanor Arraignment Courts," *Journal of Criminal Law, Criminology and Police Science* 53 (June): 215–19.

OAKS, DALLIN H., AND WARREN LEHMAN
  1968 *A Criminal Justice System and the Indigent: A Study of Chicago and Cook County.* Chicago: University of Chicago Press.

PRESIDENT'S COMMISSION ON LAW ENFORCEMENT AND ADMINISTRATION OF
JUSTICE
    1967   *Task Force Report: The Courts.* Washington, D.C.: Government Printing Office.

RANKIN, ANNE
    1964   "The Effect of Pretrial Detention," *New York University Law Review* 39 (June): 641–55.

REMINGTON, FRANK J., DONALD J. NEWMAN, EDWARD L. KIMBALL, MARYGOLD MELLI, AND HERMAN GOLDSTEIN, EDS.
    1969   *Criminal Justice Administration: Materials and Cases.* Indianapolis, Ind.: Bobbs-Merrill.

SAN FRANCISCO COMMISSION ON CRIME
    1970   *Staff Reports: The Criminal Courts.*

SILVERSTEIN, LEE
    1966   "Bail in the State Courts—A Field Study and Report," *Minnesota Law Review* 50 (March): 621–52.

SINGLE, ERIC W.
    1972   "The Consequences of Pre-Trial Detention," paper presented at the annual meeting of the American Sociological Association, New Orleans.

SKOLNICK, JEROME S.
    1967   "Social Control in the Adversary System," *Journal of Conflict Resolution* 11 (March): 51–70.

SUBIN, HARRY I.
    1966   *Criminal Justice in a Metropolitan Court.* Washington, D.C.: U.S. Department of Justice.

SUFFET, FREDERIC
    1966   "Bail Setting: A Study of Courtroom Interaction," *Crime and Delinquency* 12 (October): 318–31.

U.S. DEPARTMENT OF JUSTICE
    1975   *The Nation's Jails: A Report on the Census of Jails from the 1972 Survey of Local Jails* (May). Washington, D.C.: National Criminal Justice Information and Statistics Service.

WALD, PATRICIA
    1964   "Pretrial Detention and Ultimate Freedom: A Statistical Study," *New York University Law Review* 39 (June): 631–40.

WARREN, DONALD I.
    1971   "Justice in Recorder's Court: An Analysis of Misdemeanor Cases in Detroit." Report prepared for the Equal Justice Council of Detroit.

YOUNGER, RICHARD D.
    1963   *The People's Panel: The Grand Jury in the United States, 1634–1941.* Providence, R.I.: Brown University Press.

SELECTED READINGS

CAMPBELL, WILLIAM J., "Eliminate the Grand Jury," *Journal of Criminal Law and Criminology* 64 (June 1973): 174–82.
A critical examination of the functions of the grand jury in the contemporary system of American criminal justice.

DILL, FORREST, "Discretion, Exchange and Social Control: Bail Bondsmen in Criminal Courts," *Law and Society Review* 9 (Summer 1975): 639–74.
An investigation of the role of the bail bondsman in the criminal court. Dill also explains why a financial bail system has retained its importance in the American system of criminal justice despite efforts to replace it with more equitable arrangements.

MC INTYRE, DONALD M., "A Study of Judicial Dominance of the Charging Decision," *Journal of Criminal Law, Criminology, and Police Science* 59 (December 1968): 463–90.
An investigation of the function and operation of the preliminary hearing in Chicago.

MILESKI, MAUREEN, "Courtroom Encounters: An Observation Study of a Lower Criminal Court," *Law and Society Review* 5 (May 1971): 473–538.
An empirical examination of the lower-court operations in one east coast city, Mileski focuses on the patterns of presence and assignment of defense counsel, apprisal of rights, as well as the adjudication and sentencing of suspects charged with misdemeanors.

SUFFET, FREDERIC, "Bail Setting: A Study of Courtroom Interaction," *Crime and Delinquency* 12 (October 1966): 318–31.
An investigation of the functions of bail and the character of the bail-setting process in Manhattan.

6
ARRAIGNMENT
and PLEA
NEGOTIATION

The arraignment on an indictment or information marks the first appearance of the defendant, charged generally with a felony or serious misdemeanor, before the court to which he has been bound over for trial. In most jurisdictions, the arraignment is the occasion in which the defendant responds to the formal charging document. Although our emphasis in this section is with the arraignment of those brought to trial by an indictment or information, much of what is said is also relevant to the arraignment of suspected petty offenders at their first court appearance.[1]

ARRAIGNMENT

There are several tasks to be performed at the arraignment. When the defendant's case is first called, the presiding or trial judge once again informs the defendant of his rights. For example, he will be told that he has the right to a trial (either jury or bench) and that he

---

[1] The basic difference between the arraignment on the indictment or information and the arraignment on the warrant is that the latter is generally a more cursory and informal transaction in which certain formal requirements are glossed over by the magistrate.

has the right to be represented by an attorney. If the defendant cannot afford to hire a private attorney, the judge will ask him if he wishes the state to provide him with one.

A proportion of all criminal defendants, whether indigent or not, wish to have an attorney represent them. While McIntyre (1967:127) found that defendants seldom waived their right to counsel in Detroit, Silverstein (1965:363) found that between 60 to 90 percent of all defendants in other parts of Michigan waived counsel. Of all felony defendants processed through the U.S. District Courts in 1971, over 11 percent waived their right to representation (Hindelang et al., 1973:122). Newman provides an explanation for defendants' waiver of counsel based on his investigation of court practices in three states:

> Most defendants who are guilty of criminal conduct and willing to plead guilty waive counsel. This is consistent with a common popular conception that the function of counsel is limited to litigation. The defendant who is guilty, knows that he can be convicted, and is willing to plead guilty and get on with sentencing ordinarily sees little advantage in retaining or requesting counsel; in fact, he may see disadvantages, such as unnecessary lawyers' fees if he can afford counsel, or possibly antagonizing the prosecutor or court if counsel is furnished at public expense (1966:46).

It is not uncommon for judges to appoint counsel to indigents or request nonindigents to retain counsel even though the defendants explicitly waive this right. The judge may overrule a defendant's waiver and appoint counsel or suggest the retention of a lawyer (cf. Newman, 1966:50–51, 200–30) when the defendant is charged with a serious, heinous, or notorious crime; when the judge has doubts about the defendant's actual guilt; when there is a severe mandatory sentence contingent upon conviction; or when the defendant appears baffled by what is happening to him.

After the judge informs the defendant of his rights and makes the necessary provisions for defense counsel, he will inform the defendant of the formal charges against him. The judge will then ask him whether he understands the formal charges. In some cases, on review of the defendant's record or from his courtroom behavior, the judge may detect a psychological disorder that precludes the defendant's ability to stand trial. In such instances, the judge may adjourn the proceeding and order psychiatric evaluation:

> A man was arraigned on the charge of armed robbery and carrying a concealed weapon. When the judge briefly informed him of the charges filed against him and requested a plea, the defendant seemed oblivious of the whole situation. He stared at the foot of the judge's bench, grunted inaudible answers to

At an arraignment, defendants enter pleas and are informed of their rights. The great bulk of defendants plead guilty. (*Photo Division, CBS Television Network*)

questions, and had an appearance of being unaware of the world around him. The judge was quick to detect that the defendant was not mentally sound and referred him to the psychiatric clinic for an examination and the matter was adjourned (McIntyre, 1967:128–29).

If the psychiatric examination results in a finding that the defendant is sane and capable of standing trial, he is returned to court for processing. Assuming the defendant is assessed as sane, either by courthouse officials in the course of processing or by court psychiatrists, and he responds that he understands the formal charges, the judge will ask him to enter a plea to the state's charges.

At this point the defense assumes an active role in managing the criminal justice process. The defendant may plead *guilty* to the charges.[2] A plea of not guilty may be explicit or it may be entered by the judge if the defendant "stands mute," that is, refuses to answer the formal accusation.

---

[2] In some states and on the consent of the judge, the defendant may enter a plea of *nolo contendere* or no contest. Such a plea means that while the defendant does not dispute the formal accusation, he does not admit guilt and therefore cannot be held accountable for the offense in a civil proceeding arising from the case. Compared to pleas of guilty and not guilty, a plea of *nolo contendere* is rarely invoked.

When the defendant enters a plea of not guilty or stands mute, the judge will ask him whether he wishes a trial by jury or a trial by bench and will set a date (generally with the assistance of the court clerk) for the trial. At this point, the issue of pretrial release is again considered. If the defendant has been released on bail or on his own recognizance, the judge will probably let him remain "free" unless he encounters arguments by the defense or prosecution opposing the defendant's pretrial status.

When the defendant enters a plea of guilty, the judge is charged with several different tasks. First, he will inform the defendant that in pleading guilty, certain of his rights are relinquished, such as confronting accusers and challenging the state's witnesses. Second, he will inform the defendant of the penalties contingent upon pleading guilty. Judges rarely indicate *their* particular sentencing practices with respect to such crimes. In Michigan, Kansas, and Wisconsin, for example, Newman (1966) found that superior court judges would routinely inform defendants only of maximum sentences permitted by law for their particular crimes, not of the sentences generally administered in such cases. Third, the judge will assess the authenticity of the guilty plea. Ideally, he cannot accept a plea of guilty unless he is assured that it is genuine. Specifically, two questions are at issue: First, is the plea *accurate*—did the defendant in fact commit the particular crime? In short, he must be factually guilty. Second, is the plea *voluntary*—is the defendant expressing his guilt freely and willingly? The plea must not be the product of physical or psychological coercion, deception, or promises of leniency by criminal justice officials.

Generally, judges will decide the plea is voluntary after a verbal interchange with the defendant. The following transcript of an arraignment in a Michigan court illustrates, among other things, the typical character of the judge-defendant interchange vis-à-vis questions of accuracy and voluntariness:

The Court: You are charged in the information filed against you in this court with the crime of breaking and entering in the daytime, two counts. Do you understand what this means?

Defendant: Yes.

The Court: And how do you plead to this charge?

Defendant: Guilty.

The Court: Are you pleading guilty because you actually are guilty?

Defendant: Yes.

The Court: Has the prosecuting attorney, any of the officers of this court, or any other person threatened you or made you any promises or inducements to influence you to plead guilty?

Defendant: No.

The Court: You are pleading guilty freely and voluntarily?

Defendant: Yes.

The Court: Prior to your plea did you understand that you had a constitutional right to a trial by jury and that if you were financially unable to employ counsel that the court would appoint a lawyer for you?

Defendant: Yes.

The Court: You do not want a trial or a lawyer?

Defendant: No, sir.

The Court: You understand that upon accepting your plea of guilty it is my duty to impose sentence on you?

Defendant: I understand.

The Court: And that the penalty provided for daytime breaking and entering might involve a prison term up to five years?

Defendant: Yes.

The Court: Very well, I will accept your plea of guilty and set the date for sentencing three weeks from today, that is, on December 10 (Newman, 1966:7).

Two points need to be made with respect to the judicial determination that a guilty plea is accurate and voluntary. First, what is an "accurate" and "voluntary" plea is not clear. The litany of questions asked by the judge is a dubious method of establishing the legality of a plea. Whether there is a "factual basis" for a plea, for example, can be negotiated, as is demonstrated in the following case (Blumberg, 1967:132–35):

Mr. McManus: (*defendant's attorney*) If your Honor pleases, the defendant John Dukes desires to plead guilty, as charged, in each and every count in the indictment.

The Court: John Dukes, do you wish to plead guilty to the crimes of robbery in the first degree, the first count, grand larceny in the first degree, the second count, assault in the second degree, the third count in the indictment?

Dukes: Yes, I do.

The Court: And are you guilty of the crimes charged therein?

Dukes: Yes.

The Court: Do you admit, by your plea of guilt, that in ———— County, on May 23, 1964, in the vicinity of Texarkana Avenue at 2nd Street, about 4:10 A.M., you unlawfully took certain property owned by Nelson Stanley, having a value of about one hundred seventy dollars, from the person or the presence of

	Nelson Stanley but against his will, by means of force or violence or fear of immediate injury to his person, and were you at the time aided, that is, assisted in the commission of this robbery, by your co-defendants?
Dukes:	No, sir.
The Court:	Did you perpetrate this robbery alone?
Dukes:	Well, I was alone. It was a crowd of fifteen people there, and I went to the crowd of fifteen, and I picked the wallet up off the ground.I went to the defense of the complainant but by me being in the crowd he picked me out.
The Court:	I don't quite understand.
Dukes:	It was only supposed to be ninety dollars involved.
The Court:	I am not concerned about the amount of money involved. I am concerned only about the circumstance under which you got possession of this money. Did you take it by force from the person or the possession of this victim, Nelson Stanley?
Dukes:	No, sir.
The Court:	Did you threaten him?
Dukes:	No, sir.
The Court:	Then I cannot accept a plea to the indictment, Mr. McManus. Do you want to confer with your client?
Dukes:	Somebody else took the wallet. I picked the wallet up.
The Court:	Did this someone else help you in the commission of a robbery on Nelson Stanley? Mr. Dukes, I am not asking you to name anyone. I am asking you whether or not you, either alone or with someone else, acting in concert with you, committed a robbery on Nelson Stanley?
Dukes:	Yes.
The Court:	Now, a moment ago you said you came to his aid, you came to help him. Was that the truth when you made that statement, or were you lying to me?
Dukes:	(No response.)
The Court:	Mr. McManus, I am going to suggest that you confer with your client.
McManus:	*I have conferred, your Honor. You know, sometimes when it comes to this point, they somehow or other gag, so to speak, to use a vulgar expression* [our italics], but what confused him I think was the amount of money. He claims it was ninety dollars.
The Court:	I wouldn't care if it was two dollars. The amount of

	money involved is no element of the crime. I am going to start all over again. I want you to be truthful, do you understand?
Dukes:	Yes, your Honor.
The Court:	Do you want me to take this plea? Do you still wish to plead guilty to the three counts in the indictment?
Dukes:	Yes, sir.
The Court:	That is, robbery in the first degree, grand larceny in the first degree, and assault in the second degree?
Dukes:	Yes, sir.
The Court:	Is that your wish?
Dukes:	That's right.
The Court:	By your plea of guilty, do you admit that on May 23, 1964, at about 4:10 in the morning, in the vicinity of Texarkana Avenue and 2nd Street, you, together with one or more other persons who aided you in the commission of this crime, unlawfully took certain moneys owned by Nelson Stanley from his presence or from his person but against his will, by means of force or violence or by fear of immediate injury to his person?
Dukes:	Yes, sir. Me alone.
The Court:	Now I am going to ask you this question again. Was there another person, one or more persons, who assisted you? I am not asking you to name who they are. I am merely asking you, were you assisted in the commission of this robbery by one or more other persons who were actually present at the time? Now can you answer that question?
Dukes:	Yes, sir, there was more people present.
The Court:	I didn't ask you if there were more people present watching.
Dukes:	Yes, sir.
The Court:	Now, look, Dukes, you understand me when I question you.
Dukes:	Yes, your Honor.
The Court:	You understand that a robbery may be committed by one or it may be committed by two, three or more persons, is that right?
Dukes:	Yes.
The Court:	Now, you are pleading to an indictment which charges that you, together with others, acting in concert with you, committed a robbery. Is that the fact?
Dukes:	I didn't understand that, your Honor. Yes . . .
The Court:	Now, Dukes, do you want to start all over again?

Dukes:	Yes, sir.
The Court:	And I will speak slowly. Your lawyer made an offer to plead guilty, on your behalf, to the entire indictment—that's three counts—which charges you with the following crimes: robbery in the first degree, grand larceny in the first degree, and assault in the second degree. Do you wish to plead guilty to those crimes?
Dukes:	Yes, sir.
The Court:	By your pleas of guilt, do you admit that on May 23, 1964, at about four o'clock in the morning, in the vicinity of Texarkana and 2d Street, you stole—stole—certain moneys, that is, you unlawfully took this money from the person and owned by Nelson Stanley from his person or in his presence, but against his will, by means of force or violence or fear of immediate injury to his person, and were you at the time aided in any degree whatsoever in the commission of this robbery by one or more other persons who were actually present at the time with you?
Dukes:	Yes, sir.
The Court:	Now, is that a truthful answer?
Dukes:	Yes, sir.

Similarly, a "free and willing" admission of guilt or an admission resulting from "coercion," "deception," or "inducement," are not clearly defined. What constitutes "coercion" to the point of voiding a guilty plea, for example, is neither specified in the procedural law nor mechanically applicable to concrete cases. In one case,

> the prosecutor told the defendant that unless he pleaded guilty the defendant's fiancee would be charged as an accessory. The defendant pleaded guilty and his fiancee was not prosecuted. The appellate court did not find this inducement improper, commenting, "We are not prepared to say that it can be coercion to inform a defendant that someone close to him who is guilty of a crime will be brought to book if he does not plead. If a defendant elects to sacrifice himself for such motives, that is his choice. . . . " (*Kent v. United States*, cited in Newman, 1966:28, 21n).

Second, although it has been changing in recent years, the verbal interchange between judge and defendant has often taken on a ritualistic flavor, devoid of genuine expression and concern. In many cases, defendants plead guilty in exchange for certain inducements, such as a reduced charge or lesser sentence. Yet, when asked at the arraignment whether their plea is voluntary, such defendants state that their decision to plead guilty is genuine and without promise of leniency.[2] Judges regularly accept guilty pleas knowing that defendants are pleading guilty in exchange for certain inducements. Satisfied that such inducements are "proper," enjoying the mutual consent of both prosecution and defense, judges routinely accept the negotiated plea of guilty.[3]

There is enormous variation among jurisdictions in the proportions of defendants pleading guilty and not guilty at their arraignment. In 1971, in twelve nonmetropolitan California counties an average of 47 percent of all arraigned defendants in superior courts pleaded guilty, ranging from 73 percent in Placer County to 26 percent in Del Norte County (Beattie, 1972:20–31). Yet, while only 17 percent of the felony defendants in Baltimore pleaded guilty at their arraignment (President's Commission on Law Enforcement and Administration of Justice, 1967:127), a mere 3 percent of all felony defendants in Los Angeles entered a guilty plea at arraignment (Greenwood et al., 1973:-104).

Although there is considerable variation in the proportion of defendants pleading guilty at arraignment, it is estimated that between 70 to 90 percent of all criminal prosecutions ultimately result in guilty pleas. Using 1945 data from twenty four states and the District of Columbia, Kalven and Zeisel (1966:18–19) found that 75 percent of all prosecutions for major crimes eventuated in guilty pleas. In a comprehensive investigation of Wisconsin, Michigan, and Kansas, Newman (1966:3) estimated that guilty pleas account for 90 percent of all convictions (and convictions, as we shall see, account for some 80 to 90 percent of all dispositions). In its examination of guilty plea convictions in trial courts of general jurisdiction, the President's Commission on Law En-

---

[2] In some areas, defense counsel may instruct clients in how to respond to judicial questioning (Blumberg, 1967:89). As Casper (1972:82) found, in some other areas defendants know, from their own previous experience or experiences of others, how to "act":

Researcher: Think back to the time you went before the judge to change your plea to guilty and you pleaded guilty to attempted B and E [breaking and entering]. Did the judge ask you any questions?

Defendant: Yeah (laughs).

Researcher: Did your lawyer tell you how to answer them beforehand?

Defendant: No, but you know how to answer them. He [the judge] asked me, you know, like had you ever been—you haven't been offered any kind of deal or nothing. He didn't put in that word, but it meant the same thing. You have to say "no." If anybody's in the courtroom, you gotta make a little show for them.

[3] In recent years, there has been a growing move toward the judicial inquiry regarding the characteristics of the negotiated plea which most likely spurred the plea of guilty.

forcement and Administration of Justice (1967:9) made a similar observation:

TABLE 6-1   GUILTY PLEA CONVICTIONS IN TRIAL COURTS

State (1964 Statistics Unless Otherwise Indicated)	Total Convictions	Guilty Pleas	
		Number	Percent of Total
California (1965)	30,840	22,817	74.0
Connecticut	1,596	1,494	93.9
District of Columbia (year ending June 30, 1964)	1,115	817	73.3
Hawaii	393	360	91.5
Illinois	5,591	4,768	85.2
Kansas	3,025	2,727	90.2
Massachusetts (1963)	7,790	6,642	85.2
Minnesota (1965)	1,567	1,437	91.7
New York	17,249	16,464	95.5
Pennsylvania (1960)	25,632	17,108	66.8
U.S. District Courts	29,170	26,273	90.2
Average [excluding Pennsylvania][1]			87.0

[1]The Pennsylvania figures have been excluded from the average because they were from an earlier year, and the types of cases included did not appear fully comparable with the others.

Blumberg (1967:29) found that an average of 93 percent of all felony defendants processed in Metropolitan Court between 1950 and 1964 eventually pleaded guilty and avoided formal trial. Little over 90 percent of Casper's (1972:69) sample of Connecticut defendants eventually pleaded guilty. Neubauer (1974:201) found that 80 percent of the felony defendants processed in the Prairie City courts pleaded guilty by the time of their trial.

Studies suggest that a variable number of defendants plead not guilty sometime between arraignment and trial.[4] While 38 percent of the felony defendants Newman (1956) studied pleaded not guilty at arraignment, only 6 percent maintained their not guilty plea and went to trial. Similarly, while 37 percent of the felony defendants convicted in the U.S. District Courts between 1964 and 1971 pleaded not guilty at arraignment, only 15 percent maintained their pleas of not guilty and went to trial (Hindelang et al., 1973:6). While 97 percent of the felony defendants in Los Angeles pleaded not guilty at arraignment, only 12 percent of these defendants maintained their plea and went to bench or jury trial (Mather, 1973:195).

PROSECUTION AND ADJUDICATION

THE NEGOTIATED GUILTY PLEA

How does one account for variation between jurisdictions in the rate of guilty pleas made at arraignment? And more importantly, how does one account for the fact that some 70 to 90 percent of all criminal prosecutions ultimately result in guilty pleas? Why do so many defendants forego their right to trial and simply plead guilty? Is it because most are repentant and wish to be punished by the state? Or is it because the screening of the innocent is so thorough that only the truly guilty remain? How does one account for those cases that eventually go to trial?

To be sure, some defendants may plead guilty out of repentance for their wrongdoing, just as others may plead guilty because their chances of demonstrating their innocence at trial (in the face of overwhelming evidence of their guilt) are hopeless. But considerable research over the years has shown conclusively that most guilty pleas are the product of a complex process in which defendants plead guilty in exchange for some concession.

In some cases, defendants enter a guilty plea on the assumption that the plea will be "rewarded" by the court with some sentencing leniency. This has been termed "implicit bargain" because there is no direct communication between the defendant and the prosecutor or court regarding the concessions to be granted in return for the guilty plea. It has been found that the court generally rewards those who enter guilty pleas (Newman, 1966:61; Oaks and Lehman, 1967:57–81). Such a tacit arrangement generally occurs in minor cases—those that bring probation or simple jail time as standard penalties—and "dead-bang" cases—those for which the state has substantial proof of the defendant's factual and legal guilt (Newman, 1966:59). Also, defendants who are knowledgeable about the court's informal policies are likely to enter guilty pleas at arraignment. In his investigation of "bargain justice," Newman (1956) found that those defendants pleading guilty can be characterized as "conviction wise." That is, they have knocked about the courthouse on previous occasions, and have developed an understanding of typical court practices. Some have learned that if they plead guilty at arraignment, and consequently avoid ir-

---

[4] Some courts do not correspond entirely with the general pattern we have described. The majority of the defendants in Pittsburgh (Levin, 1970), Philadelphia (White, 1971), and Baltimore (President's Commission on Law Enforcement and Administration of Justice, 1967:121–28) pleaded not guilty at arraignment and maintain that plea. Many of these not guilty pleas, however, are "slow pleas" of guilty. Essentially, these cases are taken to an abbreviated form of trial where counsel presents material to influence the judge for leniency in sentencing. These trials are informal, of short duration, and typically result in conviction (Mather, 1973:190).

ritating officials by requesting counsel or trial, they will fare considerably better at sentencing.

There is considerable consensus among students of court processing that most guilty pleas represent the outcome of a transaction in which defendants or defense attorneys actively *negotiate* with the prosecutors to plead guilty in exchange for concessions in punishment (Newman, 1956; 1966; President's Commission on Law Enforcement and Administration of Justice, 1967). The negotiated plea of guilty is both a very common and a very complex practice, taking different forms within and between jurisdictions. There are, for example, different kinds of considerations that may be offered to defendants in exchange for their plea of guilty (Newman, 1956; Enker, 1967).

1. The prosecution may offer to reduce the charges, which may provide one of several advantages, including avoidance of a repugnant label, like "rapist" or "child molester," a more severe sentence, or a mandatory sentence.

2. The prosecution, in cooperation with the judge, can promise a defendant a more lenient sentence. Often, sentence leniency takes the form of offering probation or time served in jail while awaiting trial instead of imprisonment, as provided in the penal code.

3. The prosecution may offer to drop multiple charges contained in an indictment or information and prosecute only a major or a reduced charge. If, for example, a defendant who purportedly robbed a liquor store was charged with "armed robbery, first degree," "assault and battery," "trespassing," and "brandishing a dangerous weapon," then the prosecution could drop all but the "assault and battery" charge.

4. The prosecution, in cooperation with the trial judge, may promise a defendant that the sentences contingent upon conviction of multiple charges will be served concurrently, not consecutively. In effect, conviction on all of the multiple charges would bring one instead of several compounded sentences.

Plea negotiation may take place at different times in the criminal justice process. In some jurisdictions, pleas are negotiated prior to the arraignment; while in others, they are negotiated after arraignment and before trial. This variation in the temporal location of plea negotiation may account, in part, for the variation of guilty pleas entered at arraignment. In short, when negotiation occurs before arraignment, a large proportion of all defendants enter guilty pleas. But when it occurs after the arraignment, a large proportion of all defendants enter not guilty pleas at arraignment and subsequently change them to guilty at trial.

In the following discussion, after first examining some popular explanations of the negotiated guilty plea, we shall move to a detailed explanation of the process of plea negotiation. Then we shall examine what kinds of cases maintain not guilty pleas. Finally, we shall briefly consider the circumstances under which judges acquit the guilty.

EXPLANATIONS OF THE NEGOTIATED GUILTY PLEA

Over the last few years, three general positions have emerged to explain the dominance of the negotiated guilty plea as a means of conviction—organizational overload, the prosecutorial strategy for convictions on "weak" cases, and the individualization of the criminal law and the minimization of the severity of punishments contained in the criminal law.[5]

Organizational Overload

In the first position, the conventional settling of cases by negotiated pleas is explained in terms of organizational needs to manage work overload. The position holds that the prosecutor's office and the bench are greatly committed to the priorities of production and efficiency. A principle index of efficiency is the smooth, rapid processing of cases and the avoidance of a backlog on the court's docket (Blumberg, 1967:74–76). The commitment is nurtured by the feeling that all courthouse members must manage productive and efficient appearances before significant reference groups to maintain an air of legitimacy, secure organizational resources, and provide security or advancement in the professional careers of their members (Blumberg, 1967; Skolnick, 1967; 54–58; Chambliss and Seidman, 1971:261–69). Because trials take a long time to complete, routine case disposition by means of trial is very inefficient. Judge Lummus of the Supreme Judicial Court of Massachusetts pointed out forty years ago what is applicable today:

> If all the defendants should combine to refuse to plead guilty,
> and should dare to hold out, they could break down the
> administration of criminal justice in any state in the
> Union . . . . The prosecutor is like a man armed with a revolver
> who is cornered by a mob. A concerted rush would overwhelm

---

[5] This discussion follows generally the arguments of Rosett and Cressey (1976).

him . . . . The truth is, that a criminal court can operate only by inducing the great mass of actually guilty defendants to plead guilty, paying in leniency the price for the plea.

This, I agree, is a stark reality, not the ideal . . . . courts are not free, and never have been free, from the pressure in favor of criminals that the very volume of criminal business exerts (Lummus, 1937: 46–47).

Because disposition of too many cases by trial would create time pressure and case overload, an alternative system of settlement has developed: the negotiated guilty plea (Neubauer, 1974:194), which provides for the expedient, hence efficient, processing of cases (Blumberg, 1967:31, 46, 65–66, 74–76; Alschuler, 1968; Skolnick, 1967; Cole, 1970, 1975:298; Chambliss and Seidman, 1971:401–4; Smith and Pollack, 1973:152–56).

There have been variations on the case overload explanation of negotiated guilty pleas. First, some have argued that such pleas are the product of an *exchange between adversaries* seeking to achieve their particular, albeit opposed, ends and minimize potential losses (Alschuler, 1968; Neubauer, 1974: 194–95; Cole, 1975: 300–4). Rather than emphasizing the bureaucratic unity of legal actors, here, plea negotiation is portrayed as a "game in which the prosecutor, defense attorney, defendant, and sometimes the judge participate" (Cole, 1975:300). Each

The court calendar is greatly reduced through the use of the negotiated plea. (© *1976 by Fred W. McDarrah)*

PROSECUTION AND ADJUDICATION

participant enters the contest with particular objectives that are at odds with those of the other participants, and confronts particular obstacles to the achievement of those objectives. The prosecutor wants a conviction on maximum charges for every case, but his caseload precludes trial of every case. The trial judge wants to keep his calendar moving smoothly while ensuring that defendants are fairly adjudicated, but his enormous caseload also precludes trial. The defendant and his counsel want acquittal, but the state's evidence of the defendant's culpability is too overwhelming. Courthouse participants feel plea negotiation is a pragmatic way of countering the obstacle of time, and achieving, to a degree, their principal objectives, conviction without trial (the judge avoids a backlog and keeps his calendar moving) and leniency in punishment (the defense attorney gets a desirable outcome for his client). Yet, such objectives can be achieved only by incurring a loss: the prosecutor does not get a conviction on the full charges, the judge does not hear cases in order to ensure fairness in processing and to bolster his status in the courthouse community, the defendant gets convicted, and the defense attorney loses the case.

The prosecutor and defense attorney, in attempting to structure the negotiation session to their own advantage, come armed with a number of tactics designed to maximize their rewards and minimize their costs (Cole, 1975:300). The prosecutor initially files full charges against the defendant in anticipation of subsequent negotiation. Because conviction on the full charges suggests an unpleasant prospective sentence, the defense attorney counters by employing "strategies whose only utility lies in the threat they pose to the court's and the prosecutor's time" (Alschuler, 1968:56). In effect, the defense exploits the prosecutor's vulnerabilty, specifically, by threatening to take the case to a jury trial, filing a string of pretrial continuances, or making a series of pretrial motions that require the prosecutor's formal response if charge reduction or a comparable concession is not granted (Alschuler, 1968:56–57). To conserve organizational resources, the prosecutor may agree to grant a concession for a guilty plea.

Second, some have argued that guilty pleas are the product of a symbiotic relationship between colleagues who cooperate toward achieving compatible ends at the expense of defendants (Blumberg, 1967, 59–63, 103–6, 110–15 and 1967a; Chambliss and Seidman, 1971, 406–10; Smith and Pollack, 1973:154–56).[6] Ideally, the defense and prosecution are opponents engaged in an adversarial contest before a neutral judge, but, in fact, on the one hand, the prosecution is dependent on the defense attorney for assistance in conserving resources by avoiding trial and showing a productive appearance; on the other hand, defense attorneys, whether private or public, who regularly handle criminal cases are dependent on the prosecutor's office in performing their daily tasks. For a public defender to vigorously oppose the prosecutor would bring down the wrath of both the P. D.'s supervisor and the judge and the loss of the routine concessions typically enjoyed. For the private attorney to vigorously oppose the prosecutor would bring disrepute and a potential loss of income, as well as the loss in normal plea concessions granted (cf. Blumberg, 1967a). Consequently, for the courthouse regulars to please their organizational superiors, conserve their resources, maintain their prestige, or collect their fees, they must cooperate.

The Prosecutorial Strategy for Securing Convictions on "Weak" Cases

In the second position, the negotiated plea of guilty is explained in terms of the prosecutorial strategy for securing convictions on "weak" cases. In a survey of chief prosecuting attorneys from various states on the scope and character of plea negotiation, *The University of Pennsylvania Law Review* (1964:901) asked: "What influences staff members to plea bargain with a particular defendant?" The prosecutors, permitted to make more than one response, cited a number of influences in the following proportions:

	Influence	Percentage of Respondents (60)
1.	Particular crime charged	70.0
2.	Defendant's prior record	80.0
3.	Court has adequate scope to punish on conviction of charge to which plea was accepted	83.3
4.	Cooperative attitude of defendant	68.4
5.	Government has weak case	85.0
6.	Prosecuting witness does not wish prosecution continued	60.0
7.	Personal sympathy	26.7
8.	Prosecutor's workload	36.7
9.	Repetitious counts in indictment	55.0
10.	Popular sentiment	21.7
11.	Penalties of law are too harsh	31.7

While 37 percent of the prosecutors felt that workload was a critical contingency in negotiating for guilty pleas, 85 percent felt that the weakness of the state's case was critical. While *most* of the prosecutors Alschuler (1968:59) interviewed felt "sympathy with the defendant"

---

[6] Cole (1975:142) points out that the two variants of the organizational overload argument are not necessarily opposed. Rather, they may be two phases of an historical process. At first, courthouse members may engage in an adversarial relationship oriented toward securing their particular ends at the expense of others. In time, the members may develop a reciprocal relationship involving trust and cooperation (cf. Blau, 1964).

and "workload" were important, *all* of the prosecutors considered the weakness of the state's case important.

Essentially, when there is weakness in the state's evidence that a crime has been committed and that the defendant committed it, then rather than not prosecute or lose the case at trial, the prosecutor will grant certain concessions in order to induce a guilty plea; that is, he will engage in negotiation for a guilty plea only when his chances for securing a conviction at trial are poor. As one prosecutor remarked: "When we have a weak case for any reason, we'll reduce to almost anything rather than lose" (Alschuler, 1968:59).

Implicit in this position, like that of the overload position, is the conception that prosecutors strive to convict and exact some punishment from every defendant. This idea is underlined by the words of a Chicago defense lawyer:

> When a prosecutor has a deadbang [strong] case, he is likely to come up with an impossible offer like thirty to fifty years. When the case has a hole in it, however, the prosecutor may scale the offer all the way down to probation. The prosecutor's goal is to *get something from every defendant,* and the correctional treatment the defendant may require is the last thing on their minds (Alschuler, 1968:60, emphasis added).

Also implicit in this position is the adversary, not symbiotic, character of the negotiation. The prosecutor's objective is conviction on the maximum charges; the defense seeks acquittal. Hemmed in by weakness in the state's case, the prosecutor will offer a concession for a guilty plea. But, as Alschuler (1968:63) points out, the prosecutor seeks "the best he can get." Fearful of the consequences of a remotely possible conviction, the defense finally agrees to plead:

> San Francisco defense attorney Benjamin M. Davis recently represented a man charged with kidnapping and forcible rape. The defendant was innocent, Davis says, and after investigating the case Davis was confident of an acquittal. The prosecutor, who seems to have shared the defense attorney's opinion on this point, offered to permit a guilty plea to simply robbery. Conviction on this charge would not have led to a greater sentence than thirty days' imprisonment, and there was every likelihood that the defendant would be granted probation. When Davis informed his client of this offer, he emphasized that conviction at trial seemed highly improbable. The defendant's reply was simple: "I can't take the chance" (Alschuler, 1968:61).

The Individualization of Justice and the Minimization of the Severity of Punishments

In a recent examination of plea negotiation in the American courthouse, Rosett and Cressey (1976:34–44, 71–84, 104–13) present another position. Voiced in different forms in years past, their argument is that the conventional disposition of defendants through negotiated pleas is best understood in terms of courthouse participants' mutual concern for adjusting the formal penalties sanctioned by law to individual crimes and criminals in the interests of justice.

The former positions—case overload and weak cases—certainly have some warrant. They note:

> A system which sends to trial less than five out of a hundred felony arrestees, and which still lacks the capacity to give adequate time to investigate thoroughly even those cases which it does try, certainly seems overloaded (1976:105).

In addition, weak cases invariably find their way into the courthouse, and for some of these the prosecutor would gladly grant concessions for a conviction. Furthermore, some negotiation sessions seem strikingly adversarial. But explanations of the negotiated guilty plea practice that rely *solely* on organizational overload and its exploitation by adversarial attorneys or strategic maneuvers in prosecuting weak cases simply do not stand up to critical scrutiny.

The position formulated by Rosett and Cressey is based on several criticisms of the other arguments. First, it is erroneous to believe that if the burden of overload was lifted from the shoulders of prosecutors, they would seek the full statutory penalty for the gravest crime that could be charged to defendants and take all cases to trial if needed. On the one hand, it is not uncommon for prosecutors to grant concessions for guilty pleas even though their caseload is minimal. On the other hand, even in a congested courthouse, if the defense demands a trial or threatens delay, concessions by the prosecutor to induce a guilty plea are hardly automatic. Prosecutors burdened with large caseloads are not fearful of trial if a case warrants it:

> I never take time into consideration in deciding whether to go to trial. If he [the defendant] *should go to the penitentiary but won't plead, I'll go to trial no matter what the consequence, in terms of time, to me or the office. That's what I'm here for* (Rosett and Cressey, 1976:107; emphasis added).

This prosecutor, like others, is in the business of "judging the conditions under which it is right and just to send a criminal to the penitentiary" (Rosett and Cressey, 1976:107). If the defendant will not plead guilty to a charge bringing what the prosecutor deems the appropriate penalty, the state will then move to trial. Defendants the prosecutor believes should not go to the penitentiary are not going to go there, whether the defense uses delaying tactics or not (Rosett and Cressey, 1976:107). Some courthouse regulars, for example, fail miserably as gamesters. While they invariably threaten to take their cases to a jury trial, prosecutors know that these defenders have not tried a case in their many years of practicing law and shudder at the prospect. Nevertheless, concessions are granted to their deserving clients in exchange for a guilty plea, not because they are bluffed but because the penalties contained in such concessions are deemed appropriate (cf. Skolnick, 1967; Neubauer, 1974:214–19).

Second, it is erroneous to believe that the burden of overload necessarily outweighs issues of substantive justice for those occupying the bench. While trial judges are concerned with keeping their calendars moving smoothly and avoiding a cumbersome backlog, they do at times engage in time-consuming practices aimed at ensuring that the penalties routinely administered on a plea for a given charge are just. For example, a judge may refuse a guilty plea in the interests of the defendant, even though it adds to his caseload. Newman's observation is instructive here:

> . . . in accepting the plea the typical trial judge is not only
> concerned with the provident nature of the plea itself but with
> the appropriateness of whatever sentences are prescribed for the
> conduct. Judges are occasionally confronted with clearly guilty
> defendants willing to plead to a charge which carries a
> mandatory punishment which seems to the court excessively
> severe in view of the actual criminal conduct involved or the
> traits of the particular defendant. Faced with this, the only
> alternative short of outright acquittal is to convict the
> defendant of a lesser charge to avoid the mandatory sentence.
> In order to do this, judges assign counsel to such defendants to
> work out a plea to a reduced charge (1966:214).

Third, plea negotiation approaches the status of a constant practice in American criminal justice. The negotiated guilty plea, in one form or another, has been a conventional practice in heavily populated urban courts as well as in less populated rural ones (Laurent, 1959), a

---

[7] We propose that negotiation of some sort occurs at one or more stages of

practice as true in the past as it is in the present.[8] Raymond Moley's 1929 classic, *Politics and Criminal Prosecution,* demonstrates the widespread nature of the negotiated guilty plea in the 1920s. Examining the various crime surveys of that era, Moley (1929:149–92) found that a large proportion of all defendants pleaded guilty instead of standing trial. This trend occurred in urban courts as well as in rural courts. For example, in New York City, 88 percent of all defendants pleaded guilty; in rural upstate New York, 91 percent pleaded guilty. In Minneapolis, 90 percent of all defendants pleaded guilty and in St. Paul, 95 percent pleaded guilty; in twenty-five small counties in Minnesota, 85 percent of the defendants pleaded guilty. In Chicago, 85 percent of the defendants pleaded guilty; in seven partially urban and two rural counties in Illinois, 82 percent pleaded guilty (1929:160–61). Most of these pleas, Moley suggests, were entered in exchange for promises by the prosecution of leniency in punishment.

If we assume that rural courts are not pressed by enormous caseloads as are the larger urban courts, it appears that overload cannot totally account for plea negotiation.[9]

The weak case argument does not square with research demonstrating that prosecutors routinely grant concessions no matter what the strength of the case. Newman (1966:105–30), for example, found

---

the criminal justice process of all jurisdictions. The legal categorization of "individual" events and the decision about what to do with "individual" offenders are tasks requiring interpretation and negotiation among officials, and such tasks must be performed daily in order to process cases. Thus, while some jurisdictions may not practice plea negotiation in the manner we depict it, negotiation exists at one or more stages of the entire process. In England, for example, while there is little negotiation between defense and prosecution, there is substantial assessment and negotiation among officials who charge defendants (police), and among those who are to sentence defendants (judges and justices). See Davis (1970), Grosman (1969), and Herrmann (1974) for comparative views of courthouse discretion.

[8] Mileski (1971:535, 14n.) notes from the observations culled from H.C. Lea, *The Inquisition of the Middle Ages: Its Organization and Operation* (New York: Harper Torchbooks, 1969, p. 170, originally published in three volumes in 1887), that plea negotiation was practiced as early as the Middle Ages. Dalton (1959) provides an excellent historical discussion of discretion and negotiation in formal organizations.

[9] If organizational overload itself accounts for plea negotiation, then we would expect that a decrease in overload would be met by an increase in trials and a decrease in negotiated guilty pleas. While data testing this argument have not been gathered, we can refer to the following data culled from statistics of the federal courts (*Annual Report of the Administrative Office of the United States Courts,* 1974, 1975): Between 1973 and 1974 there was a 6.3 percent decrease in criminal filings and a 7 percent decrease in cases pending trial (pp. 282, 284). Also between 1973 and 1974, there was an overall decrease of 4.5 percent in trials held (p. 318), and 85 percent of all convicted defendants entered guilty pleas (p. 470). The point, it seems, is that while caseload decreased, so too did trial activity, and what we may take as negotiated pleas remained quite stable.

that if a particular defendant did not correspond to the prosecutor's conception of a criminal who deserved the punishment authorized for the offense committed, then some concession would be granted. Newman (1966:118) suggests that such a practice appears to be based "on the assumption that the law should not be fully invoked against otherwise 'good' persons."

Although caseload must be controlled, we agree with Rosett and Cressey, for it is a mistake to explain the conventional practice of plea negotiation solely in terms of organizational overload or the processing of weak cases. To be sure, guilty pleas and avoidance of trial help officials manage productive and efficient appearances. But, more importantly, on many occasions the negotiated guilty plea helps defendants. It enables courthouse officials to individualize justice by adjusting the often severe penalties contained in the law of individual crime and criminals. We recognize in its present form the practice is not without flaw, and is far from a perfect means of achieving justice. Nevertheless, it is a way to adjust penalties that are too severe (cf. Moley, 1929: 187–88; Sudnow, 1965:262; Newman, 1966:76–130; Rosett, 1967; Mileski, 1971; Mather, 1973; Rosett and Cressey, 1976).

Our system of law embraces two principles of justice, one stressing "government by law," the other emphasizing "government by men." The first is concerned with equality and uniformity: whosoever performs an act specified by law as criminal, whether a prince or a pauper, shall be punished by the state in a specified manner. In short, similarly situated people shall be treated similarly. This principle, however, is problematic in several respects. First, all criminal statutes are inherently general and open-ended. The definition of the conduct to which a given statute applies does not specify all the concrete instances of human action within its rubric. At most, the definition outlines a number of basic elements a piece of action must contain for it to be considered an instance of that category, and these elements are themselves general and open-ended. Take, for example, a gun law that states it is a crime for anyone to carry a handgun on the streets without authorization. Precisely what constitutes a "handgun"? Does it include toy pistols, waterguns, inoperable antique pistols, or firearms broken down into several pieces? What constitutes the "street"? Does it include public buildings, one's front and back yards, or one's car? The point is that the criminal law, like any body of rules, is not specific. Whether a concrete form of conduct is an instance of this and not that legal violation is subject to considerable interpretation and negotiation.

Second, it follows from the nature of criminal laws that all acts literally within the scope of a particular statute are exactly the same. Just as there are numerous shades of gray, so too are there numerous shades of seriousness within any given statute. In the statutes covering "assault" and "armed robbery," for example, we find events that are popularly perceived as differing in degrees of seriousness. One who assaults another for the sheer pleasure of watching the weaker victim crumble might seem to many as guilty of a more serious assault than one who is provoked by the victim to fight over the attentions of a woman. A career robber who steals $250,000 from a bank might seem to many as having committed a more serious crime than an unemployed first-time offender who robs a passerby of $50 to pay his family's rent. Any given statute, then, glosses the diversity of human action literally within its scope.

Third, it would follow from the first two points that some penalties contained in the law are too severe because they have not changed over time as values and attitudes have. For example, although some states have updated their drug laws by making possession of small amounts of marijuana a misdemeanor, other states maintain severe mandatory prison sentences for the same violation.

Some penalties are also severe because they are too rigid. Punishing all who have violated a given statute alike lumps together and treats quite dissimilar cases equally. This is especially harsh when the punishment is based on erroneous conceptions of offenders. Take, for example, "child-molesting" statutes:

> . . . the image of child molesting that the legislature has outlawed and the image of the child molester that the legislature has threatened with lengthy imprisonment and mandatory registration as a sex offender are not consistent with the courthouse subculture's typical experience of crime. Rather than encountering sex fiends or constitutional sexual psychopaths, prosecutors are likely to encounter inadequate old men who peek under little girls' skirts (Rosett and Cressey, 1976:94).

The second principle of justice, "government by men," stresses individuality and diversity: each person should be treated to his just deserts.[10] That is, officials should assess the "facts" of a particular case

---

[10] The criminal law crudely attempts to accommodate this second principle in three ways (Rosett and Cressey, 1976). (1) While the criminal law stresses equality by prohibiting all events literally subsumed within the statutes, it also stresses individual differences by subdividing and grading offenses by seriousness. Criminal homicide, for example, is graded in seriousness in the following manner: first degree murder, second degree murder, voluntary manslaughter, and involuntary manslaughter. (2) While the criminal law stresses equality by requiring punishment of all people convicted of a crime, it also sets ranges of minimum and maximum punishments, and these are graded by seriousness. For example, first degree murder may be punishable by ten years in prison to life imprisonment or execution; second degree murder may be punishable by seven years to life imprisonment: voluntary manslaughter may be punishable

—the "character" of a specific offense and offender—and impose the punishment that best fits, from their perspective, the facts of the case. Of course, what constitutes "individualizing justice" or "doing justice" differs from one courthouse community to another. But to ignore the unique features of each crime is to promote a "machine of terror": "A system of criminal justice that did not take into account people's uniqueness and personality would be so unmerciful and wasteful of human lives that few thinking citizens would support it" (Rosett and Cressey, 1976:39).

Plea negotiation is also a way for the prosecution and defense to achieve a working consensus on the character of offenders and offenses. Consequently, through plea negotiation attorneys arrive at agreement about what defendants deserve in exchange for guilty pleas.

A growing body of evidence, some of which we have already cited, gives support to this broad generalization. In his examination of plea negotiation in Michigan, Wisconsin, and Kansas, Newman (1966:105–30) found that prosecutors, as well as other courthouse officials, demonstrated concern with the adjustment of formal and informal penalties to the particular features of cases in exchange for guilty pleas. Newman discovered that such adjustment took a number of forms depending on the character of the offender and the offense. These forms include the following:

1. The prosecutor's reduction of a felony to a misdemeanor to avoid giving a young, inexperienced, or respectable person a felony record and tarnished reputation. While conviction on the original felony would probably bring the same basic penalty the defendant would receive for his conviction on a misdemeanor, the prosecutor is concerned with avoiding any collateral harm a felony record might bring. As one prosecutor remarked to Newman: "I want convictions, yes. But I have no desire to ruin a person's whole life by hanging a felony record on some young boy who has made a single mistake."

2. The prosecutor's reduction of the charges on which conviction brings mandatory prison terms to charges permitting sentence flexibility and leniency when the defendant is young and inexperienced, respectable and without prior record, or of low mentality. Although such defendants have literally violated the particular law on which they have been originally charged, they simply are not deemed "real" criminals. In one case, for example:

---

by three to seven years' imprisonment; and, involuntary manslaughter may be punishable by one to four years' imprisonment. (3) While the criminal law stresses equality by making all crimes punishable, it also authorizes judges to suspend penalties or to invoke probation instead of imprisonment. Thus, while the criminal law and its administrative organizations operate under the banner of equality and uniformity,the law also gives administrative officials considerable discretion in prosecution and sentencing.

A seventeen-year-old dishwasher in Kansas was originally charged with forcible rape of a pregnant, thirteen-year-old girl. While it was clear that the defendant used force, he was allowed to plead guilty to contributing to the delinquency of a minor both because the victim was disreputable and because the defendant was of extremely low intelligence. The deputy county attorney said, in reducing the charge: "This boy is so feebleminded he really doesn't know any better. There's no doubt in my mind that she led him on and he merely used more force than was necessary" (Newman, 1966:121).

The boy simply did not strike the prosecutor as a typical rapist.

3. The prosecutor's reduction of the charges permitting a more lenient sentence when the particular features of the offense did not correspond with the prosecutor's conceptions of that offense for which the penalties were designed. For example, a defendant may be allowed to plead guilty to assault and battery instead of felonious assault when the victim provoked the attack and consequently shared in its responsibility. From the prosecutor's perspective, a real felonious assault should consist of no provocation on the part of the victim.

4. The prosecutor's reduction of the charges permitting a more lenient sentence when the offender's conduct is conceived as "normal" within his subgroup. Such events as promiscuous sex relations, gambling, bootlegging, and assault are considered normal to certain subgroups, and are tolerated by criminal justice officials. As Newman observes:

> There is some agreement that offenders who fit within one of these categories should be treated with less severity, if at all, than should offenders who engage in the same conduct but whose racial, educational, ethnic, or income characteristics are such that the conduct represents greater deviancy when measured against the standard of their group (1966:122).

If we cannot explain plea negotiation by the "overload" or "weak case" theories, why do so many prosecutors rely on these accounts to explain plea negotiations? Rosett and Cressey (1976:110–13) have formulated one hypothesis. It is "convenient, safe, and reasonable for prosecutors and defense attorneys alike to attribute plea bargaining to mere defects in the warrior's armament—too much work and too many weak cases" (1976:112). For the prosecutor to publicly admit that he is in sympathy with certain defendants, or that he thinks certain laws are too harsh, is to invite the wrath of certain significant reference groups, such as the police. However, to pin the practice on overload or weak cases "neutralizes important and powerful interest groups who say they want adversary procedures that would maximize the amount of punishment meted out to criminals" (1976:111; cf. Skolnick, 1966: 199–202).

THE PROCESS OF PLEA NEGOTIATION

Thus far, we have considered the function of plea negotiation for the criminal justice process from several positions, and found the overload and weak case explanations to be relatively inadequate. The function is most profitably conceptualized as a social transaction between actors who want to expediently and justly manage defendants. Our aim in this section is to secure a basic understanding of the character and dynamics of this transaction.

Generally the prosecutor and defense attorney are pivotal participants in plea negotiation, but there are variations between jurisdictions. In some areas, for example, defendants themselves may negotiate with prosecutors without the assistance of counsel. In a Wisconsin county, Newman (1956) found that about a half of the felony defendants he interviewed waived their right to counsel, and over a half of this group directly negotiated with the prosecutor for some sentencing concession in return for a guilty plea. Similarly, Casper (1972:77–81) implies that his sample of Connecticut defendants actively negotiated with the prosecutor over concessions in exchange for pleas.

In most areas, however, the bulk of active negotiation is performed by the prosecutor and the defense attorney. In such places, the defendant is in a relatively poor position to effectively negotiate with the prosecutor. He requires the services of counsel, one knowledgeable of the courthouse and its operation; he needs, in short, an "inside dopester." Nevertheless, while the prosecutor and defense attorney may be the central participants in the negotiation, the defendant's acquiescence is necessary for final approval of their settlement.

The police are secondary figures in the transaction, at most, making their position on a particular case known to the prosecution.

The trial judge plays a more critical role than do the police. On the one hand, he may be expected, as in Philadelphia, to honor the prosecutor's sentencing recommendations, which are the results oi negotiation. On the other hand, the prosecutor and defense counsel may seek judicial approval of a tentative plea arrangement, a practice found in New York (White, 1971:443, 448). Furthermore, we would expect judicial participation to increase as the practice of negotiation itself becomes increasingly visible.

Our principal concern will be with the character of the negotiation involving the prosecutor and defense counsel. In most jurisdictions the negotiated plea of guilty represents the climax of a process in which the prosecutor and defense counsel achieve a working consensus on how the particular case should be typified and subsequently labeled to ensure a plea of guilty and a just and reasonable punishment. There are several critical phases to this process which warrant our consideration.

Typification

First, the defense attorney and prosecutor, independently of one another, typify and label the particular case.[11] In a classic investigation of plea negotiation, Sudnow (1965) argues that the process of typification is a crucial feature of the negotiation process. To "typify" a concrete case is to define it as an instance of a "commonsensical" class of events for which there are routine dispositions deemed by courthouse members as appropriate and just. Several aspects of this phase need elaboration.

As we pointed out earlier, courthouse officials do not interpret concrete cases strictly in terms of penal code categories. That is, the interpretation of an event does not involve a mechanical process whereby the elements of the case at hand are matched to the elements of a penal code category, because such categories are by nature abstract and general. Rather, courthouse members develop, and subsequently transmit to newcomers, a set of typifications that represent, and are labeled with, those penal code categories they recurrently use in processing cases. These typifications consist of rich, detailed elaborations of the "normal crimes" they consistently encounter, including "knowledge of the typical manner in which offenses of given classes are committed, the social characteristics of the persons who regularly commit them, the features of the settings in which they occur, the types of victims often involved, and the like" (Sudnow, 1965:259). For example,

> . . . burglary is seen as involving regular violators, no
> weapons, low-priced items, little property damage, lower class
> establishments, largely Negro defendants, independent
> operators, and a non-professional orientation to the crime. Child
> molesting is seen as typically entailing middle-aged fathers (few
> women), no actual physical penetration or severe tissue damage,
> mild fondling, petting, and stimulation, bad marriage
> circumstances, multiple offenders with the same offense
> repeatedly committed, a child complainant, via the mother, etc.
> (Sudnow, 1965:260).

[11] It should be noted that the defense attorney and prosecutor often typify the case at different points of the process. Prosecutors will typify a case at the charging stage; in large courts, moreover, the trial prosecutors will also typify the case. Defense attorneys will typify the case on their assignment or retainer, and this may come quite late in the process. Moreover, in large courts, defenders may typify the case only after arraignment; public defenders, for example, may only superficially represent indigent clients in preceding stages.

These typical features of "burglary" and "child molesting" are neither specified nor elaborated upon in the statutes covering the two crimes.

Courthouse members also develop, and transmit to newcomers, understandings as to what dispositions should correspond to different crimes. Such understandings include what concessions may be granted for a guilty plea. For example, if a particular case is interpreted as a typical instance of "child molesting," then it will be routinely reduced to "loitering around a schoolyard" in order to extract a guilty plea. Such understandings also include conceptions of what penalty is appropriate and just for the different normal crimes. "Loitering around a schoolyard," for example, may carry that degree of punishment considered by officials as appropriate for that class of events. To reduce the charge for a typical case of "child molesting" to "disturbing the peace," a less serious crime than "loitering around a schoolyard," is to fail at giving the defendant "his due" (cf. Sudnow, 1965:262–63). Mather (1973:193–94) reports that public defenders understand the basic types of concessions that different classes of crime bring, as well as the kinds of penalties normally considered as just by trial judges.

When the prosecutor and defense attorney independently encounter a case, they approach it in terms of their sets of typifications. They attend to the distinctive features of the case that make it a normal crime, that is, how the event was performed, the time and place of the performance, the character of the defendant's and victim's backgrounds, and the like. Sudnow (1965:266) found that in their very first interview with clients set for trial, public defenders seek to establish the typical character of the case. Oftentimes, competent public defenders can typify the case after only a few minutes of examination. In the following example the P.D. had no information about the defendant or the particular crime other than that provided by the penal code number. After some preliminary background information was gathered, the following interview occurred:

> 288 P.C.—[Child Molesting]
>
> **P.D.:** O.K., why don't you start out by telling me how this thing got started?
>
> **Def.:** Well, I was at the park and all I did was to ask this little girl if she wanted to sit on my lap for a while and, you know, just sit on my lap. Well, about twenty minutes later I'm walking down the street about a block away from the park and this cop pulls up and there the same little girl is, you know, sitting in the back seat with some dame. The cop asks me to stick my head in the back seat and he asks the kid if I was the one and she says yes. So he puts me in the car and takes a statement from me and here I

am in the joint. All I was doing was playing with her
a little. . . .

P.D.: (*interrupting*) . . . O.K., I get the story, let's see
what we can do (Sudnow, 1965:267).

This case was quickly typified. The P.D. interrupted the defendant
when he had enough information to confirm his sense that the case was
just an instance of child molesting. In the following case, the trial
prosecutor typified as "grand theft," a probationable offense, a case
originally charged as "armed robbery," an offense carrying a mandatory prison sentence:

> The defendants had no aggravated involvement with the law
> previously. One of them had only a few drunk arrests and a
> conviction of disorderly conduct, a minor thing. The other
> defendant had one drunk driving, I think, and a possession of
> pills that had been dismissed. He had served in the armed
> forces and received an honorable discharge. He had been
> overseas and even got a medal of some sort. They are both
> employed.
> The deal was: They had been drinking heavily and were
> outside a bar and stopped this guy. The victim said they pulled
> a gun on him and demanded his money and so forth. They took
> his wallet, keys, and something else—some change or a watch, I
> think. They were caught just a few minutes later and all the
> victim's belongings were in the defendants' car. But there was
> no gun. Now, robbers don't just throw away a gun if they had
> one. I mean, this is something of value. And they were caught
> immediately after the incident, so the evidence on the presence
> of the gun is very weak. The victim had been drinking in that
> bar all day long and was quite drunk, so he's not that much
> help. And the defendants were drunk when they were arrested
> —one had a .10 and the other an .18 blood alcohol reading. A
> person is presumed to be drunk by law when the alcohol
> reading is .10.
> So this case is not like when some fellows march into a
> liquor store with a gun and hold up the store. Or a robbery of a
> gas station or a grocery case. It's probably more of a Grand
> Theft Person—just the taking of money from a person. That's
> why a plea to Grand Theft Person is very appropriate here. We
> look at the background of the individuals, how much
> involvement they've had with the law, and the circumstances of
> the case (Mather, 1973:206–7).

As the prosecutor stated, the features of the event were not those of a
"classic robbery." It was just a "grand theft person," that is, "just the
taking of money from a person." Thus, to typify a case is to examine

Much of what happens in the courts can be best understood through an examination of the back rooms where decisions are negotiated rather than the courtroom where the decisions are made public. (© 1976 by Fred W. McDarrah)

its features vis-à-vis one's repertoire of typifications, and define and label it as an instance of a normal class of events for which there are often agreed-upon dispositions.

Exchange of Conceptions of the Case

Second, once the prosecutor and defense attorney typify and label the concrete case, they exchange their interpretations of the "facts" and their consequent labeling of the case and attempt to reach some agreement on how the case should be categorized and subsequently handled (Sudnow, 1965; Mather, 1973; Neubauer, 1974:200–1). Of course, the degree to which the prosecutor and defense attorney negotiate varies from case to case.

Only a brief exchange between the two attorneys may be enough for them to establish some agreement. As Mather suggests, such a brief exchange is prominent in cases that are deadbang. One judge provided Mather with two illustrations:

> On a three count forgery case, the defense attorney asks the D.A., "Can I have one count?" The D.A. says, "Yes, which one?" The defense attorney says "Count 2." And that's it. No bargain has been explicitly made. No promise made that counts 1 and 3 will be dismissed in exchange for *the plea to count 2. It's simply that everybody knows what the standard practice is.* Or here's another example. The defense attorney comes into court and asks the D.A., "What does Judge Hall give on bookmaking cases?" The D.A. asks if there are any priors. The attorney says "no," and the D.A. says, "He usually gives $150 on the first offense." The attorney says, "Fine. We'll enter a plea to count 1." Again no promise was made by anybody. It's just that everybody knows what customarily will happen (1973:199; emphasis added).

It is not unusual to find little explicit negotiation between defense counsel and prosecution in a large number of cases. The bulk of criminal defense lawyers (both courthouse regulars and public defenders) and prosecutors share a common perspective toward crime and criminals (Sudnow, 1965; cf. Grosman, 1969:93–96; Rosett and Cressey, 1976:90–92). Both groups of attorneys attend to similar features of the case, ask the same types of questions, and share similar conceptions of what dispositions are appropriate and just for different classes of events.

Because of their disagreement as to how a case should be categorized and handled, there are times when the prosecutor and defense attorney engage in lengthy negotiation. In contrast to the pattern of little explicit negotiation discussed above, in this pattern we find substantial negotiation about the "facts" of the case. Essentially, both attorneys will provide one another with the "logical" categorization based upon the particular features of the case. In the following case, there was considerable disagreement between the prosecutor and defense attorney about proper classification of the case.

> The guy was caught drilling a hole in the wall next to a safe in a store. There's no defense at all. And he's got five prior burglary convictions—and they're all good priors. I wanted to go to Greene (a judge in short cause) [SOT] and plead him. Maybe we could keep him out of state prison then. In other court it's prison for sure.
>
> The guy's just an old drunk. But Davis (the D.A.) wouldn't agree to going to Greene. And the D.A. has to consent to short cause. He figured with five priors and drilling a hole in the wall by the safe, that the guy's not just an old drunk. That he's a professional burglar. I don't think so, though (Mather 1973:204).

The prosecutor argued that the case was an instance of real burglary, and cited in support the "fact" that the defendant had five prior burglary convictions; in effect, he was a "professional burglar." The public defender differed with the prosecutor's conclusion, arguing that the case was not a real burglary because the defendant was "just an old drunk." "Everybody knows," the P.D.'s argument might follow, "that old drunks just aren't professional burglars." In providing one another with what they consider to be the "appropriate" categorization of the event, they also provide one another with the "appropriate" disposition. If the defendant is a "professional burglar," he deserves to go to prison; but if he is "just an old drunk," then county jail is appropriate.

Frequently, after lengthy negotiation two attorneys can achieve a working consensus on a case and dispose of it without trial. This may come about when one attorney persuades the other that his interpretation of the facts makes greater sense or when one is provided with additional information on the case that casts doubt on his initial categorization. A defendant, for example, may tell his attorney only part of what transpired, and it may be on the basis of this information alone that the lawyer categorizes the case. When the prosecutor and defense counsel meet, the prosecutor may provide a version of the case based on additional information. Given this new slant on the "facts," the defense attorney may come to agree with the prosecutor's categorization. In a case involving a liquor store burglary, for example,

> The client told his attorney that the police had stopped him several blocks from the alleged break-in, and he had nothing to

do with it. The prosecutor relayed a different version. According to the police reports, the squad car was on routine patrol checking stores. When the car pulled into the parking lot the car lights illuminated someone inside the store. The officers went to the back of the store and observed a suspect leaving the store and entering a car. They chased the car, stopped it several blocks away, discovered the car "loaded with goodies," and arrested the defendant (Neubauer, 1974:200).

Neubauer suggests that enlightened by the prosecutor's version of the case, the defense attorney returned to his client, probably admonished him for lying, and informed him that it would be futile to contest the case.

Attorneys can also achieve consensus on a case and avoid trial by consulting others. In some cases, they may consult with their immediate organizational superiors about the categorization of an event and the determination of what concession would be appropriate. In some prosecutor's offices, for example, there are weekly meetings in which deputy or assistant prosecutors present their troublesome cases to their colleagues. The purpose of these meetings is to arrive at some collective agreement on the relevant features of the case and how it should be typified and subsequently handled. In other cases, the prosecutor and defense attorney may together consult the trial judge.

In a small number of cases, however, the attorneys may simply fail to achieve any consensus. The matter will then be resolved by trial.

Advising Defendants of Settlement

Third, assuming the prosecutor and defense attorney come to some agreement as to how the case should be categorized and subsequently handled without trial, both attorneys may need to advise those whom they represent with the proposed settlement. The prosecutor and defense attorney are not independent agents: the prosecutor has office superiors and the defense attorney a client. In some cases, especially those involving serious charges, the prosecutor must obtain authorization of the settlement from his superiors. In all cases, however, the defense attorney must consult with his client about the proposed settlement. In effect, most defenders attempt to "sell" their clients on the settlement. Whether or not they "persuade" their clients to plead guilty in exchange for certain concessions is moot. They will usually put to their client the character of the settlement: "If you plead guilty, the prosecutor will reduce the charge to a misdemeanor" or "If you plead guilty, the prosecutor will recommend probation." They will usually follow this with their advice: "In my opinion, you would be better off pleading guilty because we haven't a chance at trial." Such "advice" is often coupled with the consequences of the two alternatives: "If you plead guilty, then you'll get straight probation; but if you take this to trial and we lose, then you'll go to prison as sure as I'm standing here." Threats of severe punishment, coupled with the miseries of jail, delay, and uncertainty of outcome may effectively coerce many defendants to accept the settlement (cf. Rosett and Cressey, 1976:28–31).

The Decision to Plead Not Guilty

We have seen that 80 to 90 percent of all defendants formally charged with crime eventually plead guilty. The question remains, then, how do we account for the small but very real number of cases that maintain a plea of not guilty and go to trial?

Those cases that maintain pleas of not guilty and go to trial reflect one of several conditions:

1. When the defense and prosecution cannot achieve a working consensus on the categorization and disposition of a case, then the defense will maintain a plea of not guilty and take the case to trial. Mather (1973) found that when public defenders held a "reasonable doubt" that their clients were guilty of the event charged and did not warrant the routine disposition conviction entailed, and were unable to negotiate a more reasonable settlement (a reduction in charge and penalty or outright dismissal), they would then take the cases to trial. Similarly, Neubauer (1974:232) found that when there was a "fact dispute," trial was a normal disposition. Furthermore, if the state fails to uphold its end of the settlement, the defense may withdraw its guilty plea and take the case to trial.

2. When deadbang cases involve particularly serious charges bringing mandatory or severe prison sentences. Mather (1973) found that in these cases involving prison sentences, the public defender felt the defendant had nothing to lose by going to trial because he would be sentenced to prison whether he pleaded guilty or was convicted at trial. Consequently, "justice" was best served by a trial disposition. Neubauer found a similar situation in Prairie City:

> . . . the decision to go to trial involves a rough calculation on the part of the defendant and his attorney: What are the chances of winning? What penalty if we lose? What settlement if we plea? The seriousness of the offense tends to slant the decision toward trial because the relative differences in penalties are lessened (1974:233).

3. When the defendant insists on trial, despite the considerable pressure brought to bear on his acquiescence, the defense will maintain a not guilty plea and take the case to trial. Sudnow (1965:270) found in a California public defender's office that "most of the P.D.'s cases that 'have to go to trial' are those where the P.D. is not able to sell the defendant on the 'bargain.' "[12]

4. When the case has drawn an inordinate amount of publicity or when it involves a particularly notorious and heinous crime, it will more readily go to trial (Sudnow, 1965:274–75). In such cases as the Tate-LaBianca murders committed by members of the Manson "family" in California, the negotiated guilty plea practice is suspended. Certainly the Los Angeles district attorney was cognizant of the political consequences of pleading out the Manson case. Few citizens would plead for mercy in a case that involved several promiscuous girls who used excessive amounts of drugs and lived in a commune led by a man who had spent most of his life in prison. The public expects what they consider the norm, a jury trial complete with battling adversaries, surprise witnesses, and melodramatic tactics. To avoid trial is to leave the public suspicious of the court process, a situation found when former Vice President Agnew negotiated a plea of *nolo contendere* to charges of income-tax evasion.

A final question remains. Assuming that the defendant maintains his plea of not guilty and takes the case to trial, he must decide between a trial by jury or a trial by bench. How do we account for the selection of one mode of trial over another? Why do some defendants select a jury trial while others select a trial by bench?

To preface the answer to these questions we should note that the mode of trial typically selected varies by jurisdiction and time. Between 1964 and 1971, for example, 4.8 percent of the cases processed through the federal district courts were by bench trial, while 9 percent of the cases were by jury trial (Hindelang et al., 1975:380). In 1972, only 2 percent of the cases processed through California courts were by bench trial and nearly 9 percent were tried by jury (Public Systems, Inc., 1974:101). In another investigation of criminal justice processing in several jurisdictions, McIntyre and Lippman (1970:1156–57) found that, of those defendants who took their case to trial, 17 percent in Houston and 33 percent in Brooklyn, New York, selected a bench trial.

---

[12] "Nevertheless, insistence on trial, especially by defendants in a deadbang case, is often viewed negatively by courthouse members, because it both places a strain on organizational resources and will eventuate in unjust treatment of the defendant" (Sudnow, 1965:271–74). Neubauer (1974:233) found that courthouse members viewed such insistence as "illegitimate." Participants label defendants as irrational who refuse to recognize the realities of the criminal justice system and insist on a trial even when the state has a very strong case."

Yet, 67 percent in Chicago and Detroit, 91 percent in Los Angeles, and 98 percent in Baltimore took their cases to a bench trial. There is, then, considerable variation from one jurisdiction to another in the proportion of defendants opting for bench or jury trials.

Which mode of trial is selected is not so much a whimsical matter as it is a strategic decision by the defense. It has been proposed that the defense will select that mode of trial that sports the best chance of acquittal (Oaks and Lehman, 1968:53–57). In their examination of Cook County and downstate Illinois, Oaks and Lehman (1968:54) found a "strong correlation between a defendant's choice of a jury or bench trial and the relative rates of conviction by each." Essentially, the more judges are likely to convict, the more likely defendants are to select jury trials, and the more juries are likely to convict, the more likely defendants are to select bench trials. It appears, Oaks and Lehman argue, that defense attorneys learn the conviction and acquittal patterns of judges and juries, and base their decisions on such past performances. Indeed, as the rates of conviction and acquittal by judges and juries change over time, so too do defense decisions on mode of trial change. As juries come to convict more often, defense comes to select bench trials. We should also note that when the conviction and acquittal rates of judges and juries converge, defendants generally opt for the bench trial, because sentences on conviction are generally more severe when a defendant is convicted at a jury trial than when he is convicted at a bench trial. This is due, it has been argued, to judges' penalizing defendants who, in their view, waste valuable court resources by demanding a jury trial. Using 1945 national data on fifteen types of crime, Kalven and Zeisel (1966:27–30) provide considerable support for these generalizations.

ACQUITTAL OF THE GUILTY

It has been argued that acquittal of defendants in spite of sufficient evidence to convict is a common judicial practice (Kalodner, 1956; Newman, 1966:131; Mileski, 1971). The practice itself may take one of several forms depending on the customs of the particular courthouse. In some areas, the trial judge may acquit defendants after they have entered their guilty plea; in other areas, he may dismiss the case prior to any pleading; in yet other areas, he may continue the case with eventual dismissal. But the practice typically finds its locus at the defendant's arraignment, and is generally confined to cases involving minor or misdemeanor charges. The consequence of this practice, unlike that of the negotiated guilty plea, is to remove the defendant from the criminal justice process altogether.

Acquittal of the guilty is oriented toward achieving one of two goals. First, the practice is oriented toward the individualization of justice by the trial judge. As Newman (1966:132) suggests, "It is an act of forgiveness; an attempt to achieve equity and effectiveness by the use of alternatives to formal conviction and sentencing." In his investigation of Michigan, Wisconsin, and Kansas, Newman (1966:134–72) found several types of cases in which trial judges would acquit the guilty:

1. When the criminal conduct appeared to be the product of emotional disturbance short of outright insanity. Homosexual conduct, for example, was deemed by some trial judges a manifestation of psychological disorder and not entirely within the realm of full criminal intent.
2. When the criminal conduct was judged to be a matter of private morality. Family or private disputes, sexual activities among consenting adults, and noncommercial gambling were not considered by some judges as proper matters for formal social control.
3. When the criminal conduct was judged as "normal" in the context of the defendant's social group. Among certain groups, for example, simple assault, sexual promiscuity, and gambling are considered normal activities.
4. When it was felt that the defendant did not deserve the criminal record brought by conviction. Conviction of respectable, first-time offenders is often considered unjust.
5. When better alternatives to conviction and sentencing existed. For example, a trial judge would acquit a defendant charged with writing bad checks if he agreed to make restitution to his victim.

Second, the practice is oriented toward the control or assistance of such formal social control agencies as the police (Newman, 1966: 188–99). Trial judges would acquit the guilty for purposes of informing police that certain enforcement policies did not meet with judicial approval. For example, some judges acquit those charged with engaging in certain illegal sexual activities, noncommercial gambling, or simple assault arising from family disputes as a means of informing police officers that other types of crime need their concern more than these types. Trial judges may acquit the guilty for purposes of informing police officers that their techniques of enforcement meet with judicial disapproval. They may acquit, for example, when police entice homosexuals or prostitutes to commit a crime. Trial judges may also acquit the guilty when the defendant is or can be cultivated as a police informant, thus providing the police with resources for law enforcement.

SUMMARY

"Bargain justice" is one of the most difficult aspects of the criminal justice system to understand. The mere mention of the term evokes puzzlement and angry responses from a public that has been socialized into believing the accused are innocent until proven guilty in a court of law. Unfortunately it is difficult to imagine a judicial system that does not use at least some of the elements of the negotiation process discussed in this chapter.

Throughout this text we have emphasized that the law's meaning cannot be decided without interpretation and negotiation. Indeed, the same holds true for conduct that may be considered criminal. Compared to conduct that is deemed criminal, the circumstances associated with an act that literally satisfies the elements of a law may, to reasonable and prudent persons, make it acceptable behavior or at least less than serious criminal conduct. Plea negotiations are ways to consider the circumstances of a crime.

We recognize there are inequities in a criminal justice system that relies on negotiated settlements. Informal disposition of cases is susceptible to capricious uses of power and discriminatory practices; therefore, such disposition must be controlled. But we must recognize that plea negotiations are partly the result of excessive punishments prescribed by law. Consequently, plea bargaining is not only a courthouse problem but a legislative one as well. As Rosett and Cressey (1976) have pointed out, legislative attempts to deter crime by instituting harsh punishments have actually promoted plea negotiation. Mandatory sentences are not sensitive to the unique features and circumstances of each crime.

We do not feel that the addition of more restrictive rules and policies about plea negotiation will reduce the abuses associated with our present system. Such a response to the problem only succeeds in driving negotiations deeper into the background where they may take more insidious forms. Only by admitting to the existence of plea negotiation as a legitimate means of settling cases and taking it out of hidden chambers will judges and lawyers be constrained to avoid the discriminatory and unjust aspects of the practice.

REFERENCES

ALSCHULER, ALBERT W.
  1968 "The Prosecutor's Role in Plea Bargaining," *University of Chicago Law Review* 36 (Fall): 50–112.

BEATTIE, RONALD H.

1972 *Offender-Based Criminal Statistics in 12 California Counties.* Sacramento, Calif.: Bureau of Criminal Statistics.

BLAU, PETER M.

1964 *Exchange and Power in Social Life.* New York: Wiley.

BLUMBERG, ABRAHAM S.

1967 *Criminal Justice.* Chicago: Quadrangle.

1967b "The Practice of Law as a Confidence Game: Organizational Cooptation of a Profession," *Law and Society Review* 1 (June): 15–39.

CASPER, JONATHAN D.

1972 *American Criminal Justice: The Defendant's Perspective.* Englewood Cliffs, N.J.: Prentice-Hall.

CHAMBLISS, WILLIAM J., AND ROBERT B. SEIDMAN

1971 *Law, Order, and Power.* Reading, Mass.: Addison-Wesley.

COLE, GEORGE F.

1970 "The Decision to Prosecute," *Law and Society Review* 4 (February): 331–43.

1975 *The American System of Criminal Justice.* North Scituate, Mass.: Duxbury Press.

DALTON, MELVILLE

1959 *Men Who Manage.* New York: Wiley.

DAVIS, ANTHONY

1970 "Sentences for Sale: A New Look at Plea Bargaining in England and America," *Criminal Law Review* (March and April): 150–62, 218–29.

ENKER, ARNOLD

1967 "Perspectives on Plea Bargaining," Appendix A in President's Commission on Law Enforcement and Administration of Justice, *Task Force Report: The Courts,* pp. 108–19. Washington, D.C.: Government Printing Office.

GREENWOOD, PETER W., SORREL WILDHORN, EUGENE C. POGGIO, MICHAEL J. STRUMWASSER, AND PETER DELEON

1973 *Prosecution of Adult Felony Defendants in Los Angeles County: A Policy Perspective.* Santa Monica, Calif.: Rand Corporation.

GROSMAN, BRIAN A.

1969 *The Prosecutor: An Inquiry into the Exercise of Discretion.* Toronto: University of Toronto Press.

HERRMAN, JOACHIM

1974 "The Rule of Compulsory Prosecution and the Scope of Prosecutorial Discretion in Germany," *University of Chicago Law Review* 41 (Spring): 468–505.

HINDELANG, MICHAEL J., CHRISTOPHER S. DUNN, L. PAUL SUTTON, AND ALISON L. AUMICK

1973 *Sourcebook of Criminal Justice Statistics, 1973.* Washington, D.C.: U.S. Department of Justice.

KALODNER, HOWARD I.

1956 "Metropolitan Criminal Courts of First Instance," *Harvard Law Review* 70 (December): 320–49.

KALVEN, HARRY, JR., AND HANS ZEISEL
  1966 *The American Jury.* Boston: Little, Brown.

LAURENT, FRANK
  1959 *The Business of a Trial Court: 100 Years of Cases.* Madison: University of Wisconsin Press.

LEVIN, MARTIN A.
  1972 "Urban Politics and Judicial Behavior," *Journal of Legal Studies* 1 (January): 193–221.

LUMMUS, HENRY T.
  1937 *The Trial Judge.* Mineola, N.Y.: Foundation Press.

MC INTYRE, DONALD M.
  1967 *Law Enforcement in the Metropolis.* American Bar Association.

MC INTYRE, DONALD M., AND DAVID LIPPMAN
  1970 "Prosecutors and Early Disposition of Felony Cases," *American Bar Association Journal* 56 (December): 1154–59.

MATHER, LYNN M.
  1973 "Some Determinants of the Method of Case Disposition: Decision-Making by Public Defenders in Los Angeles," *Law and Society Review* 8 (Winter): 187–216.

MILESKI, MAUREEN
  1971 "Courtroom Encounters: An Observation Study of a Lower Criminal Court," *Law and Society Review* 5 (May): 473–538.

MOLEY, RAYMOND
  1929 *Politics and Criminal Prosecution.* New York: Minton, Balch and Co.

NEUBAUER, DAVID W.
  1974 *Criminal Justice in Middle America.* Morristown, N.J.: General Learning Press.

NEWMAN, DONALD J.
  1956 "Pleading Guilty for Considerations: A Study of Bargain Justice," *Journal of Criminal Law, Criminology, and Police Science* (March–April): 780–90.

  1966 *Conviction: The Determination of Guilt or Innocence Without Trial.* Boston: Little, Brown.

NOTE
  1964 "Guilty Plea Bargaining: Compromises by Prosecutors to Secure Guilty Pleas," *University of Pennsylvania Law Review* 112 (April): 865–908.

OAKS, DALLIN H., AND WARREN LEHMAN
  1968 *A Criminal Justice System and the Indigent: A Study of Chicago and Cook County.* Chicago: University of Chicago Press.

PRESIDENT'S COMMISSION ON LAW ENFORCEMENT AND ADMINISTRATION OF JUSTICE
  1967 *Task Force Report: The Courts.* Washington, D.C.: Government Printing Office.

PUBLIC SYSTEMS, INC.
  1974   *California Correctional System Intake Study.* Sacramento, Calif.:
         Office of Criminal Justice Planning.

ROSETT, ARTHUR
  1967   "The Negotiated Guilty Plea," *Annals of the American Academy of
         Political and Social Science* 374 (November): 70–81.

ROSETT, ARTHUR, AND DONALD R. CRESSEY
  1976   *Justice by Consent: Plea Bargains in the American Courthouse.* Phila-
         delphia: Lippincott.

SILVERSTEIN, LEE
  1965   *Defense of the Poor.* American Bar Foundation.

SKOLNICK, JEROME H.
  1966   *Justice without Trial: Law Enforcement in Democratic Society.* New
         York: Wiley.
  1967   "Social Control in the Adversary System," *Journal of Conflict Resolu-
         tion* 11 (March): 51–70.

SMITH, ALEXANDER B., AND HARRIET POLLACK
  1973   *Crime and Justice in a Mass Society.* New York: Holt, Rinehart and
         Winston.

SUDNOW, DAVID
  1965   "Normal Crimes: Sociological Features of the Penal Code in a Public
         Defender Office," *Social Problems* 12 (Winter): 255–76.

WHITE, WELSH
  1971   "A Proposal for Reform of the Plea Bargaining Process," *University of
         Pennsylvania Law Review* 119 (January): 439–65.

SELECTED READINGS

MATHER, LYNN M., "Some Determinants of the Method of Case Disposition:
    Decision-Making by Public Defenders in Los Angeles," *Law and Society
    Review* 8 (Winter 1973): 187–216.
    An examination of the significance of the strength of the prosecutor's
    case and the seriousness of the case on a public defender's decision as to
    how he should manage the case. Also provides ethnographic data illus-
    trating the process of plea negotiation.

NEWMAN, DONALD J., *Conviction: The Determination of Guilt or Innocence with-
    out Trial.* Boston: Little, Brown, 1966.
    An investigation of plea negotiation in Kansas, Michigan, and Wisconsin.
    Examines the alternatives available to officials and the conditions under
    which different alternatives are employed.

ROSETT, ARTHUR, AND DONALD R. CRESSEY, *Justice by Consent: Plea Bargains in
    the American Courthouse.* Philadelphia: Lippincott, 1976.

An analysis of the role of plea negotiation in criminal justice. After examining several popular explanations of the practice, the authors argue that plea negotiation is oriented toward administering justice within an inherently punitive organization.

SUDNOW, DAVID, "Normal Crimes: Sociological Features of the Penal Code in a Public Defender Office," *Social Problems* 12 (Winter 1965): 255–76. A sociological investigation of the typification process which is involved in plea negotiation as well as in such other practical decisions as charging.

7
TRIAL

The average American probably thinks most critical decisions about defendants are made during a trial. However, we have seen in the previous chapters that only about 10 percent of those charged with a crime take their cases to trial. The criminal trial is a statistically atypical procedure for adjudicating unusual cases. It is likely that a case will go to trial when there is substantial disagreement between courthouse members about the proper categorization of the defendant's act, when charges are likely to bring a severe prison sentence, or when the case has generated a lot of publicity.

We should not, however, diminish the importance of the criminal trial, for many cases actually reach this stage of the criminal justice process. To be sure, relative to the number of cases that enter into the criminal justice process, the number of court trials is small, but a trial is not an insignificant event.

THE STAGES OF TRIAL

A criminal trial is a formal transaction in which the guilt or innocence of a defendant is decided by a judge or jury on the basis of facts developed by the prosecution and defense relating to the commission of a crime and the defendant's culpability for that crime. The transaction itself is comprised of five basic stages (Knowlton, 1962).

1. After the jury has been selected, for those defendants opting for a jury trial, the trial begins with the opening statements of the prosecutor and defense attorney. During these statements attorneys outline their respective cases.

2. The prosecutor presents the state's case against the defendant. Essentially, he tries to establish "beyond a reasonable doubt" that a crime was committed and the defendant intentionally committed it. To this end, he provides "evidence" that the defendant performed a line of action that constitutes an instance of a particular penal code violation. The prosecutor's step-by-step presentation of the state's case is subject to cross-examination by the defense. At the conclusion of the state's case, it is customary for the defense to move for a dismissal on the grounds that the prosecutor failed to provide sufficient evidence that the case is an instance of a particular penal code violation.

3. Assuming the judge does not grant a dismissal, the defense presents its case. While the prosecution must provide evidence demonstrating that the defendant did commit the crime of which he is charged, the defense need only show that the state failed to establish guilt beyond a reasonable doubt. The defense attorney may accomplish this by attacking the prosecutor's interpretations of the physical artifacts and verbal testimony of witnesses and/or providing additional artifacts and testimony he interprets as "facts" which prove his client did not commit a crime. The defense attorney's step-by-step presentation is subject to cross-examination by the prosecutor.

4. Once the defense rests its case, both the prosecution and defense make their closing arguments. This summation serves as the final argument, in which each attorney tries to persuade the judge or jury to adopt the version of the case he has presented.

5. Once the prosecution and defense have completed their closing arguments, a judgment of guilt or innocence must be made by the judge or jury. In some jurisdictions, the judge at a bench trial is required to file a memorandum in support of a guilty judgment. In cases tried by a jury, the judgment is preceded by a set of instructions from the judge, which include the responsibilities of the jury, the major issues in the case, and the relevant laws to be considered. The judge has the right to reverse a jury's verdict of guilty, but does not have the right to reverse its verdict of acquittal.

Implicit in this brief sketch of the trial is the adversarial character of the event. Unlike the cooperative tenor of much plea negotiation, the court trial often reflects an adversarial, combative transaction between defense and prosecution (cf. Remington et al., 1969:666–73; Chambliss and Seidman, 1971:416). Once the defense and prosecution decide to take a case to trial, they typically commit themselves to win: the defense strives for dismissal or acquittal and the prosecution works for conviction. To their respective ends, both are expected to employ a variety of tactics designed to advance their cause and hinder that of their opponent.

There is, of course, considerable variation between and within jurisdictions in the character of criminal trials. It makes a difference, for example, whether the trial is by jury or by bench. Jury trials require procedures, such as jury selection, sequestering, instruction, and judicial assessment of the verdict. It also makes a difference whether the trial occurs in a lower court or in a superior court. Research has shown that lower court trials are generally very quick, quite informal, and less combative in comparison to felony court trials (Kalodner, 1956; Subin, 1966; President's Commission on Law Enforcement and Administration of Justice, 1967:30–31, 133–36; Mileski, 1971).

Perhaps more than any other stage of the criminal justice process, the court trial, especially the felony court trial, has been subjected to an enormous amount of academic investigation. Most have been undertaken by jurists and legal scholars, and have centered around issues of procedural law and the insanity defense.[1] Our concern will be confined to the character of the trial process.

The Trial Process

For generations, the court trial, whether a jury or bench trial, a misdemeanor court or felony court trial, has been conceptualized as a rational "fact-finding" process aimed at discovering the "truth" about an alleged criminal event and acting upon that truth (cf. Frank, 1969: 80–102; Kaplan, 1973:337). As the noted jurist Jerome Frank points out:

> When we say that present-day trial methods are "rational," presumably we mean this: The men who compose our trial courts, judges and juries, in each lawsuit conduct an intelligent inquiry into all the practically available evidence, in order to ascertain, as near as may be, the truth about the facts of that suit (1969:80).

It is assumed that the trier intelligently examines the physical

---

[1] An entire issue of *Law and Contemporary Problems* 28 is devoted to "jurimetrics," and includes articles on the decision-making processes involved in trials.

artifacts introduced and verbal testimony elicited from witnesses by the prosecution and defense, and derives from that information the "real" facts of the case; for example, "a first-degree burglary occurred on May 5 at 10 P.M. at the residence of John Kizzae," "Mike Kilgore committed that burglary," and "Mr. Kilgore intended to commit that burglary." It is commonly assumed that the trier can best determine the facts through an adversarial or combative proceeding. In short, "truth" derives from a battle between the defense and prosecution. Once the facts are established according to our ideal model of the trial, the trier works at matching the facts of the case with the elements of the relevant penal code category. If the facts match, the trier logically finds the defendant guilty; if the facts do not match, the trier logically finds the defendant not guilty (of that particular crime at least).

We feel that the trial may not be as rational and efficient as the public often assumes it is. What constitutes the "real facts" in any given case is not self-evident. Students of the trial process have long recognized that *information* on the real facts of a particular event removed in time and space is obscure and subject to considerable distortion: (1) The physical artifacts of an event may be incomplete, and consequently alter the trier's definition of the event. (2) Eyewitnesses fail to appear at trial; therefore, information that could alter the trier's definition of the events is not always discovered. (3) Eyewitness accounts of events may be insincere and therefore inaccurate. In a number of cases, a witness may lie about features of events in order to achieve some personal end (Frank, 1969:18–19). A defendant's wife, for example, may state that on the night of the burglary, her husband was at home, when in fact he was burglarizing a home. (4) Eyewitness accounts of the event may be sincere yet inaccurate (cf. Pound, 1930: 70–72, Frank, 1969:17–18; Williams, 1963; Karlen, 1964:119–35; Chambliss and Seidman, 1971:429). Here, inaccuracy may derive from one of several conditions. People are generally poor observers, especially when they are not "prepared" to observe (Jones and Gerard, 1967:249). This point is well illustrated in classroom experiments where students, sitting quietly taking notes, suddenly witness a person enter the lecture hall, perform a bizarre act and quickly depart. In the students' report of the act there will be enormous variation and distortion of the details. This is so because people selectively perceive their environment (Shibutani, 1962:108–9). "Ordinary healthful living requires that we be highly selective in the stimuli to which we pay attention and, at the same time, that whole ranges of stimuli be consigned to the background and ignored" (Lindesmith, Strauss, and Denzin, 1975:173). Things that may not be relevant to an eyewitness and hence not attended to could be critical features of a crime. Memory is general; only the gist of events and materials is recalled (Bartlett, 1932). When asked to recall material, subjects eliminated logical inconsistencies, and retention was minimal when an event had little or no relevance to a person's life (Lindesmith, Strauss, and Denzin, 1975:189). What people observe and how they define objects in a setting are functions of their present interests and their cognitive perspectives for making sense of the world (Shibutani, 1962:118–27). As Lindesmith, Strauss, and Denzin succinctly put it:

> The individual's report of what he perceives, and his idea of what he sees or hears, includes matters of inference, interpretation, and judgment—in short, it does not discriminate between what may be called direct perception or physical stimulus, and the meaningful elaboration of the perception that occurs when it is classified, named, analyzed, and judged (1975:173).

What persons observe is not what "really" happened but what they have been equipped, through social participation in groups, to see. For example, there may be disagreement between two witnesses as to what the victim did to the defendant's wife in the tavern before his fatal demise. One says that the victim was "manhandling" and "making a sexual play" to the defendant's wife, while the other says that the victim was simply "being friendly." The former witness may be operating from a perspective in which "touching" is forbidden, except between kin and confined to certain times and places; the latter witness may be operating from a perspective in which "touching" is an expected way of showing friendship. Williams (1963:89) reports that when witnesses recount the verbal expressions of the performers, they do not report their precise verbalizations so much as their understanding of what the performers "meant," whether this coincided with the performers' intent or not. Furthermore, people often have difficulty communicating what they observed to the court. Witnesses who do not speak English fluently, for example, have trouble communicating their observations to an English-speaking court. All persons, no matter how articulate they may be, might use an improper word or phrase or make an unwitting gesture which conveys something quite different than what was intended (Frank, 1969:18).

Thus, it is difficult if not impossible to determine "what really happened." At best the truth is approximated. Even if humans were *capable* of objectively reporting all the facts of a case, the method by which facts are to be discovered, namely, the adversarial or "fight" method, may preclude objectivity. Frank (1969:80–102) has levied a critical attack on the value of the adversary or fight method as a means of determining the facts of the case. Recall that in this procedure the prosecution and defense engage in an intellectual contest. Each side uses a body of information to support his line of argumentation and denigrate the opponent's claims. As Frank points out, "the lawyer aims at victory, at winning in the fight, not at aiding the court to discover the facts. He does not want the trial court to reach a sound educated guess, if it is likely to be contrary to his client's interests" (1969:85). Indeed, "the partisanship of the opposing lawyers blocks the uncovering of vital evidence or leads to a presentation of vital testimony in a way that distorts it" (1969:81).

In effect, the adversary or fight method facilitates tactics aimed at manipulating the information on which the trier makes decisions. The following are several commonly employed tactics:

1. Attorneys coach witnesses before trial, perhaps telling them precisely what to say and what not to say in response to formal questioning. In some cases, especially those involving dishonest lawyers, attorneys might even tell witnesses to provide false testimony.

2 Attorneys coach witnesses on how to deceptively manage appearances in court. For example, "He educates the irritable witness to conceal his irritability, the cocksure witness to subdue his cocksureness. In that way, the trial court is denied the benefit of observing the witness's actual normal demeanor, and thus prevented from sizing up the witness accurately" (Frank, 1969:83).

3 Attorneys may work at controlling information that is unfavorable to their line of argumentation. The attorney, if possible, "will not ask a witness to testify who, on cross-

Trials are a stage where the defense and prosecution perform before a judge and jury. The "reality" of what happened in a given case is constructed on this stage. (*UPI Photo*)

examination, might testify to true facts helpful to his opponent" (Frank, 1969:84).

4 An attorney may bring in surprise testimony for which his opponent is unprepared. The point, of course, is to catch the adversary off guard; develop a line of information that the opponent cannot readily or methodically rebut.

Thus, the determination at trial of "what really happened" is seriously impeded not only by the ambiguous and distorted nature of the information provided by witnesses but also by the tactical manipulation of that information by the adversary attorneys. The trial does not function merely as a fact-finding procedure. As Frank (1969:23) argues, " . . . facts are not 'data,' not something that is 'given'; they are not waiting somewhere, ready made, for the court to discover, to 'find.' " Rather, the trial is a social transaction in which human actors —witnesses, attorneys, and triers—"develop" or "construct" from a plethora of cues facts that they define and compete with others to have accepted as the "real facts" of the event. As we have seen, eyewitnesses do not observe raw reality but define objects and events in terms of the cognitive perspective they have learned for making sense of their world. Similarly, trial attorneys make sense of physical artifacts and verbal statements of witnesses in terms of their particular interests and their cognitive perspectives. The trier of the case also develops the facts of the event. Indeed, as Frank (1969:233) points out, trial judges and jurors are themselves "witnesses" of the trial. They observe the presentation of information and select which witnesses to believe and which interpretations of the event seem most credible, most reasonable, and most logical given their particular orientation toward the world (Frank, 1969:24, 165–85; Chambliss and Seidman, 1971:429–31). Thus, as Quinney concludes, "the criminal trial constructs a reality— a social reality. Objective facts are not gathered in a criminal trial, but decisions are reached on 'evidence' that is meaningful to the interacting and conflicting participants" (1975:215).

Trial by Bench—Trial by Jury

Given the problematic nature of information and the adversarial character of the transaction, we propose that "trial" is best conceptualized as a "fact-developing" instead of a "fact-finding" transaction. Our interest now turns to the formal decisions of the authorized trier of criminal cases. One basic question will be addressed: On what basis do triers of criminal cases pass their verdicts? To preface this discussion, it is useful to consider briefly the character of the bench and jury trials.

In a bench trial, the trial judge is charged with two basic tasks. First, he must regulate the trial proceedings, deciding what evidence can and cannot be introduced and ruling on the motions presented by the defense and the prosecution. Second, on the basis of what has been presented to him during trial, he must decide if conviction is warranted.

The character of this proceeding is somewhat different from that of a jury trial. The trial attorneys tend to be less emotional and more methodical in their presentations before a trial judge (Chambliss and Seidman, 1971:432). They typically acknowledge that trial judges are "wise" to their emotional, sometimes dramatic, tactics aimed at swaying a lay jury. Rather than alienate the trial judge, attorneys present a more methodical case aimed at supporting a particular interpretation of the event. The bench trial is usually brief. In such areas as Pittsburgh, Philadelphia, and Los Angeles, a common form of bench trial is the "trial on the transcript," a brief proceeding in which the defense may concede certain points but contest others. But "argument is focused only on the issues in conflict, not on the entire case" (Mather, 1973:195). In all bench trials, including the more traditional forms, the proceeding is not too lengthy because attorneys do not devote a lot of time explaining the many nuances of criminal law and criminal proceedings to the judge. Instead, they present their cases on the premise that the judge understands many of the assumptions on which their arguments are based.

Judges do not approach cases as "neutral," "objective" triers. As Nagel (1962) pointed out, judges hear cases with particular cognitive perspectives including conceptions of what are "real" crimes and "real" criminals, the meaning of various penal code categories, and the meaning of procedural rules. Consequently, judgment is flavored by the judge's particular perspective. Such an idea is given support in Nagel's investigation of 313 state and federal supreme court judges. He found that when judges were former prosecutors, members of the American Bar Association, Republicans, Protestants, and voiced conservative ideologies, they sided more with the prosecution than with the defense. Conversely, when judges were not former prosecutors, not members of the A.B.A., Democrats, Catholics, and voiced liberal ideologies, they sided more with the defense than with the prosecution.

Research has also suggested that in some cases judges take into consideration the political implications of their judgment. Jacob and Vines (1963) found that judges are very sensitive to the political community of which they are a part. A judge may be influenced by local power groups who have strong feelings about those brought to court (cf. Vines, 1964). To ensure reelection, for example, judges take into account the repercussions of acquitting a notorious defendant or convicting a respected member of the community. In their investigation of nine trial judges sitting in "Central Sessions," Smith and Blumberg (1967) found that each judge maintained strong ties to various political groups. The political-mindedness of these judges often precluded what Smith and Blumberg termed "objective" consideration of the cases they were to process.

Trial judges will often state for the record that their official judgments of guilt and innocence are products of astute legal logic, a mechanical exercise of fitting facts to law. But, as Frank argues, the trial judge begins

> . . . with the decision he considers desirable, and then,
> working backwards, figure[s] out and publish[es] a F [fact] and a
> R [rule] which will make his decision appear to be logically
> sound, if only there is some oral testimony which is in accord
> with his reported F, and if he applied the proper R to that
> reported F. If so, it does not matter whether actually he
> believed that testimony, that is, whether the facts he reports
> are the facts as he believes them to be. In other words, he can,
> without fear of challenge, "fudge" the facts he finds, and thus
> "force the balance" (1969:168).

Thus, the trial judge attends to a number of contingencies and arrives at what he feels is a reasonably just decision, and then tries to find accepted (often written) principles to justify that decision.

In a jury trial, a lay body comprised of local citizens is authorized to pass judgment on a defendant's guilt or innocence.[2] Except for their delivery of judgment, jurors are passive observers of the trial. They are not allowed to question witnesses, rule on motions, censor participants, or take notes during trial. "They must observe the evidence, listen to the testimony, and form their impressions as the trial progresses" (Jacob, 1972:125). At the conclusion of the attorneys' presentations and judicial instructions, they retire to a private room to reach a decision on the verdict. On reaching a verdict, they announce their judgment, generally through the foreman, to the court. Unlike judges in some areas, the jury does not have to account to any state official for its verdict or the basis of its verdict (cf. Kadish and Kadish, 1971).

Reviewing the empirical research done by the University of Chicago's jury project, Broeder (1959) reports that most juries they investigated voted on the verdict as soon as they were sequestered. The popular belief that juries regularly partake in extensive deliberation and discussion prior to a vote is fallacious. In slightly under one-third of the cases reviewed by the Chicago project, unanimity was reached on the first ballot. In 90 percent of the remaining cases, the majority on the first ballot ultimately won out. Cases in which a single, devoted juror rises in opposition to the others and eventually wins them over are quite rare.

Strodtbeck et al. (1957) found in a study of mock jury operations that members of higher status occupations were overrepresented in the

---

[2] The trial judge has the right to direct the jury to acquit the defendant or simply overrule their conviction.

foremen positions. More importantly, they found several differences in levels of participation. Men participated more than women, and members of the higher status occupations participated more than members of the lower status occupations. Simon (1959) also found that the better educated members participated more than members of the less educated classes. These differentials are important for participation is an indicant of power (Simon, 1959). That is, those who participate more are considered by their fellows as helpful during the deliberation, and can shape the image of the group's collective feeling toward the case. Simon also found that jurors spent little time discussing the legal instructions announced by the judge compared to the time spent exchanging opinions about the trial and experiences from personal and daily life deemed pertinent to the case.

The jury is supposed to reach a verdict by applying the legal rules announced by the trial judge to the body of facts it has found in the course of the trial. In other words, their formal judgment is supposed to be a product of a mechanical process of matching legal rules to the facts of the case. That juries operate in this fashion has been seriously questioned for years. Erlanger aptly states the points at issue:

> The principal question has been whether juries confine themselves to judging issues of fact (including assigned issues of law and fact) as presented to them or whether they depart from the judge's instructions and render verdicts based on their own conception of the law or on purely irrational considerations. A concomitant issue in this debate has been the question of the jury's general competence: whether uninitiated laymen are even able to comprehend the evidence and the instructions, and whether court procedure is not so organized as to diminish rather than increase the possibilities of a rational judgment of the facts (1970:346).

Many scholars have suggested that jurors do not understand all or part of the legal instructions. In one early study, Hervey (1947) found that 40 percent of his sample of midwestern jurors reported they had not fully understood the judicial instructions. In her examination of jurors' understanding of judicial instructions on insanity defenses, Simon (1967:161–63) found that jurors confused the elements of the insanity rules provided by the judge. She studied three groups of juries. One group was instructed on the use of the M'Naghten rule in defining insanity: "The defendant is excused only if he did not know what he was doing or did not know that what he was doing was wrong." A second group was instructed to use the Durham rule in defining insanity: "A defendant is excused if his act was the product of a mental disease or defect." A third group was not instructed on any rule for defining insanity. Simon found that of those juries instructed to use the

M'Naghten rule, a third failed to use it. Furthermore, of those juries instructed to use the Durham rule, half in effect used the "right or wrong" test specified in the M'Naghten rule. It appears, then, that jurors had some problems in understanding the specific elements involved in the insanity rules.

It could be that jurors are interpreting the legal instructions in terms of their own perspectives for making sense of the world. Returning for a moment to Simon's investigation, she found that jurors did not have as much trouble understanding judicial instructions on the meaning of insanity as they had in assessing insanity in terms of their understanding of how a "reasonable" or "rational" person acts. This was illustrated by one juror who was instructed under the Durham formula and heard no judicial reference to "right from wrong" as a formula for insanity:

> Are they insane when they commit these acts? Our society brought us up in such a way as to believe that these particular acts are wrong; as any sexual perversion is wrong. Going back to Cleopatra's day, why brothers and sisters got married and had children; and it was not considered wrong. But we have been brought up to believe that it is wrong. Now in his [the defendant's] mind he knew that it was wrong according to our society's teachings, but that doesn't make him insane or mentally unbalanced. Being wrong is guilty (Simon, 1967:161–62).

Thus, "for most jurors, the defendant's admission that he knew that what he was doing was wrong proved that he was guilty and not insane," irrespective of the rule under which they were instructed or whether they were not instructed at all (Simon, 1967:162).

In their monumental investigation of jury operations, Kalven and Zeisel (1966:221–97) found that jurors would also interpret the announced penal code categories in terms of their perspectives regarding the meaning of the laws at issue. For example, often jurors would not define penal code categories like assault and battery or aggravated assault as encompassing events in which victims provoked or attacked the defendants. Kalven and Zeisel also found that jurors would routinely interpret such events as hunting on game preserves, making illegal whiskey, and some forms of gambling as not really "crimes," and would consequently acquit defendants.

Like others in the criminal justice system, jurors also assess a defendant's character, and there is some evidence indicating that their evaluation strongly influences their decision on the verdict (cf. Stephan, 1975). If jurors define the accused as "unattractive," that impression may work against the defendant. For example, Kalven and Zeisel

The character of the defendant is assessed by juries, and the bizarre antics and appearances of the defendants in the Manson trial was a factor in their conviction. (*UPI Photo*)

In the trial of Patty Hearst, the defense attorney, F. Lee Bailey, objects when prosecutor James Browning Jr. asks Patty if she considers herself a good actress. (*Wide World Photos*)

(1966) found "vulgar" comportment on the part of the defendant was associated with situations in which the judge would have ruled more leniently than did the jury. However, if jurors "sympathize" with those on trial, then this relationship may work in their favor.

Several factors, all of which influenced jurors' decisions, were identified by Kalven and Zeisel, including the defendant's age, physical attractiveness or physical condition, emotional comportment, and occupational position. These features, and undoubtedly many others, provide jurors with clues about defendants. Many times such clues may be interpreted as evidence that a person is not really a criminal, but a respectable member of the community who made a mistake. To convict and punish him, therefore, may be viewed as inappropriate.

Again, like others in the criminal justice system, jurors assess the punitive consequences of their decisions. According to Kalven and Zeisel (1966), jurors acquit or render a lenient verdict against defendants who they feel have been punished enough for their wrongdoing. For example, in cases where the defendant himself was injured in the crime, that injury may be deemed punishment enough and state-administered punishment would be excessive. Similarly, when a defendant has suffered a personal loss brought about through his wrongdoing, further punishment may be viewed as harsh and unnecessary. For example, in a prosecution for negligent auto homicide the victim was the fiancée of the defendant, a twenty-one-year-old member of the Air Force. It was clear from the judge's description of the case that the jury as well as the parents of the girl felt the death of the defendant's fiancée had been punishment enough for the event (Kalven and Zeisel, 1966:302).

When jurors evaluate the appropriateness of a penalty that would be imposed if they convicted a defendant, they may not really know what penalties are prescribed by the law. If jurors ask the judge about the potential penalty in a given case, they are usually informed that it is irrelevant. Consequently, their deliberations may only involve what they think the penalty will be. If jurors guess that the penalty is too severe, then acquittal or leniency is likely.

Assessing the propriety of sentences is an old practice. In early nineteenth-century England, some 230 criminal offenses were punishable by death. Most of these offenses, however, were considered too trivial to warrant such a harsh penalty. This popular sentiment found its way into the courtroom in the form of juries. Jurors would routinely acquit or reduce the charges to a noncapital offense in order to circumvent what they felt were unjust punishments (Radzinowicz, 1948: vol. 1, pts. IV, V). For example, jurors would find, against the evidence, that only thirty nine rather than forty shillings had been stolen by a defendant, because stealing forty shillings was a violation punished by death.

THE VALUE OF THE PETIT JURY

It has been argued that jurors may be incompetent as triers. As we have seen, they may not comprehend all or part of the legal instructions announced by the judge, or they may not always understand the factual basis of the cases they try. In his study of mock jury operations, for example, Marston (1924) argues that judges understand the factual basis of cases far better than jurors. This may be especially true in cases involving complex pieces of technical or scientific artifacts and testimony. Furthermore, a juror's understanding of the information presented at trial may be shaped to a greater extent than the judge's understanding by such nonfactual features as the demeanor and self-confidence of the witnesses (Marston, 1924), the socioeconomic background and physical attributes of the defendant (Stephan, 1975), and the prestige of the attorneys (Weld and Danzig, 1940). The question remains, of course, whether a jury is more "just" in its decisions than a judge. Is the system so riddled with problems that it should be abandoned? We think not.

In all probability jurors are just as competent as the supposedly expert trial judges in understanding the factual basis of cases. Recall that Kalven and Zeisel (1966:56) found that in 75 percent of their cases judges and juries agreed on the verdict. Kalven and Zeisel (1966:149–62) interpreted such agreement as evidence that judges and juries share a common understanding of the factual basis of most cases. They also found that jurors were generally competent in understanding even the most technical of arguments and lines of testimony. Similarly, Simon (1967:85–86) found that jurors generally had little difficulty understanding most aspects of psychiatric testimony, even though they often felt such testimony was extreme and impractical.

However, jurors often reach irrational and legally groundless verdicts. Courthouse officials in Prairie City provided Neubauer (1974) with several lines of support for this criticism. Prosecutors, for example, informed Neubauer that jurors are amateurs in criminal justice and, hence, somewhat unpredictable.

> An example of such unpredictability came in a narcotics case when two little old ladies announced during jury deliberations that "only God can judge" and refused to vote, thus hanging the jury. Another grandmother type, after a not guilty verdict, put her arm around the defendant and said, "Bob, we were sure happy to find you not guilty, but don't do it again" (Neubauer, 1974:229).

The legally groundless nature of jury verdicts is also suggested by one defense attorney who distinguished between a factually strong case and a winning case:

The state may have a strong case and sufficient evidence to prove the defendant committed the act, but still not have a winning case because a jury would not convict. He cited a hypothetical example of an eighteen-year-old charged with a sex crime, but love was involved. The evidence might be open and shut, but it is doubtful that a jury would convict (Neubauer, 1974:231).

But two points should be considered with regard to this criticism. First, as Jacob suggests, the arbitrary and groundless character of jury verdicts "seems to be based on a small number of cases that are vividly remembered because of their spectacular nature" (1972:129). Second, as Neubauer (1974:228–31) implies, just because there is an element of unpredictability in jury trials and a failure by juries to convict in some cases where the evidence of guilt is strong, this does not mean that jurors operate irrationally or arbitrarily. What is deemed reasonable and sound by courthouse officials is not necessarily what jurors consider reasonable and sound. For example, while Simon (1967) found that jurors understood psychiatric testimony, they often disregarded it for it seemed too extreme and impractical given their orientation toward what is sane and insane.

The defense and prosecution confer with the judge over a point of law during a trial. Any evidence not in accord with the law cannot be brought before the jury. (*UPI Photo*)

Over the last several hundred years, the sanctioned role of a jury has become that of a "fact-finding" body only. The jury is no longer authorized, as in the past, to determine the relevant laws for a given case or to disregard the legal instructions of the judge (Chambliss and Seidman, 1971:432–34, 440–41). Consequently, the judge formally constrains the operation of the jury by structuring the law with which they work. Yet, as we pointed out above, jurors continue to assess the legal instructions from their particular perspectives. Furthermore, jury verdicts are products of jurors fitting penalties to the concrete facts of the cases, hence, manipulating the announced laws to fit their conceptions of what cases deserve. Such findings could be taken as a serious criticism of jury operations.

Mortimer and Sanford Kadish (1971:268), however, present a persuasive argument that the jury is authorized, albeit implicitly, to depart from the legal instructions when such instructions require the implementation of unjust rules or their unjust application. As these authors argue:

> The duty of the jury is indeed to find the facts upon the basis of the evidence presented and to issue a general verdict by applying those facts to the propositions of law given by the judge. This is the rule, and it imposes an obligation to comply. But it is not therefore an absolute and unyielding obligation. Sometimes the jury's commonsense perceptions, considerations of fairness to the defendant, or appraisal of the law (in contrast to the judge's statement of it) are so weighty that they *justify* departure from the requirement that the jury defer to the judge's instructions. Some rules, that is, *permit departure* from the very rules that bind their agents when the agents are satisfied that there is not merely reason, but extremely good reason, for doing so (Kadish and Kadish, 1971:211; emphasis added).

The point, then, is that the jury remains an institution for importing various community sentiments into the trial process. That is, it provides yet another means for "doing justice" within an inherently unjust legal framework (cf. Kalven and Zeisel, 1966:494–95).[3]

---

[3] A final note is in order. We must remember that the typical jury does not import, nor does it represent, the sum total of community sentiments. We find within the confines of this state a multitude of social groups, each of which is organized around somewhat different sets of interests. The typical jury, however, underrepresents certain groups—the poor, the nonpropertied, the transient, and some ethnic and racial minorities—and overrepresents certain other groups—the propertied, the middle and upper classes. Those groups that contribute the most defendants in the criminal justice process are also those groups generally underrepresented on the typical jury. As a consequence, many defendants may be tried from the perspectives of outsiders. In some

SENTENCING

Except for those who, on conviction, take their case to the appellate courts, convicted defendants make their final court appearance at the sentencing occasion. Up to this time, court processing was *formally* oriented toward issues of guilt and innocence, but at the sentencing stage guilt is assumed. The primary issue now (as it is in fact throughout the entire process) is "what are we going to do with the defendant?"

Several types of sentences are currently authorized in handling convicted criminals. (1) A monetary fine is authorized for many petty crimes, such as traffic offenses, vagrancy, drunk and disorderly behavior, and the like. (2) Probation is a type of sentence in which the defendant is not incarcerated but is released in the community under the supervision of governmental agents (probation officers). (3) Jail time is available for many petty crimes. Generally, a city or county jail term is limited to a maximum period of one year. Jail sentences may be used as an alternative or supplement to a fine. A defendant convicted of drunk and disorderly behavior, for example, may receive a sentence of thirty days or $300. (4) Prison time is routinely available for the more serious crimes. Felony offenses normally carry terms of incarceration in state or federal prisons. (5) The death penalty has been reinstituted as a sentence for such crimes as first-degree murder. Over the years, probation, fines, and jail time have come to dominate sentencing, with prison sentences reserved for but a small percentage of those convicted (President's Commission on Law Enforcement and Administration of Justice, 1967b:27).

Broadly, sentences may be *determinate, indeterminate,* or *indefinite* (Tappan, 1960:430–35). A determinate sentence is a legislatively fixed penalty. For some criminal offenses, the state legislature has designed a mandatory penalty over which the trial judge has no control. In some states, for example, those convicted of selling narcotics must be sentenced to a specified term in prison. The determinate sentence was a prominent type of sentence in an earlier historical epoch. In eighteenth-century England, the utilitarians, in opposition to judicial discretion in sentencing, argued that an equalitarian, antiauthoritarian system of justice could be had only if punishments were standardized. Under this system, the trial judge did no more than try a defendant and determine guilt or innocence. On conviction, a specified penalty was imposed.

The growth of the treatment ideology brought a decline of the determinate sentence and a growth of the indeterminate sentence.

---

cases, the typical jury takes into consideration the perspective of the defendant, and strives to fit the verdict to what is deemed appropriate to the defendant's social group (Kalven and Zeisel, 1966:339–44). Other times, however, the defendant may be judged from the perspective of some other group, an orientation toward justice quite at odds with that of the defendant.

Essentially, in the indeterminate sentence a defendant can conceivably serve from one day to life. Neither the legislature nor the judge can set, specifically or generally, the length of time a defendant must spend in confinement, because they simply cannot predict when he will be "cured" of his criminality. Consequently, sentencing is removed from the hands of the legislature and judge and placed completely in the hands of a board or an official who monitors the defendant's progress and can best determine the appropriate time for release.

The indefinite sentence is a contemporary compromise of sorts between the determinate and indeterminate sentence. The determination of the specific length of incarceration is taken from the legislature. At most, the legislature sets the outer limits of the sentence for any given crime, that is the maximum and/or minimum terms. The trial judge then sets a more specific maximum and minimum term for any given case within the legislatively authorized boundaries.[4] The correctional board (parole board) will then determine specifically when the defendant should be released. Although indefinite sentencing still dominates, it seems to be losing ground to definite sentencing.

In the United States, several types of officials are authorized to sentence convicted criminals. The legislature can, in effect, sentence in that it may design mandatory penalties to be imposed on certain kinds of defendants. Second, the jury may be authorized to determine the sentence. Most states permit the jury to recommend or fix punishment in capital cases, and about one-quarter of the states authorize the jury to determine the type and length of punishment for some or all other offenses as well (President's Commission on Law Enforcement and Administration of Justice, 1967:26). Third, in some jurisdictions, sentencing is assisted by a sentencing council, consisting of a board of judges that meets to consider what sentences should be imposed in pending cases (President's Commission on Law Enforcement and Administration of Justice, 1967:24). Of course, the ultimate responsibility for determining the specific sentence in a given case rests with the judge before whom the case was processed. Fourth, in the overwhelming number of cases, the trial judge is the principal agent responsible for the sentencing of convicted criminals. Given the dominance of the indefinite sentence, and the fact that most defendants plead guilty and escape jury sentencing, trial judges in both the lower and superior courts consider sentencing their primary task in the criminal justice process (cf. Kaplan, 1973:439–40; Neubauer, 1974:90). Therefore, our

---

[4] Sentencing discretion may be "delegated," as when the legislature simply authorizes the judge to use his judgment in sentencing. He may be authorized to select from several possible sentences (probation, fine, imprisonment) and to specify those sentences. The judge may also provide himself with discretion in cases that call for mandatory sentences. This is accomplished by altering the charges on which the defendant is convicted to those providing delegated discretion (Ohlin and Remington, 1958:501-2; Dawson, 1969).

discussion in this final section focuses on the sentencing decisions of trial judges.

Given the number of available alternatives provided by the indefinite character of penalties for most penal code categories, how do we explain the selection of one alternative over another? For example, how do we account for the imposition of probation for a convicted thief instead of prison time?

Sentencing Disparity

Most academic investigations of sentencing have focused on the issue of disparities between sentences imposed on similar cases (Hood and Sparks, 1970:141). A brief sampling of the literature suggests marked disparity among trial judges in sentencing. In 1935, Sellin examined the differences between blacks, native-born whites, and foreign-born whites in the lengths of prison sentences received for ten offense categories. He found that blacks received longer minimum sentences than whites for all offenses except murder and longer maximum sentences for all offenses except burglary and assault. Johnson (1941) also found a disparity between sentences on the dimension of race. Examining dispositions of those convicted of murder in North Carolina, Georgia, and Virginia, he found that severity in sentencing, from the most to the least severe, was as follows: (1) black murdered white, (2) white murdered white, (3) black murdered black, (4) white murdered black. Twenty years later, Bullock (1961) investigated sentencing differentials between blacks and whites who were incarcerated in Texas State Prison at Huntsville. On the basis of his data, he argued that blacks convicted of murdering blacks received less severe sentences than whites convicted of murdering whites. Yet, blacks convicted of burglarizing whites received more severe sentences than whites convicted of burglarizing whites. The point derived from these studies is that the sentences imposed for the same offense category differ markedly depending on the nature of the offender-victim relationship.

McGuire and Holtzoff (1940) found extreme variation between federal judges in the sentencing of liquor and narcotics violators. In liquor cases they found the average term of imprisonment ranged from 40 to 851 days, and in narcotics cases from 31 to 3408 days. Furthermore, one district court placed 62 percent of its convicted criminals on probation while another placed only 4 percent on probation. One of the more influential studies of sentencing disparity (1949; cf. Gaudet, Harris, and St. John, 1933) examined the sentencing practices of six judges sitting in the same county court in New Jersey over a ten-year period and found substantial variation between the six in the imposition of imprisonment, probation, fines, and suspended sentences. The imposition of imprisonment ranged from 33.6 percent of all cases to 57.7 percent; probation ranged from 19.5 to 32.4 percent of the cases; fines varied from 1.6 to 3.1 percent; and suspended sentences were granted from 15.7 to 33.8 percent of the cases. Severity in sentencing also varied among judges with respect to the type of offense involved. Some were more severe with those convicted of property offenses than with those convicted of sex offenses, while others imposed comparatively more severe sentences on sex offenders than on property offenders. Similar findings are cited by the *President's Task Force Report: The Courts* with respect to the ten judges sitting in the Detroit Recorder's Court.

> Over a twenty-month period in which the sample cases were about equally distributed among the ten judges, one judge imposed prison terms upon 75 to 90 percent of the defendants whom he sentenced, while another judge imposed prison sentences in about 35 percent of the cases. One judge consistently imposed prison sentences twice as long as those of the most lenient judge. . . . Judges who imposed the most severe sentences for certain crimes also exhibited the most liberal sentencing policy for other offenses (1967:23).

Sentencing disparities have also been found in the lower courts. In her investigation of the lower court in one eastern city, Mileski (1971:499–510) found that 38 percent of those convicted of minor misdemeanors (drunk and disorderly behavior, vagrancy, breach of peace, and the like) received suspended sentences, 39 percent received monetary fines, 17 percent were incarcerated, 4 percent received probation, and 1 percent received a fine and probation. With respect to sentencing of intoxication cases by the two judges of the court, she found that 55 percent of these cases received suspended sentences, 25 percent received monetary fines, and 20 percent received jail time (1971:505). Further subdividing the latter disposition, 2 percent received five days or less in jail, 7 percent received six to ten days, 9 percent received eleven to fifteen days, and 2 percent received sixteen days or more. The ethnographic data presented in the earlier studies by Kalodner (1956) and Foote (1956) also suggest considerable variation in the disposition of defendants processed through lower courts.

Explanations of Sentencing Disparity

Over the years, a number of explanations for sentencing disparity, hence, the basis of sentencing, have been offered. Some have explained disparity in terms of the personal whim or idiosyncracies of sentencing judges. Sellin (1935:217), for example, explained disparities in terms of the "human equation in judicial administration." Similarly, Gaudet (1949) argued that the disparities he uncovered reflect the capriciousness of the trial judges and their uneven reliance on legal criteria for sentencing. Such explanations suggest an arbitrary decision-making process, "as it were, by tossing a coin" (Hood and Sparks, 1970:154).

Others have explained disparity in terms of the predispositions of trial judges toward attending to various "extralegal" attributes of the convicted offender in determining sentence. By "extralegal" it is generally meant those features of defendants, such as age, sex, race, and socioeconomic status, that are not emphasized in or derived from the penal code (Hagan, 1974:358). The judge's personality is again at issue, but his decision-making is not wholly arbitrary. Rather, particular attitudes regarding such dimensions as race, age, sex, and socioeconomic status influence sentencing decisions. Variations among judges in such attitudes are taken as explanations of sentencing disparity. McGuire and Holtzoff, for example, come close to this idea:

> . . . the conclusion seems inescapable that the differences [in sentences] are due primarily to diverse attitudes on the part of the individual judges toward various crimes and that severity or lightness of the punishment depends in each instance very largely on the personality of the trial judge (1940:428).

The findings of sentence disparity between blacks and whites convicted of similar offenses have been explained in terms of prejudicial attitudes toward blacks. Similarly, the age of the defendant may enter into sentencing decisions. In his study of sentencing practices in Michigan, Wisconsin, and Kansas, for example, Dawson found that "age is the most conspicuous and frequently encountered personal characteristic that influences the probation decision . . . (1969:83–84)." The youthful defendant, and perhaps the very old, fares considerably better in sentencing because judges do not like to send "boys," and "old men," to prison (Dawson, 1969:84).

To explain sentencing disparity in terms of the "human equation" or the "individuality of the judge" is quite vague conceptually. But more importantly, "to explain sentencing disparities in terms of a 'subjective' or 'indefinable' element is really to give no explanation at all—at least until it is shown just what this 'element' is, what its causes are, and how it enters into sentencing decisions" (Hood and Sparks, 1970:154). To explain sentencing disparity in terms of extralegal attributes of the defendant to which judges differentially attend may be based on a problematic assumption: the penal code is sufficiently consistent and precise so as to clearly demarcate extralegal variables. It may be, as we shall see shortly, that judges are considering legal criteria in rendering sentences, but researchers view such features as extralegal.

When combined, several other explanations that focus on organizational and social psychological contingencies may provide a more detailed, credible account of sentencing disparity and the basis of sentencing decisions.[5] Judges may be oriented toward different sentencing policies, the product being different sentences for the same offense category. That is, sentences can be oriented justifiably toward several objectives. First, they may be oriented toward deterrence of two kinds (cf. Andenaes, 1974). They may be geared toward punishing the defendant in an effort to prevent him from engaging in future criminal conduct, that is, "special deterrence." Or they may be geared toward showing others what will happen to them if they engage in comparable forms of criminal activity, that is, "general deterrence." Second, sentencing policies may be designed to reaffirm community values through formal condemnation of the convicted defendant (cf. Durkheim, 1938: 64–75). Third, sentences may be used as a protection by isolating and confining convicted criminals deemed threatening to the safety and well-being of the community. Fourth, sentences may be oriented to the goal of rehabilitation, which is to be accomplished through treatment aimed at resolving whatever social or psychological problems accounted for the defendant's nonconformity.

Sentencing may also be oriented toward achieving various organizational goals. For example, judges may reward with leniency those who plead guilty outright and thereby save the court time and expense, an orientation found in many jurisdictions (cf. "Comment," *Yale Law Journal,* 1956; McIntyre, 1967; Dawson, 1969:94–96, 179–81; Blumberg, 1967; Neubauer, 1974:240). Judges may also reward with leniency those who assist the police by providing information regarding the criminal activities of others. These two goals compete in that each may call for a somewhat different sentence in a given case.[6] For example, take a case in which a person is convicted of selling dangerous drugs. One judge oriented toward deterrence may opt for a definite prison term of five years so as to illustrate to both the defendant and the public that other instances of the same conduct will be met with like sentences. A second judge oriented toward social defense may sentence the defendant to a prison term of fifteen years so as to keep him away from the law-abiding citizenry. A third judge oriented toward rehabilitation may sentence the defendant to five years' probation with the condition that he involve himself in a local drug program.[7]

---

[5] The structure of the following discussion derives in part from the discussion in Hood and Sparks (1970:154–60).

[6] Whether these goals of sentencing are credible, let alone accessible, is irrelevant. The point is that they do serve as justifications for action (Sutherland and Cressey, 1974:325).

[7] The two conceptions of justice embraced by our criminal law and enforcement organizations further contribute to the issue at hand. One conception of justice emphasizes that like offenses be treated alike. In a "government by law" those convicted of the same offense should be treated equally, that is, uniformly sentenced. A second conception of justice emphasizes that individual defendants be given their just deserts. In a "government by men," sentences should

In his review of twenty empirical studies of sentencing, Hagan (1974) found that the relationship between sentence and such extralegal variables as the age, race, sex, and socioeconomic status of defendants is at best minimal. The perceived association between such variables and sentencing may reflect not so much a real association but rather a general failure among researchers to control for legalistic variables (cf. Green, 1961:8–20). Several studies have examined the comparative significance of both sets of variables, and have concluded that judges attend to and take into consideration a number of legalistic cues in the determination of sentence.

In the sentencing of minor and summary offenses, judges have several alternatives available, including incarceration, probation, monetary fines, commitment to a public service organization such as Alcoholics Anonymous, and such nonformalized penalties as jail work details. Determining which alternative to impose in any given case, judges are generally limited in their information to whatever is immediately available. At most, they restrict their consideration to the basic features of the crime, the defendant's criminal record, and his present courtroom appearance (Foote, 1956:605). While there is variation in priority, these three types of cues have been found to figure prominently in the sentencing of those convicted of minor and summary offenses.

In a study of sentencing in the Traffic Court section of the Detroit Recorder's Court, Jaros and Mendelsohn (1967) were concerned with two questions: (1) Do lower court judges' sentencing patterns conform to legally relevant criteria or to the particular attitudes of the judges? (2) Does the receipt of respect from defendants as a right of the judicial role influence sentencing? They found that the more serious the offense charged, the greater the probability of receiving jail time or paying a higher monetary fine. Similarly, recidivists faced a significantly greater chance of receiving jail time or paying a higher fine than first-time offenders. While only 18 percent of the first offenders were jailed, 28 percent of the recidivists were jailed. While first offenders paid an average fine of $47.34, recidivists paid an average of $62.88. Yet, the influence of age and race was minimal in comparison to the legalistic variables. The authors used two measures of "respect" shown toward judges: (1) mode of dress, ordered from manual work clothes, soiled or rumpled casual clothes, and business clothes; and (2) courtroom comportment, such as shouting, disparaging remarks toward judges, and the like. They found that the less well-dressed the defendant, the more severe the sentence. Yet, they found no statistically

---

be tailored to the particular character of the defendants; justice should be individualized. In the former conception, sentencing disparity signals a failure to do justice; in the latter, sentencing disparity is expected. In fact, in the latter conception, a lack of disparity within offense categories signals injustice.

significant relationship between courtroom comportment and sentencing severity. This latter pattern is not surprising in light of Mileski's (1971:521–31) observations of the sentencing patterns in another lower court. She found that when defendants violated the informal rules of the court, regardless of their violations of legal rules, they were susceptible to "situational condemnation," not more severe sentences. Situational sanctioning included judicial pronouncements that the defendant was a "bad person" or engaged in an "evil" activity and lectures on the seriousness of certain criminal activities.

Mileski also found that the probability of incarceration increases when defendants have prior criminal records. Focusing on intoxication cases, she observes:

> No defendants in intoxication cases who had clean records were incarcerated. Nearly all (92 percent) were released on suspended sentences. . . . Incarceration increases quite strikingly as the length and recency of records increase. The judge incarcerates 7 percent of those with light records, 20 percent of those with intermediate records, and 41 percent of those with heavy records. Thus the court tends to sanction through incarceration not so much for public intoxication per se but rather for repeated instances of court appearances for intoxication, to say nothing of actual repeated instances of public intoxication (1971:504).

Controlling for prior record and the type of offense, she found no consistent disparity between the sentencing of black and white defendants. For example, skid-row blacks charged with public intoxication are treated in much the same way as skid-row whites charged with public intoxication.

Considerably more research has addressed the sentencing practices involved in more serious, felony cases. Incarceration and probation are generally the two real alternatives available in the sentencing of convicted felons. For example, in 1969 California's state courts placed 66 percent of the state's convicted felons on probation and sentenced 16 percent to jail or payment of fines, 10 percent to prison, 4 percent to the California Youth Authority, and 4 percent to some civil institution (California Council on Criminal Justice, 1971:77). In 1969, the federal district courts sentenced their felons in the following manner: 48 percent to prison or jail, 37 percent to a period of probation, 6 percent to pay fines, and 9 percent to some "other" disposition. In 1973, the following proportions prevailed: 50 percent were sentenced to prison or jail, 43 percent were placed on probation, 5 percent were fined, and 2 percent received some "other" sentence (Hindelang et al., 1975:398). It is important to consider why some defendants are placed on probation while others are sentenced to some period of incarceration, be it prison, jail, or some other institution.

Examining decisions to grant probation in Kansas, Michigan, and Wisconsin, Dawson (1969:79–99) found that several contingencies recurrently brought decisions for probation instead of incarceration. When judges were oriented toward the goal of rehabilitation—whether, in their judgment, the defendant could make the successful adjustment to community living under probation and refrain from further criminal conduct—several contingencies recurrently brought probation. (1) If the defendant was a first-time offender, or had a petty record of misdemeanor convictions, then probation was more likely than incarceration, except when the offense was exceptionally serious (such as murder or rape). Conversely, those with several prior felony convictions were rarely placed on probation. Similarly, Mather (1973: 193–94) found that in Los Angeles a prior felony record typically brought more severity in sentencing. She states that "almost 90 percent of convicted defendants in 1970 with minor or no prior records received probation or a fine, compared with 55 percent of defendants with major or prior prison records" (p. 193). Neubauer (1974:240–41) found a similar pattern in sentencing in Prairie City. (2) If the defendant is not characterized as a "professional" criminal or as a "drug addict," then probation instead of incarceration is more likely than for those who are so characterized. Trial judges assume that a social or physical commitment to criminality lessens defendants' chances for successful probation.

Dawson suggests that when judges were oriented toward the goals of deterrence or retribution, in whole or part, then the perceived "seriousness" of the offense was a critical criterion in granting probation. Basically, the lesser the perceived seriousness of the offense, the more likely the defendant received probation instead of incarceration; conversely, the more serious the offense, the more likely the defendant received incarceration instead of probation. In addition to the rough grading provided by the penal code, several concrete cues were typically attended to in assessing the seriousness of an offense, and hence the determination of incarceration or probation.

1. Crimes that involved violence or intimidation were more likely to be defined as serious and deserving of incarceration than probation. For example, robbery involving the use of weapons or actual force would be defined as a more serious crime than a robbery in which no weapons or actual force were used, even though both crimes might entail the same statutory penalty.

2. When the victim of the crime contributed in some way or other to the criminal performance, then such a cue is taken as an indication that the event is not as serious as in cases where the victim was noncontributing. For example, in cases of statutory rape where it is clearly established that the victim actively contributed and encouraged her pregnancy, probation is much more likely than in cases of statutory rape where she did not encourage the offender. Or, if the victim con-

tributed to his injury developing from an assault by throwing the first punch, probation is a more likely outcome for the defendant.

In an investigation of sentencing in the Philadelphia Court of Quarter Sessions during 1957–58, Green (1961) studied the comparative influence of several legal and extralegal variables in the determination of sentence. The legal variables examined were the crime committed, the number of bills of indictment on which the defendant was convicted, and the defendant's prior record. The extralegal variables examined were the defendant's sex, age, race, and place of birth. These were taken as the independent variables. The dependent variable was the severity of the sentence, measured in the following order, from greater to lesser severity: imprisonment, probation, fine, and suspended sentence.

Green found that the most important variables in the determination of sentence were the seriousness of the offense charged and the defendant's prior record. While the penal code grades the gravity of different categories of offenses, this scaling is rough and sometimes inconsistent. Consequently, trial judges develop their own ways of determining seriousness. Several types of cues were routinely considered in assessing seriousness. The more specific the victim (an "individual" as opposed to "the public"), the more serious was the offense and the consequent sentence. The greater the personal contact between the defendant and victim (face-to-face interaction as opposed to no interaction), the more serious the offense and sentence. The more bodily harm done to the victim, the more serious the offense and sentence. A prior record is also taken as an indication of some commitment by the defendant toward criminality, hence an indication of a need for more severe sentencing. When Green examined the differences in sentences by age, sex, and race, he found that "females are favored as compared with males, younger offenders as compared with older offenders, and whites as compared with Negroes" (1961:63). While some would claim that such extralegal variables were associated with sentencing, and provide explanations of disparity based on prejudice or arbitrariness, the data do not support this. Rather, "these variations in the gravity of the penalties are due to differences in *criminal behavior patterns* associated with these biosocial variables. . . . " (1961:63; emphasis added). As Green explains:

The female defendants commit fewer serious crimes and have a lower rate of recidivism than the male defendants. Increasing age is accompanied by a rise in recidivism but a decline in the proportion of convictions of the more serious types of crimes. White and Negro defendants differ considerably in age-cycles in criminal behavior patterns. Youthful Negro defendants commit a much higher proportion of crimes of violence than youthful white defendants. As the two racial groups increase in age, their patterns of criminal behavior tend to become more similar (1961:63).

Thus, controlling cases by offense seriousness and prior record brought only negligible disparities.

3. Even though one can argue that trial judges use legalistic variables in determining sentences, disparities still appear. This should not be surprising, for trial judges may differentially categorize cases as a result of differential interpretation of broad legalistic variables. Differential categorization on these grounds is to be expected because the criminal law does not literally specify what cues judges should attend to and use in determining sentences. As Hood and Sparks argue, "there is little agreement as to what information about offense and offender is relevant to the choice of sentence, and even less on the relative weights to be given to different items of information" (1970: 156). Consequently, judges may develop somewhat different perspectives toward the sentencing of routinely encountered crimes and criminals, and these include what legalistic cues are deemed relevant in assessing cases and the weights of such cues.

While we have found that judges operate in terms of such benchmarks as "seriousness of the offense" and "prior record of the defendant," what these mean is not self-evident. For example, what does a particular criminal record indicate? While some judges would define a prior "drunk" and "GTA" (Grand Theft Auto) as indicative of relatively nonserious priors, others may define such a record as an indication that the defendant is committed to criminality and marching straight for prison. Thus, while judges may in fact use legalistic variables in determining sentences, there may be considerable variation in the cues they use and emphasize and how they interpret them, and this variation may account for a measure of sentencing disparity.

In the Philadelphia study, Green (1961) found substantial agreement among judges regarding the "nature of criminality" that is measured by the legalistic cues cited for very serious and very grave offenses. He did, however, find disparity among judges in their sentencing of intermediate offenses. Green accounts for this disparity in terms of the differing perceptions of "seriousness" judges have.

In an extensive investigation of 71 Ontario magistrates, Hogarth (1971:229–44, 266–78) found that different sentencing goals coupled with different attitudes held by judges led to differential assessment of concrete cues, hence differential sentencing.

4. Trial judges may receive different kinds and amounts of information on which to base their sentencing decisions, and this variation may account, in part, for variations in sentencing. Just as police and prosecutors attend to particular types of cues in developing decisions, so too do trial judges attend to and use particular types of cues in

determining sentences. It is important to recognize that cues are differentially available.

On the one hand, cues may be restricted to whatever is available in the courtroom immediately before sentencing (and immediately after receipt of guilty pleas or at the end of trial). While he processes most misdemeanor and summary offenses, the trial judge's information is generally restricted to the defendant's "rap sheet" or prior record, brief statements by the prosecutor, the defense attorney (if there is one) or defendant, and the police officer, and the comportment and dress of the defendant. In Detroit, McIntyre (1967:158–59) found that sentencing of most misdemeanants was made on the basis of these sources of information alone. It has been suggested that these sources of information are all that may be managed given the organizational resources available for the processing of misdemeanor cases.

On the other hand, judges may routinely cultivate additional sources of information when sentencing more serious cases. In his investigation of Kansas, Michigan, and Wisconsin sentencing practices, Dawson (1969:15–55) found that the post-plea-of-guilty hearing and the presentence investigation performed by the probation department were common methods for securing additional sentencing information for felony cases.

There are some basic differences in the information brought to the judge's attention between these two sources. In the post-plea-of-guilty hearing, the judge solicits information, arguments, and recommendations from the prosecuting attorney, defendant, and defense attorney regarding the appropriate sentence for the offense on which the defendant was just convicted. In Milwaukee five general areas of information are covered: (1) circumstances of the offense, (2) uncharged offenses admitted by the defendant, (3) the defendant's criminal record, (4) the degree of the defendant's cooperation with the police, and (5) the defendant's social history. In Milwaukee, the "social history of the defendant" is given scant consideration, but the circumstances of the offense and his prior record are emphasized. The information brought before the judge is secured *in* the courtroom and before the other courtroom participants. In many cases, the judge will pronounce the sentence after the termination of the hearing.

The presentence report is decidedly different. The judge may ask, if it is not mandatory, for the probation department to undertake a presentence investigation of the case pending sentencing. Essentially, this investigation consists of a report including information on the circumstances of the offense; the defendant's employment status, assets, prior criminal and juvenile record; marital history, education, military record, family, and health; the victim's background; and a recommendation to the judge as to whether the defendant should be placed on probation or imprisoned.

Dawson found that there was variation between probation departments in what aspects of the offense and offender were emphasized and considered in developing recommendations. "One major variation is in the extent to which the defendant's background is emphasized in the report; another is the extent to which the probation officer interprets and evaluates the data obtained" (1969:35–36). Similarly, Carter and Wilkins (1967) found marked variations among probation officers in the percentage of cases recommended for probation, which they accounted for in terms of variations among officers' perspectives toward the correctional process. Such variations in correctional perspectives, Carter and Wilkins argue, are the result of differences in vocational training and the length of time employed in probation. In either event, it appears that judges are provided with differential accounts of quite similar cases, and differential recommendations based on those accounts.

While the quality of information varies in terms of officers' cognitive perspectives toward corrections, information and recommendations may additionally vary as a function of organizational participation. In some departments, for example, the chief probation officer may supervise the investigations performed by the various officers. Consequently, the individual officers may examine those aspects of the offense and offender and develop recommendations in anticipation of what their supervisors expect. In other departments, where officers act autonomously, considerably more variation in recommendation may be found.

Probation officers may also differ in what information they provide as a function of the degree to which their reports are made available to others besides the sentencing judge. In the post-plea-of-guilty hearing, information regarding what sentence is appropriate is openly provided in court. The presentence report, however, is constructed by the probation department in the confines of the department. Traditionally, the report was constructed for the eyes of the judge alone, but in recent years it has been made increasingly available to the defense so as to ensure the accuracy of the information on which recommendations are based. As a consequence of this practice, probation officers may be reluctant to include information that cannot be verified or that is of a particularly controversial nature (Dawson, 1969:37). What this indicates is some difference in the information brought to the fore in confidential reports and that to be made accessible to the defense or the post-plea-of-guilty hearing information.

While we find disparity in the information and recommendations provided by the probation officers, we also find comparable disparity in the sentencing decisions made by judges with respect to probation-incarceration. Carter and Wilkins (1967) found that the recommendations of probation officers for probation were followed in 95 percent of the cases by judges. Similarly, Neubauer (1974:239–43) found that trial judges failed to follow the recommendations of probation officers in only 5 percent of the cases. The import of this discussion lay in the correspondence of recommendations and sentencing dispositions despite the variation in the recommendations themselves. Thus, it would follow that variation in decisions to place the defendant on probation or in prison may be accounted for more in terms of the variation of probation officers' recommendations.

It has been argued that this interpretation of the basic correspondence noted is best explained in terms of probation officers investigating cases and providing recommendations consistent with the particular orientations of the judge. Dawson, for example, states that "probation officers in Detroit readily acknowledge that judicial preference was a factor in making their recommendations" (1969:40). In a careful investigation of just this issue, Carter and Wilkins (1967) found that while there is some second-guessing, it is not prominent. They found a high rate of consistency in the recommendations made to trial judges of various types. If the officers were second-guessing judicial preference, we would expect some tailoring of recommendations to individual judges, hence some degree of inconsistency in recommendations by individual officers. The point is that judges, limited in the time they can spend in judging each case, rely on presentence investigations as critical sources for making decisions.

Thus, from this brief discussion, it would seem reasonable to argue that different kinds of information brought to the attention of a judge shape the cues to which he attends and the categorization of cases he is to consider.

In some areas, the prosecutor exerts a measure of influence over the sentencing decision, although Green (1961) found that his effect on sentencing was slight. Recall that the basic issue in plea negotiation is sentencing. We found that several types of concessions are routinely granted for a guilty plea, varying by type of offense and jurisdiction; these include reduction of charges, altering conviction labels, recommendations for probation or concurrent sentences, and the avoidance of negative recommendations. The former two concessions signal the prosecutorial manipulation of charges on which the defendant is convicted. Such manipulation shapes or controls the sentencing limits of judges—avoiding mandatory sentences, lowering upper limits of maximum legislative sentences, bringing in the possibility of probation— or avoids particularly stigmatizing labels. Since such practices relieve court congestion and enhance the processing of defendants, "the prosecutor may be expected to have the sympathetic understanding and support of the trial judge, who is not likely to be dissatisfied so long as he considers the sentence for the lesser offense to be *adequate* punishment for the conduct involved" (Ohlin and Remington, 1958:502).

The latter three concessions, in contrast, involve a "recommendation" to the judge concerning the disposition of the convicted criminal. In effect, the prosecutor provides information that a particular disposition is deemed appropriate for the case at hand or shields information that would call for a more serious punishment. While the judge always has the option of imposing a sentence quite at odds with the prosecutor's recommendation, it is generally rare that he does so. The question is whether the prosecutor's recommendation, like that of the probation officer, is "followed" by the judge, or whether the prosecutor negotiates a guilty plea in terms of the typical sentences administered by judges for certain kinds of cases. Neubaurer addressed this issue:

> In setting the prison sentence within the range allowed by the statutes, the key figure is the prosecutor. At the sentencing hearing the prosecutor will make a recommendation to the judge, a recommendation that is invariably followed. In turn, the prosecutor's recommendation is based on well-established policies of normal or modal penalties for a given offense. In a forgery case the usual recommendation is one to five years; in burglary one to ten; and in armed robbery two to ten. There may be an upward valuation if the defendant has a long previous record, or if the crime is viewed as particularly heinous (1974:244).

While Neubauer at first suggests that judges follow the recommendations of the prosecutor, he comes to the position that prosecutors negotiate in terms of the particular orientations of trial judges. Mather's investigation in Los Angeles also provides support for this latter point. Recall the comments of one trial judge regarding a common practice of "implicit negotiation" by the prosecutor and defense counsel:

> On a three count forgery case, the defense attorney asks the D.A., "Can I have one count?" The D.A. says, "Yes, which one?" The defense attorney says, "Count 2." And that's it. No bargain has been made. No promise made that counts 1 and 3 will be dismissed in exchange for the plea to count 2. *It's simply that everyone knows what the standard practice is.* Or here's another example. The defense attorney comes into court and asks the D.A., "What does judge Hall give on bookmaking cases?" The D.A. asks if there are any priors. The attorney says "no," and the D.A. says, "He usually gives a $150 fine on the first offense." The attorney says, "Fine. We'll enter a plea to count 1." Again no promise was made by anybody. *It's just that everyone knows what customarily will happen* (Mather, 1973:199; emphasis in the original).

Defense attorneys routinely address trial judges on the sentencing of their clients with the aim of shaping the sentencing decision. On the one hand, it is not uncommon for the defense attorney to "shop" around for those judges known to routinely impose a less severe sentence for cases such as that of the attorney. In Washington, D.C., Subin (1966:87–88) found that defense attorneys commonly employed "judge-shopping" in order to secure a more lenient sentence for their cases. On the other hand, the defense attorney may work at providing the judge with information that shapes his conception of the case, hence his sentence determination. Mather (1973:199–200) provides an apt illustration:

> The P.D. [public defender] was familiar with Judge Greene's sentencing practices . . . and court was busy that afternoon, so the attorneys did not discuss the case in chambers before disposition. When the judge called the case, the P.D. announced that his client wished to change his plea of not guilty to guilty. Then the D.A. "took the waivers," that is, he asked the defendant a series of questions to ascertain that he understood the nature and consequences of the proceedings, that he waived his rights to jury trial, cross-examination of witnesses, and self-incrimination, and that no promises or threats had been made to induce the plea of guilty. Judge Greene then accepted the plea, making it second degree burglary, and the following occurred:

> **P.D.:** Your Honor, we request immediate sentencing and waive the probation report.
> **Judge:** What's his record?
> **P.D.:** He has a prior drunk and a GTA (Grand Theft Auto). Nothing serious. This is really just a shoplifting case. He did enter the K-Mart with the intent to steal. But really all we have here is a petty theft.
> **Judge:** What do the people have?
> **D.A.:** Nothing either way.
> **Judge:** Any objections to immediate sentencing?
> **D.A.:** No.
> **Judge:** How long has he been in?
> **P.D.:** 83 days.
> **Judge:** I make this a misdemeanor by P.C. #17 and sentence you to 90 days in County Jail with credit for time served.

Interestingly, the P.D. refers to offenses in terms of their social reality rather than their legal definitions. That is, *legally* the case may be a burglary, but *really* it is just a petty theft. Likewise, Grand Theft Auto may be a serious crime according to the penal code, but because of the circumstances that typically surround it, everyone knows it's usually "nothing serious."

In sentencing, the trial judge functions as a human actor constrained not only by his cognitive perspective for making sense of cases vis-à-vis legal cues but also as an organizational functionary constrained by the information provided from various sources and the contingencies posed by organizational goals.

SUMMARY

Judging a defendant's guilt or innocence and assigning the appropriate penalty for a crime is a complex process. A trial is a bewildering experience for the defendant, who sits in the courtroom while a small group of people, mostly strangers, decides his fate. Perhaps the best way to understand the criminal trial is to view it as an information-producing and a fact-creating process.

The judge and jury listen to victims, witnesses, police officers, and attorneys talk about the defendant's alleged crime. Each account consists of bits and pieces of information selected and reported to the court. Reporting the facts of a case is not simply a matter of telling others about what "really happened." Rather, testimony consists of descriptions of what persons think they saw or heard and their reports about what their observations mean. Answering questions before the court is a social process that reflects the cognitive perspectives of the participants in a trial. One may be able to identify those biases that distort a witness's testimony, but accounts are not objectified by noting biases. The truth is always relative to a particular perspective. A sense of what is "real" does not exist independently from persons' accounts about the world around them.

During a trial persons organize their testimony to create a sense of reality, but this sense of reality cannot be sustained unless others are willing to help in the process. Judges and juries must accept the limits of descriptions formulated in ordinary language. They must be ready to "fill-in" the vagaries of testimony, let obscure comments pass and generally operate from a shared yet unarticulated set of expectations about what is reasonable and possible in the real world (cf. Garfinkel, 1967).

Judges and juries assess and respond to an infinite variety of legal and extralegal information. Each case before the court represents a unique configuration of "facts." How courtroom actors will evaluate the seriousness of an offense, the adequacy of the evidence, and the culpability of an offender will ultimately depend on how they interpret the "facts."

PROSECUTION AND ADJUDICATION

REFERENCES

ANDENAES, JOHANNES
1974 *Punishment and Deterrence.* Ann Arbor: University of Michigan Press.

BARTLETT, F. C.
1932 *Remembering.* Cambridge, Eng.: Cambridge University Press.

BLUMBERG, ABRAHAM S.
1967 *Criminal Justice.* Chicago: Quadrangle.

BROEDER, D. W.
1959 "The University of Chicago Jury Project," *Nebraska Law Review* 38 (May): 744–60.

BULLOCK, HENRY A.
1961 "Significance of the Racial Factor in the Length of Prison Sentences," *Journal of Criminal Law, Criminology, and Police Science* 52 (November–December): 411–17.

CALIFORNIA COUNCIL ON CRIMINAL JUSTICE
1971 *The California Criminal Justice System.* Sacramento.

CARTER, ROBERT M., AND LESLIE T. WILKINS
1967 "Some Factors in Sentencing Policy," *Journal of Criminal Law, Criminology and Police Science* 58 (December): 503–14.

CHAMBLISS, WILLIAM J., AND ROBERT B. SEIDMAN
1971 *Law, Order, and Power.* Reading, Mass.: Addison-Wesley.

COMMENT
1956 "The Influence of the Defendant's Plea on Judicial Determination of Sentence," *Yale Law Journal* 66 (December): 204–22.

DAWSON, ROBERT O.
1969 *Sentencing: The Decision as to Type, Length, and Conditions of Sentence.* Boston: Little, Brown.

DURKHEIM, EMILE
1938 *The Rules of Sociological Method.* New York: The Free Press.

ERLANGER, HOWARD S.
1970 "Jury Research in America: Its Past and Future," *Law and Society Review* 4 (February): 345–69.

FOOTE, CALEB
1956 "Vagrancy-Type Law and Its Administration," *University of Pennsylvania Law Review* 104 (March): 603–50.

FRANK, JEROME
1963 *Courts on Trial.* New York: Atheneum.

GARFINKEL, HAROLD
1967 *Studies in Ethnomethodology.* Englewood Cliffs, N.J.: Prentice-Hall.

GAUDET, FREDERICK J.
1949 "The Sentencing Behavior of the Judge," in V.C. Branham and S.V. Kutash, eds., *Encyclopedia of Criminology,* pp. 449–61. New York: Philosophical Library.

GAUDET, FREDERICK J., G. S. HARRIS, AND C. W. ST. JOHN
1933 "Individual Differences in the Sentencing Tendencies of Judges,"

Journal of Criminal Law and Criminology 23 (January–February): 811–18.

GOLDSTEIN, HERMAN
1968 "Trial Judges and the Police: Their Relationships in the Administration of Criminal Justice," *Crime and Delinquency* 14(1): 14–25.

GREEN, EDWARD
1961 *Judicial Attitudes in Sentencing.* London: MacMillan.

HAGAN, JOHN
1974 "Extra-Legal Attributes and Criminal Sentencing: An Assessment of a Sociological Viewpoint," *Law and Society Review* 8 (Spring): 357–83.

HERVEY, J. C.
1947 "Jurors Look at Our Judges," *Oklahoma Bar Association Journal* 18 (October): 1508–13.

HINDELANG, MICHAEL J., CHRISTOPHER S. DUNN, L. PAUL SUTTON, AND ALISON L. AUMICK
1973 *Sourcebook of Criminal Justice Statistics, 1973.* Washington, D.C.: U.S. Department of Justice.

HOGARTH, JOHN
1971 *Sentencing as a Human Process.* Toronto: University of Toronto Press.

HOOD, ROGER, AND RICHARD SPARKS
1970 *Key Issues in Criminology.* New York: McGraw-Hill.

JACOB, HERBERT
1972 *Justice in America: Courts, Lawyers, and the Judicial Process,* 2d ed. Boston: Little, Brown.

JACOB, HERBERT, AND KENNETH VINES
1963 "The Role of the Judiciary in American State Politics," in Glendon Schubert, ed., *Judicial Decision-Making,* pp. 245–56. Glencoe, Ill.: The Free Press.

JAROS, DEAN, AND ROBERT I. MENDELSOHN
1967 "The Judicial Role and Sentencing Behavior," *Midwest Journal of Political Science* 11 (November): 471–88.

JOHNSON, GUY B.
1941 "The Negro and Crime," *Annals of the American Academy of Political and Social Science* 271 (September): 93–104.

JONES, EDWARD E., AND HAROLD B. GERARD
1967 *Foundations of Social Psychology.* New York: Wiley.

KADISH, MORTIMER R., AND SANFORD H. KADISH
1971 "The Institutionalization of Conflict: Jury Acquittals," *Journal of Social Issues* 27, no. 2: 199–217.

KALODNER, HOWARD I.
1956 "Metropolitan Criminal Courts of First Instance," *Harvard Law Review* 70 (December): 320–49.

KALVEN, HARRY, JR., AND HANS ZEISEL
1966 *The American Jury.* Boston: Little, Brown.

KAPLAN, JOHN
1973 *Criminal Justice: Introductory Cases and Materials.* Mineola, Long Island: Foundation Press.

KARLEN, DELMAR
1964   *The Citizen in Court.* New York: Holt, Rinehart and Winston.

KNOWLTON, ROBERT E.
1962   "The Trial of Offenders," *Annals of the American Academy of Political and Social Science* 339 (January): 125–41.

LINDESMITH, ALFRED R., ANSELM L. STRAUSS, AND NORMAN K. DENZIN
1975   *Social Psychology,* 4th ed. Hinsdale, Ill.: Dryden Press.

MC GUIRE, MATHEW F., AND ALEXANDER HOLTZOFF
1940   "The Problem of Sentencing in the Criminal Law," *Boston University Law Review* 20 (June): 423–34.

MC INTYRE, DONALD M.
1967   *Law Enforcement in the Metropolis.* American Bar Association.

MARSTON, W. M.
1924   "Studies in Testimony," *Journal of the American Institute of Criminal Law and Criminology* 15 (May): 5–31.

MATHER, LYNN M.
1973   "Some Determinants of the Method of Case Disposition: Decision-Making by Public Defenders in Los Angeles," *Law and Society Review* 8 (Winter): 187–215.

MILESKI, MAUREEN
1971   "Courtroom Encounters: An Observation Study of a Lower Criminal Court," *Law and Society Review* 5 (May): 473–538.

NAGEL, STUART S.
1962   "Judicial Backgrounds and Criminal Cases," *Journal of Criminal Law, Criminology, and Police Science* 53 (September): 333–39.

NEUBAUER, DAVID W.
1974   *Criminal Justice in Middle America.* Morristown, N.J.: General Learning Press.

OHLIN, LLOYD E., AND FRANK J. REMINGTON
1958   "Sentencing Structure: Its Effects Upon Systems for the Administration of Criminal Justice," *Law and Contemporary Problems* 23 (Summer): 495–507.

POUND, ROSCOE
1975   *Criminal Justice in America.* New York: DaCapo.

PRESIDENT'S COMMISSION ON LAW ENFORCEMENT AND ADMINISTRATION OF JUSTICE
1967   *Task Force Report: The Courts.* Washington, D.C.: Government Printing Office.
1967b *Task Force Report: Corrections.* Washington, D.C.: Government Printing Office.

QUINNEY, RICHARD
1975   *Criminology: Analysis and Critique of Crime in America.* Boston: Little, Brown.

RADZINOWICZ, LEON
1948   *A History of English Criminal Law and Its Administration from 1750.* 4 vols. London: Stevens.

REMINGTON, FRANK J., DONALD J. NEWMAN, EDWARD L. KIMBALL, MARYGOLD
MELLI, AND HERMAN GOLDSTEIN, EDS.
  1969 *Criminal Justice Administration: Materials and Cases.* Indianapolis,
        Ind.: Bobbs-Merrill.

SELLIN, THORSTEN
  1935 "Race Prejudice in the Administration of Justice," *American Journal
        of Sociology* 41 (September): 212-17.

SHIBUTANI, TAMOTSU
  1961 *Society and Personality: An Interactionist Approach to Social Psy-
        chology.* Englewood Cliffs, N.J.: Prentice-Hall.

SIMON, RITA JAMES
  1959 "Status and Competence of Jurors," *American Journal of Sociology* 64
        (May): 563–70.
  1967 *The Jury and the Defense of Insanity.* Boston: Little, Brown.

SMITH, ALEXANDER B., AND ABRAHAM S. BLUMBERG
  1967 "The Problem of Objectivity in Judicial Decision-Making," *Social
        Forces* 46 (September): 96–105.

STEPHAN, COOKIE
  1975 "Selective Characteristics of Jurors and Litigants: Their Influences on
        Juries' Verdicts," in Rita James Simon, ed., *The Jury System in
        America: A Critical Overview,* pp. 97–121. Beverly Hills, Calif.: Sage
        Publications.

STRODTBECK, FRED L., RITA JAMES SIMON, AND C. HAWKINS
  1957 "Social Status in Jury Deliberations," *American Sociological Review*
        22 (December): 713–19.

SUBIN, HARRY I.
  1966 *Criminal Justice in a Metropolitan Court.* Washington, D.C.: U.S. De-
        partment of Justice.

SUTHERLAND, EDWIN H., AND DONALD R. CRESSEY
  1974 *Criminology,* 9th ed. Philadelphia: Lippincott.

TAPPAN, PAUL W.
  1960 *Crime, Justice and Correction.* New York: McGraw-Hill.

VINES, KENNETH N.
  1964 "Federal District Judges and Race Relations Cases in the South,"
        Journal of Politics 26 (May): 337–57.

WELD, H. P., AND E. R. DANZIG
  1940 "A Study of the Way in Which a Verdict is Reached by a Jury,"
        American Journal of Psychology 53 (October): 518–36.

WILLIAMS, GLANVILLE L.
  1963 *The Proof of Guilt: A Study of the English Criminal Trial.* London:
        Stevens.

CARTER, ROBERT A., AND LESLIE T. WILKINS, "Some Factors in Sentencing Policy," *Journal of Criminal Law, Criminology, and Police Science* 58 (December 1967): 503–14.
An empirical investigation of the significance of presentence reports prepared by probation officers on judicial sentencing decisions.

DAWSON, ROBERT O., *Sentencing: The Decision as to Type, Length and Conditions of Sentence*. Boston: Little, Brown, 1969.
A detailed examination of sentencing practices in Kansas, Michigan, and Wisconsin. Dawson outlines the types of sentences available on conviction for different kinds of crimes and analyzes the conditions under which different sentences are invoked.

ERLANGER, HOWARD S., "Jury Research in America: Its Past and Future," *Law and Society Review* 4 (February 1970): 345–70.
A survey and assessment of the academic literature relating to the function and operation of the petit jury in American criminal justice.

FRANK, JEROME, *Courts on Trial: Myth and Reality in American Justice*. New York: Atheneum, 1963; originally published in 1949.
A classic analysis of the trial court in America, Frank critically examines a number of issues, including the trial as a fact-finding process, the judge and jury as rational triers of fact, and the law as a body of finely honed rules.

GREEN, EDWARD, *Judicial Attitudes in Sentencing*. London: Macmillan, 1961.
A study of sentencing practices in Philadelphia, the focus is on the relative importance of legal and extralegal cues in sentencing decisions.

HAGAN, JOHN, "Extra-Legal Attributes and Criminal Sentencing: An Assessment of a Sociological Viewpoint," *Law and Society Review*, 8 (Spring 1974): 357–83.
A critical review of twenty empirical studies of sentencing, with special emphasis on the comparative significance of legal and extralegal variables in the explanation of sentencing disparity.

KALVEN, HARRY, JR., AND HANS ZEISEL, *The American Jury*. Boston: Little, Brown, 1966.
A classic investigation of the operation of the petit jury, the authors examine the relationship between the judge and jury as well as the conditions under which the jury arrives at decisions of conviction and acquittal.

part four

CORRECTIONS

8
PROBATION
and PAROLE

The definition of probation is twofold. First, it refers to the sentence wherein a convicted person is supervised by a probation officer as he lives in the community. Second, it refers to the work of a probation officer in the court preparing presentence reports for convicted offenders. Probation is the most common sentence for a convicted offender, and the presentence report of the probation officer may function as the deciding variable in whether a person is sent to prison or allowed to remain in the community on probation. Of the several areas of the criminal justice process, probation is the one we know the least about in terms of empirical studies. How does probation supervision work? How do probation officers decide whether an offender should go to prison or be given a chance to stay free in society? What is the guiding philosophy behind probation recommendations and supervision?

To answer these questions, we shall examine the development of the idea of probation and its underlying rationale. In addition, we shall look at those situations in which probation decisions are made to examine the situational exigencies of the decisions. However, we have less information on the supervisory activities in probation, and what information is available is sketchy and idealized. Since there is no clear-cut guiding philosophy of probation, we shall have to look at the ideals and compare them with various practices. Finally, we shall consider the political and financial realities of probation in light of the fact that probation costs about a tenth of what it costs to send a person to prison.

In contrast to probation, those who are placed on parole are persons coming out of prison, and parole itself is actually linked to a prison sentence; that is, parole consists of serving part of a prison term in the community instead of behind bars. To examine the role of parole in the criminal justice process, we must ask how convicted felons are granted parole. How does parole supervision work? And since parole can be revoked and the offender sent back to prison, we need to know about the parole revocation process. What are the conditions of parole and how are they enforced? Is the parole officer a helpful guide to the parolee or a watchdog trying to find the slightest violation of a parole condition?

To address these questions, we shall examine the operation of the parole board and parole office. Like probation, though, we shall find a vague, disorganized philosophy and haphazard patterns. In examining the parole office, however, we shall be able to see that organizational contingencies play an important role in the parole revocation process, and that the parole officer is caught between bureaucratic realities and the desire to help the deserving parolee. In those situations in which decisions regarding revocation are made, we shall examine the external matters of inter- and extraorganizational forces working to preclude any decisions of the parole officer.

PROBATION

Probation is generally considered in terms of some form of corrections and leniency, and its early history suggests that these are indeed its primary functions. The practice can be traced to early attempts to mitigate severely punitive sentences, such as by judicial reprieves and claims to the right of clergy. Even though it is commonly used, probation has occupied a tenuous position between outright discharge and incarceration. It represents a somewhat unhappy compromise between the classical school, which demands immediate punishment for wrongdoing, and a positivistic approach, which insists on treatment for those who are "sick," "disordered," or irrational. Interestingly, probation is legitimated frequently by persons who claim that supervision in the community is a good form of treatment. But those who demand a more punitive response to crime also see incarceration as a good form of treatment, while others argue that probation is a way of avoiding serious treatment.

Both probation and parole officers deal with their clients in the community. (*Wide World Photos*)

With the first probation laws in the United States emanating in Massachusetts in 1878, probation was taken to be almost synonymous with a suspended sentence (Evjen, 1975:3). In fact, when the federal courts were denied granting suspended sentences (*Ex parte United States*, 242 U.S. 27), it was suggested that federal legislation authorizing probation be enacted to remedy this restriction (Evjen, 1975:3). Eventually, and against opposition from state judges and the federal Department of Justice, federal probation, along with probation legislation in the states, emerged as a form of restitutive law (Evjen, 1975: 4–8). Conditions of probation emphasized restitution, and probation was limited to noncapital offenses. With the development of probation legislation came the development of the probation office, whose fundamental character is defined by the probation officer. Originally, the job of the probation officer was to supervise those placed on probation and to make sure that the conditions of probation were met. But, as we have seen, probation officers also assist in the determination of sentences. Consequently, the probation process includes both presentence investigations and recommendations as well as supervision (Carter and Wilkins, 1976:77). As investigators, probation officers examine the background of the defendant and develop recommendations to assist the judge in deciding what sentence to impose. In the supervisory role, probation officers oversee probationers in the community.

For our purposes, the critical decisions in probation are those in which probation officers decide whether or not a convicted defendant should receive probation and what conditions of probation should be met. We need to examine the practices whereby the probation officer constructs an image of a convicted defendant to be a good or bad probation risk and the relation of that decision to other critical situations in the sentencing process. Additionally, it is important to examine the supervisory work of the probation office. The success or failure of a probationer rests in part with how the probation office construes the person under supervision. This perception occurs in the context of a caseload and a guiding philosophy characteristic of the probation office, in addition to a political context surrounding the agency. By looking at various studies in this area, we hope not only to provide a realistic overview of what happens in probation but also to locate significant variables and processes.

Presentence Investigations

The presentence investigation the probation officer makes purportedly serves (1) to provide the court with sufficient information to make a rational decision, (2) as a guide to referral agencies that may be involved with the probationer (for example, alcoholic or drug rehabilitation services, marital counseling), (3) as a resource for prison staff and administrators planning a program for the person if sentenced to prison, and (4) as a device for parole agencies to understand the background of the offender (Cohn, 1976:361–62). From this extended use of the presentence report, we can see that a probation officer's construction of a convicted defendant's biography is consequential for other decision-makers in the criminal justice system. The problem, then, is in finding exactly how the probation officer's assesments are made. As Carter and his associates (1975:193) report, there are few studies on this decision-making process, and the data that do exist are equivocal. While the guidelines for making presentence investigations are fairly clear, it has been difficult to determine what actual dynamics operate in the investigations and the decisions. Nevertheless, several patterns can be constructed.

In the guidelines set down by federal probation authorities, a number of specific cues are supposed to be taken into account by probation officers in presentence reports. Included are the following (Division of Probation, 1974:48):

Offense

Official version
Statements of codefendants
Statements of witnesses, complainants, and victims

Defendant's version of offense
Prior record
Family history

Defendant
Parents and siblings
Marital history
Home and neighborhood
Education
Religion
Interests and leisure-time activities
Health
    Physical
    Mental and emotional
Employment
Military service
Financial condition
    Assets
    Financial obligations

The items recommended in this format are for those dispositions in which the "issues are clear" (Division of Probation, 1974:48). But, as we have seen, it is rare that any concrete case is "clear." Rather, things are made "clear" and formats, such as the one presented by the probation division, are resources for "making things clear." These devices are merely practical tools for shearing away the complexities of a social biography and the contingencies of a criminal event. However, since they provide a handle in the midst of contradictory, shifting, and equivocal information, they often become treated as *objective* facts about offenders.

Do probation officers in fact make recommendations on the basis of officially prescribed data? One study suggests that presentence decisions are made after probation officers use some, but not all, of the criteria recommended by the Division of Probation (Carter, 1967). In his experiment, Carter (1967) tried to find out which of twenty-four different criteria influenced probation officers when they made their presentence recommendations. This method allowed Carter to see which variables were most important, and which ones were used most often. He found that two variables—offense and prior record—were used more than any others, and these two were *always* chosen by the probation officers in arriving at a decision. Other variables chosen more than 50 percent of the time included the defendant's psychological/psychiatric evaluation (79.7 percent), his statement (69.6 percent), his attitude (62.3 percent), his employment history, (60.9 percent) and his age (53.6 percent).[1]

---

[1] These same factors crop up in other parts of the criminal justice process, and they can be seen as commonsense criteria for personal assessments. Piliavin and Briar (1964) found that the police use the offense and prior record as the *most* important criteria in deciding whether or not to make an arrest, and both the defendant's statement and attitude (referred to as "demeanor" in the Piliavin and Briar study) were significant considerations in the arrest decision.

Blumberg's (1967:145) list of items typically found in presentence reports includes variables Carter found important in his experiment:

> Presentence reports usually include such items as the details of the immediate offense, as obtained from the district attorney and the police; the defendant's prior criminal history, if any; the attitude of the complainant in the case; and a personal history of the defendant in terms of early development, employment, education, and personal data in connection with family or marriage. The report will include information about his mental and physical condition, probably furnished by a hospital or a private psychiatrist.

Similarly, comparing criteria used by probation officers and judges, Carter and Wilkins (1967) found the five most important variables used by both groups were the same (although not necessarily in the same order of importance). The five variables included (1) prior record, (2) confinement status, (3) number of arrests, (4) offense, and (5) longest employment (Carter and Wilkins, 1967:510). Thus, both legalistic variables and variables relating to the individual defendant are used in decision-making.

Constructing Decisions

Now that we have an idea about which variables are central to decision-making, we must look at the dynamics of decision-making. The first part of our discussion deals with the general problem of how social actors construct an image of a defendant as one sort of person or another. Goffman's work on presentation of self will serve as a starting point. According to Goffman, social actors give off information to others, and on the basis of this information, others decide how to interact with them (Goffman, 1959:1–16). Depending on how one wishes to be seen by others, one will present different information to them. Appearances, gestures, and talk are used in these interactional assessments. What a person "is" depends on what information develops, and how it is interpreted or perceived by others in the setting.

By studying presentations given off by persons under investigation and how they are interpreted by probation officers, we can examine how a person's being considered good or bad is developed in social interaction.

To preface, we will first turn to some quasiexperiments to see how social actors treat informative particulars.[2] A set of articles was selected and sealed in transparent plastic bags and given to a group of

---

Only the psychological/psychiatric report, which is unavailable to the police, was definitely *not* used by the police in routine decision-making.

[2] The findings of this experiment were presented in a paper entitled "Experiments in Accomplishing Information: Ethnomethodology and Dramaturgy" by William B. Sanders, presented at the Annual Meeting of the Southwestern Sociological Association, Dallas, Texas, 1976.

subjects who were told that all of the articles belonged to the same person. Their task was to tell what each article could reveal about the person, and after having viewed all articles separately they were to provide a composite description of the person. No information other than that the articles all belonged to the same person was provided.

The eight articles given the subjects in the experiments included (1) a paper clip and a safety pin, (2) a rolled matchbook cover burnt on one end, intended to look like a makeshift marijuana butt holder, (3) a piece of elastic strap, (4) a yellow pencil with red wax covering it, (5) a book of matches with the top torn off, (6) a wood block with a green stained potted plant printed on it, (7) a cigar band, and (8) a small white bow. In every case the subjects recognized that the articles could tell them something about the person who owned them. Moreover, they were able to provide a consistent, coherent overall picture of the person. Even though there were different readings of the items, as well as different themes developed by the subjects, the consistency and coherence of their composite descriptions was a constant feature of their report. In cases where the subjects saw inconsistency in the articles, they provided a theme that would make the articles consistent. For example, many saw the cigar band and white bow to be inconsistent at first since they assumed one belonged to a man and the other to a woman. This inconsistency was repaired by providing themes in which the two items would "normally" go together. Some said the person was a man who had raped a woman and taken the bow (along with the elastic strap), others decided the person must be a male homosexual, and still others simply concluded that the person was a woman who had kept her husband's or boyfriend's cigar band. However, no matter what sense was made of the items, a theme was developed to show that everything went together.

After the initial experiment, follow-up experiments were done to find if the order of the articles had any effect on the interpretations. In the first experiment it was found that 66 percent of the subjects used a drug theme to interpret the items. And since all of the subjects who had used a drug theme to read the articles had identified the rolled matchbook cover as a "roach holder," it was hypothesized that if the roach holder were placed near the end of the experiment, a drug theme would be used less often as an interpretive scheme. By reversing the order of presentations, the roach holder became the second to last article in the array. After the experiment was conducted using this reversed order, it was found that only 33 percent, or half the percentage of the first group, used a drug theme to interpret the articles. This established that the order of presentation influenced the interpretation of the hypothetical person.

Taking this second finding in conjunction with the initial findings, we can see that probation officers may be effectively influenced by the initial variables they are provided with over the other variables. As we indicated, researchers found that probation officers gave top priority to an individual's prior record and the nature of the offense in making a presentence recommendation. Now, given that the order of variables has an impact on the interpretation of the later variables, such as the psychological/psychiatric report and employment history, these others are interpreted not merely in terms of what is available in the psychological/psychiatric report or employment history (as well as all other variables), but instead are interpreted in terms of *themes* developed by reading the offense and prior record. Therefore, even though a long list of variables is recommended for use by the probation office, their use is not independent of certain central variables used to make up the presentence report. For example, if a person is charged with armed robbery and has a prior record of several arrests, no matter what the psychological/psychiatric report says, the charge is read in terms of the offense and prior record. A psychological/psychiatric report saying that the person is stable and mentally healthy is not taken to be evidence that the person is a good probation risk; instead, it indicates that he is an intelligent robber who, if allowed to go free, will probably do the same thing again. The probation officer might simply conclude the person is lazy, overly ambitious (especially if there is a good employment history), or any other interpretation that will justify a coherent, consistent picture that the person is not a good probation risk. On the other hand, a person convicted of a minor offense and with little or no prior record, but with a negative psychological/psychiatric report and a poor employment history, may be recommended for probation. The nature of the offense and minimal prior record could be used to interpret the psychological/psychiatric report and poor employment history to be evidence that the person needs probation and counselling to overcome these problems; incarcerating him would only serve to intensify the maladies.

The point of this discussion is to show that the construction of the presentence report is not merely reading an objective set of facts; instead, it is a process whereby the probation officer prospectively reads "the facts" while at the same time constructing these same facts. Some probation officers may place more emphasis on variables other than the ones identified, and instead of using prior record and offense to interpret the other variables, may employ some other variables as a themeing device. However, no matter what the probation officer uses as a critical variable, the variables are not objective facts but socially and organizationally produced ones. Moreover, other unlisted variables such as race might effect other variables. But no matter what interpretive scheme is used in making a presentence report, a rational one that is a consistent and coherent recommendation to the court can be developed. Thus, the variables used are not objective but are influenced by the contextual matters and interpretive practices in the situation in which they are used (Cicourel, 1968).

Given that probation officers employ an interpreted set of criteria for developing their presentence reports, the next question is whether or not the judge follows the recommendation of the probation officer. Earlier we found a high rate of agreement between the recommendation in the presentence report and the basic sentence. Tables 8–1 and 8–2 show situations in which the probation officers recommended for and against probation.

TABLE 8–1   PERCENTAGE OF PROBATION OFFICERS' RECOMMENDATIONS FOR PROBATION FOLLOWED BY CALIFORNIA SUPERIOR COURTS

Year	Percent
1959	95.6
1960	96.4
1961	96.0
1962	96.5
1963	97.2
1964	97.3
1965	96.7

SOURCES: State of California, Department of Justice. *Delinquency and Probation in California,* 1964, p. 168; and *Crime and Delinquency in California,* 1965, pp. 98-99.

TABLE 8–2   PERCENTAGE OF PROBATION OFFICERS' RECOMMENDATIONS AGAINST PROBATION NOT FOLLOWED BY CALIFORNIA SUPERIOR COURTS

Year	Percent
1959	13.5
1960	12.8
1961	14.8
1962	17.4
1963	21.6
1964	21.1
1965	19.9

SOURCES: State of California, Department of Justice. *Delinquency and Probation in California,* 1964, p. 168; and *Crime and Delinquency in California,* 1965, pp. 98-99.

Examining these two tables, we can see readily that the courts generally conform to probation officers' recommendations. There is about 97 percent agreement between judges and probation officers when the recommendation is for probation and about 83 percent agreement when the recommendation is against probation.

Carter and Wilkins (1967:507), who originally used these data to examine the impact probation officers have on sentencing, suggest four possible explanations for the parity of probation-officer recommendations and sentences:

1. The court, having such high regard for the professional qualities and competence of its probation staff, "follows" the probation recommendation—a recommendation made by the person (probation officer) who best knows the defendant by reason of the presentence investigation.
2. There are many offenders who are "obviously" probation or prison cases.
3. Probation officers write their reports and make recommendations anticipating the recommendation the court desires to receive. (In this situation, the probation officer is quite accurately "second-guessing" the court disposition.)
4. Probation officers in making their recommendations place great emphasis on the same factors as does the court in selecting a sentencing alternative.

Of these explanations, Carter and Wilkins place credence in the first and last. On the one hand, they found that probation officers and judges attend to and consider the same basic variables and in much the same order of priority in the decision (or recommendation) of basic sentence. Consequently, when a probation officer recommends one type of sentence and provides a summary account of the case legitimizing that recommendation, the judge, sharing the same basic perspective toward sentencing, may arrive at substantially the same conclusion after a consideration of the case's features. On the other hand, trial judges do (perhaps as a consequence of their shared perspective toward sentencing) have a high regard for probation officers' recommendations, and may "follow" such recommendations without careful consideration of a case's features. Carter and Wilkins show that there is wide variation between probation officers in the kinds of recommendations made. There is a range of recommendations for probation from a low of 40.0 percent to a high of 88.9 percent (Carter and Wilkins, 1967:512). In addition, the authors also found a high rate of consistency in the recommendations made to trial judges of various types. As we said before, if the officers were second-guessing judicial preferences, we would expect some tailoring of recommendations to individual judges, hence some degree of inconsistency in the recommendations by individual officers. They suggest, then, that judges follow the recommendations, not the reverse.

The problem with accepting these hypotheses is that we know that in plea negotiation the sentence is usually part of the deal. As we have seen, in some cases there may be a mere alteration of charges so as to bring legislative sentencing boundaries to what is deemed a more suitable level; in other cases, however, the prosecutor agrees to recommend a particular type of sentence (probation-incarceration, length of incarceration) in exchange for a guilty plea. In the latter situation, if the presentence report is to coincide with the deal, the probation officer must either write the presentence report to "match" the outcome arranged by the prosecutor, or he must be picking up the same clues as the prosecutor as to what the sentence should be.

We can hypothesize that a probation officer's presentence report, even though it can be used by the judge to show that he used the professional judgment of the probation officer's investigation in making his decision, is often made to conform with what is known to be the basic outcome agreed to by the defense and prosecution.

This pattern is suggested by Rosett and Cressey in their discussion of the sentencing process. The following represents the typical chain of events in sentencing:

Following his guilty plea, Peter Randolph spent another two weeks in jail awaiting sentencing. One day a probation officer called him to the lawyer's room. He seemed friendly, and he explained that he was writing a personal history of Randolph, to be used by the judge in setting Randolph's sentence. Most of his questions were routine requests for the same information Randolph had already given to others. After ten minutes of such questions, Randolph was asked for his version of the crime. The probation officer seemed to listen carefully as Randolph explained that on the night of the crime he was feeling sorry for himself, disappointed, fed up and drinking too much wine. On his note pad the probation officer wrote: "Subject says he doesn't know why he committed the burglary. Was drinking wine in the park and just wandered in the house. Inadequate personality."

Then he asked Randolph what he thought a proper sentence would be. Randolph replied that a public defender had told him that a district attorney was going to let him out of jail and put him on probation. That seemed OK. The probation worker seemed unconcerned. He made some notes.

"That's the deal, ain't it?" Randolph asked.

"The D. A. and the P. D. don't have the final say. That's up to the judge. He'll read my report and decide what to do. . . . "

At Peter Randolph's sentencing hearing the prosecutor addressed the judge first. "If it please the Court, since Your Honor has the presentence report in hand, the People at this time have no further statements or recommendations to make. Thank you, Your Honor." It was easy for the prosecutor to speak so briefly and with such confidence in the outcome. He had spent ten minutes with the probation officer before the report was written, describing the arrangements he had worked out with Randolph's lawyer. When he was given a copy of the final report, he glanced through it to make sure that it recommended the disposition they had agreed upon. He skipped the parts dealing with Randolph's background, personality, and probation plan.

Steven Ohler, the public defender assigned to Randolph at arraignment, made a slightly longer speech. "Your Honor, in the interests of justice, I would like to take just a minute to make a few remarks concerning my client, Mr. Randolph. I would remind Your Honor that this is my client's first adult conviction. He has never been in any really serious trouble before, and the offense he has pleaded to, unlawful entry, was committed in such a way that it is clear we are not dealing with an experienced criminal. In fact, I feel sure that in this case we are, so to speak, nipping a criminal career in the bud. I would also remind the Court that my client has already served more than sixty days in the county jail. He has expressed to me a deep and sincere remorse for his behavior, and this is, more than anything, what leads me to believe that this is a case in which the mercy of the Court would be most appropriate and just."

The judge then asked Randolph if he wanted to add anything. The bailiff motioned him to stand before the bench.

"No, Your Honor."

"Nothing to say?"

"Well, Judge . . . I don't know, but I sure wish you would let me out."

This the judge did, as everyone but Randolph was sure he would do. He sentenced Randolph to a jail term equal to the time already served, plus a year on probation (Rosett and Cressey (1976:31–33).

Thus, in areas where the prosecutor's negotiation with defense yields a sentence concession, the presentence investigation by the probation officer may be nothing more than a perfunctory ceremony carried out to meet the requirement of *appearing* to do a presentence investigation to determine an individual's suitability for probation. Whether this is true in all jurisdictions or not is as yet unknown, but it is typical in many.

Supervision
Once a defendant has been placed on probation, he is to be supervised by the probation officer to ensure that the conditions of probation

are maintained (Cohn, 1976:363). Probation success is measured by the "violation rate" or the number of people on probation and the number who in some way violate the conditions of probation (Carter et al., 1975:194). Although the conditions of probation vary by jurisdiction and nature of the crime, generally they deal with the following:

1. Cooperating with a program of supervision.
2. Meeting family responsibilities.
3. Maintaining steady employment or engaging or refraining from engaging in a specific employment or occupation.
4. Pursuing prescribed educational or vocational training.
5. Undergoing available medical or psychiatric treatment.
6. Maintaining residence in a prescribed area or in a special facility established for or available to persons on probation.
7. Refraining from consorting with certain types of people or frequenting certain types of places.
8. Making restitution of the fruits of the crime or reparation for loss or damage caused thereby (Cohn, 1976:363–64).

Additionally, any criminal offense is considered a probation violation.

The supervisory function of probation appears fairly clear. However, there is considerable confusion as to the philosophies and strategies of supervision and its actual practices and routines. In some vague sense the philosophy of probation may be characterized as being similar, if not identical, to that of social work (Blumberg, 1967:144), but this is not always the case. On the one hand, probation reflects a partially punitive reaction to wrongdoing: "The suspension of sentence, and hence the threat of punishment, is always present in probation . . . ." (Sutherland and Cressey, 1974:462). On the other hand, probation emphasizes that the criminal offender needs to be guided and assisted in adjusting to respectable modes of action; this focus is a reflection of a nonpunitive treatment reaction to wrongdoing (Sutherland and Cressey, 1974:462). And it is no small feat to unravel the conflicting and competing schools of social work that aim at guiding and assisting convicted criminals. One writer characterized probation as

> primarily a process of verifying the behavior of an offender
> (1) through periodic reports of the offender and members of his
> family to the probation officer and (2) by the incidence or
> absence of adverse reports from the police and other agencies.
> Secondarily, probation is a process of guiding and directing the
> behavior of an offender by means of intensive interviewing
> utilizing ill-defined casework techniques (Diana, 1960:204).

Whether or not probation has changed operationally since Diana's characterization in 1960 is uncertain. But in 1926 two writers provided the following pithy definition of probation that leads us to believe that probation has always been somewhat vague: " . . . probation is a term that gives no clue to what is done by way of treatment . . . ." (Healy and Bronner, 1926:82).

The overall goal of probation is to work with people such that they can control their own behavior in line with legal expectations. As the American Correctional Association points out:

> Probation's most important achievement is not control of
> the probationer under supervision but rather enabling the
> probationer to understand himself and gain strength in
> independent control over his own behavior (1966:107–8).

The problem is that there is little consensus as to how this is to be achieved. However, what is done to the probationer, no matter what it is, can always be called treatment, and successes can always be attributed to the treatment practices while violations can be attributed to failure to respond to treatment. In this way, as Carter and his associates (1975:190) point out, there is always evidence that the program is working since the probation office takes credit for the successful cases and attributes failure to the offender. There is the underlying assumption that *anything* done by the probation office is for the probationer's good, and since anything happening to the probationer as a result of the probation officer is glossed as "treatment," sucess is due to the treatment.

Probation's Effectiveness

One might wonder how the probation office can take credit for success and blame failures on the offender. But under the "medical model" the remedy is rarely questioned (cf. Goffman, 1961). For example, there are pills one can take that will prevent malaria, and all one has to do to avoid getting malaria is to regularly take these pills. If one does get malaria when under treatment, the fault is not with the pill; rather, it is with the patient because he did not follow the directions for taking the pill or there is something "wrong" with his physiology that prevented the pill from working. Thus, unless something is *wrong with the patient* (probationer), the treatment (probation) always works.

When evaluating the effectiveness of any "people-changing" effort, one must beware of overstating success rates. For example, by dropping drug addicts from a treatment program who continue to use narcotics, all the persons who finish the program may be declared rehabilitated. Glaser points out:

> Failure to count dropouts in determining success rates is
> most dramatic at addiction treatment agencies, but occurs also
> in other people-changing efforts. Lerman (1968) reports that a

private residential center for boys which he studied in New York rejects seventeen applicants for every one it admits, and subsequently expels 31 percent of the admittees "resisting treatment" before they complete the center's program, which has an average duration of sixteen months. An evaluation that does not take into account the rejectees and expellees could clearly be misleading (1973:163).

A second problem with the logic of success and failure in the context of probation is that the treatment (or what happens under the rubric of treatment) is so diverse that it is almost impossible to isolate the conditions that would lead to success or failure as a consequence of the treatment. As Diana concludes in his survey of probation officers:

It may well be that few correctional personnel are really aware of whatever techniques they use, and it is very highly probable that only a small percentage of the total are qualified caseworkers. It is also highly probable, and certainly seems to be the case from this writer's experience, that the image that many probation officers have of themselves is a picture of a warm and understanding though objective person, a kind of watered-down or embryonic clinician. In any event the influence of a clinical, casework ideology, along with its confused and contradictory elements, has been pervasive. Convention papers, the literature, and supervisors are filled with this ideology, so that it is constantly before the probation officer. It is no more than could be expected, then, if the probation officer feels that whatever he does and however he does it, it *is* treatment (1960:203).

Thus, again, unlike the malaria pill and the medical model, with probation treatment, we do not even have an idea whether the same pill is given, and if there is an effect whether it is due to the treatment or something else.

A final point. The issue of "caseload size" has received an increasing amount of attention over the years. At the inception of probation, the number of convicted criminals released in the community under the supervision of volunteers was variable. For example, some community members would supervise and assist one or two probationers, while others, such as Boston shoemaker John Augustus, would carry hundreds of probationers over a period of time. Fifty persons per officer has come to be institutionalized as the ideal number. A great deal of discussion has centered around caseloads that have exceeded the magic number of fifty. When research on this issue was done, it was found that the caseload size was not the main determinant of success (Adams,

1967:56–57). One study in California examined the impact of reduced caseloads. In some cases, it was found that there was a significant difference, but overall there was not the expected improvement. Apparently, the improvements that occurred were due to the type of program the probation office had, and in some cases when the caseload was reduced the offices were able to properly implement their programs; with the larger caseloads the improved programs were unable to function successfully. However, the main variable was the kind of program and not the caseload, for even with greatly reduced caseloads, probation offices with ill-defined programs had no more success than offices with large caseloads.

Conclusion

The goals of probation as well as the techniques for accomplishing them conflict. On the one hand, probation reflects a punitive, law enforcement orientation. For years, probation officers were "politically" oriented, trained to watch their probationers and punish them for violations of the "conditions of probation." They employed their commonsense and experience, drawn principally from middle-class life, in the paternalistic supervision of their wards. In recent years, however, probation has come to reflect a treatment or "helping" orientation. Probation officers have become professionally oriented and trained in various schools of social work to service the community by changing the criminal. These schools have fundamentally different orientations to probation; consequently, officers develop different perspectives about their work, and out of these differences disparate ideas about the goals of probation have developed. Although formal and official goals may be articulated in agency manuals and publications, the informal (and perhaps most important) conceptions of the job vary. Due perhaps to these differences, the methods of supervision that officers employ are inconsistent with one another (Ohlin, 1956:45–47).

PAROLE

Parole shares with probation the feature of community-based supervision, and in many ways parole and probation are analytically similar. The main differences are in the situated locations of the critical decisions and the fact that parole occurs *after* imprisonment. Thus, probationers unlike parolees are not stigmatized with the exconvict label. And while the consequential decisions for probationers are made "in the community," the decisions for prospective parolees are made while they are still behind bars.

Like probation, the granting of parole has been viewed as a "break" for the convict since parole means that he will no longer be confined in prison or jail. The purpose of parole is successful reintegration of convicts into the community (President's Commission on Law Enforcement and Administation of Justice, 1967:61–63). Thus, traditionally evaluation of parole is linked to the success of the parolee in the community, and the violation rate is taken as a measure of the success (or failure) of the parole agency. This may be an unfair index of success, since parole is not only community treatment but is also treatment linked to programs within a penal institution. A convict's release on parole is supposed to be integrated with his treatment in an institution.

The situations and processes of decision-making in parole center around (1) the decision to grant parole and (2) the decision to revoke parole and send the parolee back to prison. We shall analyze these two processes and provide some description of parole supervision.

Parole Board Decisions to Grant Parole

At the outset it can be said that most parole decisions do not appear to have a connection with a plan. If we can discover a pattern to the granting of parole at all, it is that the process is without too many operational guidelines. Carter and his associates (1975:206) demonstrate that parole boards typically make use of the presentence investigation report, correctional institution classification material, institutional progress reports, and prerelease plans, but the ways in which these informational resources are used are vague. O'Leary and Nuffield (1972:181) point out that parole boards usually employ what they call the method of "intuitive conclusion" whereby they more or less guess who would be a good parole risk. Similarly, Hoffman and Degostin argue that most jurisdictions have informal decision policies that are "unarticulated and not well developed" (1974:7). Some boards are better developed, and many penologists have been urging that statistical methodologies be employed so that parole decisions can better predict whether or not a parole candidate will be successful (Glaser, 1969:197–209). For the most part, however, decision-making is carried out in the context of *ad hoc* criteria in the specific situation in which the actual decisions are made.

Given this state of affairs, our examination of parole decision situations will have to rely on the clues we have at our disposal. One item that appears to be significant, whether intuitive or highly structured, is the seriousness of the crime. "Crime seriousness," as we have seen, is a recurrent criterion employed by criminal justice officials in making decisions at the many stages of the criminal justice process. Hoffman and Degostin (1974:12) provide detailed guidelines for determining parole suitability, and one of the main criteria is what they label "offense characteristics." The interesting aspect of this decision in the context of the parole situation, as opposed to arrest, plea negotiation and sentencing, is that by the time the convicted offender has reached the stage of being considered for parole, he has supposedly gone through some form of rehabilitation. It is assumed that the more serious the crime, either socially or in the eyes of the law, the poorer the risk for parole. Thus, even when the parole decision is being made, the potential parolee is still linked to an action that may have been performed several years earlier.

The extent to which parole boards link their decisions to the seriousness of a crime depends on how the convict's biography is established in the various records and documents the parole board examines. A retrospective reading of a "serious crime" may be mitigated by documents from the prison showing that the candidate was a model prisoner. On the one hand, change in the person may be seen as an actual change or genuine rehabilitation, and the serious crime was a mistake that was made long ago by a basically good person. On the other hand, the seriousness of the crime may be reread as being not-so-bad-after-all. For example, in cases of criminal homicide, listed by Hoffman and Degostin (1974:12) as the "greatest" in seriousness, often the victim participates in the escalation toward homicide. Rereading a homicide as being one in which the victim "had it coming," or "asked for it," the seriousness of the crime can be seen retrospectively, given other evidence of good behavior, as less serious. Therefore, the parole board can still use crime seriousness as a device in decision-making, maintaining a posture of evenhandedness; but crime seriousness is always interpreted in the context of other items of information that have been produced by various officials of the criminal justice system (Garfinkel, 1967).

A final consideration to be given parole boards is the constitution of their membership and the possible impact of their individual backgrounds on their decisions. In thirty-nine states, parole board members are appointed by governors, and most of these appointments are linked to political affiliation (President's Commission on Law Enforcement and Administration of Justice, 1967:66). Perhaps some are competent in judging rehabilitation, for some states specifically require that members have some background in the social and behavioral sciences. On the whole, however, parole board members are laymen, and as such they may or may not rely on the apparent expertise of presentence investigation reports, correctional records, and caseworker recommendations. Given the extent to which parole decisions are linked to correctional institution and caseworker reports, we can expect correctional institutions to have a great deal of influence in deciding the outcome of parole decisions. But the extent to which correctional recommendations are ignored points to the board's reliance on either the criminal

Parole is, among other things, a device for easing the transition between prison and society. (*Stern: Hamburg 1/ Reinartz*)

record, including the seriousness of the crime, the characteristics of the parole candidate, or on some other possibly unknown variable. If this unknown variable is what O'Leary and Nuffield (1972:181) refer to as the method of "intuitive conclusion," then the decision patterns may be heavily linked to the background characteristics of the board members. For example, a politically conservative board would be less likely to grant parole than would a politically liberal board, regardless of what the correctional institution did or the caseworker recommended.

Parole Supervision and Revocation

Parole supervision and revocation are linked in that the decision to revoke parole and send a parolee back to prison is made during the supervision process. Sometimes revocation takes place more or less "automatically," such as when a parolee commits a crime that is too serious to ignore.

The following is a case in point:

A convicted rapist in the jail asked to talk to one of the
burglary detectives. The rapist said that if he could talk to the

district attorney before sentencing, he would give information about a burglary. The detective agreed, and the rapist told him about a stolen pump. With this information the detective obtained a search warrant, went to the apartment of the suspect, and found not only the pump but also discovered that the pump was being used as a part of an apparatus to make psychedelic drugs. The suspect was on parole at the time, and he, working with his parole officer, had just received a large federal grant to open a half-way house for parolees. Up until the time of his arrest he had been believed to be a model parolee. Parole was revoked after the parole officer examined the evidence against his client, and later the man was convicted of burglary and producing illegal drugs (Sanders, 1977:72–73).

In the above example, the parole officer was distraught to learn of his "model" client's behavior and embarrassed that he was unaware of his illegal activities. The revocation of parole was "automatic" due to the nature of the offense and the unequivocal evidence presented by the police.

At other times, revocation occurs because of some violation of parole conditions that does not break the law. Unlike his response to serious crime violation, the parole officer has considerable discretion in handling violations of these parole conditions. While the conditions of parole are often similar to those of probation, they are typically more detailed and specific, and tailored to what the parole board and parole officer believe to be conditions under which the parolee will commit further crimes. The following represents a partial list of some types of things that are of particular interest to parole boards (Arluke, 1969: 272–73):

1. Use of liquor.
2. Change of marital status.
3. Employment.
4. Church attendance.
5. Venereal diseases.
6. Out-of-county or community travel.
7. Curfew violations.
8. Cooperation with parole officers.

The violation of specific rules associated with these concerns could be grounds for revocation of parole. Until recently, a parole officer had the authority to return a parolee to jail for such violations as staying out after curfew and not attending church. However, in 1972 the U.S. Supreme Court found, in *Morrissey v. Brewer,* that the parolee did have some rights in the matter of parole revocation and provided the following mandates for such revocations:

1. Written notice of the claimed violations of parole.
2. Disclosure to the parolee of evidence against him.
3. An opportunity for the parolee to be heard in person and to present witnesses and documentary evidence.
4. The right of the parolee to confront and cross-examine adverse witnesses (unless the hearing officer specifically finds good cause for not allowing this confrontation).
5. A "neutral and detached" hearing body such as a traditional parole board, members of which need not be judicial officers or lawyers.
6. A written statement by the factfinders as to the evidence relied on and reasons for revoking parole (National Advisory Commission, 1973:407).

Since the revocation rate is frequently used to measure the effectiveness of parole programs, a high rate may be taken as a sign of an agency's ineffectiveness (Prus and Stratton, 1976:48). Therefore, even if a parole officer has the necessary evidence to send a parole violator back to prison, he may not do so merely because he can. But, as we shall see, the parole officer cannot let everything that is seen to constitute a violation go unnoticed, and therefore must exercise considerable discretion in determining what the best course of action is.

In two studies of parole revocation, it has been found that most of the decisions made about revocation are not necessarily based on what is best for the parolee or the community; rather, they are guided by organizational concerns (McCleary, 1975; Prus and Stratton, 1976). The context of the parole violation in terms of organizational and extraorganizational concerns forces the parole officer to a decision. As we pointed out above, certain violations cannot be overlooked no matter what happens, and Table 8–3 shows the degree of freedom in decision-making the parole officer has in terms of different situations.

The example of the parolee who was caught running an LSD factory with a burglarized pump had been picked up in a situation that was doubly hopeless for any support from his parole officer. McCleary (1975:212) points out that the parole officer comes to see decisions about parole violations as "realistic" understandings of what they must do. They did not conceive of their decisions as being "fair" or "unfair," but instead they accounted for their actions in terms of the "reality of the situation." One parole officer explained his decisions in these terms when asked about "being fair":

> Realistic is a better word for it. First off, I don't make
> distinctions between guilty and innocent men. I'll help a guilty

TABLE 8–3   THE DEGREE OF FREEDOM IN PAROLE OFFICERS' DECISION-MAKING

Situation	Examples	Degree of Constraint on P. O.
Absolutely hopeless	Murder Rape Weapons assault Narcotics sales	The P. O. has no freedom whatsoever. His behavior is totally constrained by the situation. If he "bucks the system," he will be denounced by his peers.
Marginally hopeless	Burglary Simple robbery	The P. O. has relatively little freedom.
Marginally promising	Narcotics possession Simple theft	The P. O. has a relatively greater degree of freedom.
Absolutely promising	All misdemeanors "Victimless" felonies	Freedom is greatest. The parolee will not ordinarily be returned to prison in these situations unless his P. O. is forced to "sacrifice" him for some reason.

SOURCE: Richard McCleary, "How Structural Variables Constrain the Parole Officer's Use of Discretionary Powers," *Social Problems* 23 (December 1975): 213.

man beat a rap if I can and if he deserves a break, and I'll watch an innocent man go down the tubes if I have to. It's not that I don't want to help, it's that I can't. I can make a certain amount of trouble for the State's Attorney but that's an unrealistic option. I'm only stalling off the inevitable. The State's Attorney's going to get my man anyway and I'm only making a powerful enemy by stalling. What I do in a case like that is cooperate. Maybe I even give the State's Attorney some moral support. Then I come out of it with a reputation for being fair. But that's not being fair, that's just being realistic (McCleary, 1975:212).

This orientation shows two things. First, it suggests that the parole officer's discretion is mediated through consideration of organizational and extraorganizational concerns. Second, and more important, it suggests that the parole officer's orientation is often on the side of the parolee, and other than those circumstances outside of his control, he tries to keep his wards from having to return to prison. Thus, although a parole officer could have parole revoked or at least instigate revocation hearings for violations of parole conditions, it appears that he is more of a parolee advocate and protector than a "watchdog," and only in fairly hopeless circumstances will he "give over" a parolee. In other words, instead of "policing" the paroled exoffenders, parole officers protect them.

The process of parole revocation involves two different types of decisions: (1) whether a man "deserves" to have parole revoked and (2) whether revocation proceedings should be initiated (Prus and Stratton, 1976:48). Prus and Stratton point out that the parole officer makes a private definition (*typing*) and an official decision (*designation*) in the revocation process. The private typings that are made involve five basic concerns, the first of which is the protection of society. If he believes that the parolee will commit crimes that will be harmful to the community and constitutes an actual threat to society, then the parole officer will be more likely to consider the parolee a candidate for parole revocation. Usually this occurs when the parolee has been apprehended by the police, and the parole officer must actively consider what to do with him (Prus and Stratton, 1976:49). Of course, not everything the parolee does that is brought to the attention of the police is of major concern. But anything considered *serious* facilitates thinking about parole revocation.

The second private concern involves the extent to which the parolee cooperates with the parole officer. If the parole officer believes that he can work with a parolee, then not only is the parolee less likely to be considered a revocation candidate, but any incident involving him is not as likely to be considered serious (Prus and Stratton, 1976: 49–50). As we have pointed out in discussing other types of decisions in the criminal justice process, the seriousness of a crime depends on the context in which it is assessed. For the parole officer, a relevant contextual matter, then, is how cooperative the parolee is in a rehabilitation program. Thus, a parolee who is able to convince the parole officer that he is cooperative is less likely to have his parole revoked than a parolee who is viewed as less cooperative, even though both get into the same kind of trouble.

A third private concern of the parole officer is the protection of parolees (Prus and Stratton, 1976:50). This concern centers around a conception of doing his job correctly, and even though this concern is not the same as a strict organizational view of the position, it is one having to do with the nature of the work. Prus and Stratton (1976:50) describe the concern of protection in terms of three features. First, the parole officer has a personal feeling that the men under his supervision are "his guys" to be taken care of by him. Second, he sees a parolee failure as a sign of his own incompetence. Third, there is a concern for balancing justice, that is, the parole officer sees himself as "doing justice" when he judges that other aspects of the criminal justice system have failed to do so. These features all point to the concern of protecting not only the parolees but also the self-image of the parole officer. And even if a parole officer may not be overly upset about an occasional parolee's "going down the tubes," he can not easily tolerate his self-image's taking a similar course. As a result, a revocation decision not only involves the fate of the parolee but it also involves that of the parole officer.

A fourth private consideration in the revocation process is the desire to do actual rehabilitation (Prus and Stratton, 1976:50–51). On the one hand, the parole officer feels he has to take care of his wards; on the other hand, he wants them to eventually make it on their own. And for the parolee to accomplish the latter means he must change. To revoke parole and send a man back to prison is to recognize that rehabilitation has failed. Any program in which the parolee has failed can be considered an instance of the program's "not being right" for the parolee. Instead of the parolee's or the program's failing, such situations can be construed as ones in which the program and parolee did not fit. In this way, the parole officer preserves the sense that the programs are rehabilitating and that the parolee is potentially receptive to rehabilitation.

The final private concern in the decision process is the parole officer's obligation to the agency (Prus and Stratton, 1976:51). Parole agents' supervisors and departmental policy constituted a very real concern: not only are the parole officers subject to the reward system of the organization but also many of the agency's goals are identical with personal goals. If the agency policy was ostensibly announced and designed to reduce revocation rates, the personal and private considerations given to revocation could not ignore the consequences of agency policy; therefore, even privately, thinking about parolees is affected by organizational concerns.

Given these private typings, the shift from private to *public* or official designations of a parolee as a candidate for revocation can be seen in terms of still another set of concerns. The official concerns constitute not only a set of contingencies in the revocation process but they are also constraints to take the revocation process to its culmination.

The first concern in the decision to make an official designation of a parolee as a revocation candidate is the perceived likelihood that the attempt will be successful (Prus and Stratton, 1976:51). If the parole officer firmly believes privately that a parolee should have his parole revoked, but does not believe that the revocation attempt will be successful, he will be less likely to attempt it than if he believes it likely to be successful. This concern is similar to the concern of being "fair" and *realistic* as discussed by McCleary (1975:212–14). If there is little chance of a successful revocation, then it is unrealistic to pursue it.

A second concern in making an official designation involves the possible personal costs of initiating revocation proceedings. If the parole officer believes that the time and effort spent in going through hearings, confronting the parolee's defense counsel, and all the other problems involved in the revocation process are too high, then this concern mitigates against his moving to have a parole revoked (Prus and Stratton, 1976:51). The revocation hearing provides an occasion where the parole officer can be interrogated, his intent questioned (for example, racial prejudice, civil rights violation), and his career possibly damaged. Therefore, in those instances where the parole officer is seriously thinking about a revocation, even if he thinks it will be successful he must weigh this personal cost in light of the others.

As for the third concern, any revocation, no matter how successful or how well the parole officer comes out of the proceedings, can be a threat to his image as a "successful agent" (Prus and Stratton, 1976:-51–52). Agents with especially high revocation rates may be questioned as to their ability and competence as good parole officers no matter how realistic they have been in their conduct. One can always account for a high revocation rate in terms of being especially good at learning of parole violations or having the bad luck to be stuck with a bunch of "losers," but one can only show success by pointing to those clients who are in some way rehabilitated. Since rehabilitation is measured in terms of the number of revocations, then a high revocation rate can always be used to document the charge that an agent is unsuccessful.

The fourth and final concern in deciding to make an official designation about revocation deals with the parole officer's view of the worth of sending a man back to prison. Although he may privately feel that a parolee deserves to have his parole revoked and he can successfully have it done without repercussions to himself or the agency, he may not follow through because of what he believes prison will do to the returned parolee. An agent may believe that the effects of incarceration are so disruptive that the parolee who is now troublesome in the community will become totally devastated and unrepairable if returned to prison. Imprisonment completes the break between the parole agent and his client, and even though a parolee may "deserve" to be returned to prison, if this is done, the parole agent loses all opportunity to "save" the man (Prus and Stratton, 1976:53).

As we have seen in examining the studies of McCleary, Prus, and Stratton, the parole decision is not merely a reaction to something the parolee does. It is certainly not the case that the parolee is returned to prison on a whim or because of the parole officer's personality; instead, revocation decisions are imbedded in the contextual matters that comprise parole departments and the process of revocation. On the one hand, certain occasions give the parole officer no choice but to move for a parole revocation, even if he privately feels that the parolee is the victim of a "bum rap." On the other hand, before a revocation hearing can be initiated, it is necessary to consider the career ramifications and unwanted effects on the parolee that such a hearing would have. The primary concerns of rehabilitation and community protection may only play a secondary role, and even though the welfare of the parolee is certainly considered by the parole officer, McCleary (1975:217) clearly shows that parole officers find it necessary to cover themselves even at the parolee's expense.

SUMMARY

One of the ironies in the study of probation and parole is that while those who staff positions in these agencies are the most likely to have social and behavioral science backgrounds and philosophies in comparison with other agencies of the criminal justice system, they appear to be the agencies of the system least studied by social and behavioral scientists. In-house studies are in no short supply, but these works tend to concentrate on working up administrative policies and guidelines for doing the day-to-day work of probation and parole. Serious studies of the probation and parole processes show that there are vague, ambiguous guidelines with only the most general overall philosophy of goal attainment and evaluation. As a result, we have only the slightest idea of how probation and parole operate and their effectiveness.

The importance of probation officers in sentencing, at first seemingly significant, is found to be equivocal. If the probation decision is not to interfere with plea negotiation, then the presentence investigation is more ceremonial than substantive. Since the judge is as likely to know the outcome of a negotiated plea as the probation officer, it is little surprise that Carter and Wilkins and others have found a high level of agreement between recommendations and dispositions. The fact that different probation officers have different proportions of recommendations for probation does not mean that judges are greatly influenced by their recommendations, for it is not unlikely that certain probation officers are given the more serious offenders, and as a result they are more likely to recommend against probation. However, like so many other aspects of this area of the criminal justice process, further research is necessary to find out whether or not this is true.

Parole board decisions have been found to be based on the offense for which a person was incarcerated, and like other agencies of the criminal justice process, we find that after all of the ceremony is cleared away, there are certain commonsense agreements that the offense is the most important consideration in decision-making. However, the offense is not an objective fact; rather, it is an organizationally constructed characterization of an event for which one is brought into the criminal justice process. This characterization is then used as an "objective fact" to justify decisions and recommendations.

In our examination of parole office decisions, it was found that the contingencies of the organization are relevant in decision-making. In order to operate successfully, the parole officer had to consider not only organizational others but also those in other organizations. The guiding key to understanding decisions by parole officers is in their notion of "being realistic," for even though they may privately believe something other than their official act in a matter would suggest, their actions have to reflect a standard of operational pragmatism as defined by the organization. Again, however, we saw how the seriousness of the offense as it came to be characterized in the parole office was used as a measure of what a parole officer could do with his ward.

REFERENCES

ADAMS, STUART
  1967 "Some Findings from Correctional Caseload Research," *Federal Probation* (December): 48–57.

AMERICAN CORRECTIONAL ASSOCIATION
  1966 *Manual of Correctional Standards*. Washington, D.C.: American Correctional Association.

ARLUKE, NAT R.
  1969 "A Summary of Parole Rules," *Crime and Delinquency* 15 (April): 267–75.

BLUMBERG, ABRAHAM
  1967 *Criminal Justice*. Chicago: Quadrangle.

CARTER, ROBERT M.
  1967 "The Presentence Report and the Decision-Making Process," *Journal of Research in Crime and Delinquency* 4 (July): 203–11.

CARTER, ROBERT M., RICHARD A. MCGEE, AND KIM E. NELSON
  1975 *Corrections in America*. Philadelphia: Lippincott.

CARTER, ROBERT M., AND LESLIE T. WILKINS
  1967 "Some Factors in Sentencing Policy," *Journal of Criminal Law, Criminology, and Police Science* 58, no. 4: 503–14.
  1970 *Probation and Parole*. New York: Wiley.
  1976 *Probation, Parole and Community Corrections*, 2d ed. New York: Wiley.

CICOUREL, AARON
  1968 *The Social Organization of Juvenile Justice*. New York: Wiley.

COHN, ALVIN W.
  1976 *Crime and Justice Administration*. Philadelphia: Lippincott.

DIANA, LEWIS
  1960 "What is Probation?" *Journal of Criminal Law, Criminology and Police Science* 51 (July–August): 189–204.

DIVISION OF PROBATION
1974 "The Selective Presentence Investigation Report," *Federal Probation* 38 (December): 47–54.

EVJEN, VICTOR H.
1975 "The Federal Probation System: The Struggle to Achieve It and Its First 25 Years," *Federal Probation* 39 (June): 3–15.

GARFINKEL, HAROLD
1967 *Studies in Ethnomethodology.* Englewood Cliffs, N.J.: Prentice-Hall.

GLASER, DANIEL
1969 *The Effectiveness of Prison and Parole System.* Indianapolis, Ind.: Bobbs-Merrill.

GOFFMAN, ERVING
1959 *The Presentation of Self in Everyday Life.* Garden City, N.Y.: Doubleday.
1961 *Asylums.* Garden City, N.Y.: Doubleday.

HEALY, WILLIAM, AND AUGUSTA BRONNER
1926 *Delinquents and Criminals: Their Making and Unmaking.* New York: Macmillan.

HOFFMAN, PETER B., AND LUCILLE K. DEGOSTIN
1974 "Parole Decision-Making: Structuring Discretion," *Federal Probation* 38 (December): 7–15.

LERMAN, PAUL
1968 "Qualitative Studies of Institutions for Delinquents: Implications for Research and Social Policy," *Social Work* 13 (July):55–64.

MC CLEARY, RICHARD
1975 "How Structural Variables Constrain the Parole Officer's Use of Discretionary Powers," *Social Problems* 23 (December): 209–25.

NATIONAL ADVISORY COMMISSION ON CRIMINAL JUSTICE STANDARDS AND GOALS
1973 *Corrections.* Washington, D.C.: Government Printing Office.

O'LEARY, VINCENT, AND JOAN NUFFIELD
1972 *The Organization of Parole Systems in the United States,* 2d. ed. Hackensack, N.J.: National Council on Crime and Delinquency.

PILIAVIN, IRVING, AND SCOTT BRIAR
1964 "Police Encounters with Juveniles," *American Journal of Sociology* 70 (September): 206–14.

PRESIDENT'S COMMISSION ON LAW ENFORCEMENT AND ADMINISTRATION OF JUSTICE
1967 *Task Force Report: Corrections.* Washington, D.C.: Government Printing Office.

PRUS, ROBERT C., AND JOHN R. STRATTON
1976 "Parole Revocation Decision-making: Private Typings and Official Designations," *Federal Probation* 40 (March): 48–53.

SANDERS, WILLIAM B.
1977 *Detective Work: A Study of Criminal Investigations.* New York: The Free Press.

SUTHERLAND, EDWIN, AND DONALD R. CRESSEY
1974 *Criminology,* 9th ed. Philadelphia: Lippincott.

SELECTED READINGS

CARTER, ROBERT M., AND LESLIE T. WILKINS. *Probation, Parole and Community Corrections*, 2d ed. New York: Wiley, 1976
A comprehensive overview of the field and issues involved in probation and parole.

GLASER, DANIEL. *The Effectiveness of a Prison and Parole System*. Indianapolis, Ind.: Bobbs-Merrill, 1969.
Examines the relationship between prison experience and problems faced by the parolee. Also provides an evaluation of the prison and parole system.

Federal Probation: A Journal of Correctional Philosophy and Practice. Edited by the Probation Division of the Administrative Office of the United States Courts, Washington, D.C., and published quarterly by the Administrative Office in cooperation with the Bureau of Prisons of the U.S. Department of Justice.
Contains a wide variety of articles dealing with policy statements, perspectives and empirical works in probation, parole, and corrections.

MC CLEARY, RICHARD. "How Structural Variables Constrain the Parole Officer's Use of Discretionary Powers," *Social Problems* 23 (December, 1975): 209–25.
A participant observation study of the parole office, detailing how decisions regarding parole revocation are made.

9
PRISONS

Prisons, which are total institutions for the confinement of convicted offenders, are typically reserved for those whose sentence exceeds one year and exist in the form of both state and federal facilities. Jails, by contrast, are primarily used for holding criminal suspects prior to adjudication and for those who have been sentenced to less than a year's confinement. Here our focus will be on prisons, and the first question we must consider is, "What are prisons?" This simple question is obfuscated by the use of new "humane" terms such as "correctional institutions" and "rehabilitation and treatment facilities," and we shall have to first break through the language barrier before we can begin to answer the question of what prisons actually are.

Having some idea of what prisons are, we may then ask what really happens to persons in them? Are they rehabilitated? Does prison policy have much impact on the other forces that bear on prison life? Are there informal norms and sanctions that supersede the formal ones? What is life like in a prison for both inmate and staff?

To address these matters, we shall have to look at the prison as a total institution in which every facet of a person's life is regulated, for no matter what prison policy may be—benign or punitive—the regulation process is similar. The structure of the total institution forces inmates into peculiar relationships among themselves and between themselves and the prison staff. To understand these relationships, we shall examine the inmate world and the different orientations those who occupy it have to the same set of circumstances. Similarly we must attempt to understand the staff's world and their position vis-à-vis the inmates and the organization, for even though the staff is free to leave the prison, it nevertheless affects their lives. Finally, we shall examine prison violence in the context of the inmate world and staff as it develops in a total institution. In addition to looking at the violence well publicized in prison riots, we shall also consider the violence among prisoners as well as the subtle violence the institution provides in the name of "therapy."

After exploring the impact of prisons on inmates, we shall examine the major forms of rehabilitation prisons use. Can rehabilitation work in prisons, given the atmosphere of a total institution? Are some types of rehabilitation more effective than others? Since rehabilitation is a major goal of corrections, we will have to examine this matter in detail and assess the overall impact of incarceration on rehabilitation both inside and outside of the prison walls.

INCARCERATORIES

Up to this point in the book, we have concentrated on critical situations in which decisions about suspects, defendants, and convicted offenders are made. However, when we look at prisons, we find that, with the exception of appeals, pardons, and parole board decisions, just about all of the decisions have been made concerning the fate of the prisoner. We have already discussed the parole board decision, and the appeals process is a court matter and not one of corrections. Therefore, in this chapter, instead of examining decisions in prisons, we shall concentrate on prisons (or "incarceratories" as we shall be calling them) as a form of total institution.

In order to arrive at a clear picture of what happens to persons who are sent to prison, we must first recognize that even though we may give them new names, prisons are still places where people are incarcerated by the state. In comparison to such newer designations such as "correctional center," "rehabilitation facility," and similar euphemisms that imply positive outcomes, "prison" connotes a fairly harsh image. Certainly those who run prisons wish they could do something to correct the behavior of their wards. Moreover, there can be no doubt that some people sent to prison are corrected, either because of the rehabilitative programs administered or because they never want to go back. Some former convicts will even point to their prison experience as an opportunity to "go straight." For example, a mugger (who did not mend his ways) explained that he was able to finish high school in prison and learned of opportunities he would not have otherwise considered had he not been incarcerated (Willwerth, 1974). But examining the day-to-day, mundane routine of prisons, we find far more concern with other matters, and even though the names of the personnel positions and actions have been changed, most of the same old prison routines that have existed ever since prisons began still exist. Mitford cites the accomplishment of one commission in such a semantic facelift:

> "Effective July 8, 1970 . . . there were no more prisons; in their places, instead, stood six maximum security 'correctional facilities.' The prisons wardens became 'institutional superintendents' . . . and the old-line prisons guards awakened to find themselves suddenly 'correctional officers.' No one's job or essential duties changed, only his title. Certainly the institutions themselves did not change. . . . To a man spending 14 to 16 hours a day in a cell being 'rehabilitated,' it was scarcely any comfort and no reassurance to learn that he was suddenly 'an inmate in a correctional facility' instead of a convict in a prison." In the same spirit some prisons are now called "therapeutic correctional communities," convicts are "clients of the correctional system," solitary confinement and punishment cells have become "adjustment centers," "seclusion," or, in Virginia, "meditation" (1971:6).

As can be seen from the example, another language, other than the deceptive vocabulary provided by the institutions themselves, is needed to accurately depict the real events that occur in prisons.

To avoid inaccurate terminology, we will incorporate a somewhat awkward term but one we believe serves well the purposes of analysis. We shall refer to jails, prisons, adjustment centers, correctional facilities, or whatever other place is used to lock up persons as "incarceratories." Some may be better designated "dungeons" and others "rehabilitation units," but since they all share the common element of incarcerating people, the term applies no matter what officials or those locked up in it call the place. We shall occasionally use the more common terms to ease the problem of reading, and we shall differentiate between jails and prisons. However, no matter what terms are used at any given point, the focus will be on the notion of incarceration and the problems stemming from locking people up as a means of controlling their lives.

THE GOALS OF INCARCERATION

In the context of the criminal justice system, the subsystem of corrections has as its goal three distinct and sometimes interrelated purposes: (1) revenge, (2) restraint, and (3) reform (Carter, et al., 1975: 12–13).

Seeking revenge or retribution, the criminal justice system incarcerates the lawbreaker to "get even" for the harm he has caused society. As we pointed out in an earlier chapter, the prescribed punishment of the law is an action taken by society as a political whole against criminals. The denial of freedom, especially in a society that has traditionally considered freedom a basic right, is a very real matter for those who are incarcerated.

Under the auspices of "restraint," jails and prisons can be seen as nothing more than warehouses where people are placed for either a specified or unspecified period of time to keep them away from society and thereby keep society safe. This function of merely "keeping people" is the closest to the conceptual picture we are dealing with in analyzing forms of incarceration, but we are not making the same comments on goals of incarceration.

Finally, the reform, rehabilitation, or treatment goals of incarceration assume the possibility of changing the lawbreaker's behavior. This goal, frequently discussed by prison officials and penologists, is the direction implied in the new terminology used by administrators of incarceration. The kernel ideal of reform is to transform those who have broken the law into persons who will not break the law again after their release. For just about everyone, if this ideal were realized, the criminal justice system would be considered successful. Consequently, recidivism rates—the extent to which released offenders do or do not return to prison—have been used as a general measuring device for evaluating the success of correctional programs.[1]

In order to evaluate each of the three goals of incarceration—revenge, restraint, reform—we shall examine the available data to determine to what extent each function is realized in the day-to-day operations of incarceratories. Most studies of goal accomplishment in prisons have centered on the reform function, but even when looking at some of these studies one can find evidence of the other goals being met or not.

To begin our evaluation of the stated goals of incarceratories, we need a conceptual framework to understand what routinely occurs in the prison setting. Goffman's (1961) work on mental hospitals led to the development of the concept of the "total institution," and this concept allows us to look at the mundane social arrangements in any setting designed to monitor and regulate others' lives. One type of total institution consists of those organized to protect the community from criminals, and they are the focus of our interest; but they have certain features in common with all other total institutions. By examining the

---

[1] It might be argued that many of those who do not return to prison have reformed because of the punishment of incarceration, and much crime is deterred because of the fear of punishment. Thus, instead of treatment being the cause of rehabilitation, punishment merely instills fear of future sanctions, thereby deterring crime.

characteristics that are a part of all incarceration facilities in terms of total institutions, we can generalize these aspects and therby cover a wide range of settings in our analysis. Goffman summarizes the features of total institutions in juxtaposition with normal social arrangements:

> A basic social arrangement in modern society is that the individual tends to sleep, play, and work in different places, with different co-participants, under different authorities, and without an overall rational plan. The central feature of total institutions can be described as a breakdown of the barriers ordinarily separating these three spheres of life. First, all aspects of life are conducted in the same place and under the same single authority. Second, each phase of the member's daily activity is carried on in the immediate company of a large batch of others, all of whom are treated alike and required to do the same thing together. Third, all phases of the day's activities are tightly scheduled, with one activity leading at a prearranged time into the next, the whole sequence of activities being imposed from above by a system of explicit formal rulings and a body of officials. Finally, the various enforced activities are brought together into a single rational plan purportedly designed to fulfill the official aims of the institutions (1961:5–6).

The inmate of a total institution lives in a collapsed world where his life is part of a routine the institution sets that is part of a plan to accomplish institutional goals that may or may not conflict with individual needs. Intended goals or stated goals cannot be confused with the overall effects produced by life in the total institution. Therefore, it is necessary to know what effects are common to those in total institutional settings and what effect the institutional activities have on the intended rational goals.

A first aspect prison administrators must handle is that of controlling a large number of people. In part this is linked to the assumption that the inmate is a "bad sort" who will either cause trouble or escape if not controlled. This leads to custodial routines in which inmates' lives are tied into the logistics of feeding, clothing, and providing them with other life-support needs. To do this alone presents enormous problems for the administration, and the work done to provide the control and logistical functions is a form of life and trouble maintenance. In this context, "life maintenance" refers to providing the basic resources for keeping people alive. "Trouble maintenance" refers to the everyday type of disruption of routine that occurs in physical plants, such as broken or clogged pipes, in personnel, such as hiring and training new officers, as well as to the special trouble of keeping persons locked up. This latter function includes everything from interpersonal violence to riots. If there is a failure in the spheres of life and trouble maintenance, then there will be a failure in all other spheres.

In order to minimize malfunctions in life and trouble maintenance, inmates must be forced into the routines set up by the administration. Given the total aspect of social arrangements in prison, those who do not go along with the program will create trouble for either other inmates or the staff. The extent to which an individual can be "fixed" to fit into the program determines the amount of trouble he will make, for variations from the mass-production schedule constitute institutional trouble.

From the inmate's point of view, the programs designed to maintain life and minimize trouble are viewed as irrelevant to his own problems. Describing his view of a prison warden, one inmate pointed out:

> I have not talked with him [the warden] directly; however, in
> his visits to my work assignment he had addressed the inmates
> here as a whole. He is a man that appears to be an enemy of us
> inmates rather than a friend. He does not give appraisal where
> it would not give outside publicity. All his comments are
> criticism of what he thinks we inmates adhere to, all rules at
> all times. He never comments on our progress or acts friendly
> towards us in any manner or fashion. His sole concern is the
> institution and not the people in it (Chang and Armstrong,
> 1972:96).

Implied in this inmate assessment of the concerns of the administration is the primary effort to minimize trouble and keep a smooth operation. As long as the routines are not disrupted, the institution appears to be working, and, as the inmate pointed out, there is a perceived difference between the *good of the institution* and the *welfare of the inmates.* Thus, while life and trouble maintenance may be operating in terms of institutional interests, they may not be operating as far as the inmates are concerned. The orderly movement and care of inmates necessitates a certain amount of indifference to individual needs, since individual needs are often interpreted as being dysfunctional to the institutional order. For example, the sexual needs of inmates may be met in institutionally unacceptable ways, including homosexual liasons.

A more pointed discrepancy between institutional needs and individual ones can be seen in the "moral career" of the inmate (Goffman, 1961:127–69). As inmates are processed into the institutional routines, their selfs are systematically mortified so that they can "fit" with the institutional needs. In describing this process, Goffman points out:

> The barrier that total institutions place between the inmate
> and the wider world marks the first curtailment of self. In civil
> life, the sequential scheduling of the individual's roles, both in
> the life cycle and in the repeated daily round, ensures that no
> one role he plays will block his performance and ties in another.
> In total institutions, in contrast, membership automatically

5-5 ISOLATION TOTAL **21 MAXIMUM** 16

UNIT	RACE	CELL	NAME	NUMBER	IN	OUT	R'MKS	R'MKS
		101						
D	N	102	GIBSON	B-22769	8-19	9-2		
		103						
1	M	104	GARCIA	B-27573	8-18	8-28		
1	W	105	BRUNELLE	B-22352	8-17	8-30		
		106						
		107						
		108						
		109						
		110						
		111						
		112						
		113						
		114						
		115						
		116						
		117						
		118						
* 3	W	119	WHITMORE	A76524	8-18	9-16	3.3	
		120						
		121						
		122						
* 3	N	123	RANDOLPH	B-3841	8-18	8-29	AC-1	
		124						

* FEED ON PAPER PLATES

UNIT	RACE	CELL	NAME	NUMBER	REC'D	STATUS	R'MKS	R'MKS
3	W	125	MARTINEZ	B-20464	3/2/69	AC-1		
		126						
3	W	127	HARRIS	B-5609	9/6/69	AC-1		
3	W	128	SMITH	B-2369	10/23/69	P.3.6.6		
		129						
X 3	W	130	WENDEKIER	B-12961	7/26/69	AC-1		
		131						
3	W	132	VARGAS	B-15291	4/24/70	AC-1		
		133						
		134						
		135						
3	W	136	THOMPSON	B-16521	10/4/69	AC-1		
		137						
		138						
3	N	139	PINELL	A-8240	4/24/70	AC-1		
3	N	140	WHITESIDE	A-91150	4/21/69	AC-1		
3	M	141	CHACON	A-77633	7/30/69	P.3.6.6		
3	M	142	GALAVIZ	B-22535	6/1/70	AC-1		
3	N	143	FLOWERS	B-13202	7/4/70	AC-1		
3	W	144	SATCHER	A-70893	3/2/69	AC-1		
3	W	145	ESCHBACK	A-54164	4/16/68	P.3.6.6		
X 3	W	146	ARIAZ	A-63075	6/4/69	AC-1		
	W	147	KENDRICK	B-13214	1/30/69	P.O.T.C.		
1	W	148	MAHER	A-39435	7/31/70	HPT		

The overriding concern of most prisons is security. (*Stephen Shamlis from Black Star*)

> disrupts role scheduling, since the inmate's separation from the
> wider world lasts around the clock and may continue for years.
> Role dispossession therefore occurs. In many total institutions
> the privilege of having visitors or of visiting away from the
> establishment is completely withheld at first, ensuring a deep
> initial break with past roles and an appreciation of role
> dispossession (1961:14–15).

Thus, the very preparation for life in prison is clearly a conflict between institutional needs and individual ones. There is a trade-off in this realm, for no matter what the good (or even necessary) intentions of the institutional administration, there are bound to be serious losses for self and self-development. The importance of this arrangement is not so much that a great deal of damage is inflicted, but rather that it is the arrangement of the total institution and not just the administrative and staff incumbents who are responsible for the punishing effects of total institutions.

Many writers, and even prison administrators, have pointed to the background and attitudes of prison staffs as a major cause for the problems in incarceratories. For example, in exploring the problems of prisons, Mitford says,

> The character and mentality of the keepers may be of more
> importance in understanding prisons than the character and

mentality of the kept. Would that the hordes of researchers who now invade the prisons would turn their attention to these— explore their childhood traumas, flip inkblots to find out what their Rorschach tests reveal, generally try to discover what makes them tick and what made them choose this occupation in the first place. For after all, if we were to ask a small boy, "What do you want to be when you grow up?" and he were to answer, "A prison guard," should we not find that a trifle worrying—cause, perhaps, to take him off to a child guidance clinic for observation and therapy? (1971:9)

While this is certainly an interesting question, especially as it applies to the more sadistic guards, it misses the central point that no matter what kinds of guards, correctional officers, or counselors man total institutions, there are inherent conflicts between individual needs and institutional ones, and these conflicts will always create friction and misunderstanding between the keepers and kept. This is not to say that a modern prison is no better than a dungeon, but the aspects of total institutions as dungeons are not that much different from the newest rehabilitation centers.

THE INMATE WORLD

In examining what life in prison is like, next to the official program for keeping people, we encounter the unofficial life that takes on its own reality. This other life or "under life" (Goffman, 1961:173–320) is an adaptation inmates make to prison conditions. Restrictions and a scarce supply of the taken-for-granted needs of people in the outside world lead to organized strategies for regaining, controlling, and distributing resources and coping with restrictions.

To some extent adaptations take on patterns common to all total institutions, but adaptive patterns of incarcerated persons are not of a single form. On the one hand, adaptation can be divided between individual and collective modes (Irwin, 1970:67). Individual modes typically involve withdrawal and/or isolation from the others in prison, not only from other inmates but also from the staff and institutional goals. Collective modes involve participation in an inmate social system. This style enables inmates to lessen the pains of incarceration through a shared involvement in forming a solidarity against those on the inside who would harm them, as well as against the overall effects of prison life.

More important, perhaps, than an individual or collective orientation to prison life, Irwin (1970:67–68) points to the focus of orientation. Some prisoners orient themselves to the broader world outside the prison, and their identities are based on this larger-world context. Alternatively, there is an orientation to the prison world, in which the prisoner's decision-making is tied into prison-world criteria of either the staff or the inmates. This latter orientation is interesting in that no matter what side the prison-world-oriented inmate takes, that of the staff or inmate, his point of view and actions are geared to life behind walls and fences and not the larger world into which he will eventually be released.

Whatever the adaptation to prison, however, the newcomer to the inmate world is quickly awakened to the ever-present reality of other inmates locked up with him, and oftentimes, the other inmates rather than the imprisonment itself are the most omnipresent problems. One inmate describes this reality as follows:

> A new inmate (fish) upon entering the institution discovers probably for the first time in his life that the Negro is "king." "Might makes right" can be no more meaningful than behind these walls as the Negros outnumber whites by about 75 percent to 25 percent. The white inmate who has not yet learned "how to talk," or is of lesser experience, is in for the "shock of his life." He will soon learn not to get along with the officers, but to instead learn how to get along with the other inmates who will be the ones who determine his future from that point on. The inmates are the ones who can and will "beat your brains out" or "stick a shank in your back" if you don't fit into the picture, not the officers. In fact, getting along "too well" with the officers can be a serious mistake if one isn't careful. Like the law, which is for only the troublemakers, the new inmate need only be concerned with the troublemakers. They loom before his eyes, threatening his very existence every minute and day of his life; all others remain invisible to his concern. (Chang and Armstrong, 1972:206–7).

This new arrangement in which the "Negro is king," while obstensibly a racial statement, is more importantly a vastly different form of sociation compared to the outside world for black and white inmate alike. In addition to a reapportionment of ethnic distribution, there are troublemakers one must deal with in the absence of the normal recourses available outside the prison. The correctional officers are the collective enemy, not by any maladjustment in their personality, but rather because of their position vis à vis the prisoners. Other prisoners ignore their fellow inmates' dilemmas in order to stay on the unpunished side of both the guards and the troublemakers. As a result, one is forced to rely on his own resources to ward off trouble or to enter into alliances with others in a similar state of affairs.

The overall strategy for "doing time" is summarized by Irwin (1970:69) in five basic points: Inmates (1) avoid trouble, (2) find activities that occupy their time, (3) secure a few luxuries, (4) with the exception of a few complete isolates, form friendships with small groups of other convicts, and (5) do what is necessary to get out as soon as possible. Essentially, this overall strategy is one of minimizing the pain of being locked up, a far cry from the stereotype of prisoners constantly causing as much trouble as they can. The notion that "murderers and rapists" are creating havoc in prisons is a misconception popularized in part by the prison staff (Wicker, 1975:233–52). Just as in society at large the people who cause problems are few relative to the total population, so in prison are there some who are troublemakers for both inmates and prison staff. But these are deviants in that they break institutional norms. The fact that they are highly visible is due to the high density of people living together in a closed situation, and not to the great number of troublemakers. This assertion may seem to be a paradox since those who are locked up have been society's lawbreakers. However, there is a difference between being an interpersonal nuisance and a lawbreaker. For example, most convicted murderers have killed a friend or relative under situational exigencies ripe for assault. However, in normal situations such persons would no more consider murder than wear jeans to a formal dinner. Prisoners have enough problems without creating more for themselves, and a dominant theme among them is one of tension management (Goffman, 1961) and doing their time with a minimum of conflict.

Even though there is consensus among prisoners that there are acceptable ways of doing time, not all share the same identity in the prison world. Some come from very respectable backgrounds and see themselves as essentially "good citizens" who made a mistake and are thrown in with "real criminals," while others have a history of criminal conviction and identify with inmates who are in the same position. This latter group claim a criminal identity; that is, they see themselves as persons who normally engage in criminal activities, and it is important to differentiate between this group and others (Irwin, 1970:7). Additionally, there are finer distinctions among the two groups, and in the following section we shall examine those distinctions in the inmate world.

PRISON IDENTITIES

The first group—the "square John," "straights," or "do-rights" (Sutherland and Cressey, 1974:542)—consists of those members of prison society, from all social classes, who generally accept the mores and norms of conventional society. They are often surprised to find that many of their prison cohabitants are a part of a criminal subsystem and normally see criminal means as appropriate mechanisms for living. Men, such as middle-class embezzlers, who are thrown in with burglars, rapists, and robbers, are oriented to a different world from those who have committed numerous crimes and expect to commit more after release. Working-class and even lower-class persons often find themselves in situations in which they see the commission of a crime as a temporary solution to a problem they cannot otherwise solve (Cressey, 1971). They will forge a check or embezzle money, get caught, be tried, and imprisoned. They see their crime as an abnormal rather than a normal event in their lives; thus, by divorcing themselves from their act, they maintain their identities as "honest citizens." The square John considers what he did as "not like me." Instead of viewing himself as a criminal, he considers himself in terms of the conventional identities in society into which he will eventually be released.

In contrast to the square John is the "thief." Also known as the "right guy" (Sutherland and Cressey, 1974:539), the thief's orientation to prison and the rest of the world is one that accepts certain aspects of the criminal subsystem. The thief, however, is not without a moral code, and the aspects of character, as defined by thieves, are not unlike conventional codes of character (cf. Goffman, 1967: 149–270). "Rightness" is defined along the lines of integrity, and to be a thief involves being "right" or "solid" (Irwin, 1970: 9–10). For example, a thief is expected to meet his obligations, be honest, pay his debts, and never inform. These may seem like the same criteria required to be a Boy Scout, but the difference lies in the thief's overall orientation. Unlike the Boy Scout code of ethics, the thief's code transcends the law. The following excerpt of an interview with a thief proves the thief's overall orientation to the world:

> The way I see it a guy has several ways to go in this world. If he's not rich in front, he can stay honest and be a donkey. Only

There are a variety of inmate identities and strategies for "doing time." Inmates tend to associate with others who share a common prison identity. (*Black Star*)

this way he works for someone else and gets fucked the rest of his life. They cheat him and break his back. But this guy is honest.

Now another way is he can start cheating and lying to people and maybe he can make himself a lot of money in business, legally I mean. But this guy isn't honest. If he's honest and tries to make it this way he won't get nowhere.

Another way he can make it and live a halfway decent life and still be honest is to steal. Now I don't mean sneaking around and taking money or personal property from assholes who don't have nothing. I mean going after big companies. To me this is perfectly honest, because these companies are cheating people anyway. When you go and just take it from them, you are actually more honest than they are. Most of the time, anyway, they are insured and make more money from the caper than you do.

Really, I think it is too bad it is this way. I mean it. I wish a guy could make a decent living working, which he can't do because those people who have it made got that way fucking the worker. And they are going to keep it that way. And all that crap about having to have laws protecting property. These are just laws set up by those people who got all the property and are going to make sure they keep it (Irwin, 1970:11).

As can be seen from the thief's explanation, *stealing is one way of maintaining honesty*. He compares himself with the square John in pointing out that the square John is honest but cannot maintain a decent living. To make it legally is to be dishonest; therefore, the only way to make it and be honest is to be a thief.

Another part of the thief's orientation is to make the "big score," which is anything from a bank robbery (one of the favorite ways) to a large check forgery. In this scenario, the thief is transformed from the penniless man to the American dream—a thief's Horatio Alger story. What is implicit, but not stated, is the conventional orientation to society without regard to certain laws. The thief and the honest citizen want essentially the same thing in life and dream of the "big score," whether it is a successful payroll robbery or a million-dollar sale of life insurance. Both are part of the American dream, but only one involves breaking the law.

A third prison identity is that of the "hustler," a kind of thief but different from the thief just described. This mode of prison identity is best personified and carried out by black inmates, who bring it with them from the ghetto. Unlike the thief whose character revolves around "rightness," the hustler's major theme is "sharpness" (Irwin, 1970: 12). This orientation places importance on being able to outwit or con others and appearing sharp. Just about everybody in society is to be outwitted, and while there may be some "honor among thieves," the hustler believes only suckers trust others. In describing this world-view and theme, Irwin explains:

> The hustler believes that everyone is worthy of being taken, that everyone is ready to steal from everyone else if the opportunity presents itself and one must guard against being taken. It is a dog-eat-dog world, where there is little trust even among the hustlers themselves (1970:13).

This orientation contrasts with that of the thief, who views it as sneaky, dishonest, and untrustworthy for one of his kind to hustle other thieves or anyone else. However, from the hustler's point of view, his tactics simply reflect survival mechanisms.

Irwin identifies two drug-related groups in prison whose self-concepts are linked to the trouble that originally led them to prison. One group is variously known as the "junkie," "dope-fiend" or "hype" group, and the other is the "head" group. The former is characterized by its addiction to heroin or morphine and sees itself as "hooked" on dope, while the latter is characterized by the use of either marijuana or psychedelic drugs, which they consider nonaddictive. The head group has probably changed since Irwin conducted his study, since the laws dealing with marijuana have been changed along with enforcement patterns, and as a result fewer people now go to prison for possession of marijuana. Similarly, today's "dopers" are not oriented to the same drugs in the same way as were their forerunners in the 1960s. Thus, as a result of changes in the laws and law enforcement and as a consequence of changing fads, the head group is probably smaller and, if it still exists, is made up primarily of those arrested and convicted of selling head-type drugs.

The important difference between these two groups in the prison world is their contrasting orientations. Junkies use drugs to "fix" their problems by turning off their senses to the unpleasant aspects of the world, not the least of which are withdrawal symptoms. Heads, on the other hand, use drugs to expand consciousness. Junkies are preoccupied with "scoring" dope to maintain themselves in some state of equilibrium, while heads are not dependent on their drug (Irwin, 1970: 15–26). Both junkies and heads feel that the laws regarding drugs are unwarranted, and unlike the thief, hustler, and square John, who see their crimes to be justifiably against the law, junkies and heads feel their situation is due more to unfair laws than to any wrongdoing on their part.

Three other major groups of the inmate world identified by Irwin consist of the "disorganized criminal," the "state-raised youth," and the "lower-class man." The disorganized criminal makes up the largest portion of the prison population (27 percent), and occupies a marginal role in the world of crime and criminals (Irwin, 1970:23–26). On the one hand, they are not an integral part of the criminal system even though the system is available to them. They lack the skill and character to be either thieves or hustlers, and they see their involvement in crime as "fucking-up" their own lives. Without a stable career, either legitimate or criminal, the disorganized criminal has little status in either world, and his going to prison is simply an aspect of his general ineptitude.

The state-raised youth is a product of the juvenile justice system. His orientation is one of "toughness," an aspect of his background fostered in the state detention centers for youth. State-raised youths tend to form cliques as part of mutual protection and delinquent gang formation (Irwin, 1970:28). Given his experience in state youth institutions, the state-raised youth is sensitive to homosexuality since it was probably the only sex available to him during much of his adolescence. Moves by others interpreted to be possibly homosexual, however, are often met with toughness to prove his own masculinity. Thus, the themes of toughness and homosexuality are intertwined. Finally, the state-raised youth has a unique orientation to "the streets," which constitute an arena where one is temporarily freed to get into trouble. Unlike others who see their release to be at least somewhat permanent, the state-raised youth views the outside, or "outs," as a place where one is granted a short vacation. Having spent the better part of their lives in institutions, they view the streets within the same temporal frame that especially good moments in life are viewed in conventional society.

The last group discussed by Irwin is the lower-class man. The concept of being a "man" in the lower class is linked to law violations. Goffman (1967) conceptualizes the aspects of character valued highly in the lower class in terms of courage and manliness. To be a "man" in the lower class involves breaking the law almost automatically, for given the resources of lower-class men, legitimate shows of manliness are unavailable or in short supply compared to the higher social classes. Upper- and middle-class men can demonstrate manliness through power based on their economic position, but the power of the lower-class man must be provided through one resource available to all men—his body as a violent instrument (Luckenbill and Sanders, 1977). The violence, though, is not a means to an end far removed from the violence itself, as is the case with muggers who use violence to acquire money. Instead, it is a part of the action-seeking and manhood-proof activity of the lower class. For example, Irwin, in an interview with an imprisoned lower-class man, illustrates the kind of legal trouble such men encounter.

> I weren't doin' no good. Been drinkin' and talkin' all that violence. I thought this here woman took my money so I cut her. She hit me with her shoe first though.
> I never stole though. If I were to steal I could of got in the union like I wanted to (1970:31).

These dominant types of prisoners described by Irwin constitute a connection with the outside world. Within these types in the prison there are "gorillas" (toughs, violent troublemakers), "con politicians" (institutionalized inmates who have adjusted to prison life and enjoy it), as well as different types of homosexual statuses (Cressey, 1972: 117–18). These identities, whether they are linked to the outside world or the prison world, have the feature of being *identities in the prison*. That is, what a person can see himself as being in prison is limited to the identities available behind bars. If one can see oneself only as a "hustler," a "thief" a "square John," or some other prison identity, there is little chance of self-concept development or change in the prison that is noncriminal. The square John identity certainly is a noncriminal designation, and those who see themselves as such are oriented to becoming law-abiding citizens. However, since only 16 percent of those in prison see themselves in this category, fully 84 percent have identities that assume future criminal action (Irwin, 1970:34). Thus, no matter what proposals for rehabilitation are developed in prisons, the possibilities of success are limited because so few prisoners see themselves as persons who should cooperate with the institutional programs, and without their cooperation the programs are bound to fail.

THE STAFF WORLD

The other part of the prison world is that of the staff and prison administration. From this other perspective the prison world appears to be much different, for even though they share the inmates' physical setting, staff and administrative members are on the other side of bars and go home each day after serving their shift. However, in order to understand prisons in their totality, we must understand this other side of prison life and the problems they encounter.

In examining the organization of prisons, we can see the work of the staff as being oriented to the maintenance of life and security more than to rehabilitation. Of twenty-eight divisions of assignments in one outline of prison organization, only five (or 17 percent) were linked to rehabilitative efforts (Carter et al., 1975:128). The five "rehabilitative" programs include education, recreation, counseling, factory work, and farm work; however, it might be argued that by including such programs as recreation and factory and farm work, the category of rehabilitation is being somewhat stretched. Nevertheless, even with this liberal inclusion of marginal rehabilitative programs, we still see that most of the work expected of staff is directed to something other than the reform of prisoners.

The overriding staff concern appears to be prison security, and under custodial services we find nine separate functions including institutional security, guard forces, prisoner discipline, daily and weekly schedules, sanitation, inspections and investigations, contraband control, visiting, and inmate mail. Moreover, these security functions extend into all rehabilitative functions. For example, counseling occurs in a controlled setting, and the staff is responsible for seeing to it that no one escapes during counseling sessions. On the other hand, those whose major function is security are not expected to be involved in rehabilitation. That is, while performing security functions, the prison staff is not held accountable for seeing to it that inmates are reformed. It may seem absurd to expect security personnel to engage in rehabilitation counseling; conversely, it is no less absurd than expecting security functions to be performed by rehabilitation personnel.

Given the overriding concern with the essentially simple function of keeping people fed, clothed, and locked up, we would not expect that a prison staff need be especially skilled. Indeed, when we look at the background of those who make up the bulk of prison staff, we find minimal education. In describing the background of prison staff, Tom Wicker points out:

> The educational level among prison guards is not high because their pay scale is not high. New York corrections officers' salaries in 1971 began at $9,535 and reached $11,941 after fifteen years. The national average that year was only about only $6,000. College men and women are not interested in that kind of money—nor often in the prison kind of life. So only one out of two guards is a high school graduate; one out of three has better than a high school education. Many are retired from the armed services (1975:114).

More education might help raise the level of prison personnel, but unless fundamental changes are made in the prisons, the current amount of education required to perform routine staff functions is certainly adequate. After all, it doesn't take a college degree to open and close doors.

In describing the prison routine, which regulates staff as well as inmates, one prison official outlined the following daily order (Wicker, 1975:106):

6:00 A.M.	Wake up, get ready for breakfast, clean cell, be counted.
6:30	Breakfast (march in column of twos, tallest in front, shortest in rear).
7:00	Back to your cell.
7:30	Sick call.
7:45	Work call.
8:00	Work.
Noon	Lunch.
12:30	Back to your cell and be counted.
1:00	Back to work.
3:00	Lights flash. Time to quit work, line up.
3:15	Back to your cell and/or to yard for recreation.
4:00	Line up for supper.
4:15	March to mess hall.
5:00	Lock up for rest of the night. Be counted again.

7:30	Bell rings. No more talking for the rest of the night.
10:00	Lights out.
11:00	Radio earphones off. Absolute quiet.

Given this processing of daily life, the reality of prison life for inmates is monumentally numbing for both inmates and staff. In studies of assembly-line workers, researchers have pointed out the alienating impact of doing repetitive, meaningless work. The above-described routine, while not as repetitive as assembly-line work, has many of the qualities of such work, and there is no reason to believe that prison staff adapts any better to its daily rounds than any other workers who must go through a set of mindless chores.

In addition to the numbing character of its work, the prison staff works in an ever-present state of fear. Always in the back of the minds of prison guards is the possibility of violence against them as well as the daily communications, both verbal and nonverbal, of prisoners that express contempt for them. This atmosphere creates solidarity among those of the staff who are in everyday contact with the prisoners since the common threat of the inmates can be best met by a united front. In turn, the viewpoint of the staff is one characterized by emphasizing security over everything else, especially reform, which would only loosen up conditions inmates feel are oppressive. The end result is summarized by Wicker:

The prison staff share the numbing routine life of prison with the inmates. (*Black Star*)

Little wonder, therefore, that most guards believe in a tough policy of physical restraint—"maximum security"—for prisoners. And since in most states guards form a well-organized bureaucracy with civil service protection, and in some, like New York, have an employees' union in addition, they generally are a powerful and vocal force against "prisoner preform"—just as policemen are opposed to many exercises of "constitutional rights" by criminal defendants and suspects. The guards' organization in Massachusetts was primarily responsible, for example, for the ouster of Corrections Commissioner John Boone after he began "phasing out" state prisons, an obvious threat to guards' job security as well as to their view of corrections necessities (1975:115).

It is not that the guards are inherently bad or evil persons; rather, the order of their lives in the context of the prison and their dependence on the existence of the prison for a livelihood compel them to take harsh custodial attitudes rather than rehabilitative ones.

PRISON VIOLENCE

Having viewed both the staff and inmate worlds, we can now examine another prison reality—routine violence, three forms of which can be distinguished: (1) individual, (2) collective, and (3) regulatory. Individual violence is the kind that prisoners do to one another and occasionally to the staff. Knifings ("shankings") and even shootings occur in prisons. Arguments over the allocation of goods and services (for example, cigarettes, sexual favors), racial conflict, and warring gangs provide the motives for the violence, and the everyday necessities of life provide the weapons. Were it not for the character and use of the weapons devised in prisons, one would marvel at the ingenuity of their creation. Wicker, quoting a prison administrator, describes the weapons used in individual violence that the prison staff collects in its regular searches.

"Zip guns, stabbing instruments, those type of things. And quite a quantity is picked up each month. . . . They can be made from most anything, from a toothbrush handle ground down, which is a very effective stabbing instrument, to the more elaborate daggers or steel blades. Lately the zip guns we've been picking up are the muzzle-load type, made out of pipe; the explosive part would be made of matchheads, a projectile can be anything from broken glass to nails to little stones or pieces of concrete. Extremely dangerous and very, very deadly. And they shoot beautifully. . . . " (1975:114).

Although the extent of violence by inmates upon one another is often exaggerated by the prison staff to document the hazards of its work, it cannot be ignored that many inmates are victims of violence by other prisoners. In quoting one inmate, Irwin vividly illustrates this violence.

> The first day I got to Soledad I was walking from the fish tank to the mess hall and this guy comes running down the hall past me, yelling, with a knife sticking out of his back. Man, I was petrified. I thought, what the fuck kind of place is this? (1970:69)

The most spectacular form of prison violence is the prison riot. Although riots are given a disproportionate amount of attention in relation to the frequency of their occurrence, they are important to understand. Murton (1976:80–81) explains that they are not spontaneous explosions, but, rather, calculated uprisings used to focus attention on prison conditions. Benefits from riots usually come in the form of better food, visiting privileges, and the availability of other scarce goods and services, at least temporarily, sometime after the riot. Often, a riot will call attention to deplorable conditions, giving the prison commissioner an opportunity to document the need for more money to run his institutions adequately.

The pattern of riots in prisons is fairly uniform. For the first few days there is general upheaval as the "gorillas" take over and wreck buildings, engage in alcoholic, drug, and sex orgies, and settle old scores (Cressey, 1972:118). After this initial violence, the leadership changes to the "right guys" or the normal leadership of the inmate population. When this occurs, the stage is set for the end of the riot, for this new leadership realizes that any plan to escape is doomed to failure given the fact that the institution is in a state of siege, surrounded by police or National Guard. Their only hope is to bring the public's attention to the conditions they claim "caused" the riot. This leads to negotiation with the prison administration, and since their demands are often in line with what the administration wants anyway (for example, larger budgets to provide the demanded goods and services), the end of the riot is virtually guaranteed (Cressey, 1972:119).

This pattern of rioting may be changing with the recent politicalization of prisoners. Rather than viewing the situation in prison as merely the result of low budgets or perverted prison staff and administration, many groups have come to see the prison as a political tool for maintaining the status quo. The slaughter in the Attica riot in 1971 was partially attributed to this politicalization, for the group identified as the gorillas were not going to relinquish their control to the "right guys" since they did not take the few reforms promised by the prison officials to be politically significant (Cressey, 1972). This new attitude

The instruments of violence and their consequences can be seen in the collection of weapons found in a search of Stillwater (Minnesota) State Prison and the injured inmate being led away at Homesburg (Philadelphia, Pa.) prison. (*UPI Photos*)

among many prisoners denies the legitimacy of prison as a social institution, whereas the nonpolitical prisoners have always accepted the legitimacy of their imprisonment. With this new political awareness, we should expect to see a new type of prison riot in the future.

A final kind of prison violence is regulatory violence carried out under the auspices of the prison organization and administration. With the banishment of sanctioned corporal punishment in prisons (Orland, 1975), organizational violence has taken on a more subtle and sinister form. Mitford (1971) documents a number of violent measures that have been taken to "rehabilitate" prisoners under the name of "therapy" and "behavioral modification." Most notable is the use of certain drugs that trigger violent sensations. One drug, Anectine, is used systematically as part of a program to modify the behavior of uncooperative prisoners, and while it may not be effective, its proponents talk about it in a way that provides adequate evidence that it is a form of violence.

> According to Dr. Arthur Nugent, chief psychiatrist at Vacaville and an enthusiast for the drug, it induces "sensations of suffocation and drowning." The subject experiences feelings of deep horror and terror, "as though he were on the brink of death." While he is in this condition a therapist scolds him for his misdeeds and tells him to shape up or expect more of the same. Candidates for Anectine treatment were selected for a range of offenses: "frequent fights, verbal threatening, deviant sexual behavior, stealing, unresponsiveness to the group therapy programs." Dr. Nugent told the *San Francisco Chronicle,* "Even the toughest inmates have come to fear and hate the drug. I don't blame them, I wouldn't have one treatment myself for the world." Declaring he was anxious to continue the experiment, he added, "I'm at a loss as to why everybody's upset over this" (Mitford, 1971:142).

Because the violence is carried out under the auspices of "treatment" does not make it any less real. We could call a brutal beating "rubber-hose therapy," but the inmate who had received it would be no less black and blue from its having been administered. Other kinds of regulatory violence exist in prisons, but since the names have been changed to conform with the spirit of rehabilitation and treatment, not many see such violence as being in violation of the ban against corporal punishment or as cruel and unusual punishment prohibited by the Constitution.

MODALITIES OF PRISON TREATMENT

Up to this point, we have examined prisons as total institutions and the custodial impact upon those who are incarcerated. We have not considered, however, the major issue of rehabilitation programs that are incorporated in prison life to help inmates return to society. There is a reason for this inattention: primarily, we have attempted to show that no matter what type of program is instituted in the prison context, the overriding conditions of the total institution coupled with societal reactions to those who have served time in prison preclude any chance of success for virtually any program.

Advocates of various types of therapy, from psychoanalysis to reality therapy to vocational therapy, will provide good reasons why their approaches will work. Psychopaths cannot function in society, but if they receive psychoanalytic treatment they will be able to. If a person does not realistically assess his life and accept responsibility for his actions, he can neutralize his responsibility for his criminal behavior and continue a life of crime. Without vocational skills, a person cannot get a job in the outside world and is therefore forced to criminal means for his livelihood. All of these arguments for the various therapies appear valid, and under ideal conditions they might work. But the fact is that they are not administered under ideal conditions. They are administered in a total institution, and the conditions in such an institution lead to other patterns of behavior that are more pervasive and intense than what rehabilitation programs can offer.

The measure of a program's effectiveness is its ability to reduce recidivism. That is, if a program works, those who are treated in it will be less likely to return to prison than those who have not been in the program. However, as Robinson and Smith (1973:127) contend, *there are still no treatment techniques that have unequivocally demonstrated themselves capable of reducing recidivism.* In comparing different types of treatment with no treatment at all, it was found that there were no significant differences between the types of treatment administered or between some kind of treatment and no treatment at all in reducing recidivism. Himelson (1976:373) examined all of the major studies of treatment and recidivism and concluded that other than a few successful programs (whose success could have been due to sheer chance), none worked. Thus, rather than concentrating on a number of well-intentioned rehabilitation programs that have not worked, we have been attempting to show what the *significant* conditions of prison life actually are. Clearly, they are *not* the programs designed to rehabilitate inmates, but instead are conditions that contribute to criminalizing inmates further (Hartjen, 1974:140–46).

At the same time, we are not saying that under perfect conditions, even in a perfect society, the treatment and rehabilitation programs prevalent in prisons would work. However, we are in no position to evaluate the effectiveness of these treatment programs, for they are administered under conditions that almost preordain their failure. What we intend to do here is to examine the modalities of treatment philosophies and the rationale behind each. Later we shall look at some new ideas that operate independently of the total institution conditions of prisons.

The Psychological Approach

The orientation that stresses a link between the "inner man" and crime is what Himelson (1976:359) characterizes as the psychological approach to rehabilitation. Among psychologists, there is disagreement as how best to tap the inner man and make changes, and the approaches we shall discuss, *personality management* and *behavior modification,* are only two ways of characterizing the multifaceted approaches in psychology.

The programs operated under the auspices of personality management techniques assume that in the development of an individual's personality, something went wrong, leading him to criminal activities. Prison inmates are not considered "bad" and in need of punishment; instead, they are regarded as "sick" and in need of "treatment." Goffman (1961) characterizes this approach as the "medical model," and its most prevalent application has been in mental hospitals and prisons for the criminally insane, even though many other prisons have adopted it.

The ideal circumstance under which this approach is designed to work is intensive counseling or therapy between a psychologist and an inmate-patient. However, since this technique is relatively expensive, modifications have been made so that treatment can be handled simultaneously with several patients, called "group therapy" (Himelson, 1976:360–61). As applied in the prison situation, group therapy was designed to create situations in which inmates could come to see their own problems in light of the experiences of others and simultaneously solve some of their communication blocks. Since group therapy was often seen as nothing more than "rap sessions," and since the idea of a total therapeutic community was encouraged, often custodial and secretarial staff would lead inmates in these sessions. Thus, from the original idea of having a highly trained psychologist counsel a single inmate at a time, personality modification programs came to be large group meetings conducted by laymen.

Studies that show no significant difference between those who receive no treatment and the type of personality management actually implemented in prisons may reflect the misapplication of the technique. On the other hand, personality management may simply not work in total institutions even if it is fully applied because of the offsetting conditions of the total institution. Of course, it may not work at all, even in ideal settings and under proper conditions. The fact is we don't know, but what is important to us here is that it constitutes a general mode of treatment in prisons.

The second type of psychological approach, behavior modification, is based on the theories of the behaviorist school of psychology, especially as set forth in the work of B. F. Skinner (1971). For the behaviorlist, all that is important is observable behavior, and such intangibles (unmeasurables) as personality are considered inconsequential. Basing much of their research on rats, monkeys, and pigeons, the behaviorists claim that by systematic application of the proper stimuli, the desired behavior will be fostered and the undesired behavior, namely criminal behavior, will be eradicated. Aversion therapy attempts to set up a link between negative behavior and an unpleasant stimulus, while reward therapy attempts to do the same thing with positive behavior and a pleasant stimulus.

As we discussed earlier, the techniques used in prisons under the rubric of "therapy" may appear to be no different than old-fashioned punishment and reward, but the behaviorists point out that by the systematic, as opposed to haphazard, application of punishment and reward, desired ends may be met (Skinner, 1971:23–27). They argue is that because punishment and reward have been applied haphazardly, they have therefore not resulted in lowering the recidivism of offenders. By setting up a system of rewards for desired behavior, in which reinforcement plays a crucial role, prisoners will learn to associate the desired behavior with rewards. When they return to society, they will have learned how to behave appropriately.

Like personality management, behavior modification as applied

Group therapy sessions are a popular form of treatment in prisons but there appears to be little relationship between these sessions and rehabilitation. (© 1976 by Fred W. McDarrah)

in the prison situation has not worked very well. But there are a number of reasons it would not be fair to dismiss this approach altogether because of its failure in prisons. If humans respond to stimuli and systems of stimuli, any system of reward and punishment set up in prisons would have to be stronger than the prisoners' own system of reward and punishment. For example, a young man may be given a marijuana cigarette for having homosexual relations with another prisoner. No matter how good an inmate is in relation to the institution's reward and punishment system (usually tokens used to buy candy, cigarettes, and the like), the reward will not be marijuana. Aversion works the same way. The prison may punish misbehaving inmates by withholding rewards or applying some other punishment, such as solitary confinement, but fellow prisoners can beat and even kill other prisoners for violating convict norms. Thus, the reward/punishment system of the inmates may supersede that of the official system.

The Education-Socialization Approach

A second general approach to rehabilitation is far more sociological than psychological in its understanding of crime and reforming criminals (Himelson, 1976:363). This approach assumes that most criminals turn to crime because they lack the opportunity to take legitimate pathways to American success goals (Merton, 1957; Cloward and Ohlin, 1960). By providing inmates with educational opportunities (usually vocational, but also liberal arts), it is believed that they will be able to return to society and succeed through legitimate means they had lacked before. For example, a young man who has been imprisoned before having finished his high school education or having had the opportunity to acquire a skill that will provide him with an adequate livelihood has little chance of finding employment after leaving prison. However, if during his time in prison he can finish high school and learn a trade, he has a much better chance of succeeding through noncriminal means once outside.

At the same time, as it provides the inmate with the skills for making a legitimate living, education also shows him an alternative to crime; that is, it serves to socialize the offender into legitimate orientations to society. Thus, education-socialization has a double value in that it not only provides the skills for a noncriminal life but the understandings of such a life as well.

The reason this approach fails is typically explained in terms of conditions outside of prison. When a prisoner is released on parole, he often has a difficult time finding employment in an area in which he can use his new skills because of the stigma of being an ex-convict (Himelson, 1976:376). Those who do hire ex-cons will find that others who ordinarily use their services are wary of the ex-con employee. When President Carter hired an ex-convict to care for his daughter,

Counseling and job-readiness programs are two important services provided
ex-offenders by such self-help groups as the Fortune Society. (*Alden Lewis for
the Fortune Society*)

many expressed concern over the wisdom of his choice, claiming that he would have been better off to hire someone who did not present a threat to both his daughter and political career. Many employers, especially during times of high unemployment, will ask, "Why hire an ex-con when I can hire someone who's never broken the law, worked honestly all of his life, who I won't have to worry about?" Thus, even if the education-socialization approach can be applied successfully in the prison setting, it may fail in the outside world.

The Cultural Reorientation Approach

The final rehabilitative approach used in prisons is somewhat of a combination of the psychological and the education-socialization approaches. This approach points to a "criminal subculture" in which the inmate is enmeshed. In order to rehabilitate him, he must be weaned away from criminal subcultural beliefs and attitudes and enculturated with legitimate ones (Himelson, 1976:364). On the one hand, cultural orientation shares with the psychological approach the assumption that the "inner man" must be changed; on the other hand, it is a resocialization of the offender characteristic of the education-socialization approach. Of the three approaches, it appears to be the most realistic in identifying the crux of the problem, namely, that the convict's beliefs and values are in conflict with the conventional culture. Paradoxically, however, it attempts to apply the remedy in a context that is conducive to aggravating the problem. If there is such a thing as a criminal subculture, it is most pronounced in a prison setting because of the shared experience of prisoners and the convergence of those with criminal backgrounds. Attempts to segregate the younger or first-time offender from the career criminal constitute the main effort of this type of rehabilitation (Himelson and Thoma, 1968).

Like the other approaches, this approach has not met with success either. In addition to the fact that the prison setting fosters a criminal belief system or "convict code" (Wieder, 1974), the societal stigmatization and segregation of ex-convicts outside of prison also makes it difficult to break up a belief system that rejects the idea that it is possible to achieve conventional success goals through legitimate means.

Nonprison Alternatives

The approaches to criminal rehabilitation we have discussed so far are not irrational, "bleeding heart" solutions to the problem of criminal recidivism. If a person has psychological problems, has little or no education or employable skills, or firmly believes that success is best possible through criminal means, chances are that he is more prone to repeating criminal offenses than someone without those problems. If the solutions to these problems do not work either because of the failure of the technique or the setting of application, it does not mean that the problems these solutions are meant to remedy do not exist.

Here we shall briefly examine some alternatives to prison incarceration as a means of rehabilitation. Most of these alternatives are community-based noninstitutional ones, and while comparable data are difficult to gather to compare these alternatives with traditional prison settings, either because of the nature of the process of selecting the clientele or the newness of the program, there is no concrete evidence that these alternatives are successful.

The first alternative still uses the totally controlled setting of the total institution, but the institution is designed around treatment instead of incarceration. One of the best examples of this type of institution is the North Florida Treatment and Evaluation Center established for sex offenders and those considered to have mental disorders of varying degrees. The physical setting resembles a village with wide boulevards, small housing units, and abundant lawns. The staff consists of the security and treatment personnel. There is a clear division of labor between security and treatment staff, and the treatment staff has almost no custodial or security duties. As the security chief explained, "If we maintain security, then the treatment staff can do their job." There have been conscious efforts to minimize the problems of total institutions and the view of the "clients" (as the inmates are called) is one of persons in need of help rather than of criminals.

Most of the the staff positions are filled by personnel with college degrees in the social sciences and psychology,[2] and the ratio of staff to clients is high. The institution is directed by a psychologist, and a number of psychiatrists are on full- or part-time duty. New clients are given thorough screening, and treatment plans are individualized to their different needs and problems.

Since the institution was opened in 1976, not enough time has passed to evaluate its effectiveness, and since a number of the clients will have to go on to serve prison sentences after their release, there will be severe evaluation problems in the future. However, the institution has recognized the problems of total institutions, and has attempted to do something to minimize them. This will not be entirely possible since the center is a total institution itself, but a number of the problems have at least been addressed in this new type of institution.

Most of the new thinking in the area of corrections has centered around what has been called "community-based corrections" (Carter and Wilkins, 1976:481). The main thrust of community-based corrections has been in developing alternatives to sending offenders off to

---

[2] The positions were originally funded for personnel with high school degrees, but because of the availability and willingness of people with college degrees in psychology and the social sciences to work for the low wages meant for high school graduates, the college graduates were hired. The staffing picture may change if general unemployment is reduced.

state prisons, even ones such as the progressive evaluation and treatment center just described. Basic to the argument behind the community-based approach is the idea that persons convicted of crimes must readjust to the community and community standards, and the best place to make such readjustments is in the community itself (National Advisory Commission, 1973:224). Implicit in this approach is the belief that criminal offenders should not be locked up unless they cannot be otherwise controlled.

The only problem with the notion of community-based corrections is that, in a strict sense, everything from jail to probation to half-way houses can be considered "community based." For our purposes, we shall focus on the nonsecure, nonprobation/parole forms of community-based institutions, namely, half-way houses, diversion programs, and self-help groups.

Half-way houses first appeared after the Civil War as aids to ex-prisoners (Wieder, 1974:46). The houses were run by charitable groups and supported by such sources as Community Chest. More recent half-way houses have been somewhat more sophisticated in their operation and goals, but they still exist to help former prisoners get back on their feet.

As community-based corrections are idealized, the half-way house is an excellent example of why a perfectly reasonable program should work. It is also an example of why well-intentioned ideas fail. One of the key arguments behind establishing half-way houses on a massive scale was that ex-convicts needed some kind of reintegration into society. Upon release from prison, an ex-con had a little money and a suit of clothes. With these meager resources he was supposed to find a job and settle down to a legitimate life-style. But since he rarely had enough money to find a place to stay while looking for a job, and since many of the ex-cons had no family or friends who were themselves not criminals with whom to stay until they got on their feet, the chances of successful reintegration into society tended to be slim. By providing a half-way house (half way between prison and society), it was reasoned that a former prisoner could learn to better cope in society, get a job, and not be forced by circumstances to return to crime without a chance to even try a legitimate life-style.

In one sense, half-way houses have not been successful (Wieder, 1974). Although some who go from prison to them do well, there is no evidence that houses reduce recidivism. As we saw in examining the cultural reorientation approach to corrections, criminal belief systems are a cause for continuing criminality. In prisons, the convict code of behavior stresses noncooperation with effective rehabilitation. If a person is released from prison and goes off on his own away from a cohort of other ex-prisoners, the convict code is difficult to maintain as an effective interpretive scheme for action. However, if a group of ex-prisoners is taken from prison as a cohort to a half-way house, the convict code is transferred intact from prison to society. In Wieder's

(1974) study of half-way houses, he found that the convict code was used as an interpretive scheme for understanding actions not only of the residents of the house by the residents, but also that the staff employed the convict code for interpreting the residents' behavior. Thus, the half-way house concept, while an excellent idea, failed because of another force created in prisons and transferred to the half-way house. Instead of integrating ex-prisoners into the conventional culture, the half-way house served to bring the convict code into society. Thus, the failure of the half-way house to reduce recidivism.

Diversion programs have been implemented to minimize the negative effects of the criminal justice process, especially imprisonment and the accompanying stigma attached to it (Vorenberg and Vorenberg, 1973). By keeping people out of prison, they do not have the opportunity to adopt the convict code; thus, in addition to enabling offenders to avoid the stigma of being convicted criminals, diversion programs also serve to isolate them from criminal belief systems.

There has been some research on the effectiveness of diversion, but most of it is inconclusive. Cressey and McDermott (1973), for example, found that there were a number of programs that claimed to be "diversionary" but in fact were merely conventional probation programs that labeled themselves as diversion programs. Most diversion programs have been developed for youths and juveniles, and since the bulk of juveniles "grow out" of delinquency anyway (Sanders, 1976: 20–22), it is difficult to tell whether the apparent success of such programs is due to maturation and involvement in the adult social structure or something in the program itself. Future research will provide us with more answers, but the mere fact that diversion from the criminal justice system is seen as a positive step suggests that something is critically wrong with the criminal justice process itself. Since the essential rationale behind "diverting from" the criminal justice system is that the criminal justice process does more harm than good in many instances, the success of diversion is a measure of the failure of the criminal justice system.

A final type of rehabilitation that has gained widespread attention and support is the self-help group (Himelson, 1976:379). The model of self-help programs is Alcoholics Anonymous, which operates on the premise that alcoholics best understand the problems of alcoholics, and by helping one another with problems they understand, they serve to rehabilitate others in the ways they themselves have been rehabilitated.

Other groups, such as Synanon, which helps heroin addicts (Yablonsky, 1965), and Delancy House, a group of ex-offenders giving mutual support to one another, are difficult to evaluate. For those who stick with Synanon, rehabilitation is almost total, and Delancy House appears to have great success as long as the ex-offender stays with the program. However, only those who *want* to go to Synanon or Delancy House have to. Those who go to a self-help organization have already decided they want to make changes in their lives and free themselves from criminal sanctions. If prisons took only those who wanted to go to prison, their success rate would no doubt be a good deal higher. And while it is true that without such institutions as Synanon and Delancy House a person who wanted help would have no place to turn for help, it is impossible to measure the success of volunteer self-help groups against programs that force the offender to submit to the program's procedures.

SUMMARY

This chapter has been intended to explore the dominant mechanism employed in the criminal justice process to provide maximum control over offenders—the prison. We saw that no matter what the official policies are or what programs are incorporated, there are going to be certain realities in prisons as total institutions that will vary slightly no matter what the policies are. Of course, such things as regulatory violence are greatly affected by prison programs, policy, and personnel, and the overall violence in prisons can be reduced by changes in these areas. However, the identities of those who make up the prison population are little affected by what the prison administration does, nor is the relationship between staff and inmates going to change without massive restructuring of prisons. Even then, inherent conflict between the "keepers" and the "kept" will continue to exist.

In examining the different types of rehabilitation programs offered in prisons, we saw that there is no conclusive evidence that rehabilitation works. We have attempted to show that any rehabilitation program is literally overwhelmed by the conditions and patterns of life in a total institution, and any good such a program might do is negated in the prison context. Whether this is due to some flaw in a program cannot be determined, but it is clear that the programs do not work in prisons.

The alternatives to incarceration are sparse and as yet there is no evidence that they work much better than prisons in rehabilitating former offenders. Because of the failure of these nonprison programs to achieve total rehabilitation, many critics are prepared to give up on what they consider "bleeding-heart" solutions to crime control. The critics are right insofar as they advocate dropping ineffective programs, and the first ones that should go, by that criterion, are prisons. However, it is not likely we will see the demise of incarceratories of some sort, for these institutions serve to keep dangerous individuals off the streets and prevent them, temporarily at least, from committing crimes.

Our best hope for controlling crime is not in the criminal justice system or any form of rehabilitation. Rather it lies in finding the causes of crime and preventing it from happening in the first place. If the causes are found in the basic structure of society and culture, then we must be prepared either to make sweeping changes in that structure or accept a good deal of crime. If we accept the latter approach to crime control, then we are committed to making ineffective gestures that will control crime only by small fractions. Since prisons are one of the most expensive mechanisms of crime control, we can cut our costs without losing effectiveness by exploring nonprison alternatives, for it is clear, we repeat, that prisons do not rehabilitate.

As a final observation, the greatest danger in becoming too strict and parsimonious in our attempt to "do something" about crime is that we may end up building big, cheap prisons and exploiting prison labor. The extent to which we are attracted to this alternative is a measure of changing a democratic society to a totalitarian one. If we are not willing to make basic social changes to prevent crime, we should not be eager to make basic social changes to change criminals. If our control mechanisms reduce basic freedoms, we have done more harm to society as a whole than if we make basic changes to prevent crime. The logical conclusion of harsh, cheap prisons and the exploitation of prison labor is well described in the exiled Russian writer Aleksandr Solzhenitsyn's *Gulag Archipelago,* where economic development was accomplished at the price of human freedom and life. On the other hand, if we locate the causes of crime in the social structure, we can prevent vicitimization and preserve freedom by making adjustments in the social structure. Another alternative consists of either doing nothing or very little, and at this point in time we have effectively adopted this alternative of inertia.

REFERENCES

CARTER, ROBERT M., RICHARD A. MC GEE, AND KIM E. NELSON
  1975 *Corrections in America.* Philadelphia: Lippincott.

CARTER, ROBERT M., AND LESLIE T. WILKINS, EDS.
  1976 *Probation, Parole, and Community Corrections.* 2d ed. New York: Wiley.

CHANG, DAE H., AND WARREN B. ARMSTRONG
  1972 *The Prison: Voices from the Inside.* Cambridge, Mass.: Schenkman.

CLOWARD, RICHARD, AND LLOYD OHLIN
  1960 *Delinquency and Opportunity.* New York: The Free Press.

CRESSEY, DONALD R.
  1971 *Other People's Money.* Belmont, Calif.: Wadsworth
  1972 "A Confrontation of Violent Dynamics," *International Journal of Psychiatry,* 1:109–30.

CRESSEY, DONALD R., AND ROBERT A. MC DERMOTT
  1973 *Diversion from the Juvenile Justice System.* Project Report for National Assessment of Juvenile Corrections (June). Ann Arbor: University of Michigan.

GOFFMAN, ERVING
1961   *Asylums*. Garden City, N.Y.: Doubleday.
1967   *Interaction Ritual*. Garden City, N.Y.: Doubleday.

HARTJEN, CLAYTON
1974   *Crime and Criminalization*. New York: Praeger.

HIMELSON, ALFRED
1976   "Criminal Rehabilitation," in Don H. Zimmerman *et al.*, eds., *Understanding Social Problems*, pp. 355–84. New York: Praeger.

HIMELSON, ALFRED, AND BLANCHE THOMA
1968   *The Narcotic Treatment Control Program: Phase III*. Sacramento, Calif.: California Department of Corrections.

IRWIN, JOHN
1970   *The Felon*. Englewood Cliffs, N.J.: Prentice-Hall.

LUCKENBILL, DAVID F., AND WILLIAM B. SANDERS
1977   "Criminal Violence," in Edward Sagarin and Fred Montanino, eds., *Deviants: Voluntary Actors in a Hostile World*, pp. 88–156. Morristown, N.J.: General Learning Press.

MERTON, ROBERT
1957   *Social Theory and Social Structure*. New York: The Free Press.

MITFORD, JESSICA
1971   *Kind and Usual Punishment*. New York: Vintage.

MURTON, THOMAS
1976   *The Dilemma of Prison Reform*. New York: Holt, Rinehart and Winston.

NATIONAL ADVISORY COMMISSION ON CRIMINAL JUSTICE STANDARDS AND GOALS
1973   *Corrections*. Washington, D.C.: Government Printing Office.

ORLAND, LEONARD
1975   *Prisons: Houses of Darkness*. New York: The Free Press

ROBINSON, JAMES, AND GERALD SMITH
1973   "The Effectiveness of Correctional Programs," in Benjamin Frank, ed., *Contemporary Corrections*. Reston, Va: Reston Publishing Co.

SANDERS, WILLIAM B.
1976   *Juvenile Delinquency*. New York: Praeger.

SKINNER, B.F.
1971   *Beyond Freedom and Dignity*. New York: Bantam.

SUTHERLAND, EDWIN, AND DONALD R. CRESSEY
1974   *Criminology,* 9th ed. Philadelphia: Lippincott.

VORENBERG, ELIZABETH, AND JAMES VORENBERG
1973   "Early Diversion from the Criminal Justice System: Practice in Search of a Theory," in Lloyd E. Ohlin, ed., *Prisoners in America*, pp. 151–83. Englewood Cliffs, N.J.: Prentice-Hall.

WICKER, TOM
1975   *A Time to Die*. New York: Ballantine.

WIEDER, D. LAWRENCE
1974   *Language and Social Reality: The Case of Telling the Convict Code*. The Hague: Mouton.

WILLWERTH, JAMES
1974 *Jones: Portrait of a Mugger.* Greenwich, Conn.: Fawcett.

YABLONSKY, LEWIS
1965 *The Tunnel Back: Synanon.* New York: Macmillan.

SELECTED READINGS

GOFFMAN, ERVING. *Asylums: Essays on the Social Situation of Mental Patients and Other Inmates.* Chicago: Aldine, 1961.
A theoretical statement of the operation of total institutions and the impact on both inmates and staff. Even though a study of a mental institution, the framework is applicable to prisons.

IRWIN, JOHN. *The Felon.* Englewood Cliffs, N.J.: Prentice-Hall, 1970.
Analyzes the prison experience from the inmate's viewpoint. Explains the identities and strategies developed for coping with prison life.

MURTON, THOMAS. *The Dilemma of Prison Reform.* New York: Holt, Rinehart and Winston, 1976.
Traces the history of prisons and the roadblocks to making needed reforms.

ORLAND, LEONARD. *Prisons: Houses of Darkness.* New York: The Free Press, 1975.
An historic-legal portrait of prisons as they developed in the United States, Orland provides an overview of the different understandings of constitutional safeguards and meanings of "cruel and unusual punishment."

part five

A SEPARATE JUSTICE

10
JUVENILE JUSTICE

Juvenile justice is the separate justice process designed especially for juveniles. There are many parallels between the juvenile justice system and the adult criminal justice system, but the processes differ in their operation and history. But we need to know how they differ and how they are similar. To answer this first question, we will examine the entire process of juvenile justice from the police all the way through juvenile corrections.

First, we must ask why there is a separate juvenile justice system apart from the adult system. How did it begin? How did it develop? What changes have been made and why? Are there special laws for juveniles that do not apply to adults? These questions are addressed in a discussion of the history and development of the juvenile justice process. The benign intentions behind the development of the juvenile system did not lead to a just process in comparison to the adult system, and only recently have changes been made that grant juveniles the rights afforded adults.

Second, we must ask about the different agencies that process juvenile offenders. Do the police treat them the same as they do adults? Do the courts give juvenile defendants the same benefit of doubt as they do adults? Do the agencies treat juveniles with leniency or severity in comparison to adults? Are the agencies really any different than adult criminal justice agencies or do they merely have different names? And, finally, why has there been a move to keep the young out of juvenile detention centers if such places are supposed to help them?

To find the answers to these questions, we will examine the studies of the various agencies that interact with juveniles. First, we shall look at the unique problems the police have with juveniles and the wide discretion they are afforded in dealing with them. Then, we shall look at the court-processing system, including the key role played by the probation officer in making judgments about the fate of juveniles. Finally, we will strip away the semantic overlay in juvenile corrections and examine the stark reality of detention centers. In conjunction with this, we will discuss the "diversion" movement in juvenile justice to keep youth away from the "child-savers" for their own protection.

Even though the juvenile justice system is in many ways similar to the adult system, there are significant legal differences that require separate analysis. Some of the legal differences lead to different structures and processes, but we shall show that while there are clear legal differences and criteria for deciding juvenile cases, the decision process is very much the same as it is in adult cases. Therefore, we hope to show that while some legal variations lead to structural and procedural variation, other more basic processes are little affected by the law.

In order to fully understand the sociolegal context of juvenile justice, we must examine what happens to juveniles when they become entangled with law enforcement, the courts, and corrections. However, first it will be necessary to discuss what we mean by a "juvenile" in both the the social sense and the legal sense. Also, we need to examine the development of juvenile justice and special statutes that apply only to juveniles.

WHAT IS A JUVENILE?

In traditional societies, boys and girls undergo rites of passage, whereby, quite literally, one day a person is a child and the next day an adult. There is no transition other than preparation for the ceremony of status change, and there is no question in anyone's mind as to the person's status, especially the person who underwent the change.

In American society, however, as in other modern-day societies, the passage from childhood to adulthood is gradual and equivocal. A person may consider himself an adult and certain others may share his image, but still others may consider and treat him as a juvenile. Eventually, everyone (with the exception of the mentally ill or the retarded)

A SEPARATE JUSTICE

is granted adult status, but the mechanism for such recognition is vague and the complete transition may take years. In American society a juvenile is usually considered an unmarried youth who resides with his or her parents. Most would agree that such terms as "kid," "child," "adolescent," "teenager," and "boys and girls" all denote something other than a full-fledged adult. Perhaps, if we consider juveniles to be "persons still in development" we can best understand the concept of juvenile. "Development," in this context refers to both physical and social development, and as we shall see, a person's physical development does not necessarily mean he has developed socially or vice versa. The completeness of an adult in American society is vague, and while there are some benchmarks that are generally recognized, there is no definite point at which one makes the transition from youth to adulthood.

If we attempt to specify an age at which a person is considered a complete adult, or if we look for key rituals of passage from juvenile to adult status in American society, we shall become hopelessly confused. Generally, we can point to the legal voting age, the drinking age, the age at which one can obtain a driver's license as important ages, but no single age can really pinpoint the dividing line between juvenile and adult. Even such benchmarks as graduation ceremonies, marriage, having children and leaving home are vague. A fourteen-year-old girl may marry and have children, and many may consider her an adult, but few fourteen-year-olds are treated as genuine adults. On the other hand, a boy may live at home with his parents and fully depend on them through college and on through graduate school, leaving home for the first time in his late twenties. Can we, however, really conceive of a twenty-five-year-old doctoral candidate as a juvenile?

Turning to the legal criteria that define juvenile, we find more specific guidelines, but like the juvenile status in American society as a whole, the legal definition of juvenile is also often vague. First of all, the criterion of age varies from state to state. In four states, a juvenile is anyone under twenty-one years of age, and eight states set the age at under sixteen (Sellin and Wolfgang, 1964:73). The modal age for juveniles recognized in twenty-eight states is anyone under eighteen. In many states, such as California, there is a "transition age" where one is neither a complete adult nor complete juvenile. Between the ages of eighteen and twenty-one, a person in California is subject to the jurisdiction of adult criminal court, allowed to vote, and can be drafted into the military, but is unable to buy liquor until he is twenty-one. To make matters even more confusing, most states can adjudicate a juvenile as an adult if the court decides that the person should be treated as such. For example, if a sixteen-year-old robs a liquor store in a state where the legal adult age is eighteen, the courts can decide to treat him as an adult, send him to adult court, and give him an adult sentence. Likewise, if a person is over the legal age of a juvenile, he may be adjudicated as a juvenile if the court deems it proper. The criteria for adjudicating someone as an adult or juvenile reflect the societal uncertainty as to what constitutes an adult.

Although we have shown that we cannot say in so many words exactly what a juvenile is, we have seen that "being a juvenile" depends on the legal definition of the status in a given state and the definition of a person in a given situation. Thus, instead of a static definition, the concept of juvenile needs to be understood as a vague, changing, and dynamic idea. It would be nice if we could develop a concrete, unequivocal definition of juvenile, especially if we want to foster the impression of being "rigorously scientific," but as we have seen in previous chapters, the world of criminal justice is anything but static, and imposing a static definition would be anything but scientific. Instead, we shall have to take the concept of juvenile to be a situational construct wherein social actors formulate and reformulate the sense of a person's legal status depending on his or her construed action and biography (Sanders, 1976:8–10). Certainly, the law defining the age of adulthood is an important guideline; but at the same time, the social and legal understandings that allow young people to be adjudicated as an adult or juvenile depend on the situation, and the situation, while socially determining, is also socially determined (Goffman, 1963:18). Therefore, rather than dwelling merely on the law, we shall have to examine the situational exigencies and understandings on those occasions where decisions are developed and acted upon involving the question of "juveniles."

THE DEVELOPMENT OF JUVENILE JUSTICE

In the past there was no juvenile justice as such, and everyone who could be legally charged with a crime was brought before the criminal courts. However, around the turn of the century, as an offshoot of the feminist movement, which was gathering momentum at the time, the juvenile court was established and the "juvenile delinquent" was created (Platt, 1969). The new statutes for juveniles and new procedures for dealing with young people brought into being a new realm of possible sanctions that had not previously existed.

The direction and intent of the movement to "save the children" was motivated by the spirit of general reform of the time. Seeing the squalid conditions of urban life in late nineteenth-century America, reformers believed that if something were not done to alleviate the suffering of children, they would grow up without the spiritual and moral fiber that was necessary for good citizenship. Children were working for long hours at slave wages in the deadly conditions of the sweatshops and mines. The slums of the cities were their homes, and the pool halls, saloons, and streets their playgrounds. For the reformers, all of these conditions only fostered delinquency, and if something was not done to alter these conditions, urban children would become adult hoodlums.

As a result of reform movements, special courts for juveniles were established. Rather than subject them to the punitive policies of adult courts, these special courts were to arrange treatment for juvenile delinquents and predelinquents since they were considered to have behavioral problems that required special clinical attention. A consequence of this treatment philosophy in which children were to be "saved" or at least "helped" was the denial of many constitutional rights to children that they had in adult court. Since the children were not to be punished but instead "helped," the rights of due process were not seen to be important. The "help" the courts had to offer included reform schools and other total institutions, but the reformers saw only the "good" of their intentions while neglecting the negative and even punitive consequences of their efforts. The net effect was that children who came under the jurisdiction of the new juvenile court did not have the right to an attorney, the right to confront their accuser, the right of notice of change, or any of the other safeguards allowed adults. Children could be brought before the court on little evidence (or no evidence at all) and be found to be "in need of supervision." This supervision often resulted in the child's being taken from his family and placed in an institution. This was especially true for slum children;

The juvenile court was established obstensibly to "help" juveniles, but at the same time it took away most of the rights of due process enjoyed by adults. (*Bob Adelman*)

since life in the slums was by definition "debasing," any action the court took would be an improvement. Of course, children from "good" families were less likely to be in need of the court's supervision since they lived in the proper moral environment.

Perhaps the greatest impact of the juvenile justice system was the creation of special laws that applied only to juveniles. These laws, which we still call "juvenile status offenses," were developed to provide the court with a mechanism to control "predelinquents," or those children who had broken no adult law but were believed to need the court's guiding hand. Juvenile status offenses came to include running away from home, truancy, sexual experimentation, and incorrigibility, none of which was under the control of any court before the juvenile justice system was established.

Whether there was actually any relationship between "predelinquent behavior," as juvenile status offenses were called, and later delinquency or criminality had never been proven, but this fact did not deter the child-savers from their mission. In discussing the drive to rescue children from behavior that was believed to lead to criminality, Platt points out:

> The unique character of the child-saving movement was its concern for predelinquent offenders—"children who occupy the debatable ground between criminality and innocence"—and its claim that it could transform potential criminals into respectable citizens by training them in "habits of industry, self-control and obedience to law." This policy justified the diminishing of traditional procedures and allowed police, judge, probation officers, and truant officers to work together without legal hindrance. If children were to be rescued, it was important that the rescuers be free to pursue their mission without the interference of defense lawyers and due process. Delinquents had to be saved, transformed and reconstituted (1974:378).

This end was nicely expedited by the juvenile status offenses, since a child could be picked up for almost any reason. For example, one phrase found in many juvenile statutes refers to the danger of a child's "leading a lewd and immoral life."[1] What constitutes a juvenile being on this route is left up to the commonsensical understandings of the police, judges, probation officers and others involved in the juvenile court. However, the exact manner in which juvenile status offenses come to be operationalized often exceeds even commonsense morality. In one West Coast community, the law enforcement agencies defined "out of control" (a common passage in juvenile statutes) to be a juvenile

---

[1] See, for example, Section 601 of the California Welfare and Institutions Code, 1971.

who was in a different county than where his parents had legal residence. As a result, in the particular county in which this operational definition was employed, it was not unlikely for the police to arrest a juvenile who lived only thirty miles away in another county while not arresting juveniles from another city in the same county that was *seventy* miles away (Sanders, 1977).

Consequentially, juvenile status offense arrests may appear to be insignificant, assuming the courts do not *really* treat these predelinquents with the same severity as the "real" delinquents who break the laws regulating adult activities. However, juvenile status offenders are actually treated more severely. Institutional incarceration for delinquents averages from two to twenty-eight months, while incarceration of juvenile status offenders ranges from four to forty-eight months (Lerman, 1973:250–51). The average length of incarceration for delinquents is 10.7 months, while the average for the juvenile status offender is 16.3 months (Lerman, 1973:251). It is ironic that those juveniles who are considered predelinquent and have broken no laws for which an adult would be arrested are considered to be in more need of "help" in larger (and longer) doses than those who have committed criminal acts.

In 1967 the United States Supreme Court handed down a decision, *In Re Gault,*[2] which gave juveniles several rights they had been previously denied including the right to counsel, the right against self-incrimination, notice of charges, confrontation, and cross-examination. Although the *Gault* decision provided the juvenile justice system with many of the due process features of the adult criminal court, it did not provide for the right to a jury trial nor that the prosecution must present the same unequivocal evidence required in adult courts. Moreover, since this made no changes in the definition of juvenile status offenses, which were often vague and could be applied to almost any normal juvenile behavior, juveniles still suffered from the "help" provided by the juvenile court.

Since the *Gault* decision, however, juvenile justice has undergone other changes that have given juveniles more equitable treatment. In the President's Commission Report on Delinquency (1967), it was recommended that juvenile status offenders be diverted from the juvenile justice system. The report suggested that alternatives to adjudication be established for those juveniles who had broken no "adult laws," and while many of the diversion projects have been less than what was intended (Cressey and McDermott, 1973), today, juvenile status offenders are less likely to be arrested and turned over to juvenile court. In Florida, where juvenile status offenders are referred to as CINS (Children in Need of Supervision), new laws forbid placing juvenile status offenders in detention centers for first offenses. A runaway, for exam-

---

[2] 387 U.S. 1, 87 S. Ct. 1428, 18 L.Ed.2d 527 (1967).

ple, is placed in a volunteer home where a family or an individual provides a place for him to stay until he can be returned home. There is no juvenile court action, and the child has no delinquent record nor is he placed with delinquents. These new laws, if nothing else, recognize that there is a problem with being "overprotective," and they point to serious flaws in the current structure and practices of the juvenile justice system. However, like many changes in the system, the changes in the treatment of juvenile status offenders were also economically prudent. While we would like to believe that the changes in legislation were the result of revelations of sociological theory and research, humanitarianism, some of the most profound changes may have been guided by economic austerity since it is less expensive to send a runaway juvenile home than it is to lock him up. Letting off burglars, robbers, and rapists would be politically unwise given the popular feelings against such criminals. But since there is a theoretical rationale and no popular sentiment or fear of juvenile status offenders, it was relatively easy to pass laws that would let them go free. At the same time, the federal government, especially through the Law Enforcement Assistance Administration, provided funds to set up diversion programs; thus, not only could individual jurisdictions save money by not having to lock up and care for juvenile status offenders but also they were financially assisted in setting up the less expensive diversion programs.

Our discussion to this point has tried to unearth the roots of the juvenile justice system. Unlike the adult criminal justice system, the juvenile system was founded on the concept of benevolence rather than punishment. As a result, juvenile authorities have expanded their sphere of influence far beyond that which would be considered appropriate in the adult system. Not only is there massive interference of the juvenile justice system into family matters and noncriminal activities, but also the juvenile justice system frequently justifies everything it does as helpful. This is not to say that many policemen, juvenile counselors, judges, and others do not use the system for punitive measures; rather, it simply indicates that the juvenile justice system has been able to circumvent due process by claiming to be engaged in guidance or treatment rather than punishment.

In discretion situations, the accounts for *any* course of action could be explained in terms of "helping" juveniles no matter what course of action is taken (Scott and Lyman, 1968). Thus, unlike adult courts, which have no legal rationale for "doing the best thing" for a criminal defendant, juvenile courts were given the mandate to do exactly that. Of course, as we saw in the chapter on adjudication and prosecution, the criminal court often acts to "do the best thing" regardless of the specified penalties for a crime, but the philosophy of *parens patriae* (the notion that the court acts like a family to "do the best thing" for a defendant) in adult courts has always been an unofficial one, while in juvenile court it has been the official one. Under the idea of *parens patriae*, the question of innocence or guilt is secondary to "what is best"; but since what is best is often defined in terms of some form of control by the juvenile court, the decision-making in juvenile court has the same consequentiality as it does in adult court. Thus, by examining the patterns of decision-making situations and the typical accounting for decisions in those situations, we can understand the juvenile justice system as separate from the criminal justice system while at the same time seeing to what extent juvenile justice is nothing more than a criminal justice system for the young.

THE POLICE AND JUVENILES

As for the adult, the first critical situation for the juvenile is the one in which somebody decides that some official action is to be taken. In victim-linked crimes, such as shoplifting, vandalism, and auto theft —typical juvenile crimes—juveniles come to the attention of the police in very much the same way as do adults (see Chapter 3). Other offenses, however, that are unique to juveniles have no victim but are reported by someone other than the police. For example, runaways and incorrigibles are not victim-producing delinquents in the same way that robbers are, but they are reported to the police. We might say that the juvenile's parents are the victims, and we probably would have little trouble showing that running away from home and incorrigibility create the necessary anguish for someone to be considered a victim. If a girl becomes a prostitute or a boy becomes a heroin user, their parents certainly experience anguish, and if experiencing anguish because of an act defined as a "victimless crime" (Schur, 1965) is experienced by someone close to the perpetrator, then just about all crimes could be considered victim-linked. For our purposes here, and in general, it will be useful to introduce the concept of an "indirect victim," or one who is not the direct target of a crime but experiences loss or anguish because of the crime. Juvenile status offenses can be considered *indirect victim-linked crimes* for the most part, even though in all cases for the same or different offenses, there may or may not be a specific indirect victim. For example, if a child's parents do not care if he runs away from home or even encourage it, they are not indirect victims. However, for parents who report their runaway child to the police or call them to take charge of their incorrigible juvenile, they certainly fall into the definition of indirect victim.

Now we can classify three ways in which juveniles come to the attention of the police. First, the police can be called by a victim of a direct victim-linked crime such as burglary, vandalism, or shoplifting. Second, they can learn about a juvenile's offense through an indirect victim, such as parents calling to report their daughter for incorrigibility. Third they can learn about a youthful offense through proactive policing, such as drug offenses or any other unreported criminal or delinquent act. We shall examine these three forms of occasions whereby juveniles come into official contact with the police and the situated contingencies and variables that determine whether or not they will be arrested and taken further into the system.

In those situations where the police are called to deal with victim-linked crimes, they may not know at the outset whether the crime was committed by a juvenile or an adult. For example, if they are called to investigate a burglary and the victim has no idea who the burglar was, the police naturally cannot know whether the suspect is a juvenile or adult. Later on, detectives investigating the case may learn that the culprit was a juvenile, but the case is not handled as a "juvenile case" until the discovery of the suspect. On the other hand, if a school is vandalized, for example, the police assume they are dealing with juveniles and make inquiries in terms of a "juvenile investigation."

Typically, however, the police deal with juveniles in relatively petty matters such as shoplifting, disturbing the peace, and similar offenses in which they are under less pressure to make an arrest and have more options for dealing with the situation (Sanders, 1976:157–58). In these situations, the police, backed by official policy for handling juveniles, can take several courses of action not available for cases involving adults. For example, they can take the juvenile home to his parents and let them discipline him.

Piliavin and Briar (1964), in their study of police encounters with juveniles, list the following five alternative actions police may take with juveniles:

1. Outright release.
2. Release and submission of a "field interrogation report" briefly describing the circumstances initiating the police-juvenile confrontation.
3. "Official reprimand" and release to parents or guardian.
4. Citation to juvenile court.
5. Arrest and confinement in juvenile detention.

These five alternatives form a continuum from the most severe action (arrest) to the least severe (release), and by examining the situations in which police choose from these alternatives, we can identify the salient variables in police-juvenile encounters in victim-linked complaints.

In the literature on police encounters with juveniles in victim-linked complaints, the most complete was an observation survey of a metropolitian police department made by Black and Reiss (1970). In their study, Black and Reiss examined what effect the complainant had on police discretion situations; they found that more than any other element in the situation, the complainant determined what action the police would take. In none of the cases where the complainant lobbied for leniency did the police arrest a juvenile offender (Black and Reiss, 1970:71). They also found that white complainants (typically with white offenders) were more likely to request informal dispositions than were black complainants (typically with black offenders). In 58 percent of the cases observed in the Black and Reiss study, white complainants asked the police to handle the cases informally, while only 31 percent of the black complainants asked for such leniency. This accounts in part for the greater likelihood that black youths would be arrested in victim-linked crimes than white youths.

Black and Reiss' findings are consistent with those of Wilson (1968:111) that in discretion situations involving citizen-invoked law enforcement, the police have little choice whether or not to intervene. Much of the control is turned over to the complaining citizen, and even though the police have more leeway in dealing with juveniles, especially in misdemeanor cases, they still see their actions as largely dependent on the complainant's decision.

Turning now to situations in which the police are notified by indirect victims, we might expect more police control and less influence by the complainant. To the contrary, however, available data of police action in such situations indicate a limited choice of action by the police. In Sanders' (1974) study of juvenile police, it was found that in juvenile status offenses, the police department was under a great deal of pressure to arrest juveniles who were truant, runaways, or incorrigible. If a juvenile was stopped and it was subsequently learned that he had been reported a runaway, the police always arrested him and placed him in the juvenile detention facility. Usually the child was placed in confinement only until the parents arrived and was then released to the parents. But often, the parents were in another state or a considerable distance away in the same state, so that it was not unusual for the child to remain locked up for several days or even weeks while waiting for his parents to get him or to send travel fare for the trip home. Sometimes the juvenile had run away from a foster home, and the foster parents did not want him to return; or the child had run away from his natural parents, and they did not want him back. In such cases, the juvenile would be locked up until a new home could be found, a search that could could take months. However, even if the police knew of the consequences or knew that the child had a good reason for leaving home, they were obliged to make an arrest. Thus, even though the consequences of an arrest would often result in long confinement for what the police took to be a relatively minor violation, they had little choice in the matter.

Some explanation may help in understanding why the police have so little discretion in cases involving runaways, a juvenile status offense, and so much discretion in more serious misdemeanors and

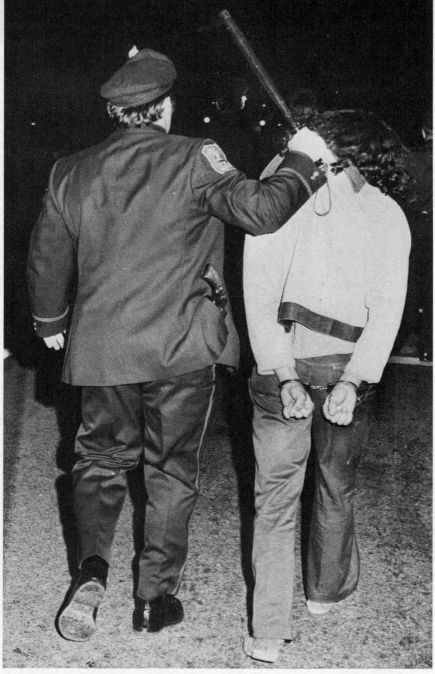

Police have more options with situations involving juveniles than they do with adults, but a serious offense by a juvenile almost always results in an arrest. (*Wide World Photos*)

A SEPARATE JUSTICE

even some felonies. If a child runs away from home, especially a home where the parents care very much about their child, they exert a great deal of pressure on the police to find the child. Unlike a stolen bicycle or a burglarized home, things that most people are willing to forget about if the culprit is not caught, a missing child is not forgotten. Parents worry about a host of pitfalls they envision will injure their runaway child, and runaways get into trouble often enough to warrant these concerns. In Houston, Texas, in 1973, when twenty-seven young boys, most of them runaways, were found murdered, pressure on the police was intensified at the time for renewed efforts to find runaway children. Even parents who normally would not have bothered with their children became concerned. One probation officer working with runaways said:

> "We used to have more trouble getting really angry parents to come down and claim their kids. . . . Sometimes they wanted to give the kid a jolt, to punish him with a few days in jail. Now, more and more parents rush straight down here, relief all over their faces, talking about Houston every time" (Stumbo, 1973).

Of course, most of the time there is no mass murder to stir parents to action, but the image of their child being ravished on the streets in a strange city is always a parental concern, a concern that is translated into pressure on the police. As a result, police administration mandates juvenile detectives to give high priority to such cases. When the police find a runaway juvenile, the parents want to see their child; thus, the police are obliged to arrest the reported runaway, whereas in other cases they might let the juvenile off with a warning. Typically, the parents are extremely grateful to the police for having found their child. So, in addition to the departmental rewards for doing their job, the police also receive the less tangible reward of the parents' gratitude.[3]

Thus, in analyzing the occasions when the police contact a juvenile offender reported by an indirect victim, it must be understood that such occasions offer the officers limited alternatives. Since the usual broad choices of courses of action are not available to them, the occasion itself demands that an arrest be made. As a result, there is a relatively high arrest rate in such instances as compared to those in which there is either a direct victim or no victim at all.

---

[3] The idea that most runaways leave home because of a "bad home" is not generally true, and most parents are not the cause of runaways. Most leave home for the action in the streets and other lures that have nothing to do with their parents. See William B. Sanders, *Juvenile Delinquency* (New York: Praeger, 1976), ch. 3.

Situations without Complainants

The final type of situation occurs when the police pick up a juvenile where no complaint has been made. Sometimes the offenses committed may be ones that would be reported if discovered, such as vandalism or burglary, but when the police contact a suspected juvenile, no report has been made.[4] Most typically, these contacts entail minor infractions, such as possession of marijuana or petty malicious mischief or theft, that probably would not be reported. Whatever the case, though, these occasions are ones in which there is no complainant present and no departmental pressure to make an arrest.

The significant variable of the occasion where the police encounter suspected delinquent juveniles (other than the seriousness of the crime and the knowledge of a juvenile's previous record, which are really outside the occasion) is the demeanor of the juvenile (Piliavin and Briar, 1964). In a sample of sixty-six cases, Piliavin and Briar found that, depending on how a juvenile acted toward the police officer and his appearance, the police were more or less likely to employ a severe disposition. Those juveniles who acted in a cooperative manner and appeared like "good kids" were less likely to be arrested than juveniles who appeared "tough" (for example, slouching, greasy hair, black leather jackets). Table 10–1 shows the relationship between demeanor and the severity of the disposition:

TABLE 10–1 SEVERITY OF POLICE DISPOSITION BY YOUTH'S DEMEANOR

Severity of Police Disposition	YOUTH'S DEMEANOR		
	Cooperative	Uncooperative	Total
Arrest (most severe)	2	14	16
Citation or official reprimand	4	5	9
Informal reprimand	15	1	16
Admonish and release (least severe)	24	1	25
Total	45	21	66

SOURCE: Irving Piliavin and Scott Briar, "Police Encounters with Juveniles," *American Journal of Sociology* 70 (September 1964): 210.

To illustrate the impact of demeanor on the outcome of a police-juvenile encounter, let us dichotomize the dispositions into "severe" and "lenient," with the two most severe dispositions being considered "severe" and the two least severe being considered "lenient." By trans-

---

[4] There are those cases in which the police have a reported crime but the complainant is not present and the discretion is entirely with the officer. In such instances there is usually departmental pressure to make an arrest.

forming the numbers into percentages along this dichotomy, we see the following:

Type of Disposition	Cooperative	Uncooperative
Severe	13	90
Lenient	87	10
Total	100	100

Thus, fully 90 percent of the uncooperative youths received severe dispositions while only 13 percent of the cooperative youths did.

We might expect that the youths who come into contact with the police are aware of the importance of such interaction variables, and studies of gang youths who come into frequent contact with the police support this expectation. As one youth explained:

> "If you kiss their ass and say, Yes sir, No sir, and all that jazz, then they'll let you go. If you don't do that, then they gonna take you in. And if you say it funny they gonna take you in. Like, Yes *sir!* No *sir!*. But if you stand up and say it straight, like Yes sir and No sir and all that, you cool" (Werthman and Piliavin, 1967:87).

Thus, cooperation with the police is not merely a sign of respect for authority; it is also a strategy to keep from being arrested. However, the same occasion can be used by juveniles to show thay they have "heart" (that is, spirit, gameness, toughness), and instead of being cooperative, they intentionally defy the police officer's authority to show other youths the kind of stuff they are made of (Goffman, 1967: 239–58). In this context, police-juvenile contacts can become "character contests," and while the price might be high for demonstrating their character—that is, arrest—some youths are willing to pay such a price for the status it brings.

In other studies of demeanor and the likelihood of arrest, demeanor has been found not always decisive. For example, in the Black and Reiss (1970) study, it was found that even though juveniles who acted civilly were less likely to be arrested than those who behaved antagonistically, the difference was slight. Moreover, they found that those who acted with an abundance of deference were more likely to be arrested than those who merely were civil to the police. The difference in the findings of these two studies may have reflected the impact of the *Gault* decision, which, we have seen, gave juveniles more rights. But it is more likely that what Black and Reiss found was based on situations in which the police had no clear probable cause to make an arrest. According to Piliavin and Briar, black youths who were uncooperative were extremely likely to be arrested, but 79 percent of the black youths who acted antagonistically toward the police officers in the Black and Reiss study were let go. This suggests that either demeanor is not as significant a variable as it was thought to be or some other intervening variable is present. One possible explanation is that the police are following an informal processing model (harassment) of control rather than using the formal processing model (arrest and, citation) that they can use officially (Black and Reiss, 1970:74).

Interaction Structures and Processes in Police–Juvenile Encounters

In other studies of police treatment of juveniles, it has been found that less "professionalized" police departments use informal sanctioning to control the young. Wilson (1968) found that the police in the less professionalized departments were not as likely to "go by the book," and as a result fewer juveniles were arrested. The first few times a juvenile came into contact with the police, he was merely likely to receive some kind of reprimand and be turned loose or over to the parents. The police believed they should give a juvenile a chance if they felt he was a "good kid" who only happened to get into trouble. As one policeman explained, "There was this fellow around here who is not vicious, not, I think, what you'd call bad; he's really sort of a good kid. He just can't move without getting into trouble" (Wilson 1968:18). Thus, juveniles can be seen as "good kids" who "get into" trouble as opposed to "bad kids" who "make" trouble. Depending on which type of youth the police see a juvenile as being determines whether or not they will make an arrest. So, instead of evaluating a juvenile offender on merely what act he has committed, they make a moral evaluation as well.

In society as a whole, juveniles are given *subordinate* status in most situations, and the police in law enforcement situations are given *superordinate* status (cf. Simmel, 1950). The result is that juveniles are placed in the "low" interactional role and the police in the "high" interactional role when police stop juveniles and begin an interactional encounter. In terms of the analysis of these situations, it must be understood that the subordinate-superordinate form of interaction is a general one, and we can learn general principles from them.

Here we shall examine the subordinate-superordinate encounter in terms of the problems created in gaining and losing "face."[5] Police action toward juveniles typically involves a type of "face game" wherein the police act so that juveniles are apt to lose face or the police officer loses face (Goffman, 1967:5–45). For example, if an officer tells some juveniles to "move along" or leave an area favored by the juveniles and they do so docilely, the juveniles may feel they have lost face.

---

[5] We are using Goffman's definition of "face" here as "the positive social value a person effectively claims for himself by the line others assume he has taken during a particular contact" (1967:5).

On the other hand, if the juveniles refuse to move or make derogatory comments to the officer, he will have lost face unless he takes official action. Reiss (1972:144–50) points out that in police-citizen encounters there generally tends to be a reciprocity of civility—that is, if officers behave in a civil manner, then so also do the people they stop and question. This is true in just about all types of encounters (Goffman, 1963). The special difficulty for police-juvenile encounters involves the officer's perspective and his mandate for "getting the job done." If juveniles meekly submit to any order by the officer, the youths lose face; but if they resist, they make the officer's job more difficult. "Difficult youth" (or "bad kids") are not seen to be deserving of civil treatment by the police officer since they have made his work harder than it already is. However, the officer's work will not be made easier if the juveniles continue to resist him; so if he wishes to work without continual difficulty, he must engage in artful interaction with the juveniles. For instance, if a group of youths is creating problems for the police, an officer will often take one of the group, preferably the leader, aside from both the group and other officers. In this way each can engage in face-saving work (Goffman, 1967:12–13). The youth can make concessions out of earshot of his friends, and the officer can do the same since he does not have to appear "in authority" to his fellow officers. Such face-saving practices make police work with juveniles easier since they make it easier for juveniles to comply with police requests.

In the absence of face-saving practices, as in all social occasions, trouble occurs. This is especially true when an audience is present who can confirm a face-loss, and in occasions of police-juvenile contact an audience is often present. The audience consists of three basic groups: (1) uninvolved bystanders, (2) advocates of the juvenile, and (3) other police officers. From the police officer's point of view, if he does not appear to be in control of the situation to any of these audiences, he will lose respect. In one incident reported to the authors, a youth was stopped for questioning by a single officer. Both the youth and the officer were civil to one another until a second officer arrived. Upon the arrival of the second officer, the first officer became abusive and the youth responded in kind. That is, as a result of the introduction of an audience to the first officer's action toward the youth, face-losing behavior ensued. It was learned that the first officer felt it was necessary to "show" the second officer that he was in control of the situation, and that he could demonstrate "control" by being abusive.

Similarly, in other observations of police-juvenile encounters, the juvenile initiated tension-producing behavior before an audience. In one case, for example, a boy picked up by juvenile detectives on suspicion of bicycle theft was civil toward the police until he was taken to his home, where he lived with his grandparents. At that time, the grandparents began degrading the police for taking in their grandson, and the boy joined in hurling slurs, resulting in a situation in which the boy's grandfather was threatened with arrest. Here again, the audiences to the occasion were significant in the outcome of the encounter while they were not, initially at least, the focus of the occasion.

Thus far we have discussed police-juvenile encounters independent of any violation of the law. It appears almost as though the police go after youths whether or not they break the law; and, as we pointed out earlier, some juvenile status offenses are worded so broadly and vaguely that almost any juvenile behavior could be considered illegal. This, of course, is not the case, and juveniles certainly break adult laws. But our focus has been on the juvenile justice process and not juvenile delinquency per se; therefore, we have been giving our attention to the elements of the occasions in which juveniles come into contact with the juvenile justice system, and not their offenses. However, basic to an understanding of the juvenile justice system is some understanding of the major patterns of delinquency, especially those patterns that go unreported. We know from studies of official juvenile records that delinquency is more predominant among lower- and working-class youths, but this may be due to the juvenile justice process, including the police, courts, and corrections, rather than actual patterns of delinquency.

Unrecorded delinquency reflects the amount of delinquency that is committed but not reported or recorded. Since, by definition, there is no record of delinquency that is unrecorded, it is necessary to conduct "self-report" surveys to discover such delinquency. In such surveys, respondents are asked whether they have committed different types of crimes and delinquent acts. The President's Commission on Law Enforcement and Administration of Justice report (1967:55) stated that, based on self-report studies, 90 percent of all young people have committed at least one act for which they could have been brought before juvenile court. However, only about 5 percent of the juvenile population appears in court in any given year (Gibbons, 1970:3). For the most part, the juveniles who appear in court are poor and members of minority groups; however, according to self-report surveys it is not just the poor and minorities who are subject to delinquency. For example, in one study of juvenile drug use, it was found that children from the upper segments of society were the most likely to have used marijuana (Sanders, 1976:18). Almost half of the high school students in the survey from the highest socioeconomic status had used marijuana at least once, while the most frequent use in any of the other social classes was only 20 percent. Thus, this study found, in the case of marijuana, there is almost an inverse relationship between social class and delinquency!

To understand why upper- and middle-class children are so underrepresented in juvenile justice records, we can turn back to our discussion of what the police used as criteria in assessing juveniles in discretion situations. Piliavin and Briar showed that a youth's appearance and demeanor were important in deciding if he should be taken in. Remembering this, we can hypothesize that the children from the higher socioeconomic strata are more likely to appear to be "good kids" and show the proper upper- and middle-class demeanor to the police. This would account for a good deal of discrimination against youths from the lower classes. Also, remembering that Black and Reiss found that blacks were more likely to demand arrest than were whites, we know that black youths are more likely to be arrested. Thus, based on the findings of two major studies of the police and youth, we would expect to find that poor youths are more likely to have official records of delinquency no matter how much or how little actual delinquency they were involved with.

Such differential treatment is documented by Chambliss (1973) in his study of the "Saints" and the "Roughnecks." The Saints were a group of upper-middle-class high school boys and the Roughnecks a lower-class group. Although both groups engaged in delinquent activities, only one got into serious trouble with the police and juvenile justice system. In fact, Chambliss points out:

> In sheer number of illegal acts, the Saints were the more delinquent. They were truant from school for at least part of the day almost every day of the week. In addition, their drinking and vandalism occurred with surprising regularity. The Roughnecks, in contrast, engaged sporadically in delinquent episodes. While these episodes were frequent, they certainly did not occur on a daily or even weekly basis (1973:146).

In accounting for the fact that the Roughnecks were more likely to be stopped and arrested than the Saints, Chambliss points out that the Saints were more likely to be polite and less likely to fight. However, the Roughnecks financial resources were considerably less than the Saints, and this led to their being more visible to the police. As Chambliss explains:

> This differential visibility was a direct function of the economic standing of the families. The Saints had access to automobiles and were able to remove themselves from the sight of the community. In as routine a decision as to where to go to have a milkshake after school, the Saints stayed away from the mainstream of community life. Lacking transportation, the Roughnecks could not make it to the edge of town. The center of town was the only practical place for them to meet since their homes were scattered throughout the town and any noncentral meeting place put an undue hardship on some members. Through necessity the Roughnecks congregated in a crowded area where everyone in the community passed frequently, including teachers and law enforcement officers. They could

easily see the Roughnecks hanging around the drugstore (1973:148).

Thus, in addition to "not looking right," the Roughnecks had the added disadvantage of high visibility. Therefore, not only were they subject to contact with the police, but their appearance and deameanor made them candidates for arrest more so than their upper-middle-class counterparts.

In summarizing this section on the police and juveniles, it is important to note that juveniles come to the attention of the police for delinquent acts. The ability of a cohort of juveniles to be visible or invisible depends on their resources for staying out of sight, and if in sight, appearing to be "good kids." It is not so much that different cohorts will be good or bad as it is a case of being seen engaging in good and bad activities or appearing as the "kind of kid" who *is* good or bad. These extralegal variables account for the patterns of officially recorded delinquency and at the same time point to the operation of the juvenile justice system on this first official level. As Black and Reiss show, there is a good deal of input by citizens in determining these patterns. Therefore, in the juvenile justice system, as in the adult criminal justice system, the police have a great deal of extralegal power in these occasions. The main difference between police contact with juveniles and with adults is that they have more informal options available to them in dealing with juveniles. Otherwise, we can assume the same occasioned social forces operate in police-juvenile encounters as do in adult-police encounters.

THE JUVENILE COURT: OFFICIAL INFORMALITY

The juvenile court, as we pointed out earlier, was developed as a unique separate entity. Unlike the police, who only had to institute some procedures that applied to juveniles (for example, officially sanctioned informal dispositions), the court constituted a new structure in the administration of justice. The *parens patriae* philosophy of the juvenile court, unlike the adult court philosophy of due process, gave the court an official mandate to proceed informally. In the adult court, the philosophy is based on the assumption of innocence, the adversary system, and the rights of the citizen, and even though the actual operation of the adult court is close to the *parens patriae* ideal, there has never been a legally or philosophically directed guideline to that effect in the official rules of procedure. More and more, the adult court has become concerned with "what to do with this person" rather than the rights of due process, and whether or not a defendant is guilty or innocent. Whereas such concerns are the ideal of conduct in the juvenile court, the adult court does this in opposition to its ideal of conduct. This has been less true since the *Gault* decision, but, nevertheless, the informal proceedings of juvenile court are rooted in its philosophy, and we cannot ignore these roots if we are to understand the juvenile court.

The route to juvenile court is an uncertain one at best, and a juvenile who is picked up by the police may or may not go to it. Typically, an errant juvenile will be brought before some type of screening officer before being referred to court. Usually, the probation department supplies such a screening authority, called an "intake" officer, who determines whether the juvenile should be released to his parents, to some kind of diversion process, or be sent to court. It is significant that the probation department takes care of this function, for probation is a part of *corrections* and not *adjudication* and *prosecution;* however, the role of probation, in this case, includes handling juveniles in official determination of guilt. As we pointed out earlier in this chapter, the juvenile court virtually assumes guilt and views itself as a helping hand, and since probation is viewed in this context, its position there is not out of place. Moreover, the amount of power the intake officer has in determining the fate of a juvenile is enormous, for his decision can either release the juvenile completely from further involvement in the juvenile justice system or push him further into it.

The importance of the role of the intake officer is often overlooked in studies of juvenile justice. We are stressing it here not only because of its neglect but also because it is the single most important role in juvenile justice. As Cressey and McDermott point out:

> The design of the buildings and the rooms used for giving justice to juveniles hides the fact the intake officer is the most important person in the juvenile justice system. This man's workroom is smaller and barer than the "chambers" of juvenile court judges, the suites used by Chief Probation Officers, and the offices of the probation department section chiefs called supervisors. In his little cubicle there are no flags, no polished wood furniture, no panelled walls, no carpet, and no statue of the blindfolded lady. The cubicle is equipped with a cheap metal desk and a couple of straightbacked chairs. A few unframed prints and a diploma or two are temporarily taped on the walls. The intake officer doesn't wear a robe or a wig. He sits at his bare desk, often wearing an open-collared shirt, and does justice (1973:11).

Cressey and McDermott list, in decreasing frequency, the options available to intake officers:

> *Counsel, warn,* and *release* is the most commonly utilized option. This disposition is an almost automatic response to cases

brought in via citations. The child is usually discharged after a warning, a lecture, or a short conference with him and his parents. The case is not carried in the official records as "dismissed," even though CWR is sometimes called "dismissed" rather than a disposition.

Informal probation is the option whereby, under Mountain State law, a juvenile might be placed on a maximum of six months' informal probation if he and his parents agree to it. In practice, the term of probation is rarely less than six months.

Probation diversion units may be used for the particular types of cases they have been established to receive. The intake officer may be required to refer certain cases (usually predelinquents or minor lawbreakers) to such a unit. In addition, or in some locations, he may opt to send other cases there. When a child is sent to a diversion unit, his case is officially logged as "dismissed." However, the child is strongly urged to participate in the special unit's program.

Referral to another agency (or to a person) is a common disposition of walk-in and phone contact cases. Such referral is an attempt to handle the case "unofficially" by sending the juvenile to someone that "is better able (qualified) to handle this case." This disposition is sometimes used for other than "walk-ins" by intake officers on night duty. These officers tend to be viewed by detention center staff members and the police as "troubleshooters." Intake officers receive cases from them that have not "officially" come to the attention of the juvenile justice system, and they dispose of them officially. It is questionable, then, whether such referrals are "dispositions," "diversions," "dismissals," or something else.

Petition for an official hearing before a juvenile court referee or judge is the "classic" disposition used in "serious" and "last resort" cases. It is something like the filing of charges in criminal cases. The papers on the case are simultaneously filed with the court and with a regular probation officer (as indicated above) who makes an investigation and reports back to the court, which then conducts a hearing.

Dismissal is the least-used option. It occurs most frequently when the intake officer decides there is not enough evidence to justify further action, or when he believes the technicalities of the arrest were improper (1973:19–20).

Given these dispositions, we can appreciate the power of the intake officer, especially since the second *least* used option is referral to juvenile court. Typically, a case does not reach the hearing stage in the course of juvenile justice, and while there is no reason to conclude that the court stage is any less haphazard than the decision of an intake officer, at least during a hearing there is some chance for the juvenile to come before a judge. In reality, however, the juvenile court (that is, judge, hearing, defense counsel) is employed sparingly, thus, in effect, placing the de facto juvenile court in the hands of the intake officer; therefore, we shall examine the occasion in which the intake officer comes into contact with a juvenile to see what determines the officer's choice of one option over another.

Juveniles come into contact with the intake officer from three major routes (Cressey and McDermott, 1973:13–14). First, they may have been picked up for what the police consider a serious offense or certain juvenile status offenses, especially runaway. Second, they will come in with their parents from home. These juveniles will have received a "citation" from the police to appear before the intake officer. Finally, there are those juveniles who come in by themselves or with their parents on their own volition. These include parents who want something done with their children because they cannot handle them themselves and youths who are seeking help for a variety of problems and have nowhere else to go.

Because the official philosophy of juvenile justice revolves around the individual needs of its clients or the "individualization" of cases, we would expect this to lead to occasions similar to those of police-juvenile encounters in which the intake officer makes a decision on the basis of interaction between himself and the juvenile. However, we find instead an even more perfunctory handling of cases. The general formula works something like this: First offenders are counseled, warned, and released; second offenders are given informal probation; and third offenders are petitioned to court. Talking with the child and his parents is not essential to the decision-making process, and as one intake officer explained, "You know what you are going to do or recommend after reading the report and records. . . . You don't have to see the kid" (Cressey and McDermott, 1973:15). This bureaucratically efficient method contrasts with the individualized ideal that is officially expoused. Therefore, the decision about what option is to be taken is determined more by a routine formula than a method of evaluating the needs of the individual juvenile.

If the officer options to counsel, warn, and release the child, then the juvenile is finished with the juvenile justice system. However, if a juvenile receives informal probation, then he is placed in a situation where the juvenile justice system exerts control without the formal proceeding of a hearing. This is done without any of the legal procedures seen either in a criminal case or in a juvenile hearing. Informal probation is "voluntary" in that the intake officer cannot place a child on informal probation without parental permission. However, if the option is between going to court and the possibility of receiving formal probation, or something worse, such as detention, parents and child are typically willing to take informal probation. The "informality" of the probation is not quite what the term implies. A child on informal probation can't choose to show up for his meeting with the probation officer at his own convenience. Instead, the informality comes to mean not going to court and not being placed on "formal" probation. The juvenile and his parents are pretty well told that the child is going to be placed on informal probation, and their agreement is more or less automatic. A typical and generic conversation between the intake officer and a youth and his parents is illustrated by the following (Cressey and McDermott, 1973:44):

Intake Officer: "I'm going to put you on informal probation for six months; what do you think?"
Youth: "Okay."
Parent: "Okay."
Intake Officer: "You'll have to sign this form agreeing to the probation department rules, okay?"
Youth: "Okay."
Parent: "Okay."

Such an interchange would occur after the probation officer has explained the seriousness of the offense and probably what would happen if the child went to court. However, there is a minimum amount of due process, and even though the intake officer sincerely believes that informal probation may offer the opportunity for useful counseling, there is no "day in court" for the youth.

The compelling force behind informal probation lies not in the good intentions of the juvenile or his parents; rather, it derives from the fact that the probation officer can refile on original charges if the youth refuses to cooperate after agreeing to the informal probation. The charges against the juvenile are *not* dropped as soon as informal probation begins, but instead are suspended until the juvenile has completed his term of probation. If the youth does not commit another offense, does not violate the conditions of probation, and successfully completes the period of informal probation, then the suspended charges are dropped. If, on the other hand, he somehow gets into trouble, the original charges can be refiled and he can be sent to court.

In some jurisdictions, the juvenile justice system has set up "diversion units" or "diversion programs." As we briefly pointed out above, diversion is an alternative to juvenile court, usually to some temporary or short-term treatment program. For example, some communities have established youth service bureaus to handle certain kinds of juvenile offenses. Typically, minor offenses or juvenile status offenses are "diverted" out of the juvenile justice system and into some other program. In Florida, runaways are diverted to short-term facilities where they stay until their parents come to pick them up. In some communities in California, the police bring runaways directly to a Youth Service Bureau where they are reunited with their parents. Under this alternative, the juvenile may never come into the juvenile justice system, or if he does, he is quickly diverted out of it.

If such diversion programs exist, the option to use them rests more with the policy of the probation department than with the discretion of any single intake officer. Runaways who are first offenders may be "automatically" placed with a diversion unit, if the policy and the diversion facilities so dictate. In certain minor cases, the intake officer may be given the discretion to refer certain other juveniles to a diversion program, but if they are given this discretion it is only because there are sufficient diversion resources and a concomitant policy allowing such actions. In situations in which either the law (as is the case in Florida) or policy come into conflict with available resources for diversion, the probation department and the police will sometimes develop courses of action to get around the law and policy. For example, the authors found that one probation department advised the police that if they picked up a runaway, they should attempt to charge the youth with something other than a juvenile status offense. What "other charges" could be brought against a juvenile who had run away from home were never specified, but the police and probation departments assumed that some charge could always be found even if there was little or no probable cause to make such a charge. In this way, the youth could be placed in juvenile detention instead of in one of the homes available for juvenile status offenders. This informal action was taken not because the probation department wanted to "get" a juvenile. Rather, with only a limited number of beds available in which to put up runaways, and because the law would not allow juvenile status offenders to be placed in detention, if a juvenile were charged with something else he would at least have somewhere to stay until he was reunited with his parents. The other charges would automatically be "dropped" as soon as the child was back with his parents.

GOING TO COURT

When a juvenile is sent to court, we again find more involvement by the probation department than we would expect in a judiciary function. Here the probation officer provides information to the court along with recommendations of what should be done with the juvenile. In essence, then, the probation officer "constructs" for the court the "facts" of a juvenile's biography (Cicourel, 1968). Since the judge's role in juvenile hearings is to decide on the basis of available information what is "best" for the juvenile, it is necessary that judges rely heavily on the "Social History Report." Since the Social History Report is compiled by the probation department, and since the probation department includes a recommendation for what is "best" for the youth, much of the actual decision-making in juvenile court is done by the probation officer. The judge or referee who does not go along with the probation department's recommendation can be accused of not being in the spirit of juvenile court's treatment orientation, for the probation department has looked into the child's biography, family, school, previous trouble, and sometimes psychological problems. This information is deemed more pertinent than any fine points of due process and/or any idiosyncratic ideas the judge might have. Therefore, to be a good judge in juvenile court is viewed in terms of agreement with the probation department's recommendation.

In describing the paramount role of the probation department in the court, Cressey and McDermott show what happens when an intake officer has decided that a petition should be filed.

Once an official petition has been filed, the juvenile's case passes from the intake officer to the discretion of a probation investigating officer. It is the latter's task to verify the facts of the case and to submit a report of his findings to the juvenile court. In addition to looking at the evidence behind the complaint and petition, the officer looks at the background of the juvenile and the circumstances of his offense. His report to the court will contain a "probation plan" if probation rather than incarceration or detention for further diagnosis (or punishment) is recommended. As part of a proposed probation plan the officer may recommend a specific program—such as

Juvenile court is less formal than adult courts, and juveniles do not have the right to a jury trial. (*Bob Adelman*)

drug abuse education—conducted either by the probation department or by some other agency, public or private. His report may, alternatively, ask for dismissal of the petition so that the juvenile can be placed on informal probation. Another alternative, rarely used, is to ask for dismissal with no further action. In one jurisdiction, the juvenile court judge grants such dismissals by signing a supply of blank request forms. Dismissal, then, may occur with a minimum of "official" action (1973:17).

As can be seen, the judge not only relies on the probation department's judgment but he also "gives over" completely to the probation department certain decisions.

Having seen that the probation officer is the central figure in the juvenile court, we shall now examine how he constructs a picture of a juvenile to be in need of one type of disposition or another. For the purposes of analysis, we shall suspend any notions of what a juvenile delinquent "really is," for even if there is such a reality outside of social constructions, it is not pertinent to the decision-making process. By formulating an image of a given juvenile, the probation officer produces what the court will make decisions about. For example, if a juvenile is picked up for shoplifting and has no record of previous misbehavior, then his image as far as the probation officer is concerned is typically not one of a "troublemaker," or a "bad kid." This image may be fostered even if the juvenile has been shoplifting as long as he has been able to walk. On the other hand, if a youth has relatives and friends who have delinquent records and he has been picked up a few times for shoplifting, even though he rarely breaks the law, he is more likely to be the subject of intense "treatment" or even punishment. The latter child is more likely to be presented as a "real" delinquent than the former, regardless of any actual delinquent history.

Any given set of "facts" is assumed to be accompanied by either good or bad behavior. In making their Social History Reports, probation officers rely on psychological and sociological concepts and theories as well as commonsensical notions of "what goes with what" (Cicourel, 1968). A juvenile from a broken home is more likely to receive more intensive counseling or be considered delinquent or predelinquent than one from an unbroken home. This is not necessarily so because children from broken homes are in fact more delinquent; rather, it is a common *belief* that children from such homes are more delinquent. Therefore, it follows from the assumptions accompanying the "fact" of a broken home that lead to more intervention by the juvenile justice system than the fact itself. Further, it follows that such children need more supervision, and more supervision leads to a greater likelihood that if a juvenile does get into further trouble, it will be noticed. This, in turn, leads to a longer delinquent record, which "validates" the theory that children from broken homes are more delinquent. Similarly, children of lower socioeconomic status are believed to be more prone to delinquency, and as a result, the "fact" of lower-class membership is taken as cause for greater intervention by the juvenile justice system. Thus, as we showed in our discussion of the Saints and Roughnecks and the police, the interpretation of the "facts" is really nothing more than a construction based on assumptions that accompany such "facts." The theories, whether commonsensical or scientific, provide the background expectations for making sense out of any set of facts, and the facts themselves are molded by the very assumptions they give rise to. Such interpretive work accounts for the skewed socioeconomic grouping of juveniles with delinquent records.

The order in juvenile justice is accomplished not merely by applying rules of due process, policy rules, or informal rules that emerge in the workaday routine of doing juvenile justice. Instead, the "rules" serve as resources for making sense out of all sorts of events and people who come before the probation officer (cf. Daudistel and Sanders, 1974). Accounts of "what happened" provided in the police report, the Social History Report, and school records are reformulated along the lines of still another set of rules used as interpretive schemes for making sense of "what happened." Thus, instead of having an orderly procedure *in fact,* either for evaluating juveniles or for administering policy (formal or informal), the order is accomplished as an ongoing ad hoc process. For example, consider the following hypothetical cases. As we noted in discussing the intake officer, there was an informal policy for dealing with first, second, and third offenders. Second offenders were placed on informal probation according to this policy. If a juvenile came into contact with the intake officer for a second time, this would serve as an "objective fact" that could be used as an account for placing the youth on informal probation. However, suppose the intake officer decides that the first offense did not count because the youth was "led" into trouble by others. Thus, he takes the second meeting to be "really," "after all," "in all fairness" to be "in fact" only the first offense. Thus, by reformulating the second meeting as the first and accounting for his action in terms of the informal policy giving first offenders a warning, the intake officer is able to preserve the sense of orderly process. Likewise, a probation officer may interpret events in terms of overly harsh or lenient police reports. For instance, he may view Officer Kelly's reports as extremely biased and Officer Smith's as understated. Therefore, the officer might go easier on a juvenile brought in by Officer Kelly since he knows that Kelly is excessively harsh in his reporting. On the other hand, he may see a child arrested by Officer Smith in need of a great deal of supervision since he knows that Smith is overly lenient, and the juvenile he brings in is "really bad."

In this section on juvenile court, we have seen that the principal character in the decision-making process is the probation officer. Since the probation office is usually viewed as a correctional agency rather than a judicial one, it is important that we understand the judicial side of this neglected agency with regard to juvenile justice. The fact that probation plays such a central role points to a nonadversary system based on the assumption that those juveniles brought into the juvenile justice system are somehow "out of order"—legal or otherwise. This is in contrast to the criminal justice system, which at least pays lip service to the assumption of innocence. Thus, since the question is not one of innocence or guilt, the decisions made revolve around "what to do" with a given juvenile. This decision occurs in the context of an organizationally constructed image of the juvenile derived from the records of the police, schools, and the probation office itself, along with images of his background gleaned from visits to his home and neighborhood. Theories of broken homes and "bad" environments lead inevitably to conclusions that discriminate against the poor and minorities. Of course, such discrimination is not unique to juvenile court, but it does account for the large number of juveniles from disadvantaged backgrounds who become caught up in the system.

JUVENILE CORRECTIONS

When speaking of "juvenile corrections," we make the assumption that when juveniles enter into a "correctional," "rehabilitation," or "reform" program, they are, as a result, "corrected," "rehabilitated," or "reformed." It is probably more accurate, however, to speak of what the juvenile court does as somehow "supervisory," for this term encompasses not only the wide range of dispositions from probation to incarceration but also implies no outcome for those juveniles who come under supervision. Therefore, when we discuss any kind of official control over juveniles, we shall use the term "juvenile supervision" to minimize any bias.

Other than counseling, warning, and release, the most common disposition for juveniles is probation, either informal or formal. In 1965, for example, 62,773 juveniles were locked up in institutions, while 285,431 were on probation (President's Commission on Law Enforcement and Administration of Justice, 1967:161). And since these figures do not include informal probation, the actual figure of juveniles on some kind of probation is much higher. As we pointed out earlier, those juveniles who were first offenders or who committed minor crimes were the most likely to be placed on probation, while the more serious offenders and repeaters were placed in institutions (Cohn, 1963).

The terms of probation vary from strict supervision and control over a juvenile's activities to fairly lenient treatment consisting of merely having the juvenile call the probation officer once a month. For example, the following terms of probation were given one boy:

1. That he violate no law or ordinance;
2. That he obey the reasonable directives of his mother and the Probation Officer at all times;
3. That he attend school regularly and obey all school rules and regulations;
4. That he not be out after dark unless accompanied by his mother or some adult person approved by her;
5. That he report once each month to the Probation Officer, either in person or in writing (Cicourel, 1968:212).

About the only thing this juvenile had to do that is not required of all juveniles is to meet with or write to his probation officer and not go out after dark without his mother or some approved adult. What correction or even supervision can be accomplished under these conditions is questionable. A monthly letter to the probation officer would certainly not mention any activities that were in violation of the terms of probation. Or if the juvenile made only monthly visits to his probation officer, it is questionable what type of effective counseling could be accomplished in such little time. This is not to say that some kind of effective counseling program could not be arranged, but given the caseloads and other duties of a probation officer or juvenile counselor, their work becomes a source of cynicism rather than inspiration. This is an especially bitter pill for young probation officers who enter their work with visions of rehabilitation and civic usefulness.

INCARCERATORIES FOR JUVENILES

Like the terminology used in other aspects of juvenile justice, terms such as "reform schools," "training schools," and "rehabilitation centers" often belie the programs in these institutions. What all of them accomplish, however, is some form of incarceration, and so as not to confuse names with substance, we shall refer to any total institution for the young as "juvenile incarceratories," and examine them in terms of their inmates in the same fashion as we did in the chapter on prisons. The following description of a Dutch incarceratory provides a backdrop for our discussion.

The most striking thing about the juvenile prison, as the Dutch called it, was its setting. They had converted a Nazi

The physical settings of juvenile detention centers are similar to those of adults.
(*Bob Adelman*)

concentration camp into what we would call a "reformatory."
The same barbed wire fences used by the Nazis, with curved
cement poles for holding the wires, were still in place. The
buildings, including a crematorium which was outside the fence,
were the same ones used to house Jews and other political
undesirables by the Nazis in the Second World War. The
interiors of the buildings were not bad, and indeed the Dutch
had done a great deal to liven up the inside of these heinous
structures. There was an abundance of trees and shrubs, and
were it not for the fact that it had once been a concentration
camp, the setting itself was quite pleasant. The director of the
prison referred to the boys as "inmates," and even though they
were treated like students, it was refreshing to hear what I
considered an honest terminology. There were more staff than
there were inmates, and there appeared to be a maximum effort
to help the boys—mostly vocational, but since the director of the
prison was a psychologist, there were counseling programs as
well. There was an attempt to be democratic in some of the
decision-making, and for this, they held weekly meetings and
discussions where any complaints were aired, and the prisoners

could vote on a number of alternatives. There was little emphasis on control and some boys joked that they had to remind the guards, who stood near the entrance, to keep others out. If any of the boys wanted to escape, they would have had little difficulty. Had the prison been in the United States and were not the setting that of a former Nazi concentration camp, it would probably be seen as a greatly enlightened and progressive "reformatory" (Sanders, 1976:201–2).

As can be inferred from this description, terminology and setting belied the incarceratory's progressive operation. On the other hand, consider the following description of the Fricot Ranch School for Boys in California:

Lights are turned on at 6:05 A.M. The group is on silence during dressing and washing up, then the boys line up in the hallway, where quiet talking is allowed until they leave for the dining room at 6:35. On the dining-hall ramp the boys stand silent at attention until the "At ease, quiet talking" order is given. In the dining room low talking is allowed, but no horseplay or trading of food. After breakfast the group is moved to the lodge yard, where the supervisor takes a count and runs a bathroom call. He selects crews to sweep and mop the lodge washroom, locker room, day room, dormitory, honor room hall and office, and supervises the work. At 8:25 the boys are ordered into formation, the supervisor takes another count and then accompanies the group to the academic school building. When classes are let out at 11:30 A.M., the boys go directly to the dining-hall ramp, met by their supervisor, who takes a count before the group enters. After lunch the boys go to the lodge, usually for a quiet period in the day room or on their beds, sometimes going on a short hike or playing outdoors. At 1:05 P.M. they are ordered into formation for a count, then move again to the school building, followed by the supervisor. School is dismissed for the day at 4:15, and the boys go directly to their lodge yard, met by their supervisor, who takes a count, then usually allows free play. By 4:30 P.M. the boys are moved into the lodge to wash up before dinner, and they leave the lodge about 5:05 to march to the dining hall. After the meal the group moves back to the lodge for a count, a bathroom call, and a brief period of free play outdoors or in the lodge. At 6:15 P.M. the group is split, following the preferences of the boys, for the evening activities, which may include a hike, organized games, or supervised crafts. Activities end at 8:00 P.M, when the boys are returned to the lodge. They brush their teeth, undress, put their shorts, socks, and tee shirts into laundry bags, and take showers by groups. As soon as they have showered, the boys go to their beds, and there is "package call"—which means that those who have received from home packages of cookies, candy, and toys may enjoy these treats until 9:30, when all boys must be in their beds. No boy is allowed out of bed after 10:30 unless it is to go to the bathroom, and during the night the supervisor quietly moves through the lodge to take a count of the boys three times every hour (Jesness, 1965:9).

The regimented order of the "ranch" appears to maximize control over the boys. They were counted several times a day, and there were numerous "activities" to keep them busy. Furthermore, the group supervisors (guards) cultivated an "exploitive truce" with the clique leaders (Jesness, 1965). Supervisors would give special favors to the leaders among the boys, and the leaders, in turn, would keep their groups in line (cf. Cressey, 1972:109–30).

If we examine one "rehabilitative" measure, we can see how easy it is to take what is probably an honest measure of rehabilitation and turn it into a control device. "Recreational therapy" is used extensively in juvenile incarceratories, and even though its theraputic value is questionable, it serves as a useful control device. It was noted by one of the authors in a juvenile detention center where he worked that recreational therapy was used as much to keep the boys and girls busy and tire them as to "rehabilitate them." One supervisor explained, "If these kids are tired from playing volleyball, they won't be as much trouble in the evening after dinner." The "trouble" the supervisor referred to was in relation to controlling the juveniles, and none of the staff believed that the daily volleyball games did anything more than to keep the youths occupied and make them easier to control. However, if anyone asked why the juveniles were playing volleyball, the benefits of recreational therapy could always be listed and praised as evidence of the progressive operation of the institution.

Similarly, a program that is now becoming popular in some areas is to provide rewards for good behavior rather than merely punishment for bad behavior. One such program rewards juveniles by letting them ride minature motorcycles ("minibikes"). One of the proponents of this program told the author: "These kids never get rewarded for positive behavior, only punishment for negative behavior. We feel that by rewarding them for responsible, productive behavior, they'll learn that there are rewards in society for doing the right thing." However, the reward of riding a minibike can be quickly changed to a punishment by withholding the activity. That is, reward and punishment are two sides of the same coin; thus, when discussing a system of rewards for positive behavior, it is impossible to do so without implying punishment for noncompliance with the desired behavior. Moreover, the control is direct in that it is manipulated by those who run the program.

Since there is no built-in evaluation of the program, or any other form of evaluation for that matter, whether it works or not is unknown. However, if it is seen generically, it is merely another version of the punishment system that never has worked in the field of corrections. As soon as the juveniles are outside of the direct control of the agencies, they are no longer subject to the artificial reward system, and unless they "see the connection" between being well-behaved and the reward system in society (the existence of which is questionable), it is unlikely that any change in their behavior can be attributed to the program.

In retrospect, juvenile corrections can be seen essentially as a control mechanism. Control and corrections are two different things, and because a program has been successful or unsuccessful in controlling a juvenile does not mean it has "corrected" him. To be "corrected" implies an individual's self-adjustment so that external control mechanisms are no longer necessary. We might concede that "corrections" is merely externally induced "self-control." Even so, there is a world of difference between self-control and control by an external agency or agent, for the former implies that there is no necessity for external control.

Thus, to best understand juvenile corrections amid all of the jargon and pronouncements, we must clearly see that at the heart of the programs and institutions is *control*. Of course, this is what agencies are supposed to do in one manner or another. However, the control is for the most part direct control with little in the way of preparation for or expectation of self-control by those juveniles who come into the juvenile justice system. Most functionaries believe that if a juvenile has come into contact with the juvenile justice system, he lacks the necessary self-control; therefore, they must design and carry out forms of external control. If there is some kind of rehabilitation program, one designed to foster self-control, it is carried out under direct control. However, the external control mechanisms that are set up to provide for the rehabilitation program often deny the very kinds of situations necessary to test and foster self-control. The result has been a lack of knowledge of what forces work successfully in rehabilitation. To be on the safe side, most correctional programs have opted for short-term external control operations. Some juveniles who come under their jurisdiction will reform on their own anyway, and so such programs can always claim some measure of success. Recidivism can be blamed on anything from sophisticated theories of family structure to simple explanations citing "permissiveness." But as long as the correctional programs include measures of external control, the agencies can cover themselves from charges that they are not "protecting society" from vicious juveniles. As a result, like other bureaucratic organizations with a difficult "product" to measure, juvenile corrections has moved from "doing good" to "looking good."

In San Francisco, Huckleberry House caseworkers confer with police officers in 1968. Huckleberry House was one of the first such establishments to serve as an alternative to incarceration for juvenile runaways. (*Bob Fitch Photo / Peoples Union*)

CHANGING PATTERNS IN JUVENILE JUSTICE

One of the most significant changes occurring in juvenile justice is a reassessment of its role in the lives of juveniles. Specifically, some have come to question whether it would be better to do nothing to certain juveniles rather than intervene in their lives. As we mentioned earlier in our discussion of the options available to intake officers, dismissal and diversion are widely used. Dismissal, in the form of perfunctory counseling and a warning before releasing the juvenile, may or may not include a promise of victim restitution. Diversion, on the other hand, ideally places the juvenile in some program or agency outside of the juvenile justice system. Both of these options are pronouncements that the system is either useless as a means of changing a juvenile violator, or that it would be unjust to put a child into it. If the system could help change a violator, or just help a child, then we would not see the massive use of the counsel, warn, and release option or the growing popularity of diversion programs. Obviously, if the juvenile justice system does more harm than good to a juvenile, then it is certainly a good idea to subject as few juveniles to it as possible. But if it is not working with a sizeable population of juvenile offenders, we must consider a radical restructuring of it altogether.

Some restructuring of the juvenile justice system has already taken place. For one thing, it is becoming more like the adult system in that many of the adversary aspects of adult court are being introduced in juvenile proceedings. But as we saw elsewhere in this book, the adversary process of adult criminal courts has eroded. New laws dealing with juvenile status offenders function to exclude a large population of juveniles from intervention by the juvenile court, and if nothing else, these new laws will certainly reduce the caseloads of juvenile courts and of the probation officers and counselors. This may free the probation officers to pay more attention to other delinquents, possibly resulting in more effective counseling and control.

SUMMARY

Beginning with a crusade-like program to save the children from the evils of society and adult criminals, the juvenile justice system has come to be a self-doubting institution adopting more and more features of the adult criminal justice system. The key role of the intake officer in the juvenile system still points to a nonadversary form of "justice," and juveniles are far more subject to the whim of a single person than are adults. But as the adult criminal courts come to be run by prosecutors and clerks, the adult and juvenile systems come to be more and more similar in actual operation. The formal ideals of the two systems are converging in that juveniles are being granted more civil rights enjoyed by adults. However, since neither system can be empirically explained by rational legalism, the comparison must be made in terms of actual operations, and it is in this comparison that we see the growing similarities.

REFERENCES

BLACK, DONALD J., AND ALBERT J. REISS, JR.
    1970 "Police Control of Juveniles," *American Sociological Review* 35 (February):63–67.

CHAMBLISS, WILLIAM
    1973 "The Saints and the Roughnecks," *Society* 11 (November–December):24–31.

CICOUREL, AARON
    1968 *The Social Organization of Juvenile Justice.* New York: Wiley.

COHN, YONA
    1963 "Criteria for the Probation Officer's Recommendation to the Juvenile Court Judge," *Crime and Delinquency* (July):262–75.

CRESSEY, DONALD R.

1972 "A Confrontation of Violent Dynamics," *International Journal of Psychiatry* 1, no. 3:109–30.

CRESSEY, DONALD R., AND ROBERT A. MC DERMOTT

1973 *Diversion from the Juvenile Justice System.* Project Report for National Assessment of Juvenile Corrections (June). Ann Arbor: University of Michigan.

DAUDISTEL, HOWARD C., AND WILLIAM B. SANDERS

1974 "Police Discretion in Application of the Law," *et al.* 3:26–40.

GIBBONS, DON C.

1970 *Delinquent Behavior.* Englewood Cliffs, N.J.: Prentice-Hall.

GOFFMAN, ERVING

1963 *Behavior in Public Places.* New York: The Free Press.
1967 *Interaction Ritual.* Garden City, N.Y.: Doubleday.

JESNESS, CARL F.

1965 *The Fricot Ranch Study.* Sacramento: State of California, Department of the Youth Authority.

LERMAN, PAUL

1973 "Delinquents with Crimes," in Abraham S. Blumberg, ed., *Law and Order: The Scales of Justice,* pp. 241–69. New Brunswick, N.J.: Transaction Books.

PILIAVIN, IRVING, AND SCOTT BRIAR

1964 "Police Encounters with Juveniles." *American Journal of Sociology* 70 (September):206–14.

PLATT, ANTHONY

1969 *The Child-Savers: The Invention of Deliquency.* Chicago: University of Chicago Press.
1974 "The Triumph of Benevolence: The Origins of the Juvenile Justice System in the United States," in Richard Quinney, ed., *Criminal Justice in America: A Critical Understanding,* pp. 356–89. Boston: Little, Brown.

PRESIDENT'S COMMISSION ON LAW ENFORCEMENT AND ADMINISTRATION OF JUSTICE

1967 *Task Force Report: Juvenile Delinquency and Youth Crime.* Washington, D.C.: Government Printing Office.

REISS, ALBERT J.

1971 *The Police and the Public.* New Haven: Yale University Press.

SANDERS, WILLIAM B.

1977 *Detective Work: A Study of Criminal Investigations.* New York: The Free Press.
1976 *Juvenile Delinquency.* New York: Praeger.

SCHUR, EDWIN

1965 *Crimes without Victims.* Englewood Cliffs, N.J.: Prentice-Hall.

SCOTT, MARVIN B. AND STANFORD M. LYMAN

1968 "Accounts," *American Sociological Review* 33:46–62.

SELLIN, THORSTEN, AND MARVIN E. WOLFGANG
  1964   *The Measurement of Delinquency.* New York: Wiley.

SIMMEL, GEORG
  1950   *The Sociology of Georg Simmel,* ed. Kurt H. Wolff. New York: The Free Press.

STUMBO, BELLA
  1973   "Spector of Houston Haunts Parents." *Los Angeles Times* (September 16).

WERTHMAN, CARL, AND IRVING PILIAVIN
  1967   "Gang Members and the Police," in David J. Bordua, ed., *The Police: Six Sociological Essays,* pp. 56–98. New York: Wiley.

WILSON, JAMES Q.
  1968   "The Police and the Delinquent in Two Cities," in Stanton Wheeler, ed., *Controlling Delinquents,* pp. 9–30. New York: Wiley.

SELECTED READINGS

CARTER, ROBERT M., AND MALCOLM W. KLEIN, EDS. *Back on the Street: The Diversion of Juvenile Offenders.* Englewood Cliffs, N.J.: Prentice-Hall, 1976.
This collection of readings is both broad and varied, providing an understanding of the theory and practice of diversion. Several diversion programs are discussed, illustrating the different ways in which diversion has been implemented.

CICOUREL, AARON. *The Social Organization of Juvenile Justice.* New York: Wiley, 1968.
The most complete work on the actual operation of the juvenile justice process. Emphasis is on the interpretive work in constructing the sense of delinquency by juvenile justice workers.

KASSEBAUM, GENE. *Delinquency and Social Policy.* Englewood Cliffs, N.J.: Prentice-Hall, 1974.
Kassebaum examines the policies which shape the meaning and disposition of juvenile delinquency in relation to the social structure.

LERMAN, PAUL, ED. *Delinquency and Social Policy.* New York: Praeger, 1970.
Not to be confused with Kassebaum's book of the same name, Lerman's reader covers a broad range of issues dealing with social policy and juvenile delinquency.

PLATT, ANTHONY. *The Child-Savers: The Invention of Delinquency.* Chicago: University of Chicago Press, 1969.
Traces the origins of the juvenile justice system in America, and explains how it developed into its current form.

EPILOGUE

During the past several years, social scientists, particularly criminologists, have developed renewed interest in "applied research." Although academics have been concerned with social problems for a long time,[1] most scholars in the 1950s and early 1960s were interested only in "pure" research on fundamental theoretical problems. Today it seems as if the tide has turned, with many social scientists now doing applied studies in the conviction that they are engaged in work that is relevant and has policy implications. Some, like Wilson (1975:53), have criticized criminologists for being too theoretical. Rather than finding ways to bring about a reduction in crime and developing techniques for measuring such change, Wilson argues, criminologists have limited their research to the causes of crime, which has resulted in theories that "could not supply a plausible basis for the advocacy of public policy."

We feel the search for causes can be relevant to crime control policy. In order to make reasoned recommendations to criminal justice administrators, it is necessary to know something about what causes persons to behave in certain ways. We have tried to offer some insight into what causes criminal justice personnel to make certain decisions. Unfortunately social scientists are a long way from being able to say with a high degree of certainty what causes legal agents to make specific decisions. Consequently most of our discussion has been descriptive, not causal.

In our discussion of the criminal justice process we have tried to draw on several studies in which researchers developed an "intimate familiarity" (Lofland, 1976) with legal settings. Sadly, only a few criminologists have done this. It seems as though those who have criticized social scientists for being too theoretical have encouraged researchers to adopt substitutes for gaining "intimate familarity" with natural settings. It may be that our new concern with doing policy research that does not involve first-hand observation in the field has actually thwarted efforts to make good recommendations about criminal justice.[2] Certainly it is valuable to engage in quantitative analysis

---

[1] Writing about American sociologists at the turn of the century Faris (1967:5) says, " . . . [there] was a hunger for a grand unity of knowledge that would be both esthetically satisfying and generally applicable in solving the major problems of humanity."

[2] Lofland (1976:20) comments: "It is only partly in jest that I suggest an

of survey and demographic data. But one cannot understand decision-making by looking at patterns of decisions. We agree with Blumer (1969:56) "that social action is built up by the acting unit through a process of noting, interpreting, and assessing things and mapping out a prospective line of action . . . (and) in order to treat and analyze social action one has to observe the process by which it is constructed." Indeed, the researcher who fails to examine the decision-making process is likely to be deceived by the quantitative data produced by the criminal justice system. Criminal justice statistics may mask how decisions are actually made and the latent goals in those decisions. Official documents and statistical reports are often developed and manipulated by criminal justice organizations to legitimate their operations (cf. Bogdan and Taylor, 1975:217; Garfinkel, 1967) no matter how ineffective these organizations may be in meeting expected goals.

As we have shown, researchers disagree about what causes criminal justice agents to decide cases in the ways they do, and their descriptions of the criminal justice process are often contradictory. However, it is reasonable to say that the majority of those who have studied legal decision-making agree that the police, prosecutors, and judges are influenced by extralegal criteria and do not strictly or literally enforce the law. If legal agents do not strictly enforce the law, can it be assumed they *could* fully enforce it if they attempted to?

We think the law could be enforced fully (even though doing so would probably be unjust). To be sure, full enforcement would be extremely difficult, requiring suppression of informal policies that call for flexibility and discretionary enforcement, requiring an enormous expansion of criminal justice resources, and necessitating the suppression of political groups that demand special treatment. Full enforcement is possible but very problematic. Bittner's discussion gives us reason to expect that full enforcement is an ideal frustrated by the nature of rules:

> All formal rules are basically defeasible. To say that rules
> are defeasible does not merely admit the existence of exceptions;
> it means asserting the stronger claim that the domain of
> presumed jurisdiction of a legal rule is essentially open ended.
> While there may be a core of clarity about its application, this
> core is always and necessarily surrounded by uncertainty
> (1970:4).

The law could be fully enforced but it would be enforcement of laws as they are interpreted by those charged with enforcing them. Therefore,

---

inchoate 'conspiracy' of sorts between social scientists and the people they seek to analyze: do not get too close, do not look too carefully, and we will give you money (jobs, research grants) as substitutes and compensations for not getting too close. We will fill out your innocuous questionnaires and supply college students for your laboratories, social scientists' reply: done."

full enforcement would still be characterized by what some take to be differential enforcement. Because laws are "open-ended," criminal justice agents use *their* typifications of crime to give law a definitive quality. Put simply, this enables law enforcement officers to operate on their interpretations of what the law intends to make criminal.

Although laws have an open-ended quality, agents of the criminal justice system still must maintain the appearance that they enforce the substantive law and do so within the boundaries of the adjective law (cf. Pepinsky, 1976:53). In addition to the fact that many jurisdictions have ordinances calling for full enforcement (Davis, 1975:52), legal agents attempt to sustain an image of full enforcement because it helps them maintain their legitimacy. Given that legitimacy is granted by others (the law and citizens), agents of the legal system must manage relations with the public so that citizens feel obligated to obey the law and legal decisions. Citizens are not likely to cooperate with criminal justice agents (in Chapter 3 we saw how important citizens' information is to the police) if they feel they are not being treated fairly and equally. We must be aware, however, that legal agents may avow allegiance to the law, "while in their actual conduct (they) are following other interests which they try to mask . . . " (Mannheim, 1936:96).

If rules themselves allow for tremendous variations in their application, how can discriminatory enforcement be avoided? Certainly further rules regarding "due process" have been written; however, research has shown that they have not successfully controlled law enforcement agents. Naturally, the open-ended quality of all rules is not altered by more rules. Given the nature of a formalized system of law and the demands for "government by law" and "government by men," we suspect that it would be extremely difficult to stop differential enforcement, and certainly it is impossible to enforce the law so that everyone feels he has been treated fairly and equally.

Given that full enforcement is only an ideal in police work, and that the courts, corrections, and discretionary enforcement are the reality, can persons wedded to the legalistic ideal feel a sense of justice? That is, given that full enforcement is hardly possible or even desirable, is it possible for an informed public to feel that there is any "justice" in the criminal justice process. This is a critical question, for as Matza (1964:102) points out, whenever there is a sense of injustice the moral binds to the law are loosened. As this occurs, there is a greater likelihood that the law will be ignored.

Statements claiming that "the system isn't perfect, but it's the best there is" are nothing more than apologies that avoid confronting the important issues. Can discretionary decisions be made in such a manner that the citizenry feels justice of some sort is being done? Probably not. Only certain persons are likely to see specific decisions as fair and just. Different persons, especially those from different socioeconomic strata, are not likely to perceive different sentences for a particular crime as just. For some our courts are too lenient; for others they are too harsh. Because our society is characterized by a multitude of value systems that are often competitive, it is not likely that all will be satisfied with our system of justice, no matter what form it takes. Indeed, because many of those who violate the law do so because they feel such behavior is appropriate (even though it is against the law), those who have the least sense of justice are the ones who have had the most contact with the criminal justice process.

At this point, it is normally time to call for more and better educated police, more judges, and more attorneys; or, to take the extreme, it is time to call for a revolution. We do neither. There are no panaceas for the problems that plague our criminal justice system. We feel, however, that careful evaluation and study of problems can improve the system. These may not be tremendous improvements but each one can be significant.

Certainly, bail reforms introduced by programs that were carefully monitored and evaluated have not eliminated the abuses in our allocation of pretrial release. Although such reforms have not satisfied everyone, we feel they have helped some feel they have been treated fairly. Importantly, improvements in the criminal justice system will have to be based on empirical investigations, not mere opinion. But, generally, we expect that improvements will have to take place at the local community level. Communities have to develop an interest in criminal justice, not only as an expensive item in their municipal budget, but also as a fundamental component of government.

We are not convinced that improvements in our system of justice will occur quickly. There are too many careers at stake, too many unfathomable bureaucracies that need to be changed before massive improvements will be realized. But unless there are concerted efforts to introduce change into the system, we expect that things will only get worse.

REFERENCES

BITTNER, EGON
    1970 *The Functions of Police in Modern Society.* Rockville: National Institute of Mental Health.

BLUMER, HERBERT
    1969 *Symbolic Interactionism: Perspective and Method.* Englewood Cliffs, N.J.: Prentice-Hall.

BODGAN, ROBERT, AND STEVEN TAYLOR
    1975 *Introduction to Qualitative Research Methods: A Phenomenological Approach to the Social Sciences.* New York: Wiley.

DAVIS, KENNETH CULP
  1975 *Police Discretion*. St Paul, Minn.: West Publishing Co.

FARIS, ROBERT
  1967 *Chicago Sociology, 1920–1932*. Chicago: University of Chicago Press.

GARFINKEL, HAROLD.
  1967 *Studies in Ethnomethodology*. Englewood Cliffs, N.J.: Prentice-Hall.

LOFLAND, JOHN
  1976 *Doing Social Life: The Qualitative Study of Human Interaction in Natural Settings*. New York: Wiley.

MATZA, DAVID
  1964 *Delinquency and Drift*. New York: Wiley.

MANNHEIM, KARL
  1936 *Ideology and Utopia*. New York: Harcourt, Brace.

PEPINSKI, HAROLD.
  1976 *Crime and Conflict: A Study of Law and Society*. New York: Academic Press.

WILSON, JAMES Q.
  1975 *Thinking about Crime*. New York: Vintage Books.

NAME INDEX

Adams, S., 289-90, 301*
Alschuler, A. W., 206, 207, *209*, 229*
American Correctional Association, 288, 301*
Andenaes, J., 255, 267*
Antell, M. P., 186, 188*
Ares, C. E., 169, 170, 172, 188*
Arluke, N. R., 294, 301*
Armstrong, W. B., *309, 312*, 335*
Aubert, V., 47, 68*
Aumick, A. L., 230*

Banton, M., 114, 118*
Barnard, C., 57, 58, 68*
Bartlett, F. C., 237, 267*
Bassiouni, C., *90*, 118*
Bayley, D., 118*
Beattie, R. H., 201, 230*
Becker, H. S., *46*, 68*, 141n
Best, J. G., 51, 68*
Biderman, A. D., 81, 118*
Bishop, C., *115*, 118*
Bittner, E., *66*, 67, 68*, 78, *105-6*, 118*, 121*, 140n, 142*, *380*, 382*
Black, D., *83*, 84*, 93, 118*, 350, 351, 355, 356, 359, 360, 376*
Blau, P. M., 57, 58*, 208n, 230*
Blumberg, A., 12, 38*, 63, 64, 68*, 71*, *197-200*, 201n, 202, 205, 206, 207, 208, 230*, 241, 255, 267*, 270*, 280, 287, 301*
Blumer, H., *380*, 382*
Bogdan, R., 380, 382*
Briar, S., 78, 83, 120*, 279n, 302*, 350, 354, 358, 377*
Broeder, D. W., 242, 267*
Bronner, A., 288, 302*
Brooks, C. F., 51, 68*

Bryjak, G., *83, 85*, 118*
Buckley, W., 45, 68*
Bullock, H. A., 252, 267*

Cain, M. E., 114, 118*
California, State of, Department of Justice, *283*
California, State of, Penal Code, *19, 21*, 30, *31*, 38*, 44, 100, *101, 128*
California Law Review, 187, 189*
Campbell, Angus, 93, *94*, 118*
Campbell, W. J., *184*, 185, *186*, 189*, 192*
Cantril, H., *88-89*, 118*
Caplow, T., 57, 68*
Carp, R. A., 182, *183*, 189*
Carter, R. M., 262, 263, 267*, 271*, 277, 278, 279, *280*, 284, 287, 288, 291, 300, 301*, 303*, 306, 318, 331, 335*, 378*
Casper, J. D., *169*, 189*, 201n, 202, 217, 230*
Chambliss, W. J., 14, 38*, 43n, 44, 49n, 50, *51-52, 53*, 65, 68*, 69*, 72*, 104, 119*, *134*, 138, 142*, 205, 206, 207, 230*, 236, 237, 240, 241, 249, 267*, *359*, 376*
Chang, D. H., *309, 312*, 335*
Cicourel, A., *28*, 38*, 282, 301, 365, 367, 370, 376*, 378*
Cloward, R., 328, 335*
Cohen, B., 94, *95, 97*, 121*
Cohen, F. S., 43, 69*
Cohn, A. W., 278, *287*, 301*
Cohn, Y., 369, 376*
Cole, G. F., *129-30*, 138, *141*, 144*, *149*, 189*, 206, 207, 208n, 230

NOTE: An asterisk indicates full citation. Italics indicates quotation.

Pollack, H., 206, 207, 232*
Pollner, M., 15, 39*
Pound, R., 67, 237, 269*
President's Commission on Law
  Enforcement and Administration
  of Justice, 91, 106, 120*, 150n2,
  151-52, 153, *201-2,* 203, 204, 231*,
  236, 250, 251, 269*, 291, 292, 302*,
  358, 369, 377*
*President's Commission Report on
  Delinquency,* 347
*President's Task Force Report: The
  Courts,* 1967, 174, 191*, *253,* 269*
Prus, R. C., 295, 297, 298, 299, 302*
Public Systems, Inc., 226, 232*

Quinney, R., *14,* 39*, 40*, 50, *60,* 61,
  70*, 116, 120*, 240, 269*, 377*

Radzinowicz, L., 246, 269*
Rankin, A., 169, 170, 172, 188*, 191*
Rawls, J., 40*
Reiss, A., 80, 81n, *92,* 93, 98, 118*,
  120*, 122*, 130, 143*, 350, 351,
  355, 356, 357, 359, 360, 376*, 377*
Remington, F. J., 42, 70*, *90,* 120*,
  124, 143*, *163-64,* 179, 191*, 236,
  251n, 263, 269*, 270*
Robinson J., 325, 336*
Rosett, A., *7,* 8, 39*, 67, 70*, 130n,
  143*, 205n, *210,* 211, 213, *214, 215,*
  216, 222, 229, 232*, *285-86*
Rubenstein, J., *98-99,* 120*, 122*

Sacks, H., 85, 86, 95, 106, 120*
St. John, C. W., 252, 267*
Sanders, W. B., 14, 16, 29, 39*, 99,
  103-104n, 107, 108, 109, 110, 119*
  120*, 122*, 280n, 294, 302*, 317,
  333, 336*, 344, 347, 350, 351, 353n,
  358, 368, *370-72,* 377*
San Francisco Commission on
  Crime, 168, 191*
Schrag, C., 136n, 144*
Schuman, H., 93, *94,* 118*
Schur, E. M., 42n, 70*, 113, 121*,
  349, 377*
Schutz, A., 15, 28, 39*
Scott, M. B., 348, 377*
Seidman, R., 14, 38*, 43n, 44, 50,
  68*, 72*, *134,* 138, 142*, 205, 206,
  207, 230*, 236, 237, 240, 241, 249,
  267*
Sellin, T., 97, 252, *253,* 270*, 343,
  378*
Selznick, P., 57, 58, 70*

Shibutani, T., *89-90,* 121*, 144*, 237,
  238, 270*
Silver A., 61, 62, 70*
Silverstein, L., 157, 166, 191*, 194,
  232*
Simmel, G., 356, 378*
Simon, R. J., 243, *244,* 247, 248,
  270*
Sinclair, A., 51, 70*
Single, E. W., 169, 170, 191*
Skinner, B. F., 327, 336*
Skolnick, J. H., 12, *34,* 39*, 63, 64,
  71* 78, 88, *89, 114,* 121*, 122*,
  129, 144*, *173,* 191*, 205, 206, 211,
  232*
Smith, A. B., 206, 207, 232*, 241,
  270*
Smith, G., 325, 336*
Socrates, 8
Solzhenitsyn, A., 335
Sparks, R., 119*, 252, *254,,* 255n,
  260, 268*
Stark, R., *47-48,* 71*, 91, 93, 121*
Stephan, C., 244, 247, 270*
Stewart, O., 94, 121*
Stinchcombe, A. L., 58, 71*, 113,
  121*
Stratton, J. R., 295, 297, 298, 299,
  302*
Strauss, A. L., 237, *238,* 269*
Strodtbeck, F. L., 242, 270*
Strumwasser, M. J., 230*
Stumbo, B., *353,* 378*
Sturz, H., 188*
Subin, H. I., 151, 153, 154, 166n,
  180, 191*, 236, 265, 270*
Sudnow, D., *128,* 144*, 213, *218,* 219,
  220, 222, 226, 232*, 233*
Suffet, F., *159,* 161, 163, 165, 166,
  191*, 192*
Sutherland, E., 4, *5,* 39*, 50, 71*,
  255n, 270*, *287,* 302*, 313, 314,
  336*
Sutton, L. P., 230*
Swett, D. H., 65-66, 71*

Tappan, P. W., 250, 270*
Taylor, S., 380, 382*
Thoma, B., 330, 336*
Turk, A., 49n, 50, 71*

Ulmer, S. S., 54, 71*
United States Commission on Civil
  Rights, 87, 91, 121*
*University of Pennsylvania Law
  Review,* 208, 231*

Vines, K., 241, 268*, 270*
Vorenberg, E., 333, 336*
Vorenberg, J., 333, 336*

Wald, P., *168*, 169, 189*, 191*
Wambaugh, J., 85, 121*
Ward, D., 6, 38*
Warren, D. I., 153, 191*
Weber, M., *56-57*, 71*
Weld, H. P., 247, 270*
Werthman, C., 121*, *355*, 378*
Westly, W., 114, 121*
White, W., 203n, 217, 232*
Wicker, T. , 313, *319*, *320-21*, 336*
Wieder, D. L., 17, *21*, *31*, 39*, 330, 332, 336*
Wildhorn, S., 230*
Wilkins, L. T., 262, 263, 267*, 277, 280, 284, 300, 301*, 303*, 331, 335*
Wilkins, R., 93, 121*
Williams, G. L., 237, 238, 270*

Willwerth, J., 305, 337*
Wilson, J. Q., 71*, 78, *101n*, 121*, 351, 356, 378*, 379, 383*
Wilson T., 15, 17, 39*
Wold, J., 18, 38*
Wolfe, A., *60*, 71*
Wolfgang, M., 94, *95*, *97*, 121*, 343 378*
Woodworth, J. R., *34*, 39*
Wright, D. B., *133*, 144*

Yablonsky, L., 333, 337*
Yale Law Journal, *156*, 190*, 255, 267*
Young, J., 142n, 144*
Younger, R., *183*, 191*

Zeigenhagen, E. A., 50, 71*
Zeisel, H., 201, 227, 231*, 244, 246, 249, 250n, 268*, 271*
Zimmerman, D. H., 15, 39*

SUBJECT INDEX

acquittal: of guilty, 227; individualization and, 228

act(s): criminal, in context, 17, 19-21, 23, 25-27, 30, 109, 128; evidence and, 24; intent and, 20-21; *see also* situation

"administrative-legal approach,"to criminal justice, 13

administrators, of prisons, 308, 309

adultery, 136

adversary system: juvenile justice and, 376; plea negotiation and, 207, 209, 210; pretrial release and, 156; promotion of, 10; in trial court, 235-36, 237, 238

age: crime definition and, 33-34; juvenile status and, 342-44; sentencing and, 254

agents and agencies (criminal justice): interest groups and, 55; justice and, 8; law-making and, 47-49, 66-67; organizational needs in, 63; rules and, 18, 63; specificity in, 5, 16, 36-37; *see also entries under individual agents and agencies*

Agnew, Spiro, 226

Alcoholics Anonymous, 256, 333

Alger, Horatio, 315

American Bar Association, 241

amicus curiae (friend of the court), 55

Anectine (drug), 324

anticontraceptive laws, 51

antiobscenity laws, 51

Anti-Saloon League, 51

antiwar movement, 62, 116

appeal: right to, 126; sources of, 43; *see also* courts (appellate)

appearance (personal): discrimination and, 95; effect of, on criminalization, 83, 85-88, 90; juries and, 244, 246; juvenile delinquents and, 354, 361; *see also* character evaluation; clothing; demeanor; typification

appearance (initial): charges and, 124; purpose of, 150

appellate courts, *see* courts (appellate)

Argersinger v. Hamlin, 10

armed robbery, 29

arraignment: acquittal and, 227; pleas at, 202, 204; trial court and, 126; on the warrant, 150

arrest: of juveniles, 351; powers of, 78

arrest rates: for juveniles, 353; as measure of competence, 63; police organization and, 64-65; social organization and, 84

arrest records: police and, 112; *see also* criminal records (individual)

assault, rates of, 80, 82

assault with a deadly weapon, 19

assembly-lines, 320

assessment process, *see* detectives, resource allocation by

Attica prison riot, 322

attorney(s): bench trial and, 241; right to, 9-10, 126, 194, 345; role of, in system, 13-14; witnesses and, 239; *see also* bar associations

attorney(s) (defense): at first appearance, 153; plea negotiation and, 207, 217; pretrial detention and, 169; pretrial release and, 166; prosecutor and, 204, 207, 222,

attorney(s) (defense) (*cont.*):
286; role of, in system, 12;
sentencing and, 261, 264-65; *see
also* defense; public defender
Attorney General (U.S.), indictment
of, 4
audience, police-juvenile encounters
and, 357
Augustus, John, 289
authority: legal system and, 42;
police and, 92, 355; youth and,
355
auto theft, *see* vehicle theft
aversion therapy, in prisons, 327

bail, 127; case type and, 161, 162,
171; courtroom actors and, 165,
166; detention without, 175-76;
forms of, 155; initial appearance
and, 124; Manhattan Bail Project,
165; O. R. Bail Project, 168;
police, and 165, 166; prior record
and, 161, 163; purposes of, 158-59,
167; race and, 163-64;
reappearance and, 156-57; reforms
in, 173-76; R.O.R. recommendation
and, 162
bailbondsman: criteria of, 167; fees
of, 156
Baltimore, 150n2, 152, 201
bar associations: legal system and,
49; *see also entries under attorneys*
"bargain justice," charge of, 203
behavior: categorization of, 17;
juvenile delinquents and, 345;
organizational, 59; police
assessment of, 19-20, 93, 102;
probation and, 288
behavior modification, in prisons,
324, 326-27
Bill of Rights, see Constitution
(U.S.), Bill of Rights
Black Death, vagrancy laws and,
51-52
blacks: arrest of, 83; discrimination
and, 46, 58, 89, 95; interrogation
of, 91, 93, 94; juvenile delinquency
and, 355-56, 359; neighborhood
and, 96-97; prisons and, 315;
sentencing of, 252, 254; Zebra case
and, 95-96; *see also* race and
ethnicity
Bogalusa (Louisiana), 58
bond(s), *see* bail
Boone, John, 321
Boston, police associations in, 48

Boston Strangler, 88
boundaries: in citizen crime reports,
28-29; of probable cause, 44
bribes, 116; grand jury and, 183
"bugs," *see* wire taps
bureaucracy: informal policy and,
33; in juvenile corrections, 374;
legislation and, 47; plea
negotiation and, 206-207; police
departments and, 62; theoretical
perspectives on, 56-60; *see also*
career; organization
Bureau of the Census (U.S.), 81
burglary, 45, 88; rates of, 80, 81, 82;
reports and, 30, 34-35, 110-11;
typification of, 218, 219
business: legal system and, 47, 54;
see also corporations; power
(economic)

Cahalan, William, 159
campaign contributions, grand jury
investigations of, 183
capital cases: jury in, 246, 251; pleas
in, 126n
career: considerations of, 205; in
courts, 63-64; judges and, 159;
parole officers and, 297-98; in
police departments, 63, 78, 97;
prosecutors and, 64, 132, 135, 138,
216-17; public defenders and, 64
Carter, Jimmy, 328
case disposition, pretrial status and,
170
categorization: of offenders, 17-18;
by police, 19-20; *see also* character
evaluation
Catholics, 241
character evaluation: by courts, 128;
by police, 29, 83, 98-107, 108, 110;
by prosecutors, 30, 133-34, 136-38;
see also appearance (personal);
clothing; demeanor; typification
charge(s): initial appearance and,
150; parole and, 291; pretrial
status and, 171; probation and,
277, 279; right to notice of, 10
charging: choice in, 134-39;
convictions and, 131, 141; of
felons, 176; full, 137-39; juvenile
delinquents and, 265; officials
responsible for, 129; probable
cause and, 130-34; prosecutor and,
124, 129
Chicago: charging in, 176n, 181;
pleas in, 212; screening in, 182

child molesting: pleas and, 204; typification and, 279

CINS petition, 347

citation, as bail reform, 174

city-ordinance violation, arraignment on the warrant for, 150

civil rights demonstrations, bail and, 158-59

class: criminal law and, 5, 14; juries and, 242-43, 249n; juvenile delinquency and, 358-60, 368; legal system and, 50; police and, 94, 101n, 106; prison populations and, 313, 316, 317; probation officers and, 290; prosecutors and, 134

classical model, of law, 36

clothing: arrest decisions and, 78, 83; see also appearance (personal); character evaluation; demeanor; typification

Code of Criminal Procedure, 185

coercion, in pleas, 200

Comanche Indians, 5-6

commercial interests: see power (economic); business; corporations

Committee for the Suppression of Vice, 51

commonsense, 28, 218, 290, 346

community: criminal courts and, 159; defendant ties to, 163, 168; judges and, 167; juries and, 249; political culture of, 63, 64-66; sentencing and, 255; see also courthouse community

community-based corrections: for adult offenders, 331-32; for juveniles, 375

community groups: criminal justice system and, 64; grand jury and, 185; legal system and, 47, 50; police and, 92; see also interest groups

computer technology, criminal records and, 116, 157

Comstock, Anthony, 51

confessions, rules for, 10

conflict-coercion perspective, 49, 50

conservative ideologies: judges and, 241; parole boards and, 293

conspiracy laws, 7n

Constitution (U.S.): Bill of Rights, 9, 10, 44-45; guarantees of, 3, 9-12; juvenile delinquency and, 345; punishment and, 324

constitutional rules, 44

context: appearance as, 86; appellate courts and, 45; criminal acts in, 17, 19-21, 23, 25-27, 30, 109, 128; plea negotiations and, 213; probation and, 282; see also situations

contraception, laws against, 51

conviction(s): bench trial and, 241; charging and, 131, 141; grand jury and, 177; preliminary hearing and, 182; pretrial detention and, 169-70; trial selection and, 227

convicts: parole and, 292; stigma of, 328-29

Cook County Grand Jury, 185

corporations: grand jury and, 183; legal system and, 47, 54; see also power (economic)

corpus delicti, 27, 33

correctional system, see prison system

corruption, grand jury and, 183

counseling: for juveniles, 370; in prisons, 318

counterinsurgency forces, police as, 116

courthouse community, 13-14, 42, 63, 142

courts: deadly force and, 93; juvenile status and, 343; politics and, 53-55; review by, 36, 90, 149

courts (appellate): influence on, by interest groups, 53; role of, 42, 44, 66, 126

courts (criminal), 78; career considerations in, 63-64; overview of, 124-27

courts (juvenile), 362, 364; adversary system in, 376; due process and, 360; establishment of, 345; probation departments and, 365-67

courts (magistrate's), 126, 151

courts (trial), arraignment at, 126, 150

courtrooms: comportment in, 256-57; description of, 151-52; as drama, 201n

crime control model, 40

crime rates: charging and, 141; class and, 106; race and, 93-95, 97-98; victimization surveys and, 81

crime reports: see criminal records (collective); police reports; victimization surveys

crime scene, 23-24; race and, 96; see also context; situation criminal justice system: approaches to 13-14; career considerations in, 63-64, 78; class and, 60-62; citizen role in, 80, 81; definition of, 4-9; English, 154, 156, 182; legal system and, 42-45; overview of, 12-13; situational approach to, 14-18; structure of, 59-60

criminal justice agents and agencies: *see* agents and agencies (criminal justice); *entries under individual agents and agencies*

criminal records (collective): computerized, 116, 157; of juveniles, 112; National Crime Information Center, 157; System of Electronic Analysis and Retrieval of Criminal Histories, 157

criminal records (individual): bail and, 161-63, 172; parole and, 292-93; police and, 112; probation and, 279, 280; ROR recommendation and, 162, 172; sentencing and, 256, 257, 258

criminal trial, 126

"critical approach," to criminal justice, 14

"critical situations," 14

cross-examination: in preliminary hearing, 177, 179; right to, of accused, 10-11; right to, of parolee, 195; in trial, 235

Crown-Zellerback Corporation, 58

Cuellar, Jess, 91

Davis v. Commonwealth, 45

"deadbang" cases: pleas and, 203, 209, 222, 225; trial and, 226n

death, legal definition of, 43

death penalty, 250

decision-making process, 380; citizen role in, 80-85; in courts, 127, 188; by judges, 126; judicial selection and, 55; juvenile delinquency and, 363, 367-69; parole and, 291, 296; by police, 78, 88, 117; in probation departments, 278, 280; in prisons, 311; rules and, 18, 37

defendants: as bail risk, 157, 161-62, 163; community ties of, 163, 164; judges and, 200-201, 211; jurors and, 244, 246, 247; plea negotiation and, 207, 213, 224-25, 226-27; preliminary hearing and, 154-55, 179; pretrial detention

defendants (*cont.*):
and, 168-69; probation and, 279-80; prosecutor and, 215-16, 217; rights of, apprised, 152-53, 193-94; sentencing and, 254-56

defense: pleas and, 195-96; preliminary hearing and, 124, 154, 155; trial selection and, 227; *see also* attorney(s) (defense); public defender

Delancy House, 333-34

demeanor: juvenile delinquency and, 354-55, 358-59; *see also* appearance (personal); character evaluation; clothing; typification

Democratic Party, judges and, 53, 54, 241

Department of Justice (U.S.), probation and, 277

detectives: criminal context and, 23, 24; proactive work of, 113-17; reactive work of, 107-13; resource allocation by, 107; *see also* police

detention: costs of, 168; effect on case, 172-73; preventive, 158, 175-76; sentence and, 172; *see also* prison system

deterrence, sentencing as, 255, 258

Detroit, 138, 150n2, 152, 194; civil disturbances in, 159; pretrial release in, 163; Recorder's Court in, 151-52, 161, 165, 178

discretion: citizen, 79-85; justice and, 19, 66, 67; juvenile delinquency and, 351; by police, 117-18; in processing, 8

discrimination, 46, 58

dismissal, move for, 235

disposition, *see* case disposition

district attorney: career considerations of, 132; public interest and, 36; report review by, 20-30, 34-35, 113; *see also* prosecutor

District of Columbia, 154; detention centers in, 168-69; preliminary hearings in, 180; public defenders in, 153; sentencing in, 265

District of Columbia Court Reform Act (1970), 175-76

diversion programs: for adult offenders, 333; for juvenile offenders, 375

documentary method, 20-21, 21-24

double jeopardy, right against, 11, 127

dragnets, 96
drugs and drug offenses:
    criminalization of, 46; informal
    policy and, 31; juvenile
    delinquency and, 349; plea
    negotiations and, 214; police and,
    78, 79, 92, 114-16; prisons and,
    316, 324; sentences for, 252, 258;
    typification and, 28, 29, 35, 101
due process, 381; agents and, 9;
    juvenile delinquency and, 347,
    360, 368
Durham rule, 243-44

education: of prison staff, 319; as
    rehabilitation, 328-30
Eighteenth Amendment, 51
Eisenhower, Dwight David, 53
embezzlement, 29, 112-13
enforcement (differential), of law, 18
English common law, bail and, 156
environment, *see* context; situation
evidence: in bench trial, 240;
    charging and, 131, 138; crime
    scene and, 23-24; grand jury and,
    177; jury trial and, 242; juvenile
    courts and, 345; plea negotiation
    and, 209; police reports and,
    27-28, 78, 110-11; preliminary
    hearing and, 179; trial and, 235

Federal Bureau of Investigation:
    Uniform Crime Reports, 81, 94;
    S.L.A. and, 91
Federal Bureau of Narcotics, 47
feedback, in legal system, 46, 47
felons and felonies: arrests for, 84;
    charging of, 176; defense of, 153,
    194; initial appearance for, 150;
    sentences for, 250
feminist movement, 344
fetus, 43
feudalism, breakdown of, 52-53
Fifth Amendment, 10; *see also*
    Constitution (U.S.)
fines, 250
First Amendment, 44-45; *see also*
    Constitution (U.S.)
first offenders, sentencing and, 256
flexibility, concept of justice and, 8
foremen (of juries), status of, 242-43
free speech cases, 54-55
Fricot Ranch School for Boys,
    372-73
friend of the court (*amicus curiae*),
    55
functional approach, 40

gambling, 228; religious groups and,
    47
gangs (juvenile), police and, 355, 359
Gault decision, 347, 355
Georgia, 44; detention centers in,
    168
gestalt psychologists, 23
ghetto, 95, 97; *see also* neighborhood
Gideon's Trumpet (Lewis), 10n
Gideon v. Wainwright, 10
goals: bureaucracy and, 56, 57, 58;
    conflict over, 12-13; criminal
    justice and, 59; plea negotiation
    and, 207; police and, 91; of
    probation departments, 288
grand jury: preliminary hearing
    and, 184; proceedings in, 125-26,
    176-77, 183; prosecutor and, 184,
    185; as "rubber stamp," 185, 186;
    selection of jurors for, 182-83
groups, *see* interest groups
guilt: probability of, 90; admission
    of, 200
Gulag Archipelago (Solzhenitsyn),
    335

half-way houses, 332-33
hashish, *see* drugs; marijuana and
    hasish
hierarchy: bureaucracy and, 56; in
    criminal justice system, 59; in
    legal system, 42
high school students, drugs and, 358
Holmes, Oliver W., 67
homicide: Comanche society and,
    5-6; investigations of, 112; rates
    of, 80
homosexuals, 92, 228; in prisons,
    309, 317, 318, 328
housing, 46

incongruity procedures, 86, 95
Indiana, detention centers in, 168
Indians, criminality of, 94
indictment: arraignment on, 193n;
    grand jury and, 126, 176, 184; rate
    of, 187
indirect victim, juvenile delinquency
    and, 349
informal policies: drugs and, 31; of
    judges toward bail, 164-65; sexual
    crimes and, 31-34
information: institutionalization of,
    105; trials and, 237
information (legal document), 176;
    arraignment on, 193n

informer system, 114-16; acquittal and, 228-29; sentencing and, 255
initial appearance, *see* appearance (initial)
initial charging, *see* charging
innocence, presumption of, 156; *see also* pleas, innocent
In Re Gault, 347, 355
insanity defense: criminal trials and, 236; juries and, 243
Institute of Judicial Administration, 173
integration, 58
integration-consensus perspective, 49, 50
intent, act and, 20-21
interest groups: appellate courts and, 53; career considerations and, 64; charging and, 138; judges and, 167; legal system and, 45, 50-51; organizations and, 58; police work and, 79; prosecutors and, 216-17; *see also* power (economic); power (political)
interpretive process, 128
interpretive scheme, 35
interrogation, police right of, 87, 90-91, 93
"intimate familiarity," 379
investigation, priority of, 107-108

jail, *see* detention; prison system
judge(s), 15; acquittal by, 227; bail and, 158, 159, 161, 164; in bench trials, 240-41; career considerations of, 64, 159; decision-making and, 126; defendants and, 200-201, 211; juries and, 249; of juvenile courts, 365-66; pleas and 196-201, 207, 217, 224; preliminary hearing and, 179, 180, 181-82; pretrial release and, 155, 167, 173; probation and, 283-84; prosecutors and, 140, 166, 241; role of, in system, 12, 124, 152-53; search and seizure and, 9; selection of, 49, 53-55; sentencing and, 172, 196, 251-56; subjectivism of, 241; waiver of counsel and, 194
judgments, trial court and, 235
jurisdiction, double jeopardy and, 127
jury: class and, 249n; competency of, 243-44, 247; evolution of, 249; foremen of, 242-43; sentencing and, 251; trials and, 150n1; verdicts of, 242, 248, 249; *see also* trial

justice: concept of, 7-8, 36; "doing," 9, 19-21, 37, 62, 130, 132, 215; individualization of, 205, 210, 213, 214, 228, 363; informal, 33; juries and, 247, 249; pleas and 203, 210; sentencing and, 255n-56n; situational, 8
justices, *see* judges
juvenile delinquents and delinquency, 32, 33, 78, 83; class and, 358-60, 368; definition of, 342-44; law and, 345-49; police and, 104, 349-53, 354-60; probation of, 369-70; probation officers and, 363-65; race and, 97; records of, 112
juvenile justice system: changes in, 375-76; decision-making in, 367-69; incarceratories for, 370-74; police and, 360; probation in, 369-70; runaways and, 364-65; state-raised youth, 317

Kansas, 154; pleas in, 201, 215; preliminary hearing in, 181; sentencing in, 196, 254, 258
Kennedy, John F., 53
Kentucky State Police, 112
Kent v. United States, 200

labor, division of, 56; *see also* strike breaking
labor force, vagrancy statutes and, 51-52
larceny: mercantilism and, 6; rates of, 80, 82
law: class and, 5, 14; created in application, 67, 130; criminal act and, 21-24, 35-36; generation of, 45-49; informal policy and, 31, 213-14; juvenile delinquency and, 346; models of, 36; reification of, 42n; substantive, 63, 64; use of, 17, 24; *see also* penal code; procedural law
legal system: operation of, 45-49; overview of, 42-45; perspectives on, 49-50; special interests and, 50-55
legislatures: drug laws and, 47; legal system and, 42, 45; police influence in, 47-48; sentences and, 250-51; usurpation of function, 116
legitimation and legitimacy, 381; criminal justice system and, 60, 67; imprisonment and, 324; informal policy and, 31; legal

Organized Crime Control Act(1970), 61

organization: conditions of, 57-58; district attorney and, 132, 135, 138

parens patriae, 348-49, 360

parole, revocation of, 295

parole departments: appointment to, 292; community and, 290-91; conditions of, 293; criteria for, 291-92; organizational concerns in, 295; probation departments and, 278; role of, 12; sentencing and, 251

parole officers, 15; career considerations of, 297-98; decision-making by, 296

patrol officers, *see* police

penal code: as conceptual scheme, 128; knowledge of, 24-27; typification and, 218; *see also* law; procedural law

penal sanction, *see* punishment

penitentiary, plea negotiations and, 211; *see also* prison system

perception, subcultural differences in, 88

phenomenology, 15

Philadelphia (Pennsylvania): bench trials in, 241; detention centers in, 169; plea negotiations in, 217; sentencing in, 261; vagrancy laws in, 65

Phoenix (Arizona), 91

photographers (police), 23

Pittsburgh (Pennsylvania), bench trials in, 241

pleas: at arraignment, 126; bargaining in, 134-36; in capital cases, 126*n*; coercion in, 200; defense and, 195-96; of guilty, 78, 124, 135, 138-39, 201, 202; at initial appearance, 124, 150; innocent, 202, 225-27; judges and, 196-201; negotiated, 64, 201, 203-205; preliminary hearing and, 155, 178; sentencing and, 203, 255, 264; waiver of counsel and, 194; *see also* negotiated guilty plea

police: abuse of power by, 116; class and, 94, 101*n*, 106; community and, 64; constitutional limits on, 9; court review of, 149, 177, 182, 228; decision-making by, 78-79, 279*n*; dispatchers, 98-105; harrassment by, 87, 91, 93, 356;

police (*cont.*):
juveniles and, 349-53, 354-60; lobbies of, 47, London, 62; as military, 62; nonrecording by, 81; parole and, 294, 297; plea negotiations and, 217; pretrial release and, 165, 166; proactive role of, 78-79, 85-98, 350; probable cause and, 44; procedural law and, 63; prosecutors and, 12, 129-30, 140, 216; race and, 83, 91, 93, 94-97; reactive role of, 78, 98-107; role of, in system, 12, 13, 19, 21, 46; sentencing and, 255; social problems role of, 3; as subculture, 88-90, 91, 117; training of, 88; *see also* detectives

police associations, 47-48

police departments: arrest rates and, 64-65; career considerations in, 63, 78, 97; hierarchy in, 59; juvenile delinquency and, 356; professionalism in, encouraged, 90; styles in, 78

police reports: evidence and, 27-28, 32-33, 111; narrative section of, 19-20, 109; review of, 25, 29-30, 34-35; sample of, 26

politicality, criminal law and, 5-6, 7

political party, appellate courts and, 53-54; *see also* Democratic Party; Republican Party

political protest: bail and, 158; police and, 62, 116-17

politics: judges and, 53-54, 241; juvenile delinquency and, 348; parole departments and, 292; plea negotiations and, 226; prison riots and, 322-23; probation and, 290; prosecutors and, 132, 138, 140-41

Politics and Criminal Prosecution (Moley), 212

polygamy, 7

post-plea-of-guilty hearing, sentencing in, 261, 262

power (economic), generation of law and, 14, 51-53; *see also* interest groups

power (political): career considerations and, 64; court system and, 53-55; judges and, 241; legal system and, 42, 49, 55; shift to industrialists, 53; *see also* interest groups

"Prairie City," 129, 131; grand jury in, 185; jury in, 247

prejudice, perception and, 89

Stanley v. Georgia, 44

state: crimes against, 4-5; legal system and, 42

statistics, *see* crime rates; criminal records (collective); criminal records (individual); victimization surveys

status offenses, juvenile delinquency and, 349

statutes, 66; writing of, 17; *see also* law; procedural law

stereotyping, 37, 103

stigma, 136, 328

stop and question, *see* interrogation

"street experience," 13

Strike Off with Leave to Reinstate, 181

strike breaking, police and, 62

subcultural perspective, of police, 88

subordinate-superordinate encounter, 356

summary offense cases, pleas in, 150

summation, trial court and, 235

summons, as bail reform, 174

Supreme Court (U.S.): juvenile delinquency and, 347; parolee rights and, 294-95; politics and, 54n; right to attorney and, 10; rules and, 44

supreme court (state), appeals to, 126

suspended sentence, probation and, 277

Symbionese Liberation Army, 91-92, 96

Synanon, 333-34

System of Electronic Analysis and Retrieval of Criminal Case Histories, 157

Tate-LaBianca murders, 226

testimony, at preliminary hearing, 177; *see also* witnesses

Texas, grand jury selection in, 183

theft, 19; rates of, 82

torts, distinguished from crimes, 4-5

"total institution" concept, 307; prison life and, 309

treatment ideology: juvenile delinquency and, 345; probation and, 276; sentencing and, 250-51

trial: actuality in, 237-40; bench, 240-42; efficiency and, 205, 206; forms of, 196; ideal of, 236-37; jury, 242-46; right to, 11, 78; selection of, 226-27; stages in, 235; variations in, 236; *see also* jury

"trial on the transcript," 241

truth, criminal trial and, 236, 237, 238

typification, 381; of child molestors, 279; drugs and, 28, 29, 35, 101; plea negotiations and, 218-24; process of, 27, 28, 29; *see also* appearance (personal); character evaluation; clothing; demeanor

unemployment, partisan attitudes and, 54

Uniform Crime Reports (FBI), 81, 94

uniformity, criminal law and, 7

United States District Courts, 194

University of Chicago jury project, 242

vagrancy: administration of, 65; history of, 51-53

values: cultural, 88-89; society and, 49

vehicle theft, rates of, 80, 82

Vera Institute (New York University), 173

verdicts, jury and, 242, 248, 249

vice, police and, 78, 113-14

victimization surveys, 80-85

violence, in prisons, 308, 321-24

vocational skills, prisons and, 325

Volstead Act, 51

waiver of counsel, 194

wardens, of prisons, 309

warrants: arraignment on, 150, 193n; issuance of, 124

Washington, D. C., *see* District of Columbia

Watts (California), 97

White, Kevin, 48

wire taps, 116

Wisconsin, 154; pleas in 201, 215; preliminary hearing in, 181; sentencing in, 196, 254, 258

witness(es): attorneys and, 239; reliability of, 237-38; right to confront, 10-11

Women's Christian Temperance Union, 51

YMCA, 51

Youth Service Bureau, 364

Zebra case, 95-96